Racing & Football Outlook

FLAT RACING
GUIDE 2019

Interviews • Statistics • Results
Previews • Training centre reports

Contributors: Richard Birch, Tom Collins, Steffan Edwards, Dylan Hill, Ben Hutton, Bruce Jackson, Tony Jakobson, Andrew King, David Milnes, Justin O'Hanlon, James Thomas, Tom Ward, Nick Watts

Designed and edited by Nick Watts and Dylan Hill

Published in 2019 by Raceform Ltd
27 Kingfisher Court, Hambridge Road, Newbury RG14 5SJ

A catalogue record for this book is available from the British Library.

ISBN 978-1-83950-004-6

Printed by CPI Group (UK) Ltd, Croydon, CRO 4YY

RACING & FOOTBALL outlook

Contents

RACING & FOOTBALL outlook

Editor's introduction

HERE come the girls! That was the theme of 2018 on the track as a succession of mighty mares and flying fillies dominated the headlines around the world.

According to the World's Best Racehorse Rankings, the best of the lot could be found across the world in Australia, where wondermare Winx kept on winning and was jointly awarded top spot in the list of 2018's top performers.

It would be fair to say that there's a great deal of scepticism around Winx's achievements at Outlook Towers. It's an incredible feat to have put together such a long winning run, but who has she really beaten? It hardly spoke highly of the Australian racing scene that exposed European performers like Yucatan were able to run away with some of their leading races last autumn.

It's just a shame that, during the debate about who should have been top that followed the publication of the rankings in January, those arguing against Winx had to bang the drum for Cracksman, who was rated alongside the Aussie mare on top.

Cracksman, of course, had tenuous claims of being rated the best in Europe, let alone the world, on the strength of his strange season in which he really deliv-

THRILLER: Enable and Sea Of Class will lock horns again in 2019

TOO DARN HOT: ante-post favourite for the 2,000 Guineas and the Derby

ered only once when surely flattered by a second soft-ground demolition job in the Champion Stakes. Indeed, there can't be many who seriously considered him the best horse in his own yard.

That's because John Gosden housed the second of last year's leading women in Enable, who stormed to a second Prix de l'Arc de Triomphe when just holding off yet another phenomenal filly in William Haggas's Sea Of Class.

The good news is that these two stay in training for 2019 and it wouldn't be remotely surprising to see them take first and second in the rankings come January 2020 – hopefully having clashed more than once over the year so that there's no arguments about the order this time – although the younger generation may have something to say about that, with Enable's stablemate Too Darn Hot leading the way on that front as ante-post favourite for the 2,000 Guineas and the Derby.

Our regional experts bring you all the news on which other big names are back to leave their mark this year and no doubt there will be more pearls like Jerry M's 25-1 tip for Kew Gardens to win the St Leger in these pages 12 months ago.

For the very best ante-post advice, though, we hand over to Steffan Edwards, who nailed Saxon Warrior for the 2,000 Guineas at 8-1 and wasn't far off with his big-priced tips for Alpha Centauri in the 1,000 Guineas and Latrobe in the Derby. Right horses, wrong races!

We've also spoken to two trainers we expect to enjoy breakthrough seasons in George Scott and Joseph Tuite to get some slightly more under-the-radar horses to follow for 2019.

Pedigree expert James Thomas looks at the first-season sires who should make an impact, while Nick Watts has searched far and wide for his list of 30 horses to follow.

As well as that, we have invaluable stable insight from Tom Collins and Richard Birch; Time Test brings you all the key speed figures; and Dylan Hill guides you through last season's leading form.

Then there are the stats, reams and reams of winner-finding numbers detailing the top trainers and jockeys also broken down course by course so you know who to follow at your local track.

Once again we have every base covered for a year packed with bumper profits – and don't forget to buy your copy of the RFO every week for the very latest news and tips.

Profiles for punters
George Scott

GEORGE SCOTT: sensational winter has built reputation as a future star

Profile by David Milnes

FINDING the next big thing before most people have cottoned on can keep a punter ahead of the game for a long time and there might well be mileage in following George Scott this season purely because his huge successes through the winter have gone somewhat under the radar because of where they occurred.

The 30-year-old Newmarket trainer took his team far and wide in search of success and was amply rewarded by the performances of Another Batt and Concierge.

Another Batt, who is famously part-owned by Southampton striker Charlie Austin, did not waste any time in getting on the board out in Dubai in January, practically running from straight off the plane to bag a 7f handicap at the first meeting of the Carnival at Meydan. He had previously shown his ability to travel when winning a hugely valuable prize in Turkey in 2017.

While the four-year-old was raking in the cash in Dubai, stablemate Concierge was doing likewise over in nearby Qatar, where he landed a 7f conditions race at Doha over Christmas.

Scott says: "Another Batt and Concierge have really kept us going this winter. It was great to have my first winner in Dubai with Another Batt and it's certainly something we will explore again next year as the prize-money is different class compared to the all-weather here."

Since sending out his first runner in November 2015, Scott's most notable performer on home shores has been James Garfield. He won the Mill Reef Stakes as a juvenile before kicking off last year with victory in the Greenham Stakes and very nearly gave Scott a Group 1 success when touched off in the Prix Maurice de Gheest at Deauville.

The son of Exceed And Excel had looked to be the type to go on as a four-year-old, but Scott's thrifty father-in-law Bill Gredley thought otherwise and sold him to stud in Ireland, where he currently stands at €7,000.

That leaves something of a void to fill, but Scott discusses several three-year-olds who look to be well handicapped in this tour and has an exciting team of juveniles, with his success abroad underlining the fact that this is a trainer going places.

That has long been the feeling about Scott from within racing and he was even headhunted back from California to team up with Lady Cecil following the sad death of Sir Henry in 2013.

He started out in the sport as a lad with Paul Nicholls, followed by a time as pupil assistant to Mark Tompkins. For the next three years he was assistant trainer to Michael Bell before learning more of his trade with Eddie Kenneally across the Atlantic. Then came his big break.

"I got a phone call from David Loder out of the blue to ask if I would return to England and help Lady Cecil at Warren Place," says Scott. "I had a wonderful two years and was involved with some great people and lovely horses owned by the Niarchos family and Khaled Abdullah, including Noble Mission, which was fantastic."

NOBLE MISSION: old favourite

The decision to go it alone near the end of 2015 came when Cecil wanted to retire, since when Scott has been in situ at Saffron Stables, a 50-box yard on the Hamilton Road in Newmarket. It had been thought he was set for grander surroundings in the town at one point and plans to move are still in the melting pot for the ambitious young trainer.

As for the horses, things appear to have come full circle from his days with Cecil and three-time Group 1 winner Noble Mission, as Scott reports: "We've a lovely unraced three-year-old filly by Noble Mission called Earth And Sky and we hope to get her out for one of the fillies' maidens that the Cecils used to like at Newbury in April."

Among the two-year-olds, the list of nearly 30 youngsters includes offspring of such premier stallions as No Nay Never, Lope De Vega, Dandy Man and Brazen Beau so there should be no hanging around on Scott's work mornings on Racecourse Side, where he can regularly be seen walking the gallops before dawn to suss out the best ground for his strong exercise, usually on the peat moss gallop.

Scott also retains the backing of top owners such as the Niarchos family, the Gredleys, Airlie Stud, Al Asayl and associates of Rabbah Bloodstock, so he is in a strong position for 2019 and beyond.

The horses

Alabama Dreaming 3yo filly
Foxwedge – Sweet Alabama

We've always liked this filly and she wasn't far behind the top-class Pretty Pollyanna on her debut at Yarmouth last June. Unfortunately she then picked up an injury at Nottingham when she was favourite next time and she missed the rest of the season. I'm hopeful she can make up for lost time this season and she should be up to winning a novice race at least.

Another Batt 4yo gelding
Windsor Knot – Mrs Batt

We hadn't had a horse suitable for the Dubai Carnival until this horse came along and thankfully he justified our decision to send him over there. He'd run some big races in Britain last season, winning at Chester and finishing third in the Free Handicap and fourth on Champions Day in the Balmoral Handicap. He'll be aimed at more top handicaps this season and he's the type to carry big weights. He's in the Lincoln, although he might need more of a break after Dubai so it's more likely he'll be prepared for Royal Ascot, where he could run in the Hunt Cup or the Wokingham. I then hope to have him on his travels again through the summer before ending up back in Dubai. We think he's a turf horse and there are no plans to run him on the all-weather.

Concierge 3yo colt
Society Rock – Warm Welcome

He's been a fantastic servant to the yard

ANOTHER BATT: wins in Dubai (pic: Dubai Racing Club / Erica Rasmussen)

CRANTOCK BAY (left): showed his talent with this near miss at Ascot on debut

already this winter having won the Al Rayyan Stakes in Qatar in December. He went back there for the Al Biddah Mile, which was won last year by Tip Two Win, but he was a bit disappointing. He was a doubt to get the mile on pedigree, but I think it was more that he didn't get the best trip in the race and, not being a big horse, he got intimidated and lost his confidence. He's come back fine and will run at Lingfield on Good Friday in the three-year-old final having won a qualifier last year. He should also be a fun horse on turf.

Crash Helmet 4yo gelding
Helmet – Hot Secret

He's very lightly raced having run only four times and could be an improver this year. He's had all his runs on the all-weather, winning at Newcastle last year under Jess Cooley, but I've always wanted to run him on a straight turf track and we haven't been able to do that yet because of a few issues. I think he's sensibly handicapped and will do better once we get him off the all-weather. Stepping up in trip will also help him.

Crantock Bay 3yo gelding
Havana Gold – Orton Park

We've always held this horse in some regard and he nearly won on his debut at Ascot last summer when beaten a neck. He disappointed next time but wasn't beaten far into ninth in the big sales race at Doncaster. I think he needed to concentrate a bit more, so we've had him gelded over the winter. I expect him to improve throughout the season.

Earth And Sky 3yo filly
Noble Mission – You're So Sweet

She's a lovely filly who will come into her own over middle distances this season.

9

BUNBURY CUP: again the aim for Gilgamesh despite last year's disappointment

She didn't run last year but she should be ready early this term and I'd like to start her off in a 1m2f fillies' maiden at the Greenham meeting at Newbury. If not, she could run at the Craven meeting, which comes a few days later this year.

Gilgamesh 5yo gelding
Foxwedge – Flaming Cliffs

He won at York last season and threatened to win a bigger pot. We really fancied him for the Bunbury Cup, but unfortunately he was disappointed and we discovered he wasn't right afterwards, which meant he missed a big chunk of the season. He was second at Newmarket when we got him back but then the ground was too soft for him in the Balmoral Handicap on Champions Day. I've got the Bunbury Cup in mind for him again and he starts the season 3lb lower than when he ran in the race last year, so hopefully he'll be on a nice mark for it, but he'll be running in all the big 6f-7f handicaps through the season.

Lyndon B 3yo colt
Charm Spirit – Kelsey Rose

He was always the type who would improve physically for another winter on his back, so it was great that he ran so well in two runs last season. We got him out twice in October and he was second in a novice at Yarmouth before finishing fourth in a 16-runner maiden at Newbury. I'm really pleased with the way he's trained since he came back in and he should be ready for a 6f-7f novice on turf in April.

Moll Davis 3yo filly
Kingman – Stupendous Miss

She's a lovely unraced Kingman filly. She was too weak to run last year and is probably only just starting to fill her frame, so it's likely she still won't be out until the second half of the season. However, she's pleased me in some very light work. She has a great attitude and is a good-moving filly.

My Excelsa 3yo filly
Exceed And Excel – Emirates Joy

I remember saying she was a horse to follow in my RFO stable tour last spring, but she just came up short and we decided to give her plenty of time. I think that will pay off because she's done really well over the winter. I also think the form of all three of her races last year is pretty strong and her opening mark of 70 could be more than workable.

Narak 3yo filly
Dubawi – Chachamaidee

She's a very well-bred filly. She's out of Sir Henry's Group 1 winner Chachamaidee and is a half-sister to Klassique, who won three times for William Haggas last year. She's unraced and only began faster work in February, but she's done fantastically well over the winter and we're very much looking forward to getting started with her.

Reloaded 3yo colt
Excelebration – Wooded Glade

He's one of the three-year-olds I'm most keen to flag up as he's a lovely horse who should improve throughout for the year. He won for us on his second start at Pontefract and we were a bit disappointed when he was then beaten at Yarmouth, but the form of that race has worked out handsomely and the ground may well have been against him. He's rated 85 and should just creep into some races that will suit him off that mark. We'll be working back from something like the Britannia at Royal Ascot – just like every other trainer in Britain!

Storm Over 5yo gelding
Elnadim – Stormy View

He's a new horse to the yard having joined from Robert Cowell. He comes with a mark of 92 having shown some smart form over five furlongs, but he's only ever run over that trip and we'll be looking to step him up a bit and see if he improves. He looks to enjoy some cut in the ground and could start off in a 6f handicap at the Lincoln meeting at Doncaster. I hope he can progress further through the year.

The Great Story 3yo gelding
Sea The Moon – Lovina

He came here midway through last year having run just once and nearly made a winning start for us at Pontefract when beaten a neck. He had one more run at York after that and has been given a mark of 77, which looks workable. He's been gelded over the winter and has relaxed nicely since then. We'll think about stepping up to a mile and maybe further based on his pedigree.

"I'm really pleased with the two-year-olds as they look a nice bunch.

*"A Zoffany colt called **Wizardry** is very much one to look out for. His dam won first time out for William Haggas so he's pretty speedily bred. He's been incredibly straightforward from day one. I'd also pick out **Amazing News**, a Toronado colt out of Angelic Air, who was a Juddmonte filly trained by John Gosden. He's a beautiful-looking horse who has plenty of potential and is ticking all the right boxes at the moment.*

*We could have an unnamed **Camacho filly** for the first weekend of the season proper when there's a 5f fillies' novice at Lingfield. She came to us from Malcolm Bastard in fantastic condition and is a very speedy type. **Chattanooga Boy**, an Acclamation colt, is another early sort and could be ready to roll in April. He's done nothing wrong in his rarly preparation.*

*"We've also benefited from a new partnership called the Black Dragon Syndicate, which includes Tim Gredley and some others. They have bought five sensibly priced yearlings with a view to racing them in the summer and maybe selling on one or two. A War Command colt called **Dragon Command** would be the most forward of the five and can hopefully get the syndicate rolling in April or May."*

Profiles for punters
Joseph Tuite

JOSEPH TUITE: had a career-best season in 2018 with 30 winners

Profile by Dylan Hill

WHEN a small trainer wins a massive prize, it more often than not remains something of an anomaly in their career, a curious one-off they will never come close to repeating.

Joseph Tuite is determined that won't be the case when people look back in years to come at his victory in the 2015 Ebor Handicap at York with Litigant.

The Ebor is now famous as the first £1 million handicap run in Britain, with the first

massive pot won by a most familiar name in John Gosden with Muntahaa, but it was still a big enough prize when won by little-known Tuite with the talented but fragile Litigant, who claimed £171,187.50 for his connections by beating Wicklow Brave that day. Even more remarkably, Litigant also went on to win the November Handicap later that year off a 7lb higher mark.

But for a blip in the second half of 2017, when his horses just weren't right and only four winners came after the end of June,

Tuite's career has been on an upward curve ever since and he credits Litigant with having a lot to do with that.

"There is no doubt about it – that was a huge moment in my career. It got my name in the headlines and we definitely got new owners as a result of his achievements."

In the first season after Litigant's two big handicap wins, Tuite sent out 22 winners, a career-best at the time, and it's a testament to how strongly he kicked off the following campaign that he still had 19 in 2017 despite its rotten end.

Last season Tuite came roaring back again, training 30 winners to storm past his previous peak.

"At the start of the year I felt it was the best bunch of horses I'd ever had, including some great two-year-olds, and I was very hopeful we'd do well," he says. "The key was that the horses stayed healthy and ran solid all through the season. It was a good year."

Tuite has acted to build on that success. He rented extra boxes last season and reports that he has a full house, including 100,000gns purchase Larchmont Lad, a Group 2 winner for Mick Channon last year.

The Irishman is certainly comfortable at dealing with top-class horses and bigger strings having been assistant to Mick Channon for eight years from 2002 to 2010, a spell during which Channon regularly sent out more than 100 winners from his 160-horse team.

"Mick would be one of the people I admire most," he says. "To achieve what he has done in two spheres [having also been a top-level footballer] is something very special."

At that time Tuite was instrumental in overseeing the preparation of stars like Youmzain, Zafeen, Music Show, Flashy Wings, Lahaleeb and Mail The Desert, remembering with particular fondness the week the yard had three winners at Royal Ascot.

"I used to love a bet at that time and I went to the local car showroom on the Monday and bought a new car!" he recalls. "We had a lot of highs, but as ever

LITIGANT: breakthrough horse

there were the lows."

Tuite had filled a similar role with Charlie Egerton before that, working his way up the ladder steadily having moved from Ireland to England in 1984, initially to get rides as a conditional jockey.

It's been a long apprenticeship since then, but the best may be yet to come and there is every chance he could take further big steps forward this season, notably with a genuine Classic possible for the first time in Angel Mead, who is set to start her campaign in the Fred Darling.

Tuite also hopes for another good year from his two-year-olds, saying: "It's early days but we have colts by Helmet, Rock Of Gibraltar and Holy Roman Emperor who would be the three who stand out at the moment."

The horses

Angel Mead 3yo filly
Archipenko – Red Sovereign

She's a very good filly and we've always thought highly of her. I knew she'd improve a ton for her debut at Windsor when she ran a lovely race to finish sixth and I then took her to Newbury, where everyone in the yard fancied her – she was backed down from 33-1 to 9-1 before settling back at 20-1 and I think I was the only one who didn't have anything on her. She duly won nicely by three-quarters of a length from Gallovie and Magnetic Charm, who both won afterwards. She picked up a knock after that, but we've been very pleased with her through the winter. She'll return in the Fred Darling back at Newbury and then we'll decide where to go from there. At this stage the million-dollar question over the 1,000 Guineas is whether she'll stay a mile and she has a nice, relaxed attitude which makes me hopeful, although I wouldn't be confident. She's exciting.

Fast Dancer 7yo gelding
Fast Company – Tereed Elhawa

We made some big plans for this horse at the start of last year and he did really well to win at Chester's May meeting. The main target was the 1m4f handicap on King George day at Ascot, but the ground was too quick and he wouldn't let himself down. He'd got a bit high in the weights by that stage, but he's a solid horse in his grade and has fallen back down again now. He'll start at Newbury and then head back to Chester, where he goes really well.

ANGEL MEAD (right): set to return in the Fred Darling at Newbury

Fortune And Glory 6yo gelding
War Front – Spain

He's done most of his racing on the all-weather but I think he's going to be a better horse on turf. He won at the sixth attempt on turf at Salisbury last year on good to firm even though he doesn't really want the ground too fast. He's not much higher in the weights now and he'll definitely win off his mark.

Kimifive 4yo gelding
Born To Sea – Appletreemagic

He did well last summer, winning a couple of 6f handicaps at Windsor, and I thought he was a bit unlucky not to win more. He was drawn on the wrong side in the big three-year-old handicap at Newmarket's July meeting when he was first on his side but only sixth overall. Then we took him back to Windsor and he was locked up with nowhere to go from stall one before flying home to take fourth, beaten less than a length. The ground had gone for him by the time I ran him in the Silver Cup – I'd thought he wanted it soft as a two-year-old, but both his wins were on good to firm and he definitely prefers top of the ground. He'll be running in good handicaps this year and I'm sure he can win one. We'll also try seven furlongs.

Larchmont Lad 5yo horse
Footstepsinthesand – Fotini

He's a new arrival who cost 100,000gns at the horses in training sale last October. He won a 7f Group 2 at the Curragh last season for David O'Meara and that looks like his ideal trip. I don't think he'll be easy to place but it's great to have a horse as good as him in the yard. He might have to run in Group 1 races and he'll also travel abroad.

Machine Learner 6yo gelding
Sir Percy – My First Romance

He was originally bought for the Ebor and hasn't quite reached that level yet, but he did win a 1m6f handicap at Ascot last year. He was a bit disappointing after that and tricked me into thinking he needs two miles when he probably doesn't quite get the trip. He's hard to train as he has respiratory problems and I never quite got the same tune out of him after the Ascot win. But if you look at the way he won that day, you'll see he's a very good horse when we get him right. He has a good handicap in him. Everyone has always thought he wanted quick ground, but Ryan Moore rode him near the end of last season and said he'd prefer a bit of ease.

Redgrave 5yo gelding
Lope De Vega – Olympic Medal

There's more to come from this horse. He wants soft ground and because of the dry summer we could only get him racing towards the end of last season, by which time he'd been in training a long time and wasn't at his best. He's well up to winning off his mark and I'd advise readers to keep him on their side.

Sophosc 3yo gelding
Society Rock – Ichiuma

He really improving after we had him gelded and won three nurseries in a row at Lingfield, Bath and Chelmsford. It was one race too many when we stepped him up to 1m2f on his final run, but I definitely see him improving again as he goes up in trip this year. He has size and scope so he could come on a good bit from two to three. He wants decent ground.

Surrey Blaze 4yo gelding
Thewayyouare – Catadalya

He had a great season, winning five times. He'd handicapped himself really as all of his runs the year before were on soft ground and he clearly isn't anywhere near as effective on it as he is on the all-weather or quicker ground. Things are tougher now as he's so much higher in the weights but he can be competitive in his grade when conditions suit him.

SURREY HOPE: could bounce back to form after being treated for ulcers

Surrey Hope 5yo gelding
Lemon Drop Kid – She Be Classy

He didn't show much on his last few runs, but we discovered he had ulcers so he's been treated for them and is on the way back. He'd been progressing well earlier in the year and I hope he'll bounce back now his ulcers have been treated.

Surrey Thunder 3yo colt
Le Havre – Zakania

He's a nice horse. He was a good third on his debut at Sandown last autumn and then won at Windsor. He's a middle-distance horse in the making, so we'll start him off over 1m2f this season and maybe step him up again after that. He could be a Group horse and we've got him in the German Derby, which was an early closer. He's a French-bred and we'll be taking him there to try to win some of the French premiums. I think he'll be best with some juice in the ground.

Sylvia's Mother 3yo filly
Foxwedge – Majestic Song

She was progressive last year and I think there's a bit more to come. The headgear made a big difference to her and in her last five runs she won twice and was second twice. She was running over sprint trips but I think she'll stay further. She can win again.

Topology 6yo gelding
Passing Glance – Bold Byzantium

It took him 25 races before he won once, but he was running well for most of last season and really deserved it when he got his head in front at Kempton. I was hoping he'd take a lot of confidence from that only for him to run badly at Lingfield next time, but he'd been on the go a while and we gave him a long break. He'll certainly win again.

Who Told Jo Jo 5yo gelding
Bushranger – Shenkara

I was disappointed with this horse last autumn, but I've now resigned myself to the fact he's a spring horse. All his wins have been in April or May, including twice last year, and we'll have him ready to go. He's down to his last winning mark and I'm sure he can do it again.

RACING & FOOTBALL outlook

Pedigrees for punters by James Thomas

WITH potential superstars like Kingman and No Nay Never having unleashed their first juveniles in 2018, this season's freshman sires have plenty to live up to.

However, with some of the hottest talents from recent times fielding their first two-year-olds, there are plenty of reasons to believe this year's crop, the most notable of which are discussed below, will prove up to the challenge.

Muhaarar
Oasis Dream – Tahrir (Linamix)

While high-class at two, including when winning the Gimcrack Stakes, Muhaarar will be best remembered for an outstanding three-year-old season.

He kicked off the year with victory in the Greenham Stakes but, having failed to land a blow in the French 2,000 Guineas, connections dropped Muhaarar back to sprinting trips, a move that saw him rattle of four consecutive Group 1 victories. The winning streak began with a breathtaking performance in the Commonwealth Cup beforfe he defeated his elders to land the July Cup and Prix Maurice de Gheest and then returned to Ascot to run away with the Champions Sprint on his swansong.

Muhaarar is by fellow July Cup winner Oasis Dream, who has made his mark as a sire of sires through Showcasing, the stallion responsible for Quiet Reflection, Tasleet and Advertise.

His debut book was befitting of his colossal talent, including 129 mares, 72 (56 per cent) of whom are stakes performers and 31 (24 per cent) Group winners.

Among his progeny are colts out of elite winners like Alexander Goldrun (named Khaalis) and Royal Highness (unnamed), and fillies out of Izzi Top (Bizzi Lizzi) and Sultanina (Manzanilla).

He also has siblings to some headline performers, including Queen's Trust (filly named Queen's Favour); Sole Power (unnamed filly); The Tin Man (unnamed colt); Chicquita and Magic Wand (unnamed colt); Signs Of Blessing (unnamed filly); and Twilight Son (colt named Run From Freedom).

Muhaarar's progeny caught the attention of some notable operators, with Shadwell spending 925,000gns to secure the half-sister to Fairyland while Blandford Bloodstock gave 500,000gns for Breton Rock's half-brother. All told, his 2018 yearlings averaged 169,195gns, almost six times his covering fee of £30,000.

With two-year-olds in training with the likes of John Gosden, Richard Hannon and Richard Fahey, and with his progeny looking likely to have inherited their fair share of their sire's class and precocity, he can get his stud career off to a flying start.

Golden Horn
Cape Cross – Fleche D'Or (Dubai Destination)

Having retired to Darley's Dalham Hall at a

fee of £60,000, Golden Horn was the most expensive recruit to stud of his generation.

Such a lofty price tag was well earned as he retired having won four Group 1s, namely the Derby, the Coral-Eclipse, the Irish Champion Stakes and the Prix de l'Arc de Triomphe during a stunning three-year-old season that concluded with a near miss in the Breeders' Cup Turf.

He was bred by Anthony Oppenheimer's Hascombe And Valiant Studs and is by Cape Cross, whose other son, Sea The Stars, has developed into one of the finest stallions around with nine Group 1 winners to his name. Golden Horn is out of an unraced sibling to six black-type performers, including Coronation Stakes winner Rebecca Sharp.

Breeders were keen to avail themselves of Golden Horn's services as his first book of mares contained 150 names, including 57 (38 per cent) stakes winners, giving him an ample measure of quality and quantity to call upon.

Among the ranks of Golden Horn's first crop are Al Zaraqaan, a three-parts brother to Awtaad; an unnamed half-sister to Dariyan; a closely related brother to Mutakayyef; Golden Hind, a half-sister to Amazing Maria; a closely related sister to Sea The Moon; and Solar Screen, a half-brother to Lumiere.

Plenty of his progeny have inherited their sire's size and scope and, with his debut book of mares containing plenty of Classic types, his first two-year-olds can be expected to follow in Golden Horn's footsteps by proving later-maturing types who improve markedly from two to three.

Gleneagles
Galileo – You'resothrilling (Storm Cat)

Gleneagles retired with four Group 1s to his name; one recorded at two, having landed the 2014 National Stakes, and a further three during his Classic campaign, namely the 2,000 Guineas and the Irish equivalent as well as the St James's Palace Stakes.

Not only is his race record right out of the top drawer but Gleneagles boasts one of the strongest pedigrees in the stud book. He is by the mighty Galileo, who has already produced Group 1 winner-siring sons such as Frankel, New Approach, Nathaniel and Ruler Of The World. His female line is also exceptional as he is out of You'resothrilling, dam of fellow Group 1 winners Marvellous and Happily. In turn

GLENEAGLES: top miler has one of the strongest pedigrees in the stud book

You'resothrilling is out of the influential producer Mariah's Storm, making her a sister to the Iron Horse, Giant's Causeway, as well as Pearling, dam of three-time Group 1 winner Decorated Knight.

That combination of pedigree and performance earned him an introductory stud fee of €60,000 and a book of 150 mares, including 26 Group/Graded winners (17 per cent).

His yearlings fetched up to 500,000gns, with Blandford Bloodstock signing for the filly out of Tarbela at Book 1 of the Tattersalls October Yearling Sale, while Sackville Donald smashed the record price at the Goffs UK Premier Sale when landing the Gleneagles colt out of Lady Eclair for £380,000.

Also, at least seven of his juveniles are in training with Gleneagles' old handler Aidan O'Brien, including a colt out of four-time Group 1 winner Peeping Fawn.

His stock seem likely to improve with time, but there should also be enough precocious performers among his debut two-year-olds to see him make a big impression this year.

NIGHT OF THUNDER: bred on the successful Galileo-Dubawi cross

---

Night Of Thunder
Dubawi – Forest Storm (Galileo)

The list of talented stallions who won the 2,000 Guineas during their racing days is a long one and this year Night Of Thunder, who landed the Classic in 2014, will bid to add his name to the roll of honour.

Night Of Thunder's success on the Rowley Mile came after an unbeaten juvenile campaign and at the expense of the likes of Kingman, Australia and Charm Spirit. A string of consistent efforts followed before he returned at four to land the Locking Stakes.

He is bred on the successful Dubawi-Galileo cross and is out of the Listed-placed Forest Storm, who descends from champion two-year-old and Irish 1,000 Guineas heroine Forest Flower.

He received 142 mares in his first book, which was covered at Darley's Kildangan Stud at a fee of €30,000, and 34 (24 per cent) of those were stakes performers.

Among his debut two-year-olds are siblings to Aclaim (a colt bought by Phoenix Thoroughbreds for 260,000gns); Obviously (colt named Herr Juergensen); an unnamed sister to Wigmore Hall; and a closely related brother to Prince Bishop called Moving Light and a half-brother to Blue Point called Desert Destination, both in training with Saeed Bin Suroor.

Night Of Thunder's most expensive yearling last year was a colt bought by Rabbah Bloodstock for €350,000. Since named Man Of The Night, the youngster has been placed under the care of Richard Hannon.

Others to note
With plenty of precocious ammunition on his side, **Gutaifan**, a son of the mighty Dark Angel, looks certain to make his presence felt in 2019, while similar comments apply to the likes of **Anjaal**, **Brazen Beau**, **Cable Bay** and **Hot Streak**.

Free Eagle and **Make Believe** are others who should not be overlooked. Free Eagles supplied a number of yearlings who proved in high demand, while Make Believe was supremely talented and comes from a farm in Ballylinch Stud who know all about nurturing a young sire's career.

RACING & FOOTBALL outlook

Ante-post preview by Steffan Edwards

2,000 Guineas

NO colt sired by Dubawi has taken part in the race since 2014, which is surprising given his record with the small sample of horses who have represented him. From just four runners, he's had two winners – Makfi at 33-1 and Night Of Thunder at 40-1 – and two placed horses at 33-1 and 16-1.

Dubawi has an excellent chance of enhancing that record this year as the two at the head of the market are both sired by him and I much prefer **QUORTO** to **Too Darn Hot** at the prices.

Too Darn Hot carried all before him last year, winning all four starts in impressive fashion, culminating in a comfortable win in the Dewhurst, to be crowned champion two-year-old. On breeding (brother to So Mi Dar and Lah Ti Dar) he should make up into an even better three-year-old and be suited by going further than a mile, yet he clearly has bundles of pace and if he's going to win a Classic then it will surely be the Guineas.

That said, there are a couple of negatives. First off, he was on the small size last year and others with more scope could have improved past him over the winter. Secondly, John Gosden hasn't won this race before, getting the likes of Kingman, Raven's Pass and Roaring Lion beaten in it. All three were arguably the best miler

in the race, but not on that first Saturday in May. Given that Too Darn Hot is such a short price, I'm happy to take him on.

Quorto impressed me in his three starts last year, winning his first two, including the Superlative Stakes, on Newmarket's July Course, before quickening up well to take the National Stakes at the Curragh, beating that solid yardstick Anthony Van Dyck into second.

His form at two closely matches that of his sire, who also went 3-3 at two, winning the same Group races, and his trainer Charlie Appleby may have had that in mind when deciding not to run him again after his trip to Ireland. Appleby, who is at the top of his game right now, has said the plan is for Quorto to go straight for the Guineas and I think he's a solid alternative to the favourite at 8-1.

Calyx and **Ten Sovereigns** are ones to take on. Both were unbeaten at two but have big negatives against them.

Calyx wasn't seen again after getting injured at Royal Ascot and, as a precocious late April foal, he wouldn't be a banker to train on – his dam certainly didn't.

Ten Sovereigns looked all speed to me, which isn't surprising given he's by No Nay Never out of an Exceed And Excel mare, and Aidan O'Brien has already expressed doubts about him getting a mile.

While Dubawi has had a good record,

the dominant sire of the race in recent years has still been Galileo. Of the last eight winners, six had Galileo as either their sire or damsire, while another one had him as a grandsire. As one might expect, he has several who could represent him this year, including the Futurity Trophy winner **MAGNA GRECIA**, who has Galileo as his dam sire.

Magna Grecia was one of only three juvenile colts to win first time out for Ballydoyle last year and, after getting narrowly beaten by Persian King in the Autumn Stakes, he ran out a gutsy winner at Doncaster. That's often a race that produces middle-distance horses of the future, but he doesn't look to be crying out for a trip (brother to a three-time 7f winner) and at this stage he looks O'Brien's strongest candidate for the Guineas.

It's also worth remembering his stable struggled with a virus last year and he made his debut on the last day of September, having three quick runs including his Group 1 victory, so he could be open to any amount of improvement over the winter. In any case, it's never a bad idea to get with the best candidate from a yard that

has sent out nine of the last 21 winners of this race.

Phoenix Of Spain progressed with every start last year, finishing a good second to Too Darn Hot in the Champagne before going down narrowly in the Futurity Trophy. He has the size to improve from two to three and is an interesting contender. The one concern is that Charlie Hills kept him away from Newmarket last year as he thought the undulations wouldn't suit – in his words – the "big, heavy horse" at that stage of his career. I guess there's a chance he could still think the same this spring, although he's surely likelier to roll the dice for a Guineas.

Another colt who has the size and scope to progress from two to three is **Persian King**. Godolphin bought a half-share of him in the off-season but he's to stay in training with Andre Fabre. He just outbattled the less experienced Magna Grecia to win the Autumn Stakes and, if anything, looks the type who will thrive over further than a mile this year. The Prix du Jockey Club might be his ideal target.

Anthony Van Dyck, who had a busy time of it last year, came up a bit short on

QUORTO: form closely matches his sire, Dubawi, who has a fine Guineas record

GREAT SCOT: could be an interesting outsider for Tom Dascombe

his tries in Group 1 company. He's a mid-May foal and might need further than a mile this year, so he's not for me.

Jash ran a big race against Ten Sovereigns in the Middle Park without necessarily suggesting he's a miler in the making, while I'm far from convinced that **Advertise** is crying out for a mile. He's by Showcasing out of a 6f winner by Pivotal and will probably get outstayed.

Madhmoon impressed in both his starts last year and his win in a Group 2 at Leopardstown reads well, with the second and fourth going on to be placed in Group 1 company. With the Guineas in mind, however, there are one or two things against him. He ran only over a mile at two, which is unusual for a Guineas winner (only Camelot and Saxon Warrior in the last 30 years) and trainer Kevin Prendergast has suggested some cut in the ground would suit him ideally. Prendergast doesn't make a habit of bringing one over for the Guineas either, tending to prefer to stay at home for the Irish version.

Charlie Appleby has said **Line Of Duty** will join Quorto in going straight to the Guineas, but I wonder whether he'll have the pace for the race. He didn't get off the mark last year until stepped up to a mile, then won a Group 3 over 1m1f in France before staying on strongly to win at the Breeders' Cup. I think he'll be using the Guineas as a stepping stone to the Derby.

The Saeed Bin Suroor-trained Group 1 winners **Royal Meeting** and **Royal Marine** have been wintering in Dubai, the latter racing on the dirt at Meydan, and it remains to be seen where they are targeted. The former isn't sure to be suited by stepping up to a mile judged by his pedigree.

Dark Vision won his first three last year, including the Vintage Stakes, after which he was sold to Godolphin, but he blew out on his first start for them in the Champagne Stakes. He has a bit to prove now.

Turgenev didn't run up to expectations when raised markedly in class in the Futurity Trophy. A son of Dubawi, he could have more to offer this term but perhaps over further than a mile (dam was at her best over 1m2f).

Sangarius looked good winning his first two but was then well held in the Dewhurst. That might just have been too big a step up for him at that stage of his career and he retains potential, but he's a May foal and the Guineas might just come a bit soon for him.

Dubai Warrior is probably more of a Derby prospect, while fellow backend maiden/novice winners **Space Blues**, **Skardu** and **Zakouski** all look promising types but may find the Guineas coming a bit quick.

Kadar is highly regarded and impressed on his debut at Haydock. Karl Burke wasn't prepared to run him on fast ground in the Royal Lodge or Autumn Stakes, though, and then he missed the Futurity despite the ground coming in his favour. By Scat Daddy but out of a Sinndar mare, he's more of a galloper than a quickener and might need further than a mile to show his best this year.

The Richard Hannon stable always likes to have a runner in the Guineas and have a couple of potential candidates.

Boitron won his first three before falling short in the Lagardere and on that form he needs to improve quite a bit, so maybe the more interesting runner from the yard is **Urban Icon**. He won a couple of novices early in the campaign and, while he wasn't seen again afterwards, his trainer felt he would benefit from time to strengthen up. He certainly didn't look like just an early type and it wouldn't be a surprise to see him show up well in a race like the Greenham, before a tilt at the Guineas. Stamina will be the issue, though, as he isn't short of speed and his pedigree isn't entirely convincing on that front either.

The Tom Dascombe-trained **Great Scot** is an interesting outsider. After winning on his debut at Chester, he followed up by giving weight and a beating to Line Of Duty at Haydock, showing a smart turn of foot. Next time out in France he was unlucky not to retain his unbeaten record, flying home off a steady pace but not quite getting up in a Listed race won by Al Hilalee. He gained compensation in another Listed race back at Haydock despite taking a fierce hold in the early stages. That failure to settle didn't cost him there, but it compromised his chance in the Futurity, in which he wasn't beaten far in fifth.

Getting back on faster ground should suit him and, off a strong gallop in the Guineas, I could see him surprising a few people.

2,000 Guineas

Newmarket, 4 May

	Bet365	Betfred	Betway	Coral	Hills	Lads	PPower	SkyBet
Too Darn Hot	5-4	5-4	5-4	5-4	5-4	5-4	**11-8**	**11-8**
Quorto	**8**	7	13-2	7	**8**	**8**	**8**	7
Ten Sovereigns	8	7	8	8	7	6	**10**	8
Calyx	8	8	8	**10**	6	9	**10**	**10**
Persian King	10	10	10	12	**14**	10	**14**	12
Advertise	10	**14**	10	12	10	10	**14**	12
Magna Grecia	12	12	12	**14**	**14**	**14**	**14**	12
Anthony Van Dyck	16	14	16	**20**	**20**	16	**20**	16
Madhmoon	14	14	16	**20**	16	16	**20**	20
Line Of Duty	18	-	18	16	**20**	**20**	16	-
Jash	16	16	16	14	16	12	**20**	16
Sangarius	25	25	25	25	25	25	**33**	20
Phoenix Of Spain	20	25	16	25	16	**33**	**33**	25
Dark Vision	33	33	33	33	25	33	**40**	33

each-way 1/5 odds, 1-2-3
Others on application, prices correct at time of going to press

1,000 Guineas

THE betting for this race is very open, with bookmakers going 10-1 the field. If they were all to line up the impressive Breeders' Cup winner **Newspaperofrecord** would be a lot shorter, but it doesn't look like she'll be travelling over for the Guineas. She's currently pencilled in for the Coronation Stakes and it's understandable that the royal meeting holds greater allure for her connections than Newmarket in May.

Consequently, **Just Wonderful**, who finished almost eight lengths behind her at Churchill Downs, heads the market. She's a strong traveller and, as she showed when taking the Group 3 Flame Of Tara and Group 2 Rockfel, her ability to quicken is impressive.

In between, however, she blew out in the Moyglare and of course she was well held on her final start at the Breeders' Cup, so she's been a bit inconsistent. Perhaps it was just immaturity and she'll fulfil her potential this year, but it's worth remembering that she's a half-sister to Lost Treasure, who is rated 112 but a 'character' who doesn't like to hit the front, so it might not be plain sailing with her.

Skitter Scatter was out early last year, making her debut in March, but she improved with every start, culminating with victory in the Moyglare.

Her trainer Patrick Prendergast has joined forces with John Oxx ahead of this year's campaign and the filly will run under Oxx's name, but by all accounts nothing much will change on the training front. A trial and then the Guineas is the plan, and a mile should be within her compass, but there might be one or two with more scope for improvement.

Lady Kaya was last off the bridle in the Moyglare and again travelled well for a long way in the Cheveley Park. Physically, she wasn't the finished article last year and there could be better to come at three. She's by Dandy Man but out of a Singspiel mare, so getting the mile isn't out of the question.

Hermosa proved a consistent performer at the top level in 2018, finishing placed in the Moyglare, Fillies' Mile and Criterium International, the latter against the colts. A sister to Hydrangea, who was effective over a variety of distances, she looks the type who could go to the Guineas and Oaks, but she's a May foal (no winner in the last 30 years) so I'm happy to take her on in the Guineas. The same worry applies to Winter's sister **Frosty**.

Fairyland stuck to 6f at two, winning the Lowther and Cheveley Park, and the obvious question is whether she'll stay a mile. Being a sister to the sprinter Ateltico, it's probably worth betting she won't.

So Perfect is another who didn't venture beyond 6f last year. There's a lot of speed on the dam's side of the pedigree and I suspect she may not even make the trip to Newmarket.

When it comes to other contenders from Ballydoyle, I'd say **Fleeting** and **Pink Dogwood** look more like Oaks fillies, while for the moment the likes of **Zagitova**, **Coral Beach** and **Peach Tree** look short of the standard required.

Secret Thoughts is the first foal of Irish Oaks winner Chiquita, who for all her talent was a long way from being straightforward. It appears her daughter has inherited some of her quirkiness as she flashed her tail on each of her three starts last year and had to be kidded along to win her maiden. She could be good but probably comes with some risks attached.

Of all the O'Brien-trained fillies, I think **GODDESS** might be the most interesting.

She was one of the biggest eyecatchers of the year on her debut at the Curragh when getting boxed in and crossing the line in ninth when with a clear run she might have won. Given a no-nonsense front-running ride second time out at Leopardstown, she bolted up by 10l. On the back of that she was promoted to Guineas favouritism and sent off heavy odds-on to win the Group 3 Silver Flash, but she trailed in last of six behind Skitter Scatter and wasn't seen again.

GODDESS: made Guineas favourite after this win and forgiven subsequent loss

O'Brien had a number of reverses around the time of her last run which were put down to a virus in the yard, so it's easy to put a line through that. She could easily bounce back this year and, while on pedigree she ought to be suited by middle distances, she didn't look short of speed, so a well-run Guineas might be ideal early in the campaign. A prominent showing in the Leopardstown Guineas Trial is all it will take for her to get back in the reckoning.

Iridessa was a bit of a shock winner of the Fillies' Mile, but she'd looked a smart prospect when winning on her debut and things hadn't gone right for her back over 7f on her next two starts. She got plenty of cover at Newmarket and, on a windy day when stamina came to the fore, she was strong at the finish. She looks more of an Oaks prospect on pedigree.

The Prix Morny winner **Pretty Pollyanna** ran well to be third in the Fillies' Mile, especially as she had her face in the wind throughout and was possibly beaten by a couple of Oaks fillies in what became quite a test.

There's still a question mark over the trip for her and her pedigree (half-sister to two 7f winners) doesn't offer much reassurance, but she's not one to write off and it's easy to see her going off shorter than the current 25-1 as she's likely to take in the Fred Darling first and will probably be favourite to win that.

Ralph Beckett has a strong bunch of three-year-old fillies and whatever he chooses to run will have to be respected.

He has a bit of a guide to the level of some of the opposition through **Sand Share**, who was third in the May Hill, and I've no doubt that she's a little way down the pecking order.

Feliciana De Vega only made her debut in November, but she followed up a 6l win at Newmarket with a Listed success on the Polytrack at Deauville in December. She looks smart and a mile should suit her well this year, but with the Guineas in mind it's slightly off-putting that her trainer believes she'll always require some cut in the ground to be at her best.

Manuela De Vega looks very much a middle-distance filly in the making, while the Prestige Stakes winner **Antonia De Vega** is another who should need further than a mile to be seen at her best. The fact she finished lame when trailing home last in the Fillies' Mile adds another question mark next to her name.

Queen Power is a daughter of Shamardal and bred to be effective over a mile this term. She won well enough first time up (second and third won next time out) and could leap into contention with a prominent showing in a trial.

However, from what I saw the pick of Beckett's fillies for the Guineas is probably **DANCING VEGA**, who travelled strongly

25

and quickened up in impressive style to win by 4l from a subsequent Listed winner on her debut at Doncaster. That race was over a mile and the concern is that she was beating future middle-distance horses rather than milers, but she didn't look short of pace and I can't imagine her having a problem with a well-run mile in the spring before possibly moving up to 1m2f later in the campaign. Given her lack of experience, she might benefit from an outing in the Nell Gwyn beforehand.

Fashion's Star won well enough on her debut in a conditions race at Newbury. She has potential, but on breeding the Guineas might be a bit short for her. The same goes for **Sparkle Roll**, who's a half-sister to Wings Of Eagles.

In contrast, the likes of **Angel's Hideaway**, **Red Impression** and **Angelic Light** are probably sprinters in the making.

The Albany winner **Main Edition** didn't really progress from Royal Ascot, although she did bag another Group 3, winning the Sweet Solera in August. Others are likely to have improved past her over the winter.

The Kevin Ryan-trained **East** quickened up in good style to win a French Group 3 in October and then went on to finish

second at the Breeders' Cup. She might just have bumped into a very good horse that day and it's unlikely she'll have to face her again at Newmarket, so she looks a player, with further improvement likely from two to three based on her breeding.

It didn't look a particularly strong edition of the Oh So Sharp that **Mot Juste** won last year. A mile should suit her, but she needs to progress further.

Hidden Message won nicely over 6f at Yarmouth on her debut, but her relative inexperience caught her out when sent off favourite for the Oh So Sharp next time, running green and also hampered entering the Dip. She'll do better, but whether she wants to go as far as a mile is open to debate.

Rainbow Heart is another William Haggas novice winner of interest. She travelled well for a long way behind Roger Varian's Qabala on her debut at Newmarket but got disorganised running into the Dip before keeping on for third. On her second start she proved far more professional and bounded clear over 7f to win by 8l.

The question with her is whether a mile will be on the short side, as she's by Born To Sea out of a mare who won at Group

NATALIE'S JOY: among a few interesting outsiders in the 1,000 Guineas

2 level over 1m4½f. It might be that she's more of an Oaks filly, but Sea Of Grace (same connections) was similarly bred and was best over a mile. Either way, she's worth keeping in mind.

Watheerah (Owen Burrows) and **Operatic Export** (Jim Bolger) are promising maiden winners but would need to show up well in a trial for me to take them seriously. The former is by Dubawi out of a half-sister to Ghanaati so certainly bred for the job.

While Charlie Appleby holds a strong hand in the colts' Classics, his fillies look weak in comparison. **Divine Image**, who's been running on the dirt in Dubai, might be switched to the turf because the likes of **La Pelosa**, **Ceratonia** and **Beyond Reason** all ended their seasons on downers and need to not only bounce back but improve significantly on their form so far to figure.

Natalie's Joy clocked a fast time when scoring by 6l on her debut at Goodwood and on the back of that was sent off a short price to win the Chesham. She flopped at Royal Ascot but bounced back to win a Listed race at Newbury (subsequent Gimcrack winner Emaraaty Ana in third). Some minor setbacks afterwards prevented her from running again, but the Mark Johnston yard are aiming her at the Guineas and

she's a possible flyer at a big price as on breeding she should be suited by the mile.

Star Terms progressed as she moved up in distance last term, taking a big jump from winning a 7f nursery on her fourth start to finishing second in the May Hill and then backing that up with a close third in the Marcel Boussac. Her pedigree is a nice mix of speed and stamina, a strongly run mile should suit her down to the ground and she's trained by someone in Richard Hannon who values the Guineas and knows how to get one ready for the race. She might be overpriced at 50-1.

Tasleya travelled well and quickened up smartly to win on her debut at Deauville. She flopped when stepped up to Group 2 company next time in the Prix du Calvados, but that wasn't her true form and she was absent for the rest of the campaign. Entries in the Cheveley Park and Fillies' Mile suggest her trainer Jean-Claude Rouget was considering bringing her over in the autumn and she could easily get back in the Guineas picture with a big run in the Prix Imprudence in April. She's nicely bred, being by Frankel out of a mare Rouget trained to win the Imprudence before being sent off joint second-favourite for the Guineas only to finish down the field behind Homecoming Queen.

1,000 Guineas

Newmarket, 5 May

	Bet365	Betfred	Betway	Coral	Hills	Lads	PPower	SkyBet
Just Wonderful	**10**	**10**	**10**	**10**	**10**	8	**10**	**10**
Newspaperofrecord	8	10	10	10	10	10	10	**12**
Skitter Scatter	**14**	**14**	**14**	12	10	**14**	12	**14**
Fairyland	12	**14**	12	12	12	**14**	**14**	**14**
So Perfect	16	16	16	16	16	16	**20**	**20**
East	**20**	**20**	**20**	**20**	16	16	14	**20**
Iridessa	14	14	16	**20**	14	16	16	**20**
Goddess	**25**	16	20	20	20	16	16	16
Pretty Pollyanna	16	16	20	**25**	20	20	20	20
Zagitova	**33**	25	**33**	**33**	25	**33**	25	25
Main Edition	20	25	20	20	25	25	**33**	25
Antonia De Vega	**33**	20	**33**	**33**	**33**	**33**	16	**33**
Dancing Vega	25	20	25	20	**50**	25	16	-
Natalie's Joy	40	33	40	33	-	40	**50**	33

each-way 1/5 odds, 1-2-3
Others on application, prices correct at time of going to press

Derby

As with the Guineas, **Too Darn Hot** heads the market, but I'm even more determined to take him on in this race. Aside from doubts about his lack of scope, his prime asset is his turn of foot and, despite his pedigree, he'll surely struggle to stay the Derby trip.

On the face of it the Ballydoyle challenge looks strong on numbers but light on quality, but that may be misleading as the stable had the virus last year, which may have hampered the progress of some, delayed the introductions of others and even denied some the opportunity of having a run. Indeed, it wouldn't come as a surprise if a colt who was unraced at two emerged as a big runner, as in 2013 when Ruler Of The World burst on the scene.

Three names to keep in mind are **Godzilla**, who's a half-brother to nine winners, **Lake McKenzie**, who's a son of Australia, and **Sir Dragonet**, who's by Camelot out of a half-sister to Oaks runner-up Wonder Of Wonders.

From those who got to run at two, **Anthony Van Dyck** was the best of them. His progress stalled towards the backend but he won his maiden over a mile before doing most of his racing over shorter later in the campaign, so it's possible he'll appreciate a step up in trip this year despite being out of a speedy mare. He's a mid-May foal, though, and a bit of a risky proposition.

Japan beat **Mount Everest** a shade cosily in the Beresford Stakes. The latter got first run but Japan finished strongest and looks the likelier of the two to thrive over the Derby trip, although both are related to horses who arguably proved at their best over short of 1m4f, including Japan's sister Secret Gesture, who was runner-up but didn't quite get home in the Oaks and was mostly campaigned over shorter afterwards. Japan still showed signs of inexperience that day, though, and we've yet to see the best of him.

I see **Magna Grecia** as more of a Guineas horse and doubt he'll stay 1m4f, while the Royal Lodge winner **Mohawk** will be suited by the Derby trip but might just lack the class required, comments that also apply to **Norway** and possibly **Circus Maximus** as well. The St Leger might suit the strong-staying **Constantinople** better than the Derby.

I don't like Too Darn Hot's claims, but John Gosden has plenty of other potential candidates to fire at the race.

Chief among them could be **Dubai Warrior**, who impressed on his debut at Chelmsford, overcoming greenness to scoot home by 4½l. He has plenty of scope and should make up into a nice three-year-old, while his pedigree (by Dansili out of a Galileo mare who won at up to 1m4f) suggests he should stay the Derby trip. The niggle about him is whether he will transfer his form to the turf as his brother Mootasadir, who won a Group 3 at Dundalk in September, is thought by connections to need an artificial surface to show his best. His dam, Mahbooba, was perfectly effective on turf, but she did win the UAE 1000 Guineas on Tapeta, so the family are clearly at home on those kind of surfaces.

Turgenev progressed steadily last term. He didn't run up to his market billing in the Vertem Futurity Trophy, but he's probably more of a three-year-old in the making anyway and middle distances should suit this term. He could be a player.

Humanitarian is bred to stay well but might just lack the tactical pace required, something that cannot be said of **Sucellus**, who came from a long way back off a steady early pace to win at Wolverhampton on his debut. He was very green that day and is a lot better than the bare form suggests. By Dansili out of a mare who won at up to 1m2f, there might be a bit of a question mark over his stamina for the trip, but at this stage he could be anything.

Charlie Appleby sent out Masar to win the Derby last year and he holds a stronger hand this time around than the current betting suggests.

Although **Quorto** looks more of a Guin-

LINE OF DUTY (left): improved with every start and won at the Breeders' Cup

eas horse to me, it's not out of the question he could go for both races and there are reasons to think he could well stay the trip given his dam was third in the Oaks and Irish Oaks, but that said I do think the yard has a stronger card to play.

LINE OF DUTY improved with every start last year and his form has worked out well. Unlucky not to make a winning debut at Sandown, it turned out that was a hot contest, the winner going on to score in Group 3 company and the third placing in the Group 1 Criterium de Saint-Cloud towards the end of the season. He then bumped into the subsequent Vertem Futurity fourth when runner-up again on his second start at Haydock. Moving up to a mile at Goodwood saw him off the mark and he didn't look back after that, showing a smart turn of foot to win a French Group 3 over 1m1f in October (third won the Criterium de Saint-Cloud next time out) and then crossing the Atlantic to win the Breeders' Cup Juvenile Turf.

He was always strongest at the finish of his races and, being by Galileo and a brother to a couple of middle-distance

horses, the Derby trip isn't going to be a problem for him.

Appleby has said he plans to run Line Of Duty in the Guineas first time out and, while I don't expect him to win it, a good run isn't out of the question and that should tee him up nicely for a tilt at the Derby – Appleby has said before that he's a strong believer in the Guineas being the best trial for Epsom, so I think it's interesting he plans to send him to Newmarket rather than to a Derby trial.

Al Hilalee is the other possible candidate from the Appleby yard.

A winner of both his starts last year, he's bred for the job, being by Dubawi out of an Authorized mare who won the Group 1 Pretty Polly. He overcame greenness to win nicely on his debut at Newmarket and then held on narrowly in a French Listed race. That was a bit of a messy affair and not the sort of race that would see a future 1m4f horse at his best, especially against pacier rivals, so it was a decent effort in the circumstances.

While his form doesn't currently match that of his Group 1-winning stablemates,

29

Derby

	Bet365	Betfred	Betway	Coral	Hills	Lads	PPower	SkyBet
Too Darn Hot	11-4	4	11-4	**9-2**	5-2	**9-2**	3	4
Anthony Van Dyck	10	12	12	12	**16**	10	12	12
Dubai Warrior	**16**	14	14	**16**	**16**	**16**	14	14
Quorto	14	**16**	14	**16**	**16**	**16**	14	**16**
Japan	16	14	16	16	**20**	16	14	16
Magna Grecia	**20**	12	16	16	14	14	16	**20**
Madhmoon	16	**20**	**20**	16	**20**	**20**	**20**	**20**
Line Of Duty	**25**	20	20	16	20	16	**25**	20
Turgenev	25	**33**	-	**33**	**33**	**33**	20	**33**
Mount Everest	25	-	25	25	25	25	**40**	-
Rakan	33	33	33	33	**40**	33	33	33
Norway	25	25	25	33	25	40	**50**	25
Mohawk	33	25	25	40	33	**50**	**50**	40
Almania	**66**	50	-	-	50	-	50	-

each-way 1/5 odds, 1-2-3
Others on application, prices correct at time of going to press

he's very much a three-year-old in the making and could well take the leap. I'd imagine he'd be a likely type for the Dante.

Sir Michael Stoute has a couple of interesting candidates, both owned by Saeed Suhail, who had such a great time of it last year with Poet's Word.

Deal A Dollar was unfancied on his debut over a mile at Kempton but ran well in defeat behind the more experienced Khuzaam. The pair finished 7l clear of the third, who won a handicap off 79 next time out. By Frankel out of a Cape Cross mare who won the Rockfel and is from the family of Imagine and Generous, Deal A Dollar could be a different proposition upped in distance this term.

However, I think his connections might have a better one in **ALMANIA**.

The word was out before his debut at Ascot that he was well regarded, but he found 6f too short and couldn't justify favouritism. Stepped up to 7f at Sandown next time out, he rallied strongly after being headed to see off Buffalo River, the pair finishing 7l clear of the third.

His trainer avoided the temptation of running him in one of the backend Group 1 races and, given his pedigree, he could take a big leap when stepped up to middle distances this term. By Derby winner

Australia out of a mare who finished fourth in the Guineas but is a half-sister to several middle-distance winners, he looks to have the right blend of speed and stamina required.

Phoenix Thoroughbreds have an unraced son of Sea The Stars in training with Stoute called **Dilmun Dynasty**, who cost one million guineas as a yearling, but they also own **Kadar**, in training with Karl Burke, who has already shone on the track, winning first time out at Haydock. Although by Scat Daddy, there's plenty of stamina on the dam's side to suggest he'll get 1m4f and he shapes like a middle-distance horse. He's worth considering.

Nivaldo looked good in winning a pair of novices last autumn. There's plenty of stamina on the dam's side of his pedigree and he'll have prospects of staying the Derby trip as long as he settles better than he did at Kempton second time out. He'd have to show something in one of the trials to get me interested, though.

The same goes for Wolverhampton winner **Great Bear** and Haynes, Hanson & Clark winner **Raakib Alhawa**. The latter did well to win first time out and was sent off at just 6-1 to follow up in the Vertem Futurity Trophy, but he never threatened at Doncaster. It's still early days and he's got a nice mix of speed and stamina in his pedigree, being by Kingman out of a Sea The Stars mare who won at 1m4f, but he has something to prove now.

I think **Persian King** will be suited by further than a mile this year, but perhaps it'll be the French Derby for him rather than Epsom. Stamina is likely to be an issue for **Sangarius**, **Set Piece**, **Phoenix Of Spain** and the promising maiden winner **Space Blues**.

Madhmoon doesn't strike me as a Derby winner on breeding and, as I mentioned in the Guineas preview, his trainer isn't normally one for travelling.

Rakan, representing the same owner but a different trainer in Dermot Weld, might make the trip if he's considered up to the task, though. He galloped on strongly, showing a fast-ground action, when scoring on his second start at Leopardstown and his pedigree is very much that of a Derby horse, being by Sea The Stars out of Oaks runner-up Tarfasha, whom Weld also trained, so there's plenty to recommend him on paper.

Weld also trains **Tankerville**, a son of Kitten's Joy who won on his debut at Gowran Park. He suggested that colt might start off in the Ballysax this year so clearly considers him a Derby prospect as well.

The Hamdan Al Maktoum-owned novice winners **Dawaam**, **Khuzaam** and **Alfaatik** all look potentially smart types in the making.

The first two are both by Kitten's Joy and of them Khuzaam would look the likeliest to appreciate the Derby trip, whereas for Alfaatik it might be a question of 1m4f being on the short side for him. He overcame greenness to win on his debut at Chelmsford in December over 1m2f and, being by Sea The Stars out of a mare who stayed 1m3f, he might just need the Leger trip to be seen at his best. That could also be the case for **Waldstern**.

ALMANIA: a serious Derby contender for Sir Michael Stoute and Saeed Suhail

IRIDESSA: favourite for the Oaks but it's worth chancing two at bigger prices

Oaks

WITH the favourite for the Oaks a 16-1 chance, the bookmakers are saying anything could win it and it's hard to disagree.

Joseph O'Brien's **Iridessa** heads the market on the back of her Fillies' Mile success and, as a daughter of Ruler Of The World, she's bred to improve for middle distances. She had also looked a smart prospect on her debut and had things go against her on her next two runs.

That said, her Fillies' Mile win was a big step up on her previous form and things fell her way, so she doesn't necessarily deserve to be favourite.

There are a whole host of fillies from Ballydoyle to consider.

Just Wonderful showed a fair amount of speed at two so doesn't strike me as one for the Oaks, while **Secret Thoughts** is by War Front and had the pace to win over 6f last year. Although she's out of an Irish Oaks winner, her sire doesn't get many who win over 1m4f.

Goddess is another who might be at her best over distances short of the Oaks trip as she showed plenty of toe last year and her sister Athena was a 1m2f filly.

Peach Tree is a potential improver up in trip, being a sister to last year's Oaks fifth Flattering, and **Pink Dogwood** isn't going to have any issues with the trip, being a sister to last year's Irish Derby winner Latrobe. She didn't run badly in the Marcel Boussac, just being done for a bit of pace, but I suspect there might be one or two stronger candidates in the yard.

Hermosa has proved herself a solid performer at Group 1 level and promises to do better up in trip this year. Her sister Hydrangea won the Matron Stakes over a mile and the Fillies & Mares at Ascot over 1m4f on Champions Day at three and she may prove just as versatile.

Fleeting was nicely on top at the finish of the May Hill, her stamina coming to the fore late on. She's by Zoffany, who's more associated with siring milers, but he did sire Architecture, who was second in the Oaks and Irish Oaks in 2016, and Fleeting's dam, who's by Motivator, won at up to 1m6f in Spain, so she should be well suited by the Oaks distance.

Narrow preference, though, is for **CHABLIS**, a rare first-time-out two-year-old winner for the yard when scoring cosily at Gowran Park in October. In total only nine horses from Ballydoyle managed that feat, but they included Ten Sovereigns, Magna Grecia and Fairyland, who all went on to win in Group 1 company, Just Wonderful and Fleeting, who won Group 2 races, and So Perfect, who scored a Group 3.

So there's a good chance Chablis is well above average and that's backed up by her pedigree, as she's a 1.55 million guineas daughter of Galileo out of the Group 1 Prix Saint-Alary winner Vadawina, which makes her a sister to The Pentagon, who was fifth in last year's Irish Derby.

There's plenty to recommend her on paper and by the time Epsom rolls around she may well have overtaken some of her higher-profile stablemates in the pecking order.

Looking at Ralph Beckett's options for the race, it seems to me that **Dancing Vega**, **Sand Share**, **Queen Power** and **Feliciana De Vega** will be at their best over shorter than 1m4f, which leaves **Antonia De Vega** and **Manuela De Vega**.

Neither of those two should have any issues going the Oaks distance, but the latter has more physical scope and might improve more from two to three. There's also the concern over the former finishing lame in the Fillies' Mile.

Although **Star Terms** is by Sea The Stars, her dam was fast and it's hard to see her staying the trip.

The same goes for **Clematis**, who is by a speedier sire than her half-sister Sepal, who stayed 1m6f. **Fashion's Star** is another by Sea The Stars and would appear to have decent claims of staying 1m4f as she's out of a half-sister to Pakistan Star, who's won Group 1s in Hong Kong at up to 1m4f, but Roger Charlton cast doubt on that after she won on her debut.

Dubai Blue, **Sparkle Roll** and **Fran-**kellina all won novices over a mile at two and have the potential to develop into contenders. The latter might be the pick of them, but William Haggas, who trains Frankellina, might have an even better one in **Rainbow Heart**, who bolted up on her second start at Newmarket. I could see her going for the Guineas and Oaks and would respect her chance in both.

Mot Juste probably won't want to go as far as 1m4f, but Roger Varian has a few other possibles, including first-time-out winners **Nearooz** and **Nausha** as well as **Tauteke**, who got off the mark second time out having suffered a wide trip at Kempton on her debut. The latter is bred to get the trip well, being a daughter of Sea The Stars out of a Sadler's Wells mare who won a Group 3 over 1m4f, but perhaps that first run of hers at Kempton is a pointer to a more interesting outsider to keep in mind.

Tauteke was third that day as the James Fanshawe-trained **AUDARYA** came within a nose of making a winning debut, just unable to catch the more experienced Roger Charlton-trained Lady Adelaide, who'd enjoyed the run of things out in front.

Little was expected as she was sent off at 50-1, but she showed a good level of ability that day and don't let her starting price kid you that it was a fluke. Speedy Boarding (third at 20-1), Seal Of Approval (second at 50-1) and Ribbons (winner at 20-1) all began their careers by outrunning market expectations before going on to win in Group 1 company for Fanshawe and he's only had nine first-time-out juvenile winners in the last ten years, so it was a big performance from Audarya.

She galloped out strongly after the line and her pedigree gives hope she'll get the Oaks trip, as her dam won over 1m4½f. The fact she's by Wootton Bassett does temper enthusiasm and it might be she's a 1m2f filly in the making, but I'm willing to take a chance on her at a silly price.

There are one or two others who will begin the season as maidens but caught the eye first time out and still have time to make their mark.

Kalanoura had a wider trip than ideal and ran green when second on her debut at Dundalk. She finished 5l clear of the third, though, and on breeding (by Casamento out of a mare who won over 1m5f and is closely related to Kalanisi) she should relish a step up to middle distances this year. The negative is that her trainer Mick Halford doesn't make a habit of travelling his horses over to Britain.

Fanny Logan was narrowly denied by her stablemate Mehdaayih on her debut at Yarmouth. A daughter of Sea The Stars, she is out of a mare who won at up to 1m4f, so stamina isn't going to be an issue for her.

Kiss For A Jewel was green but showed plenty on her debut at Galway, just getting outbattled by a Ballydoyle filly who had already had a couple of outings. She's by Kingman out of Sapphire, who won the Fillies & Mares on Champions Day for her trainer Dermot Weld in 2012. She might end up being more of a 1m2f sort, but Weld also has several unraced fillies still to come out, notably **All Our Tomorrows**, who cost 1.7 million guineas and is a half-sister to three-time Listed winner Abingdon, and **Search For A Song**, who is closely related to Prince of Wales's Stakes winner Free Eagle, so he's not short of ammunition.

Portfolio

2,000 Guineas

Quorto 3pts 8-1
(generally available)

Magna Grecia 1pt 14-1
(generally available)

1,000 Guineas

Goddess 1pt 25-1
(bet365)

Dancing Vega 1pt 50-1
(Hills)

Derby

Line Of Duty 3pts 25-1
(bet365, Paddy Power)

Almania 1pt 66-1
(bet365)

Oaks

Chablis 2pts 33-1
(generally available)

Audarya 1pt 100-1
(bet365)

Oaks

Epsom, 31 May

	Bet365	Betfred	Betway	Coral	Hills	Lads	PPower	SkyBet
Iridessa	14	**16**	**16**	**16**	**16**	14	14	**16**
Just Wonderful	16	**20**	16	**20**	16	**20**	-	16
Hermosa	14	20	16	20	20	20	**25**	16
Manuela De Vega	**25**	-	**25**	25	25	25	25	25
Goddess	**25**	25	**25**	25	25	25	25	25
Dancing Vega	**28**	20	25	-	-	-	20	25
Beyond Reason	-	20	22	20	-	25	**33**	25
Fleeting	**33**	**33**	25	25	-	25	25	20
Chablis	**33**	**33**	**33**	**33**	33	**33**	**33**	25
Rainbow Heart	**33**	**33**	**33**	**33**	33	**33**	**33**	-
Zagitova	**40**	-	33	33	-	33	33	-
Antonia De Vega	**50**	25	33	33	33	33	40	33
Sparkle Roll	33	-	28	25	33	20	**66**	25
Audarya	**100**	40	-	-	50	-	66	-

each-way 1/5 odds, 1-2-3
Others on application, prices correct at time of going to press

RACING & FOOTBALL outlook

Nick Watts's horses to follow

BACCHUS 5 ch g
Kheleyf – Rumbled (Halling)
1400-

Bacchus must be a talented horse as he won the Wokingham first time out last season, beating the good thing Dreamfield by a neck. Connections went up in class after that and he ended up running in a pair of Group 1s, failing to cut much ice in either. Maybe Group company is flying too high, but he is definitely worth watching first time up as he also won at Newbury on his return in 2017 at odds of 25-1 so he definitely goes well fresh.

Brian Meehan, Manton

CALYX 3 b c
Kingman – Helleborine (Observatory)
11-

Calyx isn't a forgotten horse, but maybe because he hasn't been seen since last June, he is not at the forefront of punters' minds going into this year. However, as long as he gets over his injury all right, then he is well worth inclusion in this list following a scintillating display in the Coventry Stakes on his last outing. He beat Group 1 winner Advertise easily, with Group 3 winner Sergei Prokofiev back in third. He might be a sprinter, which would bring in races like the Commonwealth Cup if he doesn't see out a Guineas trip.

John Gosden, Newmarket

CENTURY DREAM 5 b h
Cape Cross – Salacia (Echo Of Light)
0114443-

Century Dream has won only in Group 3 company so far, but this improving five-year-old isn't very far away from a breakthrough success at the top level and he could achieve it this season. Best with cut in the ground, he arguably put in his best run of the season at Ascot in October when third in the QEII, beaten just three-quarters of a length by Roaring Lion and I Can Fly. His jockey, William Buick, went too early on him that day and he has the ability to win a Group 1 for sure.

Simon Crisford, Newmarket

CROSSED BATON 4 b c
Dansili – Sacred Shield (Beat Hollow)
117226-

Although below-par on his final start of the season at Deauville, Crossed Baton had been very consistent prior to that and could improve this season. He won the Blue Riband Trial at Epsom last April but swerved the Derby after he was well beaten in the Dante. However, he was a good second in the Hampton Court at Royal Ascot after that before occupying the same position in a Group 2 at Maisons-Laffitte. All of his runs came over 1m2f, but with another year on his back he may well stay further this year.

John Gosden, Newmarket

DARK VISION 3 b c
Dream Ahead – Black Dahlia (Dansili)
1116-

For three of his four starts last season, Dark Vision looked like a real superstar, nailing three wins in a row, culminating with an impressive last-to-first strike in the Vintage Stakes at Glorious Goodwood. Sold to Godolphin after that, he was then aimed at the Champagne Stakes at Doncaster in September but was woeful on Town Moor, finishing last of the six runners. He is better than that, however, and it's best to take his talents from those first three runs rather than marking him down unduly for the last one.

Mark Johnston, Middleham

DASH OF SPICE 5 br h
Teofilo – Dashiba (Dashing Blade)
22110-

Although failing when 3-1 favourite for the John Smith's Cup on his final start of the campaign, this handicapper had been tough and progressive prior to that, winning two races including the Duke of Edinburgh Handicap at Royal Ascot. He won that race on good to firm ground but has also been placed on heavy, so he is adaptable regarding surface. He is also from a family that David Elsworth knows well, being related to Barshiba. It's not impossible he could grab a Group win somewhere along the line.

David Elsworth, Newmarket

EAST 3 ch f
Frankel – Vital Statistics (Indian Ridge)
112-

Considering she didn't make her debut until the end of September, East made giant strides in a short space of time. Following her debut win at Hamilton, she followed up in a Group 3 at Saint-Cloud, thereby justifying a trip to the US on her final outing in the Breeders' Cup Juvenile Fillies Turf. She acquitted herself well, finishing second behind runaway winner Newspaperofrecord, and she will be Group 1 class this season based on that. A Guineas might be on the agenda and she should stay further in time.

Kevin Ryan, Hambleton

EQUILATERAL 4 b c
Equiano – Tarentaise (Oasis Dream)
108144-

Despite winning only two minor races last year (one of those came at odds of 1-2), there is definitely more to come from Equilateral and that is a view echoed by his trainer. He was well fancied by many to land the Commonwealth Cup in June following an eight-length defeat of Foxtrot Lady on his return, but he could never get competitive in that and was then comfortably beaten in three more attempts at Group company. Hills is adamant that he will be a force this season, though, and he gets the benefit of the doubt to prove his worth in the sprinting division.

Charlie Hills, Lambourn

FALCON EIGHT 4 b c
Galileo – Polished Gem (Danehill)
113-

From one of the finest Moyglare families – related to Free Eagle and Sapphire among others – the lightly raced Falcon Eight has had only three outings but has won two of them – at the Curragh on debut and at Killarney a month later. Although beaten on his final start when stepped up to two miles, he wasn't beaten far in a Naas Group 3 and still looked very green, so there should be a lot of improvement from him this year. He seems to stay very well so Cup trips might well be within his remit before the season is out.

Dermot Weld, The Curragh

FIRST ELEVEN 4 b c
Frankel – Zenda (Zamindar)
213513-

First Eleven is a half-brother to Kingman but stays much further than his illustrious sibling. He was clueless as a two-year-old but improved rapidly last season, starting the season on a mark of 77 but ending it on 104. His most eyecatching run probably came at Royal Ascot when third behind Baghdad, beaten only a neck. He was also most unlucky as he was repeatedly denied a clear run in the final furlong. Group races on fast ground over a mile and a half should be the way forward for him and he will be a valuable stallion prospect if he can achieve that.

John Gosden, Newmarket

FLASHCARD 3 ch g
Fast Company – Portico (Pivotal)
112-

Andrew Balding's two-year-olds normally need a run or two to hit their peak, hence Flashcard being sent off at 33-1 to make a winning debut at Salisbury in August. Win it he did, however, and that instantly marked him down as useful. Better was to come as he won at Salisbury again nine days later and then went for an extremely valuable sales race at the Curragh, finishing second of 18 behind Barbill. Already gelded, he could be interesting this season both on these shores and abroad over six and seven furlongs.

Andrew Balding, Kingsclere

FOX TAL 3 b c
Sea The Stars – Maskunah (Sadler's Wells)
112-

Fox Tal made his debut at Sandown in July when he finished third, just behind Breeders' Cup winner Line Of Duty in second. Following that he got off the mark at Ffos Las and then went to Salisbury for a Listed event where he was slightly disappointing in fourth. However, his trainer ploughed on and sent him for a 1m2f Group 1 at Saint-Cloud for his final run, which proved his best one as he was beaten only a length in third. He will stay well this season and something like the Gordon Stakes at Glorious Goodwood could be a target.

Andrew Balding, Kingsclere

FREDERICKBARBAROSA 3 b c
Holy Roman Emperor – Midnight Partner (Marju)
74212-

Frederickbarbarosa probably isn't one of the stars of Clarehaven but, being owned by the China Horse Club, it is important he does well. He has started off promisingly as well, getting better on turf before successfully switching to the all-weather with a win at Newcastle in November. On his final start of 2018 he finished second to Private Rocket at Kempton, beaten only a short-head, and although raised 6lb he could exploit his mark of 88 this summer in mile handicaps. Given time, he might also stay further.

John Gosden, Newmarket

HAZRAN 3 b c
Lope De Vega – Hazaraba (Oasis Dream)
3-

This is a dark one, but Hazran's breeding makes him of interest, as does his first run at Naas. His dam is a half-sister to the Aga Khan's Derby winner Harzand and, while it is asking a lot for him to do likewise, he does have the entry and ran well on his debut. It came late in the season – November – and he finished a running-on third behind two colts from the Aidan O'Brien stable. He started the race well back and passed all but two of his rivals in the straight so the experience will have done him good. A maiden win should be a formality before better things come his way.

Mick Halford, Co Kildare

JAPAN 3 b c
Galileo – Shastye (Danehill)
711-

A feature of the Ballydoyle two-year-old army is the way they progress from run to run and Japan was no different. He was only seventh on his debut at the Curragh but then won his next two starts, culminating with a battling win in the Beresford Stakes at Naas in September. That contest has been the launchpad for many a great career, including the mighty Sea The Stars, and while Japan only just struggled home the performance bodes well for his ability to stay Derby trips. A trial run in the Ballysax or Derrinstown is surely in the offing.

Aidan O'Brien, Ballydoyle

KALOOR 3 b c
Nathaniel – Blinking (Marju)
1-

Like Andrew Balding, the Brian Meehan team only rarely get a winning juvenile first time out, so when they do they are generally decent. Kaloor was an unfancied 16-1 chance for his sole start at Salisbury, but he made a mockery of those odds to win by three and a half lengths. The form of the race is a bit of a mixed bag, but the fourth home, Ginistrelli, won his only subsequent start and is in the Derby, so it is worth viewing it positively. Kaloor has no fancy entries at this stage, but he should stay 1m2f no problem and will win more good races.

Brian Meehan, Manton

LAH TI DAR 4 b f
Dubawi – Dar Re Mi (Singspiel)
11123-

What a family. A full-sister to Too Darn Hot (discussed later on in this list), Lah Ti Dar made giant strides last season, starting off with a maiden win at Newbury in May and ending it with a placed effort in a Group 1 at Ascot in October. In between she won the Galtres Stakes at York by ten lengths and was a good second in the St Leger behind Kew Gardens. Her inexperience shone through in that race, but it was still a commendable effort and surely it is only a matter of time before she notches at the top level.

John Gosden, Newmarket

MADHMOON 3 b c
Dawn Approach – Aaraas (Haafhd)
11-

It's been a faultless start to life for Madhmoon. Two outings, both at Leopardstown, two wins, both achieved very easily and both times the form has stacked up. For his first win he beat Sydney Opera House by nearly three lengths and the runner-up came within a neck of landing a Group 1 on his final start. Then he beat Broome, who similarly came within a neck of winning a Group 1 at Longchamp on Arc day. They are good horses but Madhmoon pulverised them both. An Irish 2,000 Guineas bid must be on the cards and he might well stay middle distances.

Kevin Prendergast, Co Kildare

MANUELA DE VEGA 3 b f
Lope De Vega – Roscoff (Daylami)
11-

It's well documented what a deft touch Ralph Beckett has with the fillies and there is now quite a long list of top-class females to have emanated from his stable in the last decade or so. Manuela De Vega is the latest one. She is unbeaten and took the step up from maiden to Listed level very easily last season, winning at Salisbury before going up to Pontefract to record a comfortable black-type success. That came over a mile, but Beckett will surely try to turn her into an Oaks filly so look out for her in a trial somewhere this spring.

Ralph Beckett, Kimpton

MATEWAN 4 b g
Epaulette – Cochin (Swain)
3211-

Ian Williams is one of the best placers of a horse you will find so expect him to do well with late bloomer Matewan. He did nothing in three maidens as a two-year-old and was a different horse entirely last season as the addition of cheekpieces helped him enormously. He got off the mark at Newmarket in August over 1m2f and then went up two furlongs for his next start at Beverley with the same result. He is only rated 72 despite those two wins and there is no doubt he can rate higher and is a well-handicapped horse.

Ian Williams, Worcestershire

NORWAY 3 ch c
Galileo – Love Me True (Kingmambo)
53114-

Norway was quite aggressively campaigned as a two-year-old, running in five races and most of them good ones. It took him three goes to get off the mark, but after that he soon got the hang of things as he followed up in the increasingly important Zetland Stakes (upgraded to a Group 3 for 2019) at Newmarket in October. Perhaps he was over the top when disappointing in France on his final start of the campaign, but he is undoubtedly a top-class middle-distance colt in the making and might well be the Ballydoyle St Leger horse for 2019.

Aidan O'Brien, Ballydoyle

PINK DOGWOOD 3 br f
Camelot – Question Times (Shamardal)
2215-

Named after one of the holes at Augusta, Pink Dogwood really sprung to prominence on her third start at Gowran Park in September when she won a maiden by seven lengths. So impressed were connections that she was immediately stepped up to Group 1 company in the Prix Marcel Boussac for her final start of the campaign, but she failed to fire that day, with the race possibly coming too soon for her. She handles cut in the ground and, while she will be effective at a mile, she should stay a good deal further than that.

Aidan O'Brien, Ballydoyle

RAINBOW MOONSTONE 3 b f
Holy Roman Emperor – Moonstone Magic (Trade Fair)
01-

Like his father, Joseph O'Brien also improves his juveniles massively from run to run. Rainbow Moonstone was last of 16 on her debut at Gowran Park in October, but she obviously learned plenty as she scored at Naas on her next outing at a juicy 16-1. The progress she made was quite startling and attributed to the better ground she experienced on her second start. Both of her runs came over six furlongs, but she will stay further than that according to her breeding and should be effective over a mile. She's probably not top-class, but she might still be distinctly useful.

Joseph O'Brien, Co Kilkenny

REDICEAN 5 b g
Medicean – Red Halo (Galileo)
911-45

One of the features of recent Flat campaigns is how seriously Alan King takes the summer game. Once it was obvious Redicean was in a twilight zone over hurdles – useful but not quite good enough to take on the best – he immediately switched him to the all-weather with impressive results. He won his first two starts on the sand and, while the winning run came to an end last time out, he is very interesting for the summer when he hits turf again. He's always been considered best on good ground and a decent handicap, possibly even the Ebor, could be feasible.

Alan King, Barbury Castle

SO PERFECT 3 b f
Scat Daddy – Hopeoverexperience (Songandaprayer)
1441233-

What a consistent and classy juvenile So Perfect was. Not out of the first four in seven races, she won twice and beat Skitter Scatter in a Group 3 at the Curragh in July. Following that, she was beaten only half a length in the Group 1 Phoenix Stakes and not much further in the Cheveley Park. On her final start she placed again in the Breeders' Cup Juvenile Turf Sprint, showing her toughness, and while a mile may stretch her there is no reason she can't win a good sprint at some stage this season.

Aidan O'Brien, Ballydoyle

SOUTHERN FRANCE 4 b c
Galileo – Alta Anna (Anabaa)
2112437-

A typical Ballysoyle improver, Southern France was second in the Queen's Vase at Royal Ascot behind Kew Gardens and then placed again behind the same horse in the St Leger. He was well fancied for the Cesarewitch on the back of that, going off favourite, and while he didn't get the job done then, he ran well for one so lightly raced to finish seventh – the experience won't be lost on him. Cup trips might well be within range for him and if he builds on his exploits from last season he could be a player in that division.

Aidan O'Brien, Ballydoyle

STRATUM 6 b g
Dansili – Lunar Phase (Galileo)
31000-

Three duck eggs to round off his season don't really telll the story for Stratum, nor do him any justice at all. He first sprang to prominence in the Ascot Stakes when third behind stablemate Lagostovegas. Then, on his next start, he hacked up in a good handicap at Newbury and all of a sudden he was on everyone's radar for the Ebor, for which he started 3-1 favourite. He could only manage 12th place, but he got no kind of run at all and was below-par thereafter. A break could have done him the world of good and he can still notch that big handicap win.

Willie Mullins, Co Carlow

TOO DARN HOT 3 b c
Dubawi – Dar Re Mi (Singspiel)
1111-

Too Darn Hot looked simply amazing as a two-year-old and hopefully he trains on to show similar brilliance in his Classic season. He took every test in his stride as a juvenile, graduating from maiden win to Group 3 to Group 2 and finally Group 1 level with ease, and he left the best until last. Tackling the fastest ground he had faced in the Dewhurst, he didn't look to be going that well at one stage, but when Frankie Dettori pulled him out the result was never in doubt. His turn of foot is a joy to behold and he can go for the 2,000 Guineas and Derby. Why not?

John Gosden, Newmarket

WATAN 3 ch c
Toronado – Shotgun Gulch (Thunder Gulch)
1251-

Watan is from the first crop of the stable's Group 1 winner Toronado and he enjoyed a positive campaign as a juvenile, bookending his season with wins. In between, he arguably put in his best effort at York in the Acomb Stakes when second behind Phoenix Of Spain, who has since shown that form in a positive light. Although beaten twice, he is the type to progress with time and he should do better again this year. His best trip has yet to be ascertained but will probably be around a mile and he is Listed class at least.

Richard Hannon, East Everleigh

WISSAHICKON 4 ch c
Tapit – No Matter What (Nureyev)
118111-

It is not often you see the Cambridgeshire won in such dominant fashion as it was by Wissahickon last year. However, John Gosden has done it with some top horses in the past and this looks to be another as he won the big Newmarket handicap by a staggering margin. He has since done good things on the all-weather and, at the time of going to press, a trip to Dubai was being considered. Whatever happens with that, it is surely it is only a matter of time before he makes an impact in Group company on turf. This is a seriously classy horse who has a pedigree to match.

John Gosden, Newmarket

Top ten horses

Calyx	**Norway**
East	**Pink Dogwood**
First Eleven	**So Perfect**
Fox Tal	**Too Darn Hot**
Japan	**Wissahickon**

ENABLE: a third Arc is on the cards for John Gosden's superstar filly

Newmarket by Aborigine

JOHN GOSDEN once again has the brilliant dual Prix de l'Arc de Triomphe winner Enable to spearhead his bid to retain his trainer's title and his smart three-year-old Classic contenders Too Darn Hot and Calyx are also particularly exciting prospects.

The five-year-old **Enable** – beaten only once in her 11 starts to date – rounded a curtailed season off with that incredibly game Arc win, bravely fighting off the determined late challenge of Sea Of Class. She then went and conquered the US in the Breeders' Cup.

Gosden will not be hurrying her and has plenty of options for her mid-season build-up to a bid for an Arc hat-trick in the autumn.

Too Darn Hot will provide Gosden with plenty of interest earlier in the year as he could hit the target in the Qipco 2,000 Guineas.

The Dubawi colt won all four of his races last season, finishing his juvenile campaign off with a flourish beating Advertise by two and three-quarter lengths in the Dewhurst.

Being out of dual 1m4f Group 1

43

winner Dar Re Mi, herself a Singspiel mare, it is easy to understand his position at the head of the Derby market as well.

Stablemate **Calyx** also holds the 2,000 Guineas entry but may not get further than the mile.

The son of Gosden's superstar Kingman showed great speed in winning his two starts, but sadly his season did not get further than Royal Ascot, where he won the Coventry Stakes by a length from Advertise.

Gosden has given him plenty of time to recover and his turn of foot suggests he could always take the Commonwealth Cup route as an alternative to chasing Classic success.

WILLIAM HAGGAS had another marvellous year, earning his patrons a majestic £2,996,293, and he will be aiming to break the £3 million barrier this year.

Pride of place among his winners goes to **Sea Of Class**, who won the Irish Oaks and the Yorkshire Oaks.

On her final run it was only an agonising short-neck by which she failed to overhaul Enable in the Arc and she will once again

be trained for the Longchamp showpiece.

Plans beforehand come down to what Haggas learns when she gets back into faster work, but all roads lead to her attempt to gain revenge on Enable in the Arc.

I share Haggas's enthusiasm about **One Master**, who was brought up through the ranks during 2018 and earned her a bit of the Paris limelight on Arc day.

She came with a devastating late run to beat Inns Of Court in the Group 1 Prix de la Foret and it was then off across the Atlantic to Churchill Downs, where she had anything but a clear run in the Breeders' Cup Mile, having to settle for fifth place to Expert Eye.

She was well fancied in her next race on the other side of the globe in the Longines Hong Kong Mile but Ryan Moore rode a rare poor race. Held up, she was never in with a chance and was unable to use her exhilarating turn of foot.

She had been on the go for long enough when eighth to the Oriental superstar Beauty Generation next time but will attempt more global gallivanting after a

ONE MASTER (13): won the Foret last season, showing a great turn of foot

SKARDU: big things are expected of him this season for William Haggas

crack at the Queen Anne at Royal Ascot.

Sticking with the Haggas fillies, make certain you watch out for **Rainbow Heart**.

The Born To Sea filly took some time to come to hand but showed promise on her debut when keeping on to be second to Pythia over 7f at Newmarket before winning on her final start of the campaign.

This likeable individual has strengthened during the winter and her trainer's high opinion of her is reflected by the fact he is preparing her for the Poule d'Essai des Pouliches.

Skardu is another Somerville Lodge three-year-old with quality. He was ridden with great confidence on his debut before quickening for a two-length success from Velorum at Newmarket. It will certainly be a question of onwards and upwards.

Further ammunition in the Haggas lockers is supplied by the multiple Group 3 winner **Young Rascal** and it is interesting

Haggas describes him to me as "a work still in progress". There is clearly more in his locker.

If you are looking for a sleeper at Somerville Lodge, **Faylaq** is the one for you.

The Dubawi colt first caught the eye in the sales ring, costing 1.5 million guineas. There was to be no quick return on the outlay as he was a very slow developer, running only twice, but he showed a modicum of promise on his second run when beaten only two and a half lengths in fifth behind Ginistrelli over a mile at Newmarket.

His dam, the Arc and King George winner Danedream, was herself a slow burner and the way Faylaq is currently shaping suggests he will leave his juvenile form well behind. By the end of the year his original purchase price might not look so frightening.

Among the Haggas older horses, the

ex-Brian Meehan Bahrain Trophy winner **Raheen House** has wintered well.

ED VAUGHAN is one of the most under-rated trainers in Newmarket but continues to make the most of the material at his disposal.

This year could be a big one for the Irishman and I am particular keen on the prospects of his $950,000 Scat Daddy colt **Magic J**.

He was well backed on his one run at Yarmouth after some eyecatching work and eased home a comfortable winner from Swindler over 6f. Vaughan holds out high hopes fror him and plans to run him in a Guineas trial.

Also going for a trial, although in this instance a fillies' one, is *MARK TOMPKINS*'s **Garrel Glen**.

This is easy to understand in view of her juvenile form. The Mount Nelson filly stepped up on a promising Yarmouth debut with a length-and-three-quarters win from Tronada over Newmarket's 7f in the autumn.

The canny Tompkins confirms that she has wintered to his satisfaction and the plan is to go for one of the trials on the way to a bid for Classic glory in the Qipco 1,000 Guineas, back on the track to which her long, raking stride is well suited.

On the handicapping front Tompkins has a potential money-spinner in **Roof Garden**.

Twice a winner last year, he was put away to build up his strength over the winter and he will work his way up the ladder. The 2020 Lincoln, a race Tompkins has won before, is the long-term objective – remember where you heard the name first!

MICHAEL BELL holds out high hopes for **Eagles By Day**.

An attractive son of Sea The Stars, he was slow to come to hand, going into winter quarters after his Nottingham second in October, but Bell plans to aim him at some major middle-distance races.

Others worth a mention are the Queen's **Eightsome Reel**, who was well fancied despite his 50-1 odds when going in at Wolverhampton in November, and **Babbo's Boy**.

Bell may also have secured a real bargain in the ex-Ralph Beckett Bated Breath filly **Plait**, who was an empathic winner at Chelmsford on her first run for her new trainer.

JOHN RYAN has found a rich seam of gold in buying Aidan O'Brien rejects and **Aircraft Carrier** represents his best purchase to date.

A winner of his last three starts, he earned himself a tilt at Easter riches when completing a hat-trick at Wolverhampton.

That first attempt at two miles was impressive and the Marathon at Lingfield on Good Friday is on the cards. Whatever his fate there, he will continue to pay his way.

A similar comment applies to the highly capable multiple winner **Grey Britain** and Ryan will also be firing off the game **Battle Of Marathon** early in the year to take advantage of the soft ground he loves.

WILLIAM JARVIS handled **Chief Ironside** brilliantly last year, winning two races with him and also getting him placed in Pattern company.

The indications are that he will achieve even more this year as he has grown into his frame. All the jockeys who rode him believe he will go onwards and upwards and Jarvis is sure to tap his full potential.

DAVID ELSWORTH continues to pursue his profession with great success and **Dandhu** has the ability to hit the heights for the veteran handler.

The Dandy Man filly cost 75,000gns and might just be a steal. A win at Kempton prefaced a running-on length-and-three-quarters second to Just Wonderful in the Rockfel Stakes. It will be back to the Rowley Mile for the 1,000 Guineas and she is a serious longshot.

On the handicap front, do not desert Elsie's Royal Ascot winner **Dash Of Spice** as he has wintered a treat and is expected to achieve even more this season.

Hot off the Heath

Dandhu

Eagles By Day

Magic J

TONY JAKOBSON

WHO ELSE KNEW?
NAVAL INTELLIGENCE 33-1

**With gems like that, there is nowhere else to
go for brilliant Newmarket tipping advice**

Call 0906 911 0232

BT UK calls cost £1 per minute. ROI call 1560 719 760 (Eircom calls
€1.25/min). Calls from mobiles and other networks will vary.

Ireland
by Jerry M

YOU won't get a medal for working out where the main strength in the three-year-old division lies in Ireland, but whether *AIDAN O'BRIEN* has a superstar in his midst, something that could compete with the likes of Too Darn Hot or even Quorto in the Classics, is another matter.

The speediest and flashiest of last season's juveniles was undoubtedly **Ten Sovereigns**, who seems more of a candidate for champion sprinter. Brilliant on his Curragh debut, decisive in the Round Tower

BROOME: looks like a middle-distance type for this season

Stakes and workmanlike in the Middle Park, he will probably get an opportunity over a mile but sprinting seems far more likely to prove his game.

It is not that easy to pick out a potential 2,000 Guineas candidate from Ballydoyle. Some of O'Brien's potential Derby candidates, such as Anthony Van Dyck, are likely to take their chance, but his main challenge for the Rowley Mile looks likely to come from **Magna Grecia**.

Just touched off in the Group 3 Autumn Stakes at Newmarket, he probably didn't have to improve that much to land an ordinary renewal of the Vertem Futurity Trophy at Doncaster. There is scope for him to improve a good deal over the winter.

Whether Magna Grecia stays 1m4f is open to question and the stable may well have stronger Derby candidates.

Anthony Van Dyck won over a mile during the summer and fared quite well when dropping back to 7f. No match for Quorto in the National Stakes or Too Darn Hot in the Dewhurst, he ran better than his finishing position suggests in the Breeders' Cup Juvenile Turf. The 2,000 Guineas may well be his Derby trial.

Japan progressed from winning a heavy-ground Listowel maiden to touching off stablemate **Mount Everest** in the Beresford Stakes at Naas. Both colts will be contesting Derby trials and could be genuine contenders.

Broome progressed through last season. He was very game when just denied in the Prix Jean-Luc Lagardere on Arc weekend and looks a middle-distance type.

O'Brien looks strong in the three-year-old filly department and **Just Wonderful** went into winter quarters as favourite for the 1,000 Guineas. She put a disappointing effort in the Moyglare Stud Stakes

48

MAGICAL: seen here winning at Ascot, she is back for more this year

behind her with a very smooth success in the Rockfel Stakes at Newmarket and her chance in the Breeders' Cup went when she blew the start. She looks to be the top contender for the race.

Fairyland never went beyond 6f last season in a campaign which saw her colours lowered only once, but she is not particularly a speedster and really stayed on well when winning the Cheveley Park. Her staying a mile is certainly not out of the question.

So Perfect is another for whom stamina is uncertain as she also never raced beyond 6f, but a lot of that was because she refused to settle. If that is something O'Brien can get under control, she could well get further and the strength of her form against top juveniles like Skitter Scatter, Fairyland and top colt Advertise is of the highest order.

Where a filly like **Goddess** comes in will be interesting to see. She looked top-class when winning her maiden at Leopardstown before she flopped in the Silver Flash Stakes.

Over middle distances, **Hermosa** could be a lively Oaks candidate. She got a mile well last season, finishing the season with very creditable seconds at Newmarket and Chantilly, and is the type to go from strength to strength.

The older brigade at Ballydoyle doesn't look as strong as in previous years, but there is plenty of depth in the middle-distance and staying divisions.

Magical will be back for another season after her three-year-old campaign ended so strongly with victory in the Champions Fillies & Mares Stakes at Ascot and a close second to Enable at Churchill Downs.

Also returning is 2017 Irish Derby winner **Capri**, whose campaign never really got going last season.

The retirement of Order Of St George should have left a big hole in the stable's ammunition in the staying department, but Doncaster and Curragh St Leger winners **Kew Gardens** and **Flag Of Honour** will both be back and should make their mark.

The evidence of last season is that the biggest threat to O'Brien's supremacy for the foreseeable future will come from his son *JOSEPH O'BRIEN*.

Most of the younger O'Brien's successes last season came with progressive handicappers and promising maiden types, in addition to big hitters like Irish

49

HAZAPOUR: didn't stay in the Derby but could be a Group 1 colt at around 1m2f

Derby hero **Latrobe**, who will be back for this season with all of the good races at about 1m4f open to him as well as a possible Melbourne Cup bid.

The best of the Carriganog three-year-olds would seem to be **Iridessa**. She improved throughout last season and won both of her starts over a mile, most notably when beating Hermosa in the Group 1 Fillies' Mile at Newmarket. She went into the winter as favourite for the Oaks and there would seem to be a good chance of her also taking her chance in the 1,000 Guineas.

Promising three-year-olds such as **Cava**, **Cnoc An Oir** and **Kiss For Luck** are all likely to run in Classic trials and could make their mark.

DERMOT WELD came back strongly last season after a disastrous 2017 and, while his two-year-olds didn't manage to win a stakes race, there are a number of promising sorts.

Masaff is a decent middle-distance prospect, rounding off last season with a close second in the 1m1f Eyrefield Stakes at Leopardstown. He could well be an Irish Derby prospect.

Also noteworthy as a middle-distance prospect is **Zuenoon**, winner of two of his three starts last season, while impressive October maiden winners **Rakan** and **Tankerville** are exciting.

Of the older horses, the most interesting could well be **Hazapour**, who didn't appear to stay in the Derby and was well short of his best on his one subsequent start. He could well be a Group 2 or even a Group 1 performer at about 1m2f.

Yulong Gold Fairy and **Making Light** also return and will continue to be solid performers at Listed and Group 3 level.

JIM BOLGER had a disappointing season by his standards, but there are some encouraging signs for this season, particularly with some two-year-olds who improved at the end of the year.

Guaranteed is one such example as he rounded off the season with a strong-staying victory in the Killavullan Stakes at Leopardstown and a Derby trial would appear an obvious first step. That may also be the direction of **Bold Approach**, winner of his sole maiden and not seen after finishing second in the Tyros Stakes in July.

Operatic Export, winner of his sole maiden at Leopardstown in August, is another promising type.

Among the older horses, **Verbal Dexterity** will be returning. The firm ground last summer probably scuppered his season somewhat and hopes are high that he can show his true form this season.

The Godolphin-owned filly **Luceita**, winner of her sole start in a big-field Curragh maiden in August, is exciting too.

GER LYONS has been a very consistent trainer over the past few years.

Among his three-year-olds, the best prospects may be among his fillies, particularly the Khalid Abdullah-owned pair of **Viadera** and **Fulminate**, who may get their chances in 1,000 Guineas trials.

The older horses will be strong. **Who's Steph** could make her presence felt in high-class fillies' company from 1m to 1m2f. **Blue Uluru** could make a mark as a sprinter, while **Mustajeer** and **Psychedelic Funk**, who has been gelded, will pay their way.

JESSICA HARRINGTON enjoyed her best ever season last year due to the exploits of the brilliant Alpha Centauri. There would not appear to be anything remotely similar to her this season in terms of ability and she also lost top stayer Torcedor, while good older horses like I'm So Fancy, Pincheck and Beautiful Morning won't be returning, so some promising three-year-olds will have to take up the slack.

Best of those could be **Indigo Balance**, who shows real promise as a sprinter, as does **Servalan**, who was a Listed winner early in the season before losing her way a little after Royal Ascot. The dark one could well be **Trethias**, who could be very effective over a mile and beyond.

What an outcome it would be if the first two Irish Classics were won by *KEVIN PRENDERGAST* and *JOHN OXX* – and it is a distinct possibility.

Prendergast has the unbeaten colt **Madhmoon**, winner of both starts at two including an impressive performance in a Group 2 on Irish Champions Weekend.

By joining forces with Patrick Prendergast, Oxx has inherited the care of champion two-year-old filly **Skitter Scatter**. For a filly who made her debut in March, she showed remarkable improvement all through the season and rounded off the campaign with a decisive success in the Moyglare. If she can continue her progress, she could do something quite special this season.

Invincible Irish
Iridessa
Madhmoon
Skitter Scatter

SKITTER SCATTER (left): showed remarkable improvement

Berkshire by Downsman

CHARLIE HILLS knows a thing or two about training top sprinters and thinks he could have another star on his hands in **Khaadem**.

The 750,000gns son of Dark Angel is a full brother to Log Out Island, who was an extremely quick horse for Richard Hannon and ran away with the Carnarvon Stakes at Newbury as a three-year-old before being disqualified due to a prohibited substance.

Khaadem won his final two races last season, most notably a conditions race at Doncaster, and Hills immediately nominated the Commonwealth Cup as his big target for 2019.

The trainer would have liked to test the waters with him at the top level in the Middle Park Stakes but he was ruled out after a late setback.

However, Hills reports that this big, imposing colt has developed into a "monster" over the winter and he has high hopes he can take the big Royal Ascot

sprint that the yard won with subsequent July Cup hero Muhaarar in 2016.

The big sprint star for now at Faringdon Place is **Battaash**, a dual winner of the King George Stakes at Glorious Goodwood.

The five-year-old's record became slightly patchy either side of that second success on the Sussex Downs last year, but on his day he is without question the quickest horse in training, as confirmed by his stunning Prix de l'Abbaye triumph in 2017.

Battaash's two failures in the Nunthorpe are the biggest stain on his record, but that race comes only a few weeks after Goodwood and it might be the case that he needs more time between his races. If he skips York this time around, that might bring the Flying Five at the Curragh, upgraded to a Group 1 for the first time last year, into the equation.

There might be more to come in top sprints from **Equilateral**, who was sent off

KHAADEM: has the Commonwealth Cup on his agenda this season

ACCIDENTAL AGENT: aim is to prove his Queen Anne win was no fluke

just 6-1 for last year's Commonwealth Cup on the strength of an eight-length novice win at Doncaster but ultimately proved disappointing last year.

Royal Ascot was only the fourth run of his life and Hills feels he was lacking in experience and will benefit from being much more streetwise this season.

The four-year-old is also likely to step back up to 6f having been campaigned for his last three races over the minimum trip.

One sprinter on the comeback trail is **Magical Memory**, who hasn't run since last year's Abernant Stakes after picking up a knock but is expected to be back in the second half of last season.

While so much strength in the Hills yard comes from the speedsters, **Phoenix Of Spain** is a young colt who could do better as he goes up in trip.

Hills was hugely frustrated by his near miss in the Vertem Futurity Trophy last autumn as he might well have won without receiving a bump from the winner, Magna Grecia, but now the dust has settled there is great encouragement to be taken from the Acomb winner's performance in the Doncaster Group 1.

There won't be many horses who see out the mile of the 2,000 Guineas any better and Phoenix Of Spain could then do even better when he steps up to 1m2f, although he's by no means certain to get the Derby trip.

EVE JOHNSON HOUGHTON reports that **Accidental Agent** is back for more this season and connections are determined that he can prove his Queen Anne victory was no fluke.

The best way to do that, of course, would be to win the race again and that's exactly where Accidental Agent looks to have his best chance of further success this year because he has taken such a shine to Ascot.

He beat Queen Anne runner-up Lord Glitters in a £150,000 handicap off level weights at the course in 2017 and was unlucky not to finish closer than fourth in the Balmoral that year having not got the best of runs.

Course form counts for plenty on Ascot's unique straight track and, while not at his best after the royal meeting last year, don't rule out Accidental Agent surprising more than a few people again there in June.

It's a testament to the skills of *OWEN BURROWS* that his figures read so well last season when his horses weren't right for the key months of the summer.

Burrows sent out 38 winners at a strike-rate of 21 per cent, showing a small level-stakes profit for his followers, and that's because he kept his patience when things were going against him, allowing the horses to come roaring back in the autumn.

Chief among them was **Laraaib**, who returned from a three-month layoff to win the Cumberland Lodge Stakes at Ascot in October.

LIMATO: will win more races

Burrows had had high hopes for him after he chased home Poet's Word first time out at Sandown and he could yet make up for lost time as a five-year-old, perhaps even matching his Sandown conqueror by progressing to Group 1 level.

Tabdeed won a handicap on that same card and has more to offer, while **Wadilsafa** is another Burrows older horse with Group 1 potential. He won three out of four last season, including a Listed race at Sandown when last seen in September.

Elwazir didn't make it back in the autumn, but he is also due to return in 2019 and is worth another chance at Pattern level after blowing out in a Group 3 at Haydock in August. He had won his last two, including a handicap at Ascot.

HUGHIE MORRISON has revealed to Downsman that Nearly Caught has had a setback and may not run again, but another much-travelled stayer, **Marmelo**, will be back this year.

Although he won a Listed race at York last season, Marmelo hasn't been seen much in Britain in the last couple of years but has progressed massively in that time and may well be capable of competing in Cup races en route to another crack at the Melbourne Cup, in which he was a terrific second to Cross Counter in November.

Morrison is also bringing through the next generation of stayers and maintains that **Corgi**, **Buzz** and **Star Rock** are horses to follow this season.

Corgi was second in big 1m4f three-year-old handicaps at Royal Ascot and Glorious Goodwood last season and has been gelded since his latest sixth in the Melrose when stepped up to 1m6f at York.

Buzz and Star Rock are a year older but still going the right way. Buzz gained his biggest win in a 1m2f handicap at Newbury last autumn but gets at least 1m4f, while Star Rock twice came within a length of Group 2 wins last year and will chase more black type.

Morrison excels at getting horses to improve with age and, as so much of this guide is taken up with pinpointing exciting younger types, it's also worth highlighting another older horse with more to offer in **Limato**.

ROYAL INTERVENTION: could run well in the top fillies' races this season

Brilliantly handled throughout his career by *HENRY CANDY*, the seven-year-old may not quite be the Group 1 sprinter of old, but there still aren't many better than him at 6f-7f and he will continue to win his fair share of races.

ED WALKER confirms that his exciting filly **Royal Intervention** is back from injury having been ruled out since the Princess Margaret Stakes in July.

The three-year-old went wrong that day, but she had previously looked special when running away with a Listed race at Newmarket and could run well in top fillies' races.

ARCHIE WATSON is another young trainer with a potentially exciting three-year-old on his hands in **Soldier's Call**.

The Flying Childers winner was unlucky not to beat his elders in the Prix de l'Abbaye when he got involved in a dust-up for the early lead with Battaash and fared better than the favourite only to be done by a couple of fast finishers.

Things might be quite a bit tougher without the big juvenile allowance now, but it will be fascinating to see how he gets on for a trainer who is most definitely going places.

For a darker horse to follow, *DANIEL*

KUBLER gave Downsman the word for **Frontal**, a four-year-old who has been given an opening mark of 75 after three runs in novice/maiden company in the second half of last season.

The son of Frankel is from a family that improve with age and he could be able to do some damage this year starting off a workable mark.

DOMINIC FFRENCH DAVIS has moved into Kubler's old yard, meaning an expansion for the 53-year-old, who is determined to build on his best ever season in terms of prize-money.

Majboor won four times for Ffrench Davis last year and, while he has moved on, his owners have reinvested in **Indeed**, a four-year-old French recruit who was fifth in a Listed race when last seen and could thrive when he gets cut in the ground.

Berkshire's best
Corgi
Frontal
Khaadem

55

The North by Borderer

THE northern powerhouse was seen to full effect in 2018 with several wins at the highest level, notably from **Laurens**, who posted four Group 1 wins for trainer *KARL BURKE* and owner John Dance.

It was her first ever encounter with soft ground when she ran below-par in the Queen Elizabeth II Stakes at Ascot in October and after a break she should be set for another superb season this time around.

The four-year-old will be a major player in the leading fillies' and mares' events from 1m to 1m2f and she is also well worth another crack against males to prove what she can do.

Dance's admirable recruitment policy means he does not have many bad horses and Burke has plenty (many of them fillies) who will be racing in the white and purple colours. **Koduro's** two-year-old campaign ended in July but this well-bred Carlisle winner is a filly to keep on your side when she returns this season.

Burke's best two-year-old last season was **True Mason**, a strong-travelling sort who finished second in the Group 2 Mill Reef Stakes at Newbury in September. Slow ground and a focus on speed, as opposed to stamina, should bring out the best in him.

RICHARD FAHEY was another northern trainer who celebrated Group 1 success last season, with **Sands Of Mali** winning the Champions Sprint, and the four-year-old should be a force in the big 6f sprints this year, especially in the Diamond Jubilee given his obvious liking for Ascot. He has run well on a variety of ground but might not want it too quick.

Forest Ranger took his form to the next

LAURENS (right): the brilliant filly will be back for more this season

FOREST RANGER (noseband): one to watch early in the season

level last spring after being gelded, winning the Group 3 Earl of Sefton Stakes at Newmarket and then the Group 2 Huxley Stakes at Chester. The same horses tend to do well in those early-season races year after year and Forest Ranger can again be expected to immediately hit the ground running.

Fool For You (owned by John Dance) progressed steadily over 5f during her three-year-old campaign and appeals as a type to continue to improve, with both her running style and pedigree suggesting a step up to 6f can bear further fruit.

More Than This was unbeaten as a two-year-old last year, his third and final win coming in good style in a 7f handicap at Glorious Goodwood. He has more to offer this season at a mile and possibly beyond.

Another Musley Bank juvenile from last season who possesses significant potential is **Sabre**, who looks to be suited by a strongly run 6f in a big field.

As always, *MARK JOHNSTON* has a battalion of promising three-year-olds.

Dark Vision ended his juvenile campaign with a flop in the Champagne Stakes at Doncaster, but that was too bad to be true and he had previously shown serious promise when making it three wins from three starts in the Group 2 Vintage Stakes at Glorious Goodwood.

He won that 7f contest with authority despite not enjoying the best of runs and if he can tap back into that potential he could be an each-way player in the 2,000 Guineas.

Natalie's Joy bounced back from her Royal Ascot disappointment when readily taking Listed honours at Newbury in July and is a filly we should hear more from, while **Arctic Sound** was a highly progressive juvenile, his Group 3 triumph at Newmarket in September making it four wins from six starts, and is another one to look forward to.

Johnston's three-year-olds often come into their own when they are stepped up in trip to middle distances and beyond and the likes of **Persian Moon**, **Nayef Road**, **Cape Islay**, **West End Charmer**, **Themaxwecan**, **Mind The Crack** and **Gravistas** are all open to improvement this year when an emphasis on staying becomes more pronounced.

In a similar vein, two darker horses who it could pay to follow are **Bo Samraan** and **Caplin**.

Bo Samraan is by Sea The Stars and should relish a test of stamina, while Caplin can leave his juvenile form behind when getting a trip.

Of his more established horses, things

WELLS FARHH GO: back in mid-June

never really clicked for **Dee Ex Bee** after his second place in the Derby but he retains potential when he gets a staying test with a bit of ease in the ground.

Elarqam could not go on from his 2,000 Guineas fourth but seemed to be still growing up and could be a different proposition this season.

Another four-year-old to keep an eye on is **Austrian School**, for whom trips of 2m and beyond will be ideal.

Last year yielded a Group 3 win for **Wells Farhh Go** in the Bahrain Trophy at Newmarket, but *TIM EASTERBY* would have been hoping for more, with an injury setback forcing his stable star to miss the St Leger.

Now four, Wells Farhh Go is unlikely to return until mid-June but still has bundles of staying potential for the second half of last season.

Vintage Brut had a mixed juvenile season but everything fell into place when he hacked up in the Listed Rockingham Stakes at York in October and, with that win having come over 6f on soft ground, there is an obvious clue regarding the conditions in which he will flourish this year.

TOM DASCOMBE will be looking forward to 2019 as he has several interesting three-year-olds in his stable.

The pick of them could be **Great Scot**, a mile Listed winner who was a close fifth in the Group 1 Vertem Futurity Trophy at Doncaster in October. These performances were achieved despite him failing to settle and when he is more amenable to restraint (or fitted with a hood) there could be even more to come.

Arthur Kitt took the Chesham at Royal Ascot and ended his season with a solid fourth place in the Breeders' Cup Juvenile Turf. He looks set for another good campaign.

Iconic Choice and **Light My Fire** are others who can win some useful races.

Kachy has looked unstoppable on the all-weather but he is also a classy tool on turf. Particularly adept around a bend, he will take lots of beating whenever he runs at Chester, although his narrow defeat in the Group 2 Temple Stakes at Haydock highlights his versatility.

Lord Glitters again did *DAVID O'MEARA* proud last term, going close in the Group 1 Queen Anne at Royal Ascot and posting a Group 3 win at York in August. He is particularly potent at Ascot and should be in the mix in the top mile races there.

Suedois is another likeable type and, although winless in 2018, he went close in a couple of Group 2s and deserves to pick up a race in 2019.

O'Meara's top juvenile was **Blue Gardenia**, who is owned by Robert Ogden, and her best days should lie ahead of her following a Listed win at Newmarket in November.

KEVIN RYAN has had numerous big days at York with his two-year-olds and last year was no exception, with **Emaraaty Ana** taking the Gimcrack in August. He was not at the same level in the Middle Park next time but there are some nice prizes to be picked up with this three-year-old.

Stable flagbearer **Brando** won Newmarket's Group 3 Abernant Stakes last April for the second year running and will be a strong fancy to make it three in a row this spring. Ryan will then be hopeful that the seven-year-old can double his Group 1 tally later in the year.

There was a thrilling finish to the Nunthorpe last year, with *BRYAN SMART*'s 40-1 shot **Alpha Delphini** narrowly pipping the *MICHAEL DODS*-trained **Mabs Cross**, and the runner-up deservedly bagged a Group 1 next time in the shape of the Prix de l'Abbaye.

The eight-year-old Alpha Delphini may be able to pop up again at some stage this year, but confidence about further Group 1 success is particularly high with Mabs Cross, whose star is firmly on the rise.

The hugely admirable **Signora Cabello** had a great first campaign, with her four consecutive wins for *JOHN QUINN* including Group 2 triumphs at Royal Ascot and Maisons-Laffitte. She also went close in the Group 1 Prix Morny at Deauville and is capable of further Pattern success.

There are also more races to be won with the *KEITH DALGLEISH*-trained **Summer Daydream**, who landed the Redcar Two Year Old Trophy in October on just her third start.

Finally, *PAUL MIDGLEY* is an excellent trainer of sprinters and **Tarboosh's** blistering end to 2018 bodes very well for some high-profile wins this season.

Angels of the north
Laurens
Mabs Cross
Wells Farhh Go

THRILLER: Mabs Cross (left) and Alpha Delphini lock horns in the Nunthorpe

The West by Hastings

RICHARD HANNON landed last year's 1,000 Guineas at Newmarket with 66-1 shot **Billesdon Brook**, who remains in training, and he has a couple of potential dark horses for the season's opening Classics again this time around.

Much was expected of **Urban Icon** last summer after he won his first two starts at Windsor and Salisbury with something in hand on each occasion.

Unfortunately the son of Cityscape's season was cut short by a slight setback and he was not seen in public again, but he is back in training and connections are hopeful they can look forward to a productive three-year-old term with him.

On the plus side, he missed the hurly-burly of the busy summer spell, especially Royal Ascot, which does not suit every two-year-old as many have left their season and their futures behind after hard races at the Berkshire spectacular.

Hannon has always considered Urban Icon as a horse who would be better with age and his enforced rest last year may act in his favour as he remains a relatively unexposed contender for the bigger prizes this spring and summer.

He is entered in the Irish 2,000 Guineas and, while that is a possible early-season target, it would be no great shock if he turned up at Newmarket for the British equivalent first.

Among the fillies, the well-regarded **Star Terms** is Hannon's hope of repeating last year's 1,000 Guineas success.

She ended last term with a rather unlucky third in the Prix Marcel Boussac, beaten only a neck after meeting some

DANEHILL KODIAC (left): beat Waldgeist in 2017 and will be back this summer

HEADMAN: looked to have a lot more to offer when winning on his debut

trouble in running at a critical point in the race, and Hannon feels she will have a chance in May.

Although a Derby entry for **Mordred** may look a little optimistic at present, there is no reason why the son of Camelot cannot make his presence felt in the top company this summer.

His only success last year came at Chester over 7f, but on breeding he could excel when faced with more of a test and graduate from handicap company to something better by the autumn.

Of the Hannon older horses, Group 3 winner **Danehill Kodiac** is worth bearing in mind for good middle-distance races at home and abroad from mid-summer into the autumn as he is now back cantering and doing roadwork after missing much of last season.

He seems to act on any going but is ideally suited by a little cut in the ground, so missing the fast conditions that prevailed all last summer was not a big thing and connections remain hopeful that there is a decent prize in him this term.

ROGER CHARLTON often brings his better horses along with stealth and patience as youngsters before they are asked to prove themselves the following season and he has a couple of fascinating three-year-olds for the coming months in **Red Impression** and **Headman**, who both looked like they had a lot more to offer when winning last backend for the master of Beckhampton.

Red Impression could hardly have been more impressive on his debut when scoring without a serious question being asked at Kempton in October and then followed up in equally facile fashion at Lingfield a month later. The two victories marked him as a definite horse to follow.

Headman is also owned by Khalid Abdulla and fits the same model as he also didn't see any racecourse action until the start of last November when he made a belated winning debut at Newcastle. He was surprisingly beaten at Kempton only three weeks later when sent off a long odds-on favourite, but that race probably came too soon for such an inexperienced

HERCULEAN: still well regarded and can make the most of a mark of 91

horse and is best forgotten, so he remains of much interest.

Another Abdullah horse, **Herculean**, could prove the best of Charlton's older horses.

He remains unexposed having had just three outings last year after winning on his sole run as a two-year-old at Ascot in September 2017, after which the owner's racing manager Lord Grimthorpe had described him as "a big, immature horse" who would need plenty of time.

It didn't quite happen for him last term, but he is still well regarded and can make the most of a mark of 91. One of the Royal Ascot handicaps could be on his agenda.

MARTYN MEADE moved back to Wiltshire with the purchase of the Manton Estate in 2017 following a spell training in Newmarket and the first year was seen as a bedding-in spell for the trainer at the new premises. Now that transition period is over, the winners are expected to flow from the yard.

Meade heads into the new turf season with a proper 2,000 Guineas candidate on his hands as **Advertise** looks to have a

very bright season ahead of him.

He won the Group 1 Phoenix Stakes at the Curragh before finding only the very smart Too Darn Hot too good in the Dewhurst at Newmarket in October.

Meade also has another top-class three-year-old on his hands in **Confiding**, who is potentially just as good as his stablemate yet is a little more under the radar.

His breeding suggests he should get further than a mile in time and it would be no surprise to see him stepping up to middle distances as the season progresses.

Plenty of water has flowed under the bridge since *MARCUS TREGONING* tasted Derby glory with Sir Percy back in 2006, including a change of yard, but the Whitsbury trainer finally has another very nice prospect on his hands in **Mohaather**.

He handed Tregoning's current training career a real filip when supplying him with his first Group success for four seasons after taking the spoils in fine style in the Group 3 Horris Hill at Newbury last October and there is no reason why he cannot progress even further as a three-year-old.

His connections will have the choice

of campaigning him at around a mile or stepping him up in distance, which would almost certainly suit as he certainly was not stopping over the stiff 7f at Newbury and gave the distinct impression he would have no difficulties with more of a stamina test following his winter break.

Another trainer hoping to emerge from a few seasons in the relative doldrums is *BRIAN MEEHAN* and he has plenty to look forward to with **Kaloor**, who really caught the eye with a ready debut victory at Salisbury last autumn. He looked all over a horse who could only progress for the experience and winter break on his back.

The overall form of the race has worked out pretty well with winners emerging down the line and he can build on the performance when tried over further than the mile he encountered on that occasion.

He is definitely one for the notebooks for the new term as Meehan has not usually been associated with two-year-old first-time-out winners in recent years.

Devon-based *ROD MILLMAN* does very well with the ammunition at his disposal and was unlucky that Duke Of Bronte had to miss last summer after picking up a knee injury following his run at York in June.

Millman was hoping he was up to winning a decent handicap prize at that time and, with the five-year-old now set to return to the fray over the mid-summer period, he is certain something like the Ebor at York in August is still within the horse's compass. He seems to act on any type of going.

Duke Of Bronte's half-brother **Prince Of Harts** is also in the care of the trainer and this slow-maturing horse is just the type who may be able to nick a couple of smaller handicaps through the season.

Western wonders
Urban Icon
Red Impression
Duke Of Bronte

MOHAATHER: Marcus Tregoning's first Group winner in four years

The South
by Southerner

LAST year should have been one of unconfined joy for *ANDREW BALD-ING* after setting new personal bests in winners (123) and prize-money (£2.6m) in Britain, but it was tinged late with deep sadness.

The loss of Leicester City's talismanic chairman Vichai Srivaddhanaprabha in a helicopter crash in October was felt as keenly in the Kingsclere community as in Leicester.

Balding hopes to build his powerful owner's legacy with not only his classy older horses but also the young successors the Thai billionaire had bought to compete in racing's premier league.

The likes of **Fox Tal**, who has the looks and middle-distance pedigree to back up his Investec Derby entry, are giving Balding good reason for optimism. The Sea The Stars colt left behind his early form when third in the Group 1 Criterium de Saint-Cloud in Paris last October and will start in one of the Derby trials.

"He's done well physically over the winter and what he achieved last year as a shell of a horse shows he's very smart," said Balding, rating his three-year-old team as good as any he has had with ratings to back that up at the top of the pecking order.

The Thai owner's blue and white colours could also be carried with distinction by **Bye Bye Hong Kong**, who has ground to make up on Too Darn Hot on their Champagne Stakes running but will start in a Guineas trial, possibly at Newbury, with the French Guineas in mind rather than Newmarket.

Happy Power is another well regarded after signing off with an impressive win at Doncaster and he could be underestimated even on a rating of 97 when getting his preferred softer ground.

Shine So Bright, third in the Mill Reef, could start back in the Free Handicap at Newmarket in April to test whether this son of Oasis Dream will get the mile to open up more Group-race opportunities.

Balding sees a lot of his faithful and consistent servant Tullius in **Flashcard**. Beaten only on his third outing in a big sales race in Ireland, Flashcard has been gelded and is expected to build on a rating of 93.

Dashing Willoughby is another to look out for as a promising young stayer who could develop into a Queen's Vase candidate at Royal Ascot.

Balding has a trio of three-year-old fillies to keep on your side in Listed winner **Look Around**, who did not show her form in the Prestige at Goodwood and returned sore to finish her season early, smart little spinter **Firelight**, who has wintered well, and **Dutch Treat**, who has a Listed mission.

Balding has lost a few of his trusty old guard, notably the retired Horseplay and Absolutely So and new Australian residents Duretto and Count Octave, but he has a strong Group-race team.

Beat The Bank, recovered from a rough trip to Hong Kong, has the aim of a Group 1 win to go with his three Group 2 successes, with another tilt at the Queen Anne an aim as Balding feels he was unlucky in the race last year, failing to get the crucial gaps.

Mud-loving **Here Comes When** will be a danger to all in swamp-like conditions and Jeff Smith's home-bred fillies **Dancing Star**, who could try a mile after enjoying a first run at 7f, and last season's rapid improver **Foxtrot Lady** are to be respected.

St Simon Stakes winner **Morando** is a likely candidate for the John Porter back at Newbury, while St Leger ninth **Maid Up**, one of the improvers of the year after starting with a rating of 67, will be on the Group-race trail.

BEAT THE BANK: another tilt at the Queen Anne looks on the cards

RALPH BECKETT also did the south proud last year, registering his second-best score and prize-money haul, and he looks ready to go again with a strong squad of three-year-olds.

Beckett will be hoping it is V for Vega and more victories as he has four classy fillies for new owners Waverley Racing in **Feliciana De Vega**, **Manuela De Vega**, **Antonia De Vega** and **Dancing Vega**. All could be involved in Classic trials.

Manuela De Vega, who already holds the Irish Oaks entry, is a type for the Musidora, while the Deauville Listed winner Feliciana De Vega has the Fred Darling at Newbury pencilled in to test her credentials.

Dancing Vega will also feature in a trial and Antonia De Vega, who fractured a pastern when finishing last in the Fillies' Mile after an impressive win in the Group 3 Prestige at Goodwood, will start back over a mile but could get 1m2f.

Sand Share, third in the May Hill, is another contender for the Fred Darling and her owner-breeder Khalid Abdullah has another classy filly in **Chaleur**, who bizarrely grew a winter coat during one of the hottest summers after her Duchess of Cambridge third!

Radley runner-up **Glance** is another to note as Beckett said: "I thought she did well to achieve as much as she did at two and her family generally get better with age. She'll appreciate a bit of juice in the ground."

Skymax has a staying pedigree and is another from a late-developing family, so his October win in a mile Newmarket nursery augurs well.

Chester could be a happy hunting ground for Beckett as he has the Dee Stakes in mind for the unbeaten **Nivaldo** and the Chester Cup for **Here And Now**.

The older brigade looks powerful with an Ebor possible in **Rock Eagle** and **Mitchum Swagger**, a Listed mile winner who needs cut in the ground, trying for Group 3 honours with the Earl Of Sefton a possible early target.

Battered has the Lincoln in his sights after a nice return on the all-weather at Newcastle, while Ascot lover **Di Fede** will explore the Berkshire track again for more riches.

On a personal note, further down the pecking order it is good to hear the giant filly **Thimbleweed** is back after a wind op which could help her progress again.

DAVID MENUISIER deservedly put his name on the map last year with the exploits of **Thundering Blue**, who has had an equally merited long holiday having finished last year with trips far west and

DANCETERIA: has strengthened up

then far east for second in the Canadian International and down the field in the Japan Cup.

Menuisier welcomed his handsome grey back at the end of January and is in no hurry to name targets, although he would love to take him back to North America at some stage as well as add a Group 1 win to his Group 2 York Stakes win.

Danceteria was another improver last year, winning four on the bounce before coming up short in the Cambridgeshire and a Listed race in France, and he has reportedly strengthened up over the winter to suggest he can kick on.

History Writer, who has not been the easiest to train, being a hot individual mentally, is another to note as he has been gelded over the winter which could turn him around.

His grey half-brother **Edmond Dantes**, also gelded this winter, may be rated just 65 but has an interesting new owner in retired trainer Criquette Head, who visited her former assistant.

Menuisier picked out **Nuits St Georges**

as an interesting staying prospect, while **Migration** has done well for his break and **Dragons Voice**, who had three runs for him after the retirement of Philip Hide, should do better.

GEORGE BAKER is new to the Southerner beat after his move last year to Robins Farm, Chiddingfold, in Surrey and the former Manton trainer has shown signs he is finding his feet after a difficult first year.

His 125-1 Goodwood maiden winner Feel Glorious has been sold to race on in the US, but Baker has made shrewd buys at the horses in training sales in the past and is hoping to hit gold with two more.

Borderforce, bought out of Karl Burke's stables, is eligible for French premiums and will cross the Channel this summer. First he has the William Hill Lincoln entry and could start in the consolation race off his rating of 92, especially if he gets the cut in the ground he favours.

Cristal Spirit, formerly trained by William Haggas and winner of his last race at Kempton, is the other new recruit and Baker sees him as a smart staying prospect.

Another to look out for is Highclere Racing's **Culture**, who has done well over the winter and wasn't suited to the Amiens track in France when still a close third on her last start. She is likely to begin over a mile later in April.

The Baker team works hard to keep **Crazy Horse** at the races as he has plenty of ability along with his share of physical problems and is expected to continue to make his presence felt home and abroad in Group company.

Two others to note, both of whom have had wind ops, are **Infanta Isabella**, a big mare who at five is reaching her physical peak, and **La Maquina**, who showed promise at two but has had his niggles.

Midlands
by John Bull

IAN WILLIAMS enjoyed his best year on the Flat in 2018 and hopes there is more to come this campaign as he readies his biggest team for the turf.

Williams hit the £1 million mark in prize-money for the first time and enjoyed a career-high total of 66 winners across the turf and all-weather.

He told John Bull: "We enjoyed a great year on the Flat and this is the biggest and hopefully best team I've had this time around. I'm very much hoping we can build on last year's success."

Stable star **Magic Circle** breezed to victory in the Chester Cup and Henry II Stakes before breaking a blood vessel when down the field in the Melbourne Cup in November.

A return to Chester and Sandown is in the offing for the talented seven-year-old owned by Marwan Koukash, a big supporter of the Williams yard.

Williams said: "Magic Circle is well in himself after his Australian adventure and could go for the Ormonde Stakes at Chester before returning to Sandown for the Henry II Stakes.

"We'd like to go back and have another crack at the Melbourne Cup but he's got to earn his place again first."

Williams is eyeing another Chester Cup bid with new recruit **Shabeeb**, who cost 58,000gns at the Tattersalls July Sale having won at Newmarket off 95 on his final run for Roger Varian.

The trainer nominated several other horses to follow during the campaign, including 200,000gns purchase **Breath Caught**, who won twice last year for Ralph Beckett and was fifth in a £100,000 handicap at Newmarket when last seen.

Williams said: "Breath Caught was a nice three-year-old last year and is an exciting recruit. We've also brought in **Time To Study**, **No More Regrets** and **Consequences** and I'm looking forward to them."

Among those who flew the flag for

MAGIC CIRCLE: spreadeagles his field in the Henry II Stakes at Sandown

Williams last year, he can't wait to see **Blue Laureate** get going again after he was second in a couple of top three-year-old middle-distance handicaps last year.

"Blue Laureate did well for us last year," he said, "but I'm hoping that will be a shadow of what he achieves this season."

Old favourite **Sir Maximilian** is on the way back from injury and gets a positive mention, as do **Restorer**, **Byron Flyer**, **Heart Of Soul** and **Stars Over The Sea**.

Big Country continues to fly the flag for the *MICK APPLEBY* yard, with the Oakham trainer eyeing more international enterprise this year.

The six-year-old contested Group 3 and Listed races in Norway and Sweden last year and could be heading across Europe once more.

Appleby said: "The big handicaps over here are options for him on the turf as the prize-money is often better than in Listed company, while there will be options for him in Sweden, Norway and Germany, where there is a Listed race that might suit him."

Sputnik Planum is unbeaten in two starts for Appleby and may head for a handicap at Doncaster's Lincoln meeting, while progressive sprinter **Saaheq** is another handicapper to note.

Appleby hopes there is more to come from **Lincoln Park**, who won two nurseries towards the end of last season, and **Jackpot Royale**, who secured a hat-trick as a three-year-old.

He said: "Lincoln Park has come on really well over the winter and I'm hopeful

there's more improvement in him – he's a nice horse and may well stay a mile. Jackpot Royale will have to improve again this year but he's progressive."

Lion Hearted has been in fine form since joining Appleby and is another who could rise through the ranks, with Appleby saying: "Lion Hearted has done well since joining us and works a hell of a lot better than the mark he arrived on. He's an interesting one for the turf.

Asked for a dark horse, the trainer nominated **Quila Saeda**, adding: "She's a new recruit from Germany who I quite like and she could prove to be a decent mare."

IVAN FURTADO has moved to Averham Park – a racehorse training centre for owner John Fretwell – and is targeting high-profile success this campaign with his biggest team including 25 two-year-olds.

Furtado said: "We've moved to fantastic facilities and I'm really looking forward to the Flat campaign. We've got 65 horses in and I'm hoping to hit the jackpot with a few more Saturday winners to help raise our profile."

Among the main hopes are **Cox Bazar**, a sharp 96-rated sprinter bought from France who will be aimed at the Epsom Dash, and **Medahim**, a 98-rated handicapper who won at Glorious Goodwood last year for Richard Hannon.

The progressive trio of **Sparklealot**, **Laith Alareen** and **Belisa** notched nine wins between them for Furtado last year and hopes are high once again for that trio.

Furtado said: "Sparklealot proved himself to be tough and versatile, winning on varying ground last year, and he was still a little green. He's not the biggest horse but those who rode him said he rides bigger than he is. We'll look to start him off on soft ground and he's likely to head to Chester during the season.

"Laith Alareen had a great season and is a fast-ground horse. He's come back from a break stronger and a big field and straight track suit him best.

"Belisa is a massive filly and still open to improvement. She suffered a pelvis injury on her final start but is fine now. She's very progressive, will stay 1m6f and should

TONY CARROLL: best ever campaign

BIG COUNTRY (left): flying the flag for Mick Appleby in some big handicaps

come into her own at the backend of the season on soft ground."

Four-year-old **Kings Highway**, a novice winner for James Tate at Kempton in September, is another eyecatching recruit for Furtado, who said: "He's big, strong and has got form in the book."

The trainer also likes lightly raced three-year-old **Gennaro**, saying: "Gennaro was massive as a two-year-old and should come into his own over further this year. He works like a nice horse and I'll be disappointed if he doesn't go on this year."

Cropthorne trainer *TONY CARROLL* celebrated a career-best tally of 61 winners on the Flat last year and has several handicappers to follow for this campaign.

Temur Khan and **Happy Escape** are already multiple winners on the all-weather and will be worth following on turf, while **Doc Sportello** has bounced back to form and is one to keep on your side in sprint handicaps.

Oeil De Tigre is another tough and admirable sprint handicapper and has a particular liking for Goodwood, where he secured a hat-trick last year, while **Wiley Post** boasts a very consistent profile and should make his presence felt off a mark of 78.

KEVIN FROST could do well with **Tarbeyah**, who ran a fine race when fourth on

her sole start at Pontefract in October and has seen the form franked by third-placed Matterhorn. Frost also has three smart handicappers in **Francis Xavier**, **The Throstles** and **Documenting** who could all go from strength to strength.

Two horses to note from other yards in the region are speedy sprinter Dark Shot and middle-distance performer Panko.

Dark Shot was purchased by *SCOTT DIXON* for 40,000gns in November 2017 and ran several fine races for the yard last year, including when a neck second to El Astronaute at York, fifth in the Epsom Dash and a close fourth in the Stewards' Cup consolation race at Glorious Goodwood. He should be able to strike off a mark of 82.

The *ALEX HALES*-trained **Panko** scored twice in his first Flat campaign for the Edgcote trainer and is best suited by a quick surface. He will provide his owners with plenty of fun once again this summer.

Midlands magic
Big Country
Magic Circle
Temur Khan

RACING & FOOTBALL outlook

Tipping Point
Tom Collins

Shake off the tweed with this stellar list of hopefuls

I DON'T know about you but I can't wait for the Flat turf season to get into full swing.

Not only because finding winners over the jumps has generally proved harder than working out a Brexit deal but I miss the buzz of watching a delightful cocktail of speed and power, whether it is a Class 6 handicap at Redcar or a Group 1 at Newmarket. And the Flat season brings with it the added bonus of summer weather. What more could you want?

Unsurprisingly, last year was dominated by trainer John Gosden with an added sprinkle of Charlie Appleby, who landed his first Derby with Masar, and Aidan O'Brien. Much like most Flat campaigns, really.

Stradivarius, Roaring Lion and Enable were just three horses to stand out for Gosden, who has already started 2019 in blistering form with multiple successes on the all-weather, while you can't forget about crack two-year-old and current 2,000 Guineas and Derby favourite Too Darn Hot. He is a banker for many in the Classics.

O'Brien will surely have something to say about that, though, as he readies his traditionally strong team – likely to include exciting Ten Sovereigns and Magna Grecia – in a bid to deny the unbeaten colt a couple of red-letter days.

Just thinking about Guineas weekend has made me as excited as a child at Christmas.

It's not just about the big guns and many will have their eye on the first proper meeting of the year at Doncaster in late March with the Lincoln, a handicap won last year by subsequent Group 2 scorer Addeybb, ranking the feature event.

Furthermore, my favourite punting tracks – Windsor, Brighton and Salisbury – return so I would be disappointed if the betting accounts didn't start looking rosy again. I hope you have the same optimism!

If you are still completely engrossed in the jumps season and have forgotten what a Flat horse looks like, it is probably time to take the tweed off and dust off those notebooks from last summer.

Here are five suggestions who will hopefully prove profitable this year.

Ghaiyyath 4yo colt
311-1- (Charlie Appleby)

Charlie Appleby and Godolphin touted this colt as their top Derby prospect last season but, unfortunately for connections, a setback meant he didn't make the track as a three-year-old until late September.

The fact he was considered their number one shows how much ability and potential they must think he has – and they managed to still win the Epsom Classic with Masar, who wasn't a bad replacement.

Despite missing almost a year, Ghaiyyath proved that he had trained on from his highly encouraging and successful juvenile campaign when landing the Group 3 Prix du Prince d'Orange at Longchamp by three lengths and William Buick, interviewed in Meydan in February, said that he "looks a proper horse for this year".

A fast pace is ideal for Ghaiyyath and, given the fact he will be running in high-class contests with early speed assured throughout the campaign, he is the horse I am probably looking forward to most in 2019.

Lah Ti Dar 4yo filly
11123- (John Gosden)

Owner Andrew Lloyd Webber has plenty of exciting horses to look out for this season and Too Darn Hot probably tops his list, but I am more excited about what this unexposed filly can do over staying trips and think she could be nigh-on unbeatable in 2019.

The gorgeous and athletic Lah Ti Dar barely had to come out of first gear on her first three starts and had valid excuses the last twice when tasting defeat.

Placed in the Leger, Lah Ti Dar gave first run to a true stayer in Kew Gardens but galloped all the way to the line despite many thinking the trip would be her undoing, while racing keenly did her no favours when third on Champions Day.

She was an unfurnished sort last year but will have grown plenty over the winter and is the latest superstar filly for Gosden.

Mabs Cross 5yo mare
2143321- (Michael Dods)

How consistent is Mabs Cross? Six wins,

GHAIYYATH: he could make up for lost time this year for Godolphin

including the Group 1 Prix de l'Abbaye, and five places from 13 career starts is an incredible record for a sprinter who regularly takes on the best around, especially given Mabs Cross is a mare tackling the boys.

Despite having the stamina for a step up to six furlongs, Mabs Cross was described as an "out-and-out sprinter" by trainer Michael Dods last season and she seems to be improving with age.

I would be far from shocked should she land further Group prizes over the minimum trip this year and I already have her down as the likely winner of the Temple Stakes at Haydock in May.

Mount Everest 3yo colt
6212- (Aidan O'Brien)

He may not stand out as the best three-year-old in Aidan O'Brien's Tipperary yard

MOUNT EVEREST: promising

at this early stage, but I have high expectations of this impeccably bred colt and have backed him accordingly in the ante-post markets for the Derby and St Leger.

By Galileo out of three-time Group 1 winner Six Perfections, and thus related to Yucatan, Mount Everest boasts a big frame and will have needed this winter to allow him to strengthen and sharpen up both mentally and physically.

Despite the fact he was an unfurnished juvenile, he still ran well in a couple of high-class races and was probably unlucky not to end the season with a Group 2 victory in the Beresford Stakes when narrowly denied by stablemate Japan.

A step up in trip will be the order of the day when he comes back to the track and the early signs are promising as he has been the recipient of a number of glowing reports from the yard.

Sea Of Class 4yo filly
211112- (William Haggas)

This filly is just incredible. If I could own one horse, it would be her.

Unlucky on debut at Newmarket when finding a more experienced rival too good after sweeping from last to challenge under hands and heels – a staple of future performances – Sea Of Class shot to horseracing fame.

The daughter of Sea The Stars showed all the pace and stamina of her Derby-winning sire when recording four victories in a row in mid-summer, which included the Irish and Yorkshire Oaks.

Then came the big match-up with Enable in a competitive 19-runner Arc. She didn't win the race but she won plenty of fans.

Jockey James Doyle found trouble in the Longchamp straight when weaving to find a run after a patient ride and, had the line come 50 yards later, Sea Of Class would have defeated Gosden's reigning champion.

Nevertheless, she ran into a class filly on the day and a rematch between the two will be much sought after a year on.

Anything Enable can do, Sea Of Class could do better.

RACING & FOOTBALL outlook

Richard Birch
Read Richard every week in the RFO

Determined to get rid of the seconditis that hurt my 2018 campaign

AFTER a 2018 plagued by seconditis, I'm determined to give it to the bookies with both barrels in 2019 and here are ten I'll be keeping on my side. Happy punting!

Breathable 4yo gelding
586212244- (Tim Easterby)

The son of Bated Breath took a while to get off the mark as a three-year-old but made no mistake on his fifth start, cruising home in a 1m2f Beverley handicap under Emily Easterby.

He almost completed a double at Ripon a fortnight later, but Roundhead beat him by a short-head that day and then things didn't really go his way in three subsequent runs.

A big horse who should improve again as a four-year-old, he starts 2019 competitively rated on a mark of 69 and needs to get up to 75+ to qualify for the Cumberland Plate at Carlisle, which looks a likely target in June.

Camile 6yo mare
0121- (Iain Jardine)

I would imagine it's hard to get more out of an ex-Joseph O'Brien-trained horse, but Camile looked an improved performer on her first start for Iain Jardine over hurdles at Ayr in February when beating Gold Runner by a length and three-quarters after nearly being brought down by a faller at the last.

She had earlier shown a nice burst of acceleration to land a moderately contested Leicester event and can start the Flat turf season off a mark of just 59.

She should quickly take advantage of that rating in middle-distance handicaps.

Chica Buena 4yo filly
700- (Keith Dalgleish)

Chica Buena made gigantic strides over the winter after moving to Keith Dalgleish from Brendan Duke.

The filly won three hurdle events, including an Aintree Listed race by 23 lengths from Liffeydale Dreamer, and is now rated 136.

The fact that she can start her Flat career with Dalgleish off a mark of just 49 should have punters rushing to empty all their bank accounts to get on. Common sense dictates she will rack up a sequence at some time and the first three of those are likely to come in rapid succession. Keep your eyes firmly focused on the entries!

Christmas Night 4yo gelding
23153-7 (Ollie Pears)

He's no star, but the 65-rated Christmas Night is just the type to win two or three low-grade handicaps each season when conditions are in his favour.

Even though he scored at Wolverhampton in August, I have included him in this list in the belief the four-year-old will develop into a Beverley specialist in 2019. His attacking style from the front is perfect for the Yorkshire track and there will be no end of opportunities for him at around 7f there throughout the summer. He gets on particularly well with Ben Robinson.

De Vegas Kid 5yo gelding
17433- (Tony Carroll)

Tony Carroll places his runners particular-ly well on a general level, but he excels at finding the right races at Brighton.

De Vegas Kid, winner of back-to-back Class 5 handicaps at the seaside track in September, has a profile which suggests he'll do even better as a five-year-old and I expect him to be laid out for the valuable Brighton Mile in August – I also expect him to win it.

Garcon De Soleil 3yo colt
9637170- (Michael Blanshard)

Heavy ground is the key to Garcon De Soleil. The one time he got it at Salisbury last April he bolted up in a 1m6f handicap by nine lengths from Patent.

He competed off a basement mark of 46 that day and retains considerable handicapping scope off 7lb higher.

Given a wet spring, the six-year-old can win two or three staying handicaps before the ground dries up.

Give It Some Teddy 5yo gelding
31051- (Tim Easterby)

My number one horse to follow in 2018, he more than justified his star billing with victories at York (7-1), Ripon (11-4) and Redcar (20-1).

CHICA BUENA: a good handicap mark on the Flat is sure to help her cause

74

SO NEAR SO FARHH: stayer will have Birchy laughing all the way to the bank

A strong traveller with a good turn of foot, he seems best at 1m or 1m1f and definitely didn't get home over 1m2½f when only third to Delph Crescent at York in July after travelling halfway up the straight like much the best horse at the weights.

He is rated only 6lb higher than at the start of last season and there is definitely more to come. He'll win a £25,000+ mile handicap in the north this term.

Little Jo 5yo gelding
11131- (Brian Ellison)

Wind surgery and the fitting of cheekpieces provided the catalyst for Little Jo's rapid improvement last season.

His mark went from 53 at the end of July to 83 following victories at Pontefract, Newmarket (twice) and Newcastle and it could have been more if he had stayed 1m1f in the Silver Cambridgeshire in September. He looked likely to win decisively when quickening to the front over a furlong out, but his stamina appeared to run out close home and he was only third.

Little Jo will have plenty of options in valuable mile handicaps and I think he'll be rated in the 90s by mid-summer.

Luxford 5yo mare
59822-7 (Gary Moore)

The move from John Best's stable to Gary

Moore last autumn didn't provide the immediate transformation in the mare's fortunes that I was expecting, although she was only narrowly beaten when backed off the boards at Chelmsford and also finished second at Kempton.

That failure to win for the Horsham yard could turn out to be a blessing in disguise when it comes to her summer campaign this year as she is certainly well enough treated to land two or three handicaps at her beloved Brighton. She acts on any ground.

So Near So Farhh 4yo filly
31128- (Mick Channon)

If somebody had predicted after her September romp at Pontefract that So Near So Farhh would start the 2019 turf season on a mark of 64 I would have roared with laughter.

However, this out-and-out stayer failed to add to her tally in two subsequent visits to Pontefract and now I'm going to be laughing all the way to the bank after she kicks off her four-year-old campaign with a sequence of wins in staying and marathon handicaps.

Ideally suited by 2m and beyond, she will find opportunities in April and May for her at Pontefract and Goodwood and I wouldn't be at all surprised if she was rated in the low 80s by mid-summer.

**RACING &
FOOTBALL** outlook

*Time Test
speed ratings*

Persian could be too hot for Guineas favourite

THE market may already have rushed to crown **Too Darn Hot** the great horse of his generation, but the clock suggests that this year's Classics are going to far from a procession for the son of Dubawi.

A best Time Test figure of 76, achieved first in the Solario Stakes and matched when he completed his unbeaten juvenile campaign in the Dewhurst, leaves him only sixth in the list of last season's leading two-year-olds.

Top of the pile is another unbeaten colt, **Ten Sovereigns**, who ran to a mark of 79 when winning the Middle Park Stakes from **Jash** (77).

Ten Sovereigns looks a top-class horse in the making for Aidan O'Brien, but the suspicion is that he will prove best as a sprinter, putting him to forefront of the mind when thinking about the Commonwealth Cup at Royal Ascot.

Jash might just have more chance of staying a mile, but **Persian King** is more interesting for the 2,000 Guineas.

Andre Fabre often sends over his most likely Guineas horses for a taste of the Rowley Mile in the autumn of their juvenile season, most recently doing it with Miss France.

Persian King looks every bit as good as that subsequent 1,000 Guineas winner after earning a figure of 78 with his victory over **Magna Grecia** (77) in the Autumn Stakes and the runner-up has already backed up the findings of the clock with his Vertem Futurity Trophy success.

Magna Grecia didn't even need to run to his best form to follow up at Doncaster but still clocked a time good enough to see narrow runner-up **Phoenix Of Spain** (71) make the top ten two-year-olds.

Victory also means he is proven in all sorts of conditions and he will be a leading player for Ballydoyle in what will doubtless be another multi-weaponed assault on the Classics in Britain and Ireland.

Another to bear in mind is Godolphin's unbeaten **Quorto**, who also ran to a figure of 77 when taking the National Stakes at the Curragh.

Calyx was another two-year-old with an unblemished record, but that didn't come under threat against the big players in the second half of the season as his campaign

CRYSTAL OCEAN: winning at Ascot, where he ran a big race in the King George

ended early because of injury after his win in the Coventry Stakes. He still has plenty to prove, with that Royal Ascot victory worth a Time Test 62.

It was a really disappointing year for the fillies, with only one race standing out on the clock. That was **Fairyland**'s win over **The Mackem Bullet** in the Cheveley Park Stakes, which has produced seven of the top ten fillies on Time Test ratings.

With The Mackem Bullet having left Brian Ellison to move abroad, Fairyland (77) could be in a good position to dominate the mile fillies' division if she stays the trip. She is certainly preferred to her stablemate Just Wonderful, the 1,000 Guineas favourite, who has never achieved a mark better than 59.

That said, there is plenty of scope for something to come out of the woodwork and mop up among the fillies. While it's interesting to see Fillies' Mile winner and

Oaks favourite **Iridessa** (68) show up well in the list of last year's leading juvenile fillies, that figure wouldn't have got her in the top ten in 2017.

Among the older horses, history could repeat itself with a five-year-old trained by Sir Michael Stoute expected to make his Group 1 breakthrough at this late stage of his career.

Crystal Ocean (89) produced the best performance of 2018 on the clock by any horse still in training when narrowly beaten by his stablemate Poet's Word in the King George at Ascot. That horse was winning his second Group 1 of the season having previously been something of a nearly horse and it could be the same for Crystal Ocean.

He was unsuited by a slow gallop and small field when no match for Enable at Kempton after his Ascot second and then had excuses in the Champion Stakes, with

STRADIVARIUS: could come unstuck in a really strongly run race

trip and ground against him. Give him a mile and a half on quick ground and he can bounce back.

That said, it could be a vintage middle-distance division this season with **Masar** (88), **Enable** (84) and **Sea Of Class** (81) staying in training.

With Enable and Sea Of Class getting the sex allowance, there's hardly anything between these superstars on the clock and it's also worth bearing in mind that Enable had beaten her figure of 84 three times during her stellar 2017 campaign.

In contrast, the staying division looks to be one of the weakest going into 2019 and, according to the figures, established champion **Stradivarius** could be there for the taking if certain rivals are directed down the Cup route.

Stradivarius's peak Time Test figure of 80 last season was achieved when no more than workmanlike in winning the Lonsdale Cup at 4-11 and his best ever speed rating came in defeat when only third in the St Leger. That suggests he could be vulnerable in strongly run races.

Last year's Great Voltigeur Stakes looked a really strong race and could throw up one or two future staying stars, with the second and third, **Cross Counter** (77) and **Kew Gardens** (78), going on to win the Melbourne Cup and the St Leger respectively.

The victorious **Old Persian** (80) looked a non-stayer in the St Leger, but Cross Counter and Kew Gardens would have little to find with Stradivarius if heading down that route and are open to improvement.

Top two-year-old colts of 2018

	Horse	Speed rating	Distance in furlongs	Going	Track	Date achieved
1	**Ten Sovereigns**	**79**	**6**	**GF**	**Newmarket**	**Sep 29**
2	Persian King	78	8	GF	Newmarket	Oct 12
3	Jash	77	6	GF	Newmarket	Sep 29
3	Magna Grecia	77	8	GF	Newmarket	Oct 12
3	Quorto	77	7	GY	Curragh	Sep 16
6	Too Darn Hot	76	7	GD	Sandown	Sep 1
7	Mohawk	74	8	GF	Newmarket	Sep 29
8	Anthony Van Dyck	73	7	GY	Curragh	Sep 16
8	Soldier's Call	73	5	GD	Doncaster	Sep 14
10	Phoenix Of Spain	71	8	GS	Doncaster	Oct 27
10	Sergei Prokofiev	71	5	GF	Newmarket	Oct 12

Top two-year-old fillies of 2018

	Horse	Speed rating	Distance in furlongs	Going	Track	Date achieved
1	**Fairyland**	**77**	**6**	**GF**	**Newmarket**	**Sep 29**
2	The Mackem Bullet	76	6	GF	Newmarket	Sep 29
3	So Perfect	74	6	GF	Newmarket	Sep 29
4	Pretty Pollyanna	73	6	GF	Newmarket	Jul 13
5	Gossamer Wings	68	6	GF	Newmarket	Sep 29
5	Iridessa	68	8	GF	Newmarket	Oct 12
7	Lady Kaya	67	6	GF	Newmarket	Sep 29
8	Queen Of Bermuda	66	6	GF	Newmarket	Sep 29
9	Angel's Hideaway	63	6	GF	Newmarket	Sep 29
9	Hermosa	63	8	GF	Newmarket	Oct 12

The sprinting division is in better health, although the standout performer, Battaash (88), was somewhat infuriating at times. For the second year in a row, his win in the King George Stakes at Goodwood marked him out as something special, but we never know what is coming next from the Charlie Hills-trained five-year-old.

Admittedly it took a fine performance from Godolphin speedster **Blue Point** (87) to beat him in the King's Stand Stakes at Royal Ascot. He has to be feared again back at his beloved Ascot.

Sands Of Mali was a 28-1 winner of the Champions Sprint at Ascot and a figure 85 proves that was certainly no fluke. He could have a big season.

Ten Sovereigns and Jash lead the way among the three-year-olds, but the best performances over the minimum trip among last season's juveniles came from **Soldier's Call** (73) and **Sergei Prokofiev** (71), whose wins in the Flying Childers and Cornwallis respectively showed both races lived up to their name as the premier two-year-old races over the distance.

RACING & FOOTBALL outlook

Group 1 review
by Dylan Hill

1 Qipco 2,000 Guineas Stakes (1m)
Newmarket May 5 (Good)
1 **Saxon Warrior** 3-9-0   Donnacha O'Brien
2 **Tip Two Win** 3-9-0   David Probert
3 **Masar** 3-9-0   William Buick
3/1, 50/1, 5/2F. 1½l, hd. 14 ran. 1m 36.55s
(A P O'Brien).

A false dawn for **Saxon Warrior** as what was supposed to be the start of a dominant year, winning over a trip widely perceived as shorter than ideal, was instead his final victory. Time would show that Saxon Warrior beat a field made up of class acts who needed further and a moderate bunch of out-and-out milers, with the only horse capable of giving him a race over the trip, **Roaring Lion**, seemingly slow to come to hand in the spring. **Tip Two Win** managed to claim a shock second over **Masar** and **Elarqam**, with Roaring Lion fifth ahead of **Gustav Klimt**. **James Garfield** didn't get home in seventh, with **Expert Eye** well below his best behind.

2 Qipco 1,000 Guineas Stakes (Fillies) (1m)
Newmarket May 6 (Good To Firm)
1 **Billesdon Brook** 3-9-0   Sean Levey
2 **Laurens** 3-9-0   P J McDonald
3 **Happily** 3-9-0   Ryan Moore
66/1, 7/1, 11/4F. 1¾l, ½l. 15 ran. 1m 36.62s
(Richard Hannon).

The biggest upset in the history of the race and a result that makes just as little sense in retrospect as 66-1 shot **Billesdon Brook**, no better than fourth in three subsequent runs, beat the prolific **Laurens**. Billesdon Brook at least had excuses on those occasions and

seemed to relish this strongly run mile, powering through for a decisive win. While standout miler Alpha Centauri was absent, the form behind was rock-solid, with Laurens running a fine race in second ahead of **Happily**, **Wild Illusion**, **Altyn Orda** and **Soliloquy**, those five covered by just 1½l.

3 Al Shaqab Lockinge Stakes (1m)
Newbury May 19 (Good To Firm)
1 **Rhododendron** 4-8-11   Ryan Moore
2 **Lightning Spear** 7-9-0   Oisin Murphy
3 **Lancaster Bomber** 4-9-0   S Heffernan
100/30F, 16/1, 10/1. shd, 2¾l. 14 ran. 1m 35.07s
(A P O'Brien).

This looked wide-open with the division lacking a real star, but two proven Group 1 performers stepped forward to fight out a pulsating finish as **Rhododendron** pipped **Lightning Spear**. Rhododendron regressed afterwards, but she did really well to beat a resurgent Lightning Spear, who bounced back from a below-par 2017 campaign. The pair pulled clear of **Lancaster Bomber**, who took third ahead of **Dutch Connection** and **Deauville**, while **Accidental Agent** finished best in sixth. **Addeybb** had been progressive but found the ground too quick.

4 Tattersalls Irish 2,000 Guineas (1m)
Curragh (IRE) May 26 (Good To Firm)
1 **Romanised** 3-9-0   Shane Foley
2 **US Navy Flag** 3-9-0   Ryan Moore
3 **Gustav Klimt** 3-9-0   Donnacha O'Brien
25/1, 100/30, 9/2. 2¼l, 1¼l. 11 ran. 1m 38.93s
(K J Condon).

With the best three-year-old milers already stepping up in trip and **Elarqam** failing to fill the void, this was left without an obvious star and **Romanised** made the most of his chance. Romanised also benefited from being delivered latest off a strong pace set by **US Navy Flag**, coming from last to first as those in front of him fell in a hole, though US Navy Flag at least kept on well enough to take second ahead of **Gustav Klimt**. Elarqam was well below his best in sixth.

5 Tattersalls Irish 1,000 Guineas (Fillies) (1m)
Curragh (IRE) May 27 (Good)
1 **Alpha Centauri** 3-9-0 Colm O'Donoghue
2 **Could It Be Love** 3-9-0 Donnacha O'Brien
3 **Happily** 3-9-0 Ryan Moore
12/1, 33/1, 5/4F. 1¾l, ¾l. 12 ran. 1m 38.71s
(Mrs John Harrington).

The emergence of a true superstar as **Alpha Centauri** ran out a clearcut winner to get her stunning campaign up and running. Blunted by heavy ground on her return, Alpha Centauri showed her true colours this time as she cut down the runaway leader **Could It Be Love** and won well. Could It Be Love was probably flattered in second having been allowed a huge lead, with better fillies in **Happily** and **Soliloquy** filling the next two places.

6 Tattersalls Gold Cup (1m2f110y)
Curragh (IRE) May 27 (Good To Firm)
1 **Lancaster Bomber** 4-9-3 S Heffernan
2 **Cliffs Of Moher** 4-9-3 Ryan Moore
3 **Defoe** 4-9-3 Andrea Atzeni
100/30, 7/4, 5/4F. 2l, 1½l. 5 ran. 2m 14.05s
(A P O'Brien).

A thoroughly deserved Group 1 success for **Lancaster Bomber**, who produced perhaps his best ever performance in what would frustratingly prove his last race just as connections seemed to have found his trip. Second five times at the top level over shorter, Lancaster Bomber made the running in his usual fashion and won easily from **Cliffs Of Moher**. That said, the time was only modest for the conditions and Cliffs Of Moher was probably given too much to do, while **Defoe** found the ground quicker than ideal.

7 Investec Oaks (Fillies) (1m4f6y)
Epsom June 1 (Soft)
1 **Forever Together** 3-9-0 Donnacha O'Brien
2 **Wild Illusion** 3-9-0 William Buick
3 **Bye Bye Baby** 3-9-0 Wayne Lordan
7/1, 5/2F, 8/1. 4½l, 3½l. 9 ran. 2m 40.39s
(A P O'Brien).

With the standout filly in this division, Sea Of Class, not ready in time and many other leading contenders below their best, this proved easy pickings for **Forever Together**, who still did well to win so easily. Forever Together comprehensively outstayed the subsequent Nassau winner **Wild Illusion**, whose stamina limitations over this longer trip were exacerbated by the soft ground. **Bye Bye Baby**, ridden like a pacemaker and well exposed at the top level by the end of the season, was able to keep on well enough for third as **Magic Wand** struggled in the conditions and **I Can Fly** was a patent non-stayer.

8 Investec Coronation Cup (1m4f6y)
Epsom June 1 (Soft)
1 **Cracksman** 4-9-0 Frankie Dettori
2 **Salouen** 4-9-0 Silvestre De Sousa
3 **Windstoss** 4-9-0 Adrie de Vries
2/7F, 33/1, 20/1. hd, 3¾l. 6 ran. 2m 38.49s
(John Gosden).

A bizarre performance from **Cracksman**, who had the ground in his favour yet struggled to take advantage of what should have been a straightforward opportunity, getting up on the line to pip **Salouen** with the track and a bump in the stalls put forward as possible excuses. Salouen would at least prove to have been a higher-class opponent than many felt at the time, producing another big run when sixth in the Arc, but the race behind fell apart, with German raider **Windstoss** beaten further in four subsequent attempts at Group 1 level after taking third ahead of the below-par **Idaho** and **Hawkbill**.

9 Investec Derby (1m4f6y)
Epsom June 2 (Good)
1 **Masar** 3-9-0 William Buick
2 **Dee Ex Bee** 3-9-0 Silvestre De Sousa
3 **Roaring Lion** 3-9-0 Oisin Murphy
16/1, 20/1, 6/1. 1½l, ½l. 12 ran. 2m 34.93s
(Charlie Appleby).

Much like the 2,000 Guineas, a classy field turned out to contain many not cut out for the trip, but **Masar** deserves another chance to prove himself the best of the bunch having missed the rest of the season through injury. Third at Newmarket, Masar saw out the extra half-mile much better than **Roaring Lion** and **Saxon Warrior** to win well, although the proximity of **Dee Ex Bee** in second holds down the bare form. Roaring Lion was a close third, just coming up short in the final furlong but pulling 2½l clear of Saxon Warrior, and there were bigger gaps behind with St Leger winner **Kew Gardens** among the also-rans.

10 Queen Anne Stakes (1m)
Ascot June 19 (Good To Firm)

1 **Accidental Agent** 4-9-0   Charles Bishop
2 **Lord Glitters** 5-9-0   Jamie Spencer
3 **Lightning Spear** 7-9-0   Oisin Murphy
33/1, 20/1, 10/1. ½l, nk. 15 ran. 1m 38.85s
(Eve Johnson Houghton).

Six horses covered by just 1¾l typified the wide-open nature of the older mile division and **Accidental Agent** probably dropped lucky. Progressive at a much lower level and proven at the track, Accidental Agent stormed through late and beat **Lord Glitters** as the first two appeared to benefit from a late pace collapse. **Lightning Spear** just did best of those in the firing line earlier ahead of **Century Dream**, with US raider **Yoshida** and **Beat The Bank** making up the first six. Subsequent Prix du Moulin winner **Recoletos** had boiled over beforehand and wasn't at his best in seventh, while **Rhododendron** and **Benbatl** were also disappointing.

11 King's Stand Stakes (5f)
Ascot June 19 (Good To Firm)

1 **Blue Point** 4-9-4   William Buick
2 **Battaash** 4-9-4   Jim Crowley
3 **Mabs Cross** 4-9-1   Paul Mulrennan
6/1, 9/4, 20/1. 1¾l, nk. 14 ran. 58.14s
(Charlie Appleby).

Stamina came to the fore even over the minimum trip as **Blue Point** turned over **Battaash** in probably the sprint clash of the season. The lightning-quick odds-on favourite set a fierce gallop, but racing a little keenly just found him out, as would be even more the case when taken on in front and a close fourth behind **Mabs Cross** in the Prix de l'Abbaye, and Blue Point picked up the pieces at a track where he goes particularly well (form figures of 1311). Mabs Cross struggled to go the early pace but finished strongly in third and probably ran up to the form she showed when within a nose of a Group 1 double later in the year, with the first three pulling 2¾l clear of the rest.

12 St James's Palace Stakes (7f213y)
Ascot June 19 (Good To Firm)

1 **Without Parole** 3-9-0   Frankie Dettori
2 **Gustav Klimt** 3-9-0   Donnacha O'Brien
3 **Wootton** 3-9-0   Mickael Barzalona
9/4F, 8/1, 8/1. ½l, 3¼l. 10 ran. 1m 38.64s
(John Gosden).

Another sub-standard three-year-old Group 1 mile race that saw **Without Parole** maintain his unbeaten record despite not managing to finish better than sixth in three subsequent races. Without Parole held off the more patiently ridden **Gustav Klimt**, who got as close as he came to a top-flight win in eight attempts. The pair were 3¼l clear of **Wootton**, who was unlucky in running but finished well to pip **Tip Two Win** for third.

13 Prince of Wales's Stakes (1m1f212y)
Ascot June 20 (Good To Firm)

1 **Poet's Word** 5-9-0   James Doyle
2 **Cracksman** 4-9-0   Frankie Dettori
3 **Hawkbill** 5-9-0   William Buick
11/2, 2/5F, 11/1. 2¼l, 8l. 7 ran. 2m 3.51s
(Sir Michael Stoute).

A big upset as **Cracksman** was turned over at 2-5, though he still pulled 8l clear of the third and turned out to have met a rising star in **Poet's Word**. Cracksman, twice devastating over this course and distance in the Champion Stakes, perhaps found it too sharp on quicker ground and had to be roused along early, but he got going in the straight and still couldn't live with **Poet's Word**, who had been steadily progressive for some time and would confirm his latest leap forward by following up in the King George. **Hawkbill** was a distant third ahead of **Cliffs Of Moher**.

14 Gold Cup (2m3f210y)
Ascot June 21 (Good To Firm)

1 **Stradivarius** 4-9-1   Frankie Dettori
2 **Vazirabad** 6-9-2   Christophe Soumillon
3 **Torcedor** 6-9-2   Colm O'Donoghue
7/4J, 9/2, 14/1. ¾l, hd. 9 ran. 4m 21.08s
(John Gosden).

Stradivarius swept all before him in 2018, winning five times and claiming a £1 million bonus, and fittingly this was arguably his best performance in the staying championship as quick ground and the marathon trip played to his strengths. Stradivarius went toe to toe with another real star in **Vazirabad** and came up trumps, going away in the final half-furlong for a terrific victory. **Torcedor** ran a stormer in third and **Order Of St George** would also have gone close but for getting squeezed out, those horses the only ones to finish within 11l.

15 Commonwealth Cup (6f)
Ascot June 22 (Good To Firm)

1 **Eqtidaar** 3-9-3   Jim Crowley
2 **Sands Of Mali** 3-9-3   Paul Hanagan
3 **Emblazoned** 3-9-3   Frankie Dettori
12/1, 15/2, 12/1. ½l, 1l. 21 ran. 1m 12.12s
(Sir Michael Stoute).

BLUE POINT: outstayed the overly free-going Battaash in the King's Stand

Fiercely competitive but probably not the strongest renewal of this race, with only **Sands Of Mali** doing much for the form and perhaps unlucky not to beat **Eqtidaar**. Sands Of Mali raced on the opposite side of the track to the other principals and was a comfortable winner in his group, but he couldn't reel in Eqtidaar, who held on well yet was no better than fifth in two subsequent runs. **Emblazoned** didn't run again after his third but maintained a consistent profile having been beaten slightly further by Sands Of Mali at Haydock previously.

16 Coronation Stakes (Fillies) (7f213y)
Ascot June 22 (Good To Firm)
1 **Alpha Centauri** 3-9-0   Colm O'Donoghue
2 **Threading** 3-9-0   William Buick
3 **Veracious** 3-9-0   Frankie Dettori
11/4F, 7/1, 14/1. 6l, 1¾l. 12 ran. 1m 35.89s
(Mrs John Harrington).

Even better from **Alpha Centauri**, who was racing on good to firm ground for the first time since winning at the meeting 12 months earlier and stepped forward again with a devastating success. Alpha Centauri showed an astonishing turn of foot to leave her rivals for dead in the straight, storming clear of **Threading** and **Veracious** as only the first four finished within 12l of her. **Billesdon Brook** stayed on into fourth having struggled for room as she made her ground from the rear, with **Clemmie** fifth. French Guineas runner-up **Coeur De Beaute** was sixth, with an even worse run from Longchamp winner **Teppal** pointing to the holes in that form.

17 Diamond Jubilee Stakes (6f) Ascot June 23 (Good To Firm)
1 **Merchant Navy** 4-9-3   Ryan Moore
2 **City Light** 4-9-3   Christophe Soumillon
3 **Bound For Nowhere** 4-9-3   Joel Rosario
4/1, 12/1, 16/1. shd, ¾l. 12 ran. 1m 12.09s
(A P O'Brien).

Mission accomplished for **Merchant Navy**, who was campaigned in Europe with the goal of proving himself outside his native Australia and duly retired to stud a Group 1 winner in both hemispheres, albeit in a messy contest. **Harry Angel** blew his chance when rearing up in the stalls, finishing tailed off and lame, and there were further hard-luck stories, most notably **The Tin Man**, who was shuffled back to the rear at a key stage before finishing fast in fourth. However, Merchant Navy still did well to just hold off in-form French raider **City Light** despite being carried left by US raider **Bound For Nowhere**, who finished third.

18 Dubai Duty Free Irish Derby (1m4f)
Curragh (IRE) June 30 (Good To Firm)
1 **Latrobe** 3-9-0   Donnacha O'Brien
2 **Rostropovich** 3-9-0   P B Beggy
3 **Saxon Warrior** 3-9-0   Ryan Moore
14/1, 25/1, EvensF. ½l, nk. 12 ran. 2m 32.62s
(Joseph Patrick O'Brien).

A desperately weak race, with the first two both found out as a notch below the best several times later in the season, and one that confirmed **Saxon Warrior**'s shortcomings over the trip as he couldn't take advantage.

Saxon Warrior was always well positioned as stablemate **Rostropovich** dictated a steady gallop, but he failed to pick up and was only third behind **Latrobe**, who just battled the past the long-time leader. It was hard to make up ground from behind, with subsequent Great Voltigeur winner **Old Persian** and **Dee Ex Bee** among those who failed to land a blow.

19 Juddmonte Pretty Polly Stakes (Fillies & Mares) (1m2f)
Curragh (IRE) July 1 (Good To Firm)
1 **Urban Fox** 4-9-8   Daniel Tudhope
2 **Forever Together** 3-8-12   Ryan Moore
3 **Athena** 3-8-12   Donnacha O'Brien
9/1, 4/6F, 7/1. 3¼l, 2¼l. 6 ran. 2m 6.98s
(William Haggas).

Few horses in 2018 improved more than **Urban Fox**, who had arrived at William Haggas's yard at the start of the year as a 97-rated miler but flourished for the step up in trip and hacked up at the expense of **Forever Together**. Urban Fox was helped by the Oaks winner failing to handle the shorter distance and the lack of serious challengers outside Ballydoyle, but she won comfortably and backed up her performance by finishing second at Group 1 level in her next two runs.

20 Coral-Eclipse (1m1f209y) Sandown July 7 (Good To Firm)
1 **Roaring Lion** 3-8-11   Oisin Murphy
2 **Saxon Warrior** 3-8-11 Donnacha O'Brien
3 **Cliffs Of Moher** 4-9-7   Seamie Heffernan
7/4F, 9/4, 12/1. nk, 2½l. 7 ran. 2m 4.04s
(John Gosden).

An epic clash between two top-class three-year-olds saw **Roaring Lion** just edged out the back-to-form **Saxon Warrior**. Down to what would prove his optimum trip after not quite getting home in the Derby – his only previous run at around 1m2f had seen him win the Dante – Roaring Lion showed a tremendous turn of foot to cut down Saxon Warrior close home as the pair pulled clear of the rest. It was 2½l back to **Cliffs Of Moher**, who stayed on past the front-running **Hawkbill** into third, with **Happily** in fifth.

21 Tattersalls Falmouth Stakes (Fillies & Mares) (1m)
Newmarket (July) July 13 (Good To Firm)
1 **Alpha Centauri** 3-8-12 Colm O'Donoghue
2 **Altyn Orda** 3-8-12   Frankie Dettori
3 **Clemmie** 3-8-12   Ryan Moore
4/9F, 16/1, 6/1. 4½l, 1l. 7 ran. 1m 37.45s
(Mrs John Harrington).

Another Group 1 victory for **Alpha Centauri** but made a lot easier by the absence of any decent older horses – the only two were sent off at 33-1 and 40-1 – and any of the first four from the 1,000 Guineas. **Altyn Orda** was instead left to represent the Guineas form and at least held on for second ahead of **Clemmie**, while **Threading** flopped for the third time at the two Newmarket tracks.

22 Darley July Cup (6f) Newmarket (July) July 14 (Good To Firm)
1 **US Navy Flag** 3-9-0   Ryan Moore
2 **Brando** 6-9-6   Tom Eaves
3 **Fleet Review** 3-9-0   Wayne Lordan
8/1, 14/1, 50/1. 1¾l, ¾l. 13 ran. 1m 11.32s
(A P O'Brien).

A triumphant return to sprinting for **US Navy Flag**, who had come up short over a mile earlier in the season but returned to the form of his Group 1 two-year-old form to win what proved a slightly disappointing renewal. With Royal Ascot winners **Blue Point** and **Eqtidaar** well below their best, only **Brando** seriously challenged US Navy Flag, who made all the running and was going away powerfully at the line. Brando was still unlucky not to get closer, with his jockey wisely veering towards the main group on the far side having mainly raced in a smaller group from which **Redkirk Warrior** was next best in tenth. **Fleet Review** claimed a surprise third at 50-1 ahead of **Sir Dancealot**, who was beaten further in three other runs over the trip at Group 1 level.

23 Darley Irish Oaks (Fillies) (1m4f) Curragh (IRE) July 21 (Good To Firm)
1 **Sea Of Class** 3-9-0   James Doyle
2 **Forever Together** 3-9-0Donnacha O'Brien
3 **Mary Tudor** 3-9-0   W J Lee
11/4, 7/2, 25/1. nk, 1½l. 7 ran. 2m 32.54s
(William Haggas).

Oaks winner **Forever Together** returned to form back over her best trip, but she met her match in **Sea Of Class**, who proved herself the best middle-distance three-year-old filly. Ridden with the same exaggerated waiting tactics that controversially saw her pipped in the Arc, Sea Of Class showed a terrific turn of foot to make up lots of ground under only a hands-and-heels ride, looking a cosy winner at the line despite the narrow margin. Forever Together proved herself on quicker ground with a clear second from **Mary Tudor**, while **Bye Bye Baby** was next ahead of the disappointing Ribblesdale winner **Magic Wand**.

24 King George VI and Queen Elizabeth Stakes (1m3f211y)
Ascot July 28 (Good To Firm)

1 **Poet's Word** 5-9-7   James Doyle
2 **Crystal Ocean** 4-9-7   William Buick
3 **Coronet** 4-9-4   Olivier Peslier
7/4, 6/4F, 15/2. nk, 9l. 7 ran. 2m 25.84s
(Sir Michael Stoute).

This race lacked depth, with Cracksman pulled out because of the ground and only **Rostropovich** representing the Classic generation, but it produced an engrossing battle between **Poet's Word** and **Crystal Ocean**. The pair were given contrasting rides as Crystal Ocean kicked for home early whereas Poet's Word was held up with plenty to do, but the Prince of Wales's Stakes winner made up the ground with a remarkable sustained run, proving equally effective over the longer trip. Crystal Ocean might just have been flattered by the way the race was run given he couldn't build on it, failing to give a half-fit Enable a race on her comeback before a thumping at the hands of Cracksman, but a strongly run 1m4f clearly played to his strengths as he pulled 9l clear of **Coronet** and **Salouen**, with Rostropovich behind.

25 Qatar Goodwood Cup (2m)
Goodwood July 31 (Good)

1 **Stradivarius** 4-9-9   Andrea Atzeni
2 **Torcedor** 6-9-9   Colm O'Donoghue
3 **Idaho** 5-9-9   Ryan Moore
4/5F, 100/30, 8/1. ½l, 6l. 7 ran. 3m 30.56s
(John Gosden).

Another Group 1 victory for **Stradivarius**, who just about confirmed Ascot superiority over **Torcedor**. The Irish raider backed up that effort with another huge run from the front and looked to have Stradivarius in trouble when he kicked clear, but the Gold Cup winner reeled him in and won a shade cosily in the end. Just like at Ascot, the principals were in a different league to the rest, with a 6l gap back to **Idaho** in third.

26 Qatar Sussex Stakes (1m)
Goodwood August 1 (Good)

1 **Lightning Spear** 7-9-8   Oisin Murphy
2 **Expert Eye** 3-9-1   James Doyle
3 **Lord Glitters** 5-9-8   Daniel Tudhope
9/1, 4/1, 10/1. 1½l, ½l. 8 ran. 1m 39.89s
(David Simcock).

Without a Group 1 win in 15 attempts, **Lightning Spear** finally had his day. With the shortcomings of the Classic generation exposed for the first time against older horses – **Expert Eye**, much the best of the three-year-olds,

hadn't even run over the trip since his Guineas flop – Lightning Spear probably didn't need to improve on his Lockinge near miss, quickening up smartly for a comfortable win. **Lord Glitters** wasn't suited by a lack of early pace, running on late into third past **Gustav Klimt** and **Beat The Bank**, with those five 2¾l clear of **So Beloved** and the bitterly disappointing favourite **Without Parole**.

27 Qatar Nassau Stakes (Fillies & Mares) (1m1f197y)
Goodwood August 2 (Good)

1 **Wild Illusion** 3-8-13   William Buick
2 **Urban Fox** 4-9-7   Daniel Tudhope
3 **Veracious** 3-8-13   Frankie Dettori
4/1, 3/1, 5/1. 2l, shd. 6 ran. 2m 6.22s
(Charlie Appleby).

Twice second over 1m4f since her Guineas fourth, **Wild Illusion** found her niche over this intermediate distance and sparked a Group 1 double, with further success in the Prix de l'Opera following. Wild Illusion made all the running having been given the run of the race in front, though she was clearly the best filly with runner-up **Urban Fox** closest to her almost throughout. **Veracious** did well to throw down a challenge before losing second on the line, while **Billesdon Brook** had little chance in fourth having been held up in rear. **Rhododendron** trailed home last.

28 Juddmonte International Stakes (1m2f56y)
York August 22 (Good To Firm)

1 **Roaring Lion** 3-8-13   Oisin Murphy
2 **Poet's Word** 5-9-6   James Doyle
3 **Thundering Blue** 5-9-6   Fran Berry
3/1, 8/5F, 50/1. 3¼l, ½l. 8 ran. 2m 7.70s
(John Gosden).

Roaring Lion's crowning glory as he easily saw off the leading middle-distance older horse of the summer in **Poet's Word.** Roaring Lion benefited from always better positioned than Poet's Word, who found plenty of trouble early in the straight, but he also picked up much better once the pair were in the clear and stretched his advantage all the way to the line. **Thundering Blue** ran on late into third past **Saxon Warrior**, who failed to fire at a time when many of Aidan O'Brien's horses were out of sorts, while **Benbatl** was fifth ahead of **Without Parole** and **Latrobe**.

29 Darley Yorkshire Oaks (Fillies & Mares) (1m3f188y)
York August 23 (Good To Firm)

1 **Sea Of Class** 3-8-12   James Doyle
2 **Coronet** 4-9-7   Frankie Dettori

3 **Eziyra** 4-9-7   William Buick
7/4F, 4/1, 8/1. 2¼l, 1l. 8 ran. 2m 30.44s
(William Haggas).

A much easier win for **Sea Of Class** with her main rivals flopping, allowing her to coast home in impressive fashion with a typical turn of foot from the rear. Sea Of Class stormed clear of a trio of 2018 Group 2 winners in **Coronet**, **Eziyra** and **Horseplay**, but the mixed form of the Aidan O'Brien yard led to all three of his fillies running poorly, including **Magic Wand** and **Bye Bye Baby**, while **Laurens**, up in trip after a couple of Group 1 wins at around 1m2f in France, failed to get home.

30 Coolmore Nunthorpe Stakes (5f)
York August 24 (Good To Firm)
1 **Alpha Delphini** 7-9-11   Graham Lee
2 **Mabs Cross** 4-9-8   Tom Eaves
3 **Blue Point** 4-9-11   William Buick
40/1, 14/1, 7/2. nse, 2¼l. 15 ran. 57.18s
(Bryan Smart).

A massive upset as **Alpha Delphini**, yet to win even a Group 3, produced a clear career-best and made the most of below-par runs from **Blue Point** and **Battaash**. **Mabs Cross** had looked next in the pecking order on her King's Stand third, as she would show when winning the Prix de l'Abbaye but she couldn't quite get past Alpha Delphini, who held on in

THE TIN MAN: three Group 1 wins

a thriller with Blue Point, who perhaps found a quicker 5f against him, in third. Battaash ran a flat race for the second a year in a row, both coming after his best performances at Goodwood to suggest he may need to be fresher, but still finished ahead of subsequent Flying Five first and third **Havana Grey** and **Sioux Nation**.

31 32Red Sprint Cup (6f)
Haydock September 8 (Heavy)
1 **The Tin Man** 6-9-3   Oisin Murphy
2 **Brando** 6-9-3   Tom Eaves
3 **Gustav Klimt** 3-9-1   Ryan Moore
7/1, 14/1, 16/1. ½l, nk. 12 ran. 1m 14.13s
(James Fanshawe).

Although **The Tin Man** has never looked a truly outstanding sprinter, this meant Group 1 victories in three successive seasons as he was again in pole position when granted a suitable opening. Appreciating a strong gallop as favourite **Harry Angel** raced too keenly in front on his return from a layoff, The Tin Man came through strongly to beat another grand old campaigner in **Brando**, with **Gustav Klimt**, running perhaps his best run when finally dropped in trip, and **Donjuan Triumphant** next. **Sands Of Mali** got back on track after a couple of poor runs, doing best of those ridden prominently in fifth, with Harry Angel next.

32 William Hill St Leger (1m6f115y)
Doncaster September 15 (Good)
1 **Kew Gardens** 3-9-1   Ryan Moore
2 **Lah Ti Dar** 3-8-12   Frankie Dettori
3 **Southern France** 3-9-1 Seamie Heffernan
3/1, 7/4F, 20/1. 2¼l, 4½l. 12 ran. 3m 3.34s
(A P O'Brien).

Kew Gardens had flourished since being well beaten in the Derby and stepped forward again when stepping back up in trip, producing a tremendous performance to beat a high-class filly in **Lah Ti Dar**. There was probably less between the two class acts than the margin suggests, but Kew Gardens was ridden slightly more prominently and never relinquished his advantage, staying on strongly as Lah Ti Dar gamely tried to bridge the gap. The pair pulled clear of **Southern France**, who was the only horse to finish within 9l of them, with **Dee Ex Bee** fourth ahead of **Old Persian**, **Raymond Tusk** and **Nelson**.

33 Qipco Irish Champion Stakes (1m2f)
Leopardstown (IRE) September 15 (Good To Firm)
1 **Roaring Lion** 3-9-1   Oisin Murphy

2 **Saxon Warrior** 3-9-1   Ryan Moore
3 **Deauville** 5-9-7   Wayne Lordan
8/11F, 5/2, 40/1. nk, 2¾l. 7 ran. 2m 7.21s
(John Gosden).

A premature final chapter in the rivalry between **Roaring Lion** and **Saxon Warrior** as the 2,000 Guineas winner suffered a career-ending injury, which might have proved key in his failure to regain superiority over his Eclipse and Juddmonte conqueror. Roaring Lion produced a typically outstanding turn of foot and looked a cosy winner at the line, but it transpired Saxon Warrior had suffered a tendon injury, which explained the way he hung into the rail after appearing to have opened up a decisive lead under a more forceful ride than in his previous attempts at the trip. **Deauville** was best of a modest bunch behind, with Prix du Jockey Club winner **Study Of Man** a notable disappointment and **Rhododendron** also well below her best.

34 Coolmore Fastnet Rock Matron Stakes (Fillies & Mares) (1m)
Leopardstown (IRE) September 15 (Good To Firm)
1 **Laurens** 3-9-0   Daniel Tudhope
2 **Alpha Centauri** 3-9-0   Colm O'Donoghue
3 **Clemmie** 3-9-0   Seamie Heffernan
10/1, 30/100F, 20/1. ¾l, 1¼l. 7 ran. 1m 39.23s
(K R Burke).

A huge upset as **Alpha Centauri** was beaten by **Laurens**, with a post-race check revealing she had chipped a joint in her fetlock to force a premature retirement. With the injury clearly contributing to a below-par performance from Alpha Centauri, it became relatively easy pickings for Laurens, who would at least follow up in the Sun Chariot to confirm herself a top-class miler despite having spent much of the season racing over further. **Clemmie** was third ahead of **Magical**, whose subsequent improvement came over much longer trips, and **Happily**, who was notably unpopular in the market and may have needed the run after a mid-season break.

35 Comer Group International Irish St Leger (1m6f)
Curragh (IRE) September 16 (Good)
1 **Flag Of Honour** 3-9-1   Ryan Moore
2 **Latrobe** 3-9-1   Donnacha O'Brien
3 **Weekender** 4-9-9   Frankie Dettori
2/1F, 11/4, 3/1. 2¾l, 1¾l. 6 ran. 3m 5.72s
(A P O'Brien).

The lack of a top older horse made this race's clash with the St Leger at Doncaster even more of an issue and it was dominated by a couple of three-year-olds who had been quite well down the pecking order for that race, with **Flag Of Honour** beating **Latrobe**. Completing a hat-trick since stepped up to staying trips but no match for Stradivarius at Ascot on his following start, Flag Of Honour made all the running and comfortably saw off Latrobe, with Ebor runner-up **Weekender** third.

36 Derrinstown Stud Flying Five Stakes (5f)
Curragh (IRE) September 16 (Good To Yielding)
1 **Havana Grey** 3-9-3   Richard Kingscote
2 **Son Of Rest** 4-9-4   Chris Hayes
3 **Sioux Nation** 3-9-3   Ryan Moore
15/8F, 22/1, 5/1. ½l, nk. 9 ran. 59.59s
(K R Burke).

A strange addition to the Group 1 roster and a race that did nothing to argue the case for its hike, with **Havana Grey** winning a desperately weak contest for the grade. Havana Grey barely had to step up on the level of his Nunthorpe fifth, running almost to the pound with **Sioux Nation**, while **Son Of Rest** split the pair before dead-heating for the Ayr Gold Cup off a mark of just 101.

37 Kingdom Of Bahrain Sun Chariot Stakes (Fillies & Mares) (1m)
Newmarket October 6 (Good)
1 **Laurens** 3-9-0   Daniel Tudhope
2 **Happily** 3-9-0   Donnacha O'Brien
3 **Altyn Orda** 3-9-0   Silvestre De Sousa
11/4F, 8/1, 25/1. hd, 2¼l. 9 ran. 1m 37.94s
(K R Burke).

A terrific battle between **Laurens** and **Happily**, with Laurens just confirming her superiority over her old rival with probably the best win among her five at the top level. Known for her narrow victories, with her only Group 1 win by more than a neck coming against the crocked Alpha Centauri, Laurens showed she had more under the bonnet when pushed all the way by the back-to-form Happily, the pair putting some big gaps into the rest of a strong field. **Altyn Orda** was a fine third, finishing 3l clear of subsequent QEII runner-up **I Can Fly**, while **Billesdon Brook** came home with a rattle in fifth having been held up too far back off a steady gallop. **Veracious** and **Clemmie** were among those behind.

38 Qatar Prix de l'Arc de Triomphe (1m4f)
Longchamp (FR) October 7 (Good)
1 **Enable** 4-9-2   Frankie Dettori
2 **Sea Of Class** 3-8-9   James Doyle
3 **Cloth Of Stars** 5-9-5   Vincent Cheminaud

EvensF, 6/1, 28/1. snk, ¾l. 19 ran. 2m 29.24s (John Gosden).

Probably the most discussed race of recent times as **Enable** claimed her second Arc by holding off **Sea Of Class**, felt by seemingly equal numbers on either side to have been given a great or awful ride as she just failed to get up from the rear in a race that favoured those racing prominently according to the sectional times. Whatever the truth of it, Sea Of Class proved herself right out of the top drawer with a mighty effort in coming past most of the field in the straight, whereas Enable was aided by a much kinder draw and just about got away with being only 85 per cent fit according to her trainer after an extremely late start to her campaign and a further setback following her prep run at Kempton. **Cloth Of Stars** and **Waldgeist** were next ahead of **Capri**, who couldn't make the most of a good pitch, with **Salouen** sixth. **Kew Gardens** finished strongly in seventh after he was caught well adrift, as was **Magical**, getting a contrasting run to their stablemate **Nelson**, who set the pace and emphasised the benefit of racing prominently by sticking on well enough to be beaten little over 4l in ninth.

39 Qipco British Champions Sprint Stakes (6f)
Ascot October 20 (Soft)
1 **Sands Of Mali** 3-9-1   Paul Hanagan
2 **Harry Angel** 4-9-2   Adam Kirby
3 **Donjuan Triumphant** 5-9-2   James Doyle
28/1, 4/1, 16/1. 1l, 1¼l. 14 ran. 1m 14.21s (Richard Fahey).

Arguably the best 6f race run all season and a fine win for **Sands Of Mali**, who confirmed his liking for the course and distance when holding off **Harry Angel**. Unlike at Haydock, the first two were able to maintain prominent positions throughout whereas those held up struggled to land a blow, but an impressive time figure suggests they weren't given a soft lead and this was instead top-class sprint form. **Donjuan Triumphant** was third ahead of **Brando**, with **The Tin Man** only seventh.

40 Qipco British Champions Fillies & Mares Stakes (1m3f211y)
Ascot October 20 (Soft)
1 **Magical** 3-8-13   Ryan Moore
2 **Coronet** 4-9-5   Olivier Peslier
3 **Lah Ti Dar** 3-8-13   Frankie Dettori
5/1, 6/1, EvensF. 1l, ¾l. 11 ran. 2m 33.28s (A P O'Brien).

Magical had been slightly disappointing earlier in the year, but stepping up in trip

proved the making of her and she proved a top-class middle-distance filly. Having run beyond 1m1f for the first time when unlucky in the Arc, things went far more smoothly for Magical as she shook off **Coronet** and **Lah Ti Dar** before underlining the quality of this form by running Enable close in the Breeders' Cup Turf. Coronet, consistent all season on quicker ground, produced her best run when finally getting plenty of cut, as she had done when third in the race in 2017, surpassing that form by finishing ahead of Lah Ti Dar, who disappointingly couldn't build on her Leger run. That said, she still pulled 3½l clear of Prix Vermeille winner **Kitesurf** with another 5l gap back to 2017 winner **Hydrangea**.

41 Queen Elizabeth II Stakes (1m) Ascot October 20 (Soft)
1 **Roaring Lion** 3-9-1   Oisin Murphy
2 **I Can Fly** 3-9-0   Donnacha O'Brien
3 **Century Dream** 4-9-4   William Buick
2/1F, 33/1, 25/1. nk, ½l. 13 ran. 1m 42.48s (John Gosden).

Soft ground saw **Roaring Lion** drop back in trip rather than run in the Champion Stakes and, despite appearing to hate the conditions, he just about got away with it in a poor renewal. Roaring Lion failed to quicken in his usual manner but wore down **Century Dream** and was always holding the strong-finishing **I Can Fly**. **Stormy Antarctic** and **Recoletos** were next, with those five covered by just 1¾l and three sent off at 25-1 or bigger, while **Lord Glitters** came home sixth. There were several disappointments behind, including **Lightning Spear**, **Laurens**, **Romanised**, **Beat The Bank** and **Addeybb**.

42 Qipco Champion Stakes (1m1f212y)
Ascot October 20 (Soft)
1 **Cracksman** 4-9-5   Frankie Dettori
2 **Crystal Ocean** 4-9-5   William Buick
3 **Subway Dancer** 6-9-5   Radek Koplik
5/6F, 11/4, 66/1. 6l, ¾l. 8 ran. 2m 8.79s (John Gosden).

Cracksman ended a somewhat underwhelming year on a magnificent high note as he stormed to a second Champion Stakes success when back in his element on soft ground. Even in the conditions, chief rivals **Crystal Ocean** and **Capri** perhaps found the trip shorter than ideal, looking one-paced as they were split by 66-1 Czech outsider **Subway Dancer** in a tight contest for the places, with the out-of-form **Rhododendron** next.

Group 1 index

All horses placed or commented on in our Group 1 review section, with race numbers

CRYSTAL OCEAN: second on all three runs at Group 1 level, twice last year

MAGICAL: thrived when stepped up in trip during the autumn

RACING & FOOTBALL outlook

Two-year-old review by Dylan Hill

1 **Coolmore Stud Irish EBF Fillies' Sprint Stakes (Listed) (6f)**
Naas (IRE) May 20 (Good To Firm)
1 **Servalan** 2-9-0   Seamie Heffernan
2 **Chicas Amigas** 2-9-0   Colm O'Donoghue
3 **Skitter Scatter** 2-9-0   Ronan Whelan
10/1, 9/1, 8/1. 1¼l, 1¾l. 7 ran. 1m 13.17s
(Mrs John Harrington).

This was more notable in retrospect for **Skitter Scatter** and **So Perfect**, first and second at Group 1 level later in the year, finishing only third and fourth. That suggests a huge effort from the victorious **Servalan**, but she disappointed subsequently, as did runner-up **Chicas Amigas**, so there's little doubt the class acts were well below their best.

2 **Matchbook Commission Free On All Sports National Stakes (Listed) (5f10y)**
Sandown May 24 (Good)
1 **Vintage Brut** 2-9-3   David Allan
2 **Sabre** 2-9-3   Tony Hamilton
3 **Konchek** 2-9-3   Adam Kirby
7/2J, 8/1, 9/2. nk, hd. 9 ran. 1m 2.50s
(Tim Easterby).

A really competitive Listed race won in gritty fashion by **Vintage Brut**, with the first three all going on to prove smart juveniles. Vintage Brut just got up to beat **Sabre**, while **Konchek** looked the best horse in the race as he finished strongest after a terrible draw and a significant early bump. **Blown By Wind** was a close fourth.

3 **Cold Move Irish EBF Marble Hill Stakes (Listed) (6f)**
Curragh (IRE) May 26 (Good To Firm)

1 **Fairyland** 2-8-12   Seamie Heffernan
2 **Van Beethoven** 2-9-3   Ryan Moore
3 **Land Force** 2-9-3   Donnacha O'Brien
4/1, 4/6F, 8/1. 2¼l, nk. 9 ran. 1m 13.20s
(A P O'Brien).

A red-hot contest for this early stage of the season with Cheveley Park winner **Fairyland** too good for a pair of subsequent Group 2 winners in **Van Beethoven** and **Land Force**. The filly was always going well and comfortably mastered Land Force, while Van Beethoven ran on into second and **Gee Rex** powered home from the rear in fourth.

4 **Coventry Stakes (Group 2) (6f)**
Ascot June 19 (Good To Firm)
1 **Calyx** 2-9-1   Frankie Dettori
2 **Advertise** 2-9-1   Oisin Murphy
3 **Sergei Prokofiev** 2-9-1   Ryan Moore
2/1F, 10/1, 3/1. 1l, nk. 23 ran. 1m 13.51s
(John Gosden).

Calyx produced a visually stunning victory as he overcame an apparent draw bias – the next five were all drawn on the far side – to beat high-class pair **Advertise** and **Sergei Prokofiev**. It remains hard to assess just how highly to rate Calyx's performance given he raced on the opposite side of the track to the other principals and wasn't seen again due to injury, but he pulled 6½l clear of the rest of those in his group, led by a pair who had already shown solid Listed form in **Blown By Wind** and **Gee Rex**, with **Cosmic Law** and **Getchagetchagetcha**, who both did significantly better in the Vintage Stakes, next ahead of **The Irish Rover**. There were also big gaps among those on the far side, with

Advertise, Sergei Prokofiev and **Vange** much the best of them ahead of **Shine So Bright**.

5 Queen Mary Stakes (Group 2) (Fillies) (5f)
Ascot June 20 (Good To Firm)
1 **Signora Cabello** 2-9-0   Oisin Murphy
2 **Gossamer Wings** 2-9-0Donnacha O'Brien
3 **Shades Of Blue** 2-9-0   Adam Kirby
25/1, 25/1, 5/1. shd, shd. 22 ran. 1m 0.65s (John Quinn).

A blanket finish saw just 1¼l cover the first seven with a 25-1 shot the best of them, but there's little doubt the best filly won as the consistently underrated **Signora Cabello** defied her odds again. Successful at 20-1 in a Listed race at York, Signora Cabello was more streetwise than most and would continue to progress through the summer after pipping **Gossamer Wings** and **Shades Of Blue**. **So Perfect** was a close fourth, reversing Naas form with **Servalan** in sixth.

6 Norfolk Stakes (Group 2) (5f)
Ascot June 21 (Good To Firm)
1 **Shang Shang Shang** 2-8-12 Joel Rosario
2 **Pocket Dynamo** 2-9-1 Mickael Barzalona
3 **Land Force** 2-9-1   Ryan Moore
5/1, 20/1, 7/1. nse, ½l. 10 ran. 59.83s (Wesley A Ward).

Yet another Royal Ascot success for American trainer Wesley Ward, though **Shang Shang Shang** won't be remembered with his great winners after just seeing off a modest bunch of rivals. Shang Shang Shang made all the running and just held off **Pocket Dynamo**, while **Land Force** stayed on into third past **Rumble Inthejungle**, who weakened having pressed the winner closest for much of the race. **Konchek** found things happening too quickly but kept on well into fifth.

7 Albany Stakes (Group 3) (Fillies) (6f)
Ascot June 22 (Good To Firm)
1 **Main Edition** 2-9-0   James Doyle
2 **La Pelosa** 2-9-0   William Buick
3 **Fairyland** 2-9-0   Seamie Heffernan
7/1, 12/1, 5/2. nk, ½l. 18 ran. 1m 13.67s (Mark Johnston).

A terrific race in which the first five all went on to further Group success, with **Main Edition** coming out on top. **Fairyland** and **Pretty Pollyanna** would prove the best of the bunch in time and were arguably unlucky, but Main Edition was a fine winner and would confirm her superiority over a third subsequent top-flight winner, Canadian Grade 1 scorer **La Pelosa**, in the Sweet Solera. Fairyland did

best of those who raced on the far side ahead of **Angel's Hideaway**, while Pretty Pollyanna the only horse able to get into the race from the rear in fifth. **Just Wonderful** was the big disappointment behind.

8 Chesham Stakes (Listed) (7f)
Ascot June 23 (Good To Firm)
1 **Arthur Kitt** 2-9-3   Richard Kingscote
2 **Nate The Great** 2-9-3   Daniel Tudhope
3 **Duke Of Hazzard** 2-9-3   Luke Morris
13/2, 11/1, 25/1. nk, 3¼l. 11 ran. 1m 28.08s (Tom Dascombe).

A really strong race for the grade and the first two pulled clear, with **Arthur Kitt** seeing off **Nate The Great**. Though briefly outpaced, Arthur Kitt produced a fine turn of foot and was too quick for Nate The Great, who stayed on strongly and would produce his best subsequent run when stepped all the way up to 1m2f later in the year. It was 3¾l back to **Duke Of Hazzard**, **Beyond Reason** and **Cardini**, with the rest well strung out including below-par favourite **Natalie's Joy**.

9 Windsor Castle Stakes (Listed) (5f)
Ascot June 23 (Good To Firm)
1 **Soldier's Call** 2-9-3   Daniel Tudhope
2 **Sabre** 2-9-3   Paul Hanagan
3 **Dom Carlos** 2-9-3   Donnacha O'Brien
12/1, 12/1, 16/1. ½l, 1¾l. 28 ran. 1m 0.25s (Archie Watson).

While the lesser of the two 5f juvenile races at Royal Ascot in terms of grade and prize-money, this was a far stronger race than the Norfolk, with a field of 28 rather than ten for starters, and was won by the best two-year-old over the trip all season in **Soldier's Call** as he held off **Sabre**. The pair both came down the near side, but there could be no suggestion they were in any way favoured by the draw as the next six home were on the far side, led by Irish pair **Dom Carlos** and **Van Beethoven** with **Well Done Fox** back in eighth, and the next horse on the near side was subsequent Molecomb runner-up **Life Of Riley**.

10 Betway Empress Fillies' Stakes (Listed) (6f)
Newmarket (July) June 30 (Good To Firm)
1 **Royal Intervention** 2-9-0   Gerald Mosse
2 **Strings Of Life** 2-9-0   James Doyle
3 **Impulsion** 2-9-0   Andrea Atzeni
9/1, 11/2, 6/1. 4½l, ¾l. 12 ran. 1m 13.09s (Ed Walker).

A hugely impressive win for **Royal Intervention**, who made most of the running before storming clear in the closing stages and can

SIGNORA CABELLO (second right): consistently underrated last season

be forgiven her subsequent defeat in the Princess Margaret Stakes when suffering a season-ending injury. Those behind proved a largely moderate bunch, though, with only **Impulsion**'s unlucky fourth in the Sweet Solera doing anything for the form.

11 GAIN Railway Stakes (Group 2) (6f)
Curragh (IRE) June 30 (Good To Firm)
1 **Van Beethoven** 2-9-3   Ryan Moore
2 **Marie's Diamond** 2-9-3 Silvestre De Sousa
3 **Certain Lad** 2-9-3   Ronan Whelan
9/10F, 7/1, 6/1. ½l, 1¼l. 7 ran. 1m 12.45s
(A P O'Brien).

Van Beethoven had already been exposed as just below the best Ballydoyle juveniles, so the fact he was made an odds-on favourite speaks volumes about the opposition and he duly proved good enough. Van Beethoven picked up well and held off **Marie's Diamond**, who was a clear second ahead of **Chelsea Lad** and **Highland Fortune**.

12 Grangecon Stud Stakes (Group 3) (Fillies) (6f)
Curragh (IRE) July 1 (Good To Firm)
1 **So Perfect** 2-9-0   Ryan Moore
2 **Skitter Scatter** 2-9-0   Ronan Whelan
3 **Cava** 2-9-0   Donnacha O'Brien
6/4F, 16/1, 13/2. ½l, ½l. 7 ran. 1m 12.34s
(A P O'Brien).

A terrific clash between two high-class fillies as **So Perfect** claimed the scalp of subsequent Moyglare winner **Skitter Scatter**. Although the Ballydoyle filly had to be driven

along early and got up close home, the trip perhaps played more to her strengths than those of Skitter Scatter, who would flourish when stepped up in distance. **Cava** was a fine third, pulling 3l clear of subsequent Listed winner **Lethal Promise**.

13 Arqana July Stakes (Group 2) (6f)
Newmarket (July) July 12 (Good To Firm)
1 **Advertise** 2-9-0   Frankie Dettori
2 **Konchek** 2-9-0   Adam Kirby
3 **Charming Kid** 2-9-0   Paul Hanagan
11/10F, 10/1, 25/1. 2l, nk. 8 ran. 1m 11.63s
(Martyn Meade).

Advertise stood out on the form of his Coventry second and made his class tell with a commanding victory over **Konchek**, who improved for the step up in trip as he beat **Charming Kid** and **Dunkerron** into second. Subsequent Group 3 winner **Sporting Chance** was next ahead of the disappointing **Legends Of War** and **Van Beethoven**.

14 Duchess of Cambridge Stakes (Group 2) (Fillies) (6f)
Newmarket (July) July 13 (Good To Firm)
1 **Pretty Pollyanna** 2-9-0 Silvestre De Sousa
2 **Angel's Hideaway** 2-9-0   Frankie Dettori
3 **Chaleur** 2-9-0   Harry Bentley
20/1, 13/2, 11/2. 7l, 6l. 9 ran. 1m 11.51s
(Michael Bell).

Utter carnage as **Pretty Pollyanna** was helped by **Angel's Hideaway** taking out most of her rivals, but even so this was still a terrific performance. Always prominent, Pretty

DARK VISION (6): form of his eyecatching Vintage Stakes win didn't work out

Pollyanna was already in front when the trouble occurred behind and would surely have won well anyway given the way she powered home, pointing to the fact she would want further by the autumn. Angel's Hideaway was perhaps fortunate to come second having badly cut up **La Pelosa** and **Main Edition**, who both looked likely to finish close to her, and that interference led to another big gap back to **Chaleur**, who picked up the pieces in third from **Gossamer Wings**.

15 bet365 Superlative Stakes (Group 2) (7f)
Newmarket (July) July 14 (Good To Firm)
1 **Quorto** 2-9-1   William Buick
2 **Cape Of Good Hope** 2-9-1   Ryan Moore
3 **Neverland Rock** 2-9-1   Pat Dobbs
5/4F, 6/1, 8/1. 3¾l, ½l. 7 ran. 1m 25.48s (Charlie Appleby).

The emergence of a new star as **Quorto** hacked up. **Cape Of Good Hope** set a solid gallop that had a fair field really well strung out, yet Quorto was always travelling strongly and powered clear in the final furlong. Cape Of Good Hope ran a fine race in second – better than he showed in the autumn when off for a long time before coming third in the Royal Lodge – as he just held off **Neverland Rock**, who never again got this quick ground before being moved to the US. That pair were 4½l ahead of **Certain Lad** and there was an even bigger gap back to the rest.

16 Irish Thoroughbred Marketing Rose Bowl Stakes (Listed) (6f)
Newbury July 20 (Good To Firm)
1 **Natalie's Joy** 2-8-9   Frankie Dettori

2 **Chuck Willis** 2-9-0   Callum Shepherd
3 **Emaraaty Ana** 2-9-0   Tom Queally
11/10F, 12/1, 15/8. 1¾l, ½l. 5 ran. 1m 11.19s (Mark Johnston).

Natalie's Joy proved her Royal Ascot running all wrong as she got back on track with a hugely impressive victory, making all the running and easily beating a field that included subsequent Gimcrack winner **Emaraaty Ana**. That said, Natalie's Joy, who missed the rest of the season, may be flattered by such a literal reading of the form as Emaraaty Ana, running for the first time since a winning debut in April, was well below his best judging by the fact he couldn't even get past runner-up **Chuck Willis**. **Barbill** was a close fourth.

17 Jebel Ali Racecourse And Stables Anglesey Stakes (Group 3) (6f63y)
Curragh (IRE) July 21 (Good)
1 **Marie's Diamond** 2-9-3   James Doyle
2 **Viadera** 2-9-0   Colin Keane
3 **Just Wonderful** 2-9-0   Ryan Moore
7/2, 9/4, 13/8F. ½l, 2¼l. 6 ran. 1m 15.27s (Mark Johnston).

A deserved Group win for solid yardstick **Marie's Diamond**, who took advantage of another below-par performance from the favourite **Just Wonderful**. Marie's Diamond outfought **Viadera**, while Just Wonderful, who would show her talent later in the season but continued to lack consistency, was left behind in third.

18 British Stallion Studs EBF Star Stakes (Listed) (Fillies) (7f)
Sandown July 26 (Good To Firm)
1 **Look Around** 2-9-0   Oisin Murphy

2 **Ajrar** 2-9-0   Pat Dobbs
3 **La Pelosa** 2-9-0   William Buick
8/1, 6/1, 8/11F. 1¼l, shd. 7 ran. 1m 30.08s
(Andrew Balding).

A surprise result with odds-on favourite **La Pelosa** only third and subsequent events confirmed this wasn't anywhere near her true running. **Look Around** and **Ajrar** finished in front of the Godolphin filly, who in turn pulled 5l clear of the rest, but the first two were both found out at a higher level.

19 **Princess Margaret Keeneland Stakes (Group 3) (Fillies) (6f)**
Ascot July 28 (Good To Firm)
1 **Angel's Hideaway** 2-9-0   Robert Havlin
2 **Royal Intervention** 2-9-0   Gerald Mosse
3 **The Mackem Bullet** 2-9-0   Oisin Murphy
11/4, 6/4F, 20/1. 2½l, nk. 7 ran. 1m 14.59s
(John Gosden).

An impressive victory from **Angel's Hideaway**, who produced a fine turn of foot to storm through from the rear and would prove herself a very smart filly when second in the Oh So Sharp, although she was surely flattered to beat **Royal Intervention** and **The Mackem Bullet** quite so easily. Royal Intervention was felt to be hanging right by her trainer and subsequently found to be lame, while The Mackem Bullet was yet to reach the level of her Cheveley Park and Lowther runs.

20 **Wooldridge Group Pat Eddery Stakes (Listed) (formerly the Winkfield Stakes) (7f)**
Ascot July 28 (Good To Firm)
1 **Victory Command** 2-9-3   S De Sousa
2 **Glorious Lover** 2-9-3   Gerald Mosse
3 **Nate The Great** 2-9-3   Daniel Tudhope
9/2, 10/1, 6/4F. 2l, hd. 6 ran. 1m 29.25s
(Mark Johnston).

A soft win for **Victory Command**, who had to do little for the clear lead he had built by halfway and had his limitations confirmed later in the year. **Glorious Lover**, who was held up in rear, had little chance of bridging the gap but did well to come through for second ahead of the disappointing favourite **Nate The Great**, who was most unsuited by the lack of pace given he already needed further.

21 **Qatar Vintage Stakes (Group 2) (7f)**
Goodwood July 31 (Good)
1 **Dark Vision** 2-9-1   Silvestre De Sousa
2 **Dunkerron** 2-9-1   Martin Harley
3 **Confiding** 2-9-1   Callum Shepherd
100/30F, 9/1, 8/1. 1¾l, 1¼l. 12 ran. 1m 28.23s

(Mark Johnston).

A hugely impressive win from **Dark Vision** and one that promised much more than he delivered when flopping in the Champagne Stakes on his only subsequent run. While clearly much better than he showed that day, time would show he didn't beat a great deal here and he was also favoured by a significant pace bias as he came late and fast off a fierce early gallop. **Dunkerron** and **Confiding** filled the places ahead of **Getchagetchagetcha** and the unlucky **Van Beethoven**, who found all the trouble as he picked a way through. **Cosmic Law** was much the best of those ridden prominently in sixth and could perhaps have done with sticking to this trip given several lesser efforts over shorter, with **Junius Brutus** among a few to tail off.

22 **Markel Insurance Molecomb Stakes (Group 3) (5f)**
Goodwood August 1 (Good)
1 **Rumble Inthejungle** 2-9-1   Tom Queally
2 **Life Of Riley** 2-9-1   Ben Curtis
3 **Soldier's Call** 2-9-1   Daniel Tudhope
5/1, 16/1, 6/4F. 2½l, nk. 11 ran. 58.22s
(Richard Spencer).

Rumble Inthejungle looked to strengthen up as the season went on, even stepping up to 6f with distinction in the Middle Park, and saw this out much better than in the Norfolk as he stormed to a comfortable victory. Rumble Inthejungle was helped by below-par displays from favourite **Soldier's Call** and **Well Done Fox**, but there were plenty of other useful sprinters in opposition and he took them apart in hugely impressive fashion. **Life Of Riley** just got the better of a tight battle for second, with **Vintage Brut**, **Queen Of Bermuda** and **Barbill** also close up.

23 **Qatar Richmond Stakes (Group 2) (6f)**
Goodwood August 2 (Good)
1 **Land Force** 2-9-0   Ryan Moore
2 **Marie's Diamond** 2-9-0   Silvestre De Sousa
3 **Shine So Bright** 2-9-0   Oisin Murphy
5/2F, 9/2, 13/2. 1l, nk. 9 ran. 1m 11.50s
(A P O'Brien).

This had plenty of depth but lacked a standout performer and presented a good opportunity to two solid performers at this sort of level, with **Land Force** seeing off **Marie's Diamond**. A Listed winner at Tipperary since his close Norfolk third, Land Force proved better stepping back up in trip and stayed on strongly as several of his main rivals found trouble in a messy race behind. Marie's Diamond and

Shine So Bright finished strongly to fill the places ahead of **Konchek**, with **Sabre**, **Neverland Rock** and **Sporting Chance** also finishing within 3l.

24 Coolmore Caravaggio Stakes (Listed) (7f100y)
Tipperary (IRE) August 10 (Good)
1 **Christmas** 2-9-3   Donnacha O'Brien
2 **Highland Fortune** 2-9-3   W J Lee
3 **Wargrave** 2-9-3   Chris Hayes
5/2J, 5/2J, 7/1. nk, 1½l. 7 ran. 1m 36.03s
(A P O'Brien).

A fairly competitive Listed race, although the fact that Railway fourth **Highland Fortune** was made favourite suggested it may lack a star and that proved the case. **Christmas** ended up just beating Highland Fortune, rallying well after he had dictated a much steadier gallop than he would set when racing more like a pacemaker in subsequent starts.

25 german-thoroughbred.com Sweet Solera Stakes (Group 3) (Fillies) (7f)
Newmarket (July) August 11 (Good To Soft)
1 **Main Edition** 2-9-3   P J McDonald
2 **La Pelosa** 2-9-0   Brett Doyle
3 **Model Guest** 2-9-0   Shane Kelly
7/4F, 7/2, 33/1. 1¼l, 2½l. 7 ran. 1m 27.31s
(Mark Johnston).

A fascinating edition of this Group 3 with Albany one-two **Main Edition** and **La Pelosa** reopposing over an extra furlong and Main Edition increased her superiority even with a penalty. With connections seemingly unconcerned about her stamina, Main Edition made all the running in a good time, while La Pelosa was perhaps unsuited by softer ground given all her best form, including a subsequent Grade 1 win in Canada on firm, came on much quicker. **Model Guest**, not for the first time, left the rest of her form behind when faced with a stronger race, while **Impulsion** ran a cracker in fourth having lost 6l at the start. **Ajrar** was a disappointing fifth.

26 Keeneland Phoenix Stakes (Group 1) (6f)
Curragh (IRE) August 12 (Good)
1 **Advertise** 2-9-3   Frankie Dettori
2 **So Perfect** 2-9-0   Seamie Heffernan
3 **The Irish Rover** 2-9-3   Donnacha O'Brien
11/10F, 7/1, 12/1. ½l, ½l. 5 ran. 1m 12.29s
(Martyn Meade).

A weak Group 1 with Aidan O'Brien's big hope **Sergei Prokofiev** getting far too lit up, which allowed **Advertise** to win without needing to run to his best. Always well placed, Advertise was in front before the furlong pole and looked to hold the filly **So Perfect** at bay with a bit in hand. **The Irish Rover** did well to keep on into a close third having been headed before the furlong pole, but his proximity holds down the form and **Indigo Balance** proved better back at 5f after finishing fourth. Sergei Prokofiev was never a factor and finished a distant last of five.

27 Byerley Stud Stakes (registered as the St Hugh's Stakes) (Listed) (Fillies) (5f34y)
Newbury August 17 (Good)
1 **Shumookhi** 2-9-0   Oisin Murphy
2 **Heartwarming** 2-9-0   Adam Kirby
3 **Come On Leicester** 2-9-0   Ryan Moore
15/2, 7/2, 7/1. 3l, ¾l. 14 ran. 1m 2.03s
(Archie Watson).

A tremendous performance from **Shumookhi**, who was much too good for a decent field for the grade as she readily went clear of the strong-travelling runner-up **Heartwarming**. Close Queen Mary fifth **Come On Leicester** was third, pipping **Gypsy Spirit**, who was second in a stronger Listed race against colts next time. Irish raider **Lethal Promise** was well beaten.

28 Denford Stakes (Listed) (7f)
Newbury August 18 (Good)
1 **Boitron** 2-9-1   Silvestre De Sousa
2 **Dutch Treat** 2-8-10   David Probert
3 **Good Fortune** 2-9-1   James Doyle
5/4F, 8/1, 2/1. 1¾l, 5l. 5 ran. 1m 26.19s
(Richard Hannon).

There was desperately little depth to this race but it was won in good style by **Boitron**, who did enough to earn his step up to Group 1 level when fourth in the Prix Jean-Luc Lagardere. Boitron was always in command and was eased down to beat **Dutch Treat**, who couldn't land a blow in decent fillies' races after this. It was 5l back to the winner's main market rival **Good Fortune**.

29 Darley Prix Morny (Group 1) (6f)
Deauville (FR) August 19 (Good)
1 **Pretty Pollyanna** 2-8-10   S De Sousa
2 **Signora Cabello** 2-8-10   Frankie Dettori
3 **True Mason** 2-9-0   P J McDonald
8/5F, 42/10, 25/1. ¾l, 4l. 9 ran. 1m 10.24s
(Michael Bell).

A race dominated by two high-class fillies in **Pretty Pollyanna** and **Signora Cabello** and, while the gloss was taken off by three defeats between them at Group 1 level in the autumn, they probably deserve a positive view of this form. Pretty Pollyanna seemingly found 6f too sharp in the Cheveley Park and was always likely to find stepping sharply up in distance a tough task in the Fillies' Mile, but the shorter trip proved fine this time with an emphasis on stamina given how the first two had the rest well strung out. Signora Cabello was a gallant runner-up and was 4l ahead of **True Mason**, who in turn pulled 2½l clear of the disappointing **Land Force**.

30 Tattersalls Acomb Stakes (Group 3) (7f)
York August 22 (Good To Firm)
1 **Phoenix Of Spain** 2-9-1   Jamie Spencer
2 **Watan** 2-9-1   Oisin Murphy
3 **Persian Moon** 2-9-1   Silvestre De Sousa
9/2, 5/2F, 100/30. 1½l, 2l. 8 ran. 1m 24.19s
(Charles Hills).

A good Group 3 with three fancied runners coming clear, led by **Phoenix Of Spain**. The subsequent Vertem Futurity Trophy runner-up appreciated a strong gallop as he came from well off the pace to win well from **Watan**. **Persian Moon** was the best of those ridden handily in third and was 2¾l ahead of **Pogo** in fourth, with **Broome** the most notable disappointment.

31 Sky Bet Lowther Stakes (Group 2) (Fillies) (6f)
York August 23 (Good To Firm)
1 **Fairyland** 2-9-0   Ryan Moore
2 **The Mackem Bullet** 2-9-0   Ben Robinson
3 **Queen Jo Jo** 2-9-0   Daniel Tudhope
6/4F, 25/1, 16/1. nse, 2l. 9 ran. 1m 11.23s
(A P O'Brien).

A thrilling battle between **Fairyland** and **The Mackem Bullet**, a precursor to their rematch in the Cheveley Park, which showed that Fairyland had done well to see off a much-improved rival here despite not impressing every observer. Having set out to make all the running, Fairyland was headed well inside the final furlong by The Mackem Bullet but fought back to get up again on the line. The pair pulled 2l clear of **Queen Jo Jo** and **Firelight**, with **Little Kim** and **Orange Blossom** next. **Angel's Hideaway** was the big disappointment, dropping out to finish last.

32 Al Basti Equiworld Gimcrack Stakes (Group 2) (6f)
York August 24 (Good To Firm)
1 **Emaraaty Ana** 2-9-0   Frankie Dettori
2 **Legends Of War** 2-9-0   Oisin Murphy
3 **Shine So Bright** 2-9-0   William Buick

5/1, 14/1, 9/4F. ½l, ¾l. 9 ran. 1m 10.79s
(Kevin Ryan).

Emaraaty Ana put a poor run at Newbury behind him and showed his true colours with a fine all-the-way victory, albeit in what was no more than an ordinary race for the grade. Emaraaty Ana just held off **Legends Of War**, while **Shine So Bright** was beaten an identical distance in third as when filling the same spot in the Richmond. That trio pulled 2l clear of **The Irish Rover**.

33 Longines Irish Champions Weekend EBF Stonehenge Stakes (Listed) (1m)
Salisbury August 24 (Good)
1 **Kuwait Currency** 2-9-1   Tom Marquand
2 **Dark Jedi** 2-9-1   Robert Winston
3 **Dubai Dominion** 2-9-1   Ronan Whelan
5/1, 14/1, 13/2. 1¾l, 1l. 6 ran. 1m 42.92s
(Richard Hannon).

A clearcut win for **Kuwait Currency**, but he was perhaps flattered by the way the race was run as he picked up the pieces off an overly strong gallop and was subsequently well beaten twice at Group 1 level. Market leaders **Nate The Great** and **Arctic Sound** seemed to pay the price for going too hard in front, the latter cutting out particularly quickly and subsequently dropping back in trip for a Group 3 win at Newmarket. **Fox Tal** was also disappointing, racing too keenly in fourth.

34 Julia Graves Roses Stakes (Listed) (5f)
York August 25 (Good To Firm)
1 **Well Done Fox** 2-9-3   Jim Crowley
2 **Deia Glory** 2-8-9   Kieran O'Neill
3 **Sabre** 2-9-0   Paul Hanagan
13/2, 50/1, 2/1F. ½l, ¾l. 11 ran. 58.90s
(Richard Hannon).

Well Done Fox took a big step forward as he defied a penalty for a Listed win at Sandown earlier in the summer to gain his second success in the grade. Plenty went against Well Done Fox, who was drawn one and forced to race away from the main action with a bit to do, but he produced a strong run to hit the front in the final 100 yards. **Deia Glory** was flattered to split Well Done Fox and **Sabre**, who also came from a long way back and ran as if needing further.

35 Ladbrokes Prestige Stakes (Group 3) (Fillies) (7f)
Goodwood August 25 (Good)
1 **Antonia De Vega** 2-9-0   Harry Bentley
2 **Accordance** 2-9-0   Joe Fanning

3 **Chynna** 2-9-0 Scott McCullagh
5/2J, 7/1, 50/1. 1¼l, nk. 8 ran. 1m 27.58s
(Ralph Beckett).

An impressive performance from **Antonia De Vega**, up there with the most exciting by a British-trained staying juvenile filly all year as she powered home to cut down **Accordance**, although that would prove some way below the best of the Irish, most notably on a line through subsequent Flame of Tara fourth **Chynna**. **Look Around** was below her best, but a line through **Ajrar**, who was found out for the second time at Group level when only fifth, suggests she would have needed significant improvement to land a blow anyway.

36 Curragh Stakes (Listed) (5f)
Curragh (IRE) August 25 (Good)
1 **Indigo Balance** 2-9-3 Colm O'Donoghue
2 **Gossamer Wings** 2-9-0 Donnacha O'Brien
3 **Fantasy** 2-8-12 Seamie Heffernan
9/4, 2/1F, 10/1. 1¾l, ½l. 8 ran. 59.64s
(Mrs John Harrington).

Gossamer Wings brought the strongest form into this race and would prove the best horse subsequently, but she had missed a previous target after suffering a temperature and certainly wasn't at her best as she was well beaten by **Indigo Balance**. Seemingly better down in trip after his Phoenix fourth, Indigo Balance produced a far superior turn of foot as Gossamer Wings got going too late and struggled into second past **Fantasy**.

37 Galileo Irish EBF Futurity Stakes (Group 2) (7f)
Curragh (IRE) August 26 (Yielding)
1 **Anthony Van Dyck** 2-9-3 Ryan Moore
2 **Christmas** 2-9-3 Seamie Heffernan
3 **Mohawk** 2-9-3 Donnacha O'Brien
4/6F, 13/2, 12/1. ½l, 2¼l. 6 ran. 1m 24.37s
(A P O'Brien).

Competition to the Aidan O'Brien team was disappointingly thin on the ground and first string **Anthony Van Dyck** managed to come out on top without needing to run up to his best. An easy winner of a weak Tyros Stakes on his previous start, Anthony Van Dyck took his time to claw back the long-time leader **Christmas** but looked to have plenty in hand by the line and would beat the runner-up and third-placed **Mohawk** by much further when second in the National Stakes. **Could Be King** was just ½l further back in fourth, pulling 12l clear of **Guaranteed**.

38 Debutante Stakes (Group 2) (Fillies) (7f)
Curragh (IRE) August 26 (Yielding)
1 **Skitter Scatter** 2-9-0 Ronan Whelan
2 **Bandiuc Eile** 2-9-0 Kevin Manning
3 **Zagitova** 2-9-0 Ryan Moore
7/1, 50/1, 2/1F. 2¼l, ½l. 9 ran. 1m 24.83s
(P J Prendergast).

Skitter Scatter confirmed herself as a seriously smart and progressive filly as she put a high-class field to the sword. Having ap-

ANTONIA DE VEGA: hugely impressive when winning at Goodwood

peared to improve for the step up in trip when winning a Group 3 at Leopardstown on her previous start, Skitter Scatter stepped forward again as she comfortably saw off **Bandiuc Eile** and hot favourite **Zagitova**. While the placed horses failed to frank the form, the next three – **Lady Kaya**, **Iridessa** and **Hermosa** – all finished first or second at Group 1 level later in the season, while Listed winner **Peach Tree** was behind.

39 British Stallion Studs EBF Ripon Champion Two-Year-Old Trophy (Listed) (6f)

Ripon August 27 (Good To Soft)
1 **Sporting Chance** 2-9-3 Silvestre De Sousa
2 **Gypsy Spirit** 2-8-12 Jack Mitchell
3 **Sunsprite** 2-9-3 Shane Kelly
6/1, 20/1, 10/1. hd, 1¼l. 7 ran. 1m 12.48s
(Simon Crisford).

A tight but competitive Listed race, with just 2½l covering the entire field and **Sporting Chance**, a Group 3 winner at Maisons-Laffitte next time, just holding off **Gypsy Spirit**. The pair pulled ahead of a blanket finish behind and arguably the two class acts were below their best – **Kessaar** became unbalanced on the undulations and **Neverland Rock** was unsuited by the ground – but they were still a fair bunch, with **Life Of Riley** fourth and fifth-placed **Barbill** getting better with racing.

40 188Bet Solario Stakes (Group 3) (7f)

Sandown September 1 (Good)
1 **Too Darn Hot** 2-9-1 Frankie Dettori
2 **Arthur Kitt** 2-9-1 Richard Kingscote
3 **Confiding** 2-9-1 Oisin Murphy
EvensF, 6/1, 6/1. 4l, 3¾l. 6 ran. 1m 28.52s
(John Gosden).

The first big impression made by **Too Darn Hot**, who tore apart a decent field. Too Darn Hot was nudged along to make headway but powered clear once hitting top gear, leaving Chesham winner and subsequent Breeders' Cup fourth **Arthur Kitt** trailing in his wake. Arthur Kitt was still a clear second from **Confiding** and **Victory Command**, with another big gap back to **Watan** in fifth.

41 Flame of Tara Irish EBF Stakes (Group 3) (Fillies) (1m)

Curragh (IRE) September 1 (Good To Yielding)
1 **Just Wonderful** 2-9-0 Donnacha O'Brien
2 **Peach Tree** 2-9-0 Seamie Heffernan
3 **Fleeting** 2-9-0 Wayne Lordan
7/4F, 8/1, 20/1. 1½l, 1½l. 8 ran. 1m 38.78s
(A P O'Brien).

Just Wonderful restored her reputation with an emphatic win in a strong race for the grade. Just Wonderful was last at halfway but went through the gears without being hard ridden and came clear of **Peach Tree**, who was able to win an admittedly weak Listed race in the autumn, and **Fleeting**, more significantly a Group 2 winner next time in the May Hill. It was another 2¾l back to **Chynna**, while **Bandiuc Eile** was a disappointing sixth.

42 John Sisk & Son Round Tower Stakes (Group 3) 6f

Curragh (IRE) September 1 (Good To Yielding)
1 **Ten Sovereigns** 2-9-3 Donnacha O'Brien
2 **Bruce Wayne** 2-9-3 Leigh Roche
3 **Fantasy** 2-9-0 Seamie Heffernan
1/3F, 14/1, 16/1. 3¾l, 2l. 8 ran. 1m 12.02s
(A P O'Brien).

Ten Sovereigns had already caught the imagination with a stunning seven-length maiden win and had little more trouble in this higher grade, albeit in a race rendered much easier by below-par performances from main rivals **Could Be King** and **Servalan**. Ten Sovereigns was always going well and was pushed clear for an easy win as **Bruce Wayne**, sixth in the same maiden, stepped forward to take second ahead of **Fantasy**.

43 Shadwell Dick Poole Fillies' Stakes (Group 3) (Fillies) (6f)

Salisbury September 6 (Good To Firm)
1 **Yourtimeisnow** 2-9-0 Andrea Atzeni
2 **Lady Aria** 2-9-0 Silvestre De Sousa
3 **Come On Leicester** 2-9-0 Ryan Moore
4/1, 8/1, 9/2. ½l, 2¼l. 9 ran. 1m 15.01s
(Roger Varian).

This looked a good Group 3 and the first two pulled clear, with **Yourtimeisnow**, who had excuses when flopping on her only subsequent run in the Rockfel, making all the running and holding off **Lady Aria**. The Lowther form was well represented behind and, though favourite **Firelight** looked below her best, taking an age to pick up before running on into fourth, York sixth **Orange Blossom** was only marginally closer when sixth again.

44 188Bet Casino Sirenia Stakes (Group 3) (6f)

Kempton (AW) September 8 (Standard To Slow)
1 **Kessaar** 2-9-1 Kieran O'Neill
2 **Junius Brutus** 2-9-1 Harry Bentley
3 **Fuente** 2-9-1 Josephine Gordon
9/1, 3/1, 25/1. 2½l, 1¼l. 5 ran. 1m 11.65s
(John Gosden).

Kessaar had disappointed on his previous start at Redcar, but he bounced back to run out a convincing winner of what was admittedly a moderate Group 3. The subsequent Mill Reef winner stormed clear of **Junius Brutus** as the two market principals disappointed behind, with **Konchek** a tame fourth and favourite **Quiet Endeavour**, stepping up in grade on a five-timer, last of the five runners.

45 32Red Casino Ascendant Stakes (Listed) (1m)
Haydock September 8 (Heavy)
1 **Great Scot** 2-9-2   Richard Kingscote
2 **Floating Artist** 2-9-2   Oisin Murphy
3 **Certain Lad** 2-9-2   Ryan Moore
13/8F, 3/1, 5/1. 2l, 1¼l. 5 ran. 1m 49.89s
(Tom Dascombe).

An impressive performance from **Great Scot**, who stayed on strongly and easily beat **Floating Artist** despite racing keenly in desperate conditions. Great Scot was helped by market rival **Persian Moon** failing to act on the heavy ground, but there was a solid yardstick in **Chelsea Lad**, third in the Railway Stakes and successful abroad later in the season, in third and he would prove worth his place in a Group 1 in the Vertem Futurity Trophy.

46 William Hill May Hill Stakes (Group 2) (Fillies) (1m)
Doncaster September 13 (Good)
1 **Fleeting** 2-9-0   Donnacha O'Brien
2 **Star Terms** 2-9-0   Andrea Atzeni
3 **Sand Share** 2-9-0   Harry Bentley
12/1, 12/1, 14/1. 1½l, ½l. 11 ran. 1m 38.71s
(A P O'Brien).

Fleeting had looked some way below the best of the Irish-trained fillies, but she was still good enough to see off a weak home challenge, epitomised by a desperate performance from the well-backed Newmarket novice winner **Dubai Beauty**. Fleeting stayed on too strongly for **Star Terms**, who held off **Sand Share** and **Magnetic Charm** for second. There was a 3l gap back to **Dutch Treat** and **Accordance**, who lost her chance when dwelling in the stalls.

47 Weatherbys Racing Bank £300,000 2YO Stakes (6f111y)
Doncaster September 13 (Good)
1 **The Great Heir** 2-8-9   Andrew Mullen
2 **Dirty Rascal** 2-9-2   Tom Marquand
3 **Wasntexpectingthat** 2-8-6 Paddy Mathers
33/1, 25/1, 33/1. ½l, ¾l. 22 ran. 1m 19.78s
(Kevin Ryan).

By far the strongest of the numerous valuable
100

THE GREAT HEIR: won probably the strongest sales race of the year

two-year-old sales races run over the year and a fine win for **The Great Heir**, who left behind his previous form when stepped up in trip and faced with such a big field. **Dirty Rascal** and **No Needs Never** came out best at the weights and both won next time out, the latter in a Listed race having just pipped **The Irish Rover** and **Aim Power** for fourth.

48 Wainwrights Flying Childers Stakes (Group 2) (5f3y)
Doncaster September 14 (Good)
1 **Soldier's Call** 2-9-1   Daniel Tudhope
2 **Well Done Fox** 2-9-1   James Doyle
3 **Gossamer Wings** 2-8-12   Ryan Moore
4/1, 10/1, 9/1. 2¼l, ½l. 9 ran. 59.08s
(Archie Watson).

With no two-year-old Group 1 at this trip, this is essentially the 5f championship for juveniles and certainly produced a performance worthy of the title from **Soldier's Call**, who proved himself the fastest two-year-old in Europe by some distance. Making all the running, Soldier's Call was always in total command and backed up his brilliance with a stunning third in the Prix de l'Abbaye having softened up none other than Battaash up front before a forgivable Breeders' Cup flop when blowing the start. **Well Done Fox** ran a cracker to edge a tight battle for second ahead of **Gossamer Wings** and **Legends Of War** before a 1¼l gap back to the below-par

Shumookhi and **Indigo Balance**, though neither of that pair was as disappointing as **Rumble Inthejungle**, who trailed home last.

49 Weatherbys Global Stallions App Flying Scotsman Stakes (Listed)
(7f6y)
Doncaster September 14 (Good To Soft)
1 **Sangarius** 2-9-0   Ryan Moore
2 **Dubai Dominion** 2-9-0   Oisin Murphy
3 **Pogo** 2-9-0   Callum Shepherd
11/10F, 6/1, 20/1. 2¼l, 1¼l. 8 ran. 1m 26.55s (Sir Michael Stoute).

A comfortable win for **Sangarius**, backing up a tall reputation that saw him head to the Dewhurst at a single-figure price, although this form was only weak and still leaves him with a bit to prove after his well-beaten Newmarket fourth. **Dubai Dominion** had been beaten further in this grade at Salisbury and the next two, **Pogo** and **You Can Never Tell**, had several wide-margin defeats against them by the end of the season.

50 Howcroft Industrial Supplies Champagne Stakes (Group 2)
(7f6y)
Doncaster September 15 (Good)
1 **Too Darn Hot** 2-9-0   Frankie Dettori
2 **Phoenix Of Spain** 2-9-0   James Doyle
3 **Cardini** 2-9-0   Seamie Heffernan
4/11F, 8/1, 40/1. 1¾l, 2½l. 6 ran. 1m 23.92s (John Gosden).

Another step up the ladder for **Too Darn Hot**, who readily saw off a high-class opponent in **Phoenix Of Spain** despite plenty going against him. Too Darn Hot was left with plenty to do having tracked a rival who faded badly through the field in **Dark Vision**, who was reported to have found the ground too loose, but he picked up superbly and stayed on really strongly. Phoenix Of Spain was a fine second, pulling 2½l clear of **Cardini**, who ran his best race and beat the Ballydoyle first string **Van Beethoven** into third, but **Bye Bye Hong Kong** was too keen in fifth.

51 KPMG Champions Juvenile Stakes (Group 2) (1m)
Leopardstown (IRE) September 15 (Good To Firm)
1 **Madhmoon** 2-9-3   Chris Hayes
2 **Broome** 2-9-3   Donnacha O'Brien
3 **Masaff** 2-9-3   Declan McDonogh
6/5F, 7/2, 7/1. 2½l, 1¼l. 7 ran. 1m 41.00s (Kevin Prendergast).

A strong Group 2 won in terrific fashion by **Madhmoon**, who had a couple of horses

placed at Group 1 level and two more who finished second in other Group races behind him. Madhmoon beat them all easily, travelling strongly in third and keeping on well to pull clear even as the two who raced in front of him, **Western Australia** and **Sydney Opera House**, weakened close home. Subsequent Prix Jean-Luc Lagardere runner-up **Broome** ran on to claim second ahead of the staying-on **Masaff**.

52 Ballylinch Stud Irish EBF Ingabelle Stakes (Listed) (Fillies) (7f)
Leopardstown (IRE) September 15 (Good To Firm)
1 **Sparkle'n'Joy** 2-9-0   Shane Foley
2 **Foxtrot Liv** 2-9-0   W J Lee
3 **Iridessa** 2-9-0   Donnacha O'Brien
12/1, 5/2F, 13/2. hd, 1½l. 16 ran. 1m 28.80s (Mrs J Harrington).

A fiercely competitive Listed race with a sad post-script as **Sparkle'n'Joy** died later in the year after claiming a narrow victory. The filly had beaten a couple of other progressive types in **Foxtrot Liv** and **Iridessa**, the latter even going on to claim the Fillies' Mile having found this trip on the short side, while **Trethias** finished strongly in fourth.

53 Goffs Vincent O'Brien National Stakes (Group 1) (7f)
Curragh (IRE) September 16 (Good To Yielding)
1 **Quorto** 2-9-3   William Buick
2 **Anthony Van Dyck** 2-9-3   Ryan Moore
3 **Christmas** 2-9-3   Emmet McNamara
11/8F, 6/4, 9/1. 1¼l, 4½l. 7 ran. 1m 24.81s (Charlie Appleby).

Quorto produced another hugely impressive victory as he got the better of a terrific duel with **Anthony Van Dyck**, possessing too much class for a high-class runner-up with the rest of a decent field well strung out. Anthony Van Dyck ran his best race of the season with stamina brought to the fore in a strongly run race, massively extending his superiority over old rivals **Christmas** and **Mohawk** with **Land Force** and **Highland Fortune** further back.

54 Moyglare Stud Stakes (Group 1) (Fillies) (7f)
Curragh (IRE) September 16 (Good To Yielding)
1 **Skitter Scatter** 2-9-0   Ronan Whelan
2 **Lady Kaya** 2-9-0   Robbie Colgan
3 **Hermosa** 2-9-0   Seamie Heffernan
7/2F, 8/1, 20/1. 2l, 1¼l. 10 ran. 1m 25.60s (P J Prendergast).

Another ultimately comfortable victory for **Skitter Scatter**, although her rivals didn't help themselves this time as she picked up the pieces off an overly strong early gallop. **Main Edition** went too fast in front and was chased for much of the way by **Zagitova** and **Lady Kaya**, with none of them able to see out the trip anything like as well as Skitter Scatter, who was off the bridle early but came through powerfully. Lady Kaya stepped up on her Debutante run and reversed form with Zagitova, who would probably have finished third again but for being impeded by the winner in the final furlong. **Hermosa** ran on better this time in fourth, while Main Edition was fifth with **Beyond Reason**, **Just Wonderful** and **Bandiuc Eile** disappointing behind.

55 Shadwell Stud/EBF Stallions Harry Rosebery Stakes (Listed) (5f)
Ayr September 21 (Heavy)

1	**Dave Dexter** 2-9-3	Graham Lee
2	**Vintage Brut** 2-9-6	David Allan
3	**Secret Venture** 2-9-3	Daniel Tudhope

8/1, 5/1, 9/1. nk, 1¾l. 12 ran. 1m 4.06s (Ralph Beckett).

A good win from **Dave Dexter**, who lost ground at the start but produced a strong late run to get up close home. There wasn't much depth to the race behind as heavy ground counted against most of the form horses, yet it certainly suited **Vintage Brut**, who had been disappointing since a Listed win at Sandown in May but bounced back to form in more testing conditions, paving the way for a resurgent autumn campaign. **Secret Venture** was third ahead of **Cosmic Law**, who found the trip too sharp even in the conditions, with **Life Of Riley** and **Junius Brutus** among those to disappoint.

56 Dubai Duty Free Mill Reef Stakes (Group 2) (6f)
Newbury September 22 (Soft)

1	**Kessaar** 2-9-1	Frankie Dettori
2	**True Mason** 2-9-1	Ben Curtis
3	**Shine So Bright** 2-9-1	Oisin Murphy

100/30, 4/1, 3/1F. 2¾l, 2¼l. 7 ran. 1m 14.23s (John Gosden).

This looked a really tight race on paper, with just 3lb covering five of the seven runners on official ratings, but **Kessaar** took a big step forward to run out a ready winner, albeit with his main rivals perhaps unsuited by the soft ground. **True Mason**, having travelled strongly, didn't quite get home and **Shine So Bright** perhaps struggled slightly to pick up in the conditions, although he was facing

stronger opposition than when third in two other Group 2 races. **Konchek** and **The Irish Rover** were tailed off.

57 William Hill Firth Of Clyde Stakes (Group 3) (Fillies) (6f)
Ayr September 22 (Heavy)

1	**Queen Of Bermuda** 2-9-0	Joe Fanning
2	**Shumookhi** 2-9-0	Edward Greatrex
3	**Light My Fire** 2-9-0	Richard Kingscote

9/2F, 11/2, 5/1. 2l, 1l. 11 ran. 1m 16.74s (William Haggas).

A really strong Group 3 won well by **Queen Of Bermuda**, who revelled in heavy ground and went on to perform well enough at the Breeders' Cup to confirm a move to the US. Queen Of Bermuda quickened past the front-running **Shumookhi** and **Light My Fire**, who edged a tight battle for the places as Lowther third **Queen Jo Jo** was next ahead of **Summer Daydream** and **Gypsy Spirit**, both proven in Listed company by the end of the season and in testing conditions. **Glass Slippers** split that pair and the first seven were 2¾l clear of **Firelight**, who was too keen to get home in the conditions.

58 Ballyhane Blenheim Stakes (Listed) (6f)
Fairyhouse (IRE) September 24 (Good To Yielding)

1	**Lethal Promise** 2-8-12	W J Lee
2	**Inverleigh** 2-9-3	Gary Carroll
3	**Mia Mento** 2-8-12	N G McCullagh

8/1, 2/1F, 33/1. 1¾l, 1½l. 10 ran. 1m 14.49s (W McCreery).

No more than an ordinary race for the grade but one won well by **Lethal Promise**, who had twice disappointed since a wide-margin maiden success but made most of the running in commanding fashion. That said, **Inverleigh** was beaten further in a stronger Listed race on his next run and **All The King's Men**, who did most for the form when winning at this level at Navan after this fifth-placed effort, merely took advantage of a desperately weak opening there.

59 Tattersalls Stakes (registered as the Somerville Tattersall Stakes) (Group 3) (7f)
Newmarket September 27 (Good)

1	**Arctic Sound** 2-9-0	Silvestre De Sousa
2	**Bye Bye Hong Kong** 2-9-0	Oisin Murphy
3	**Prince Eiji** 2-9-0	Andrea Atzeni

5/1, 9/2, 11/4. 1l, 1¼l. 7 ran. 1m 23.38s (Mark Johnston).

Smart form on paper with the first three pull-

ARCTIC SOUND: benefited from a pace collapse in the Tattersalls Stakes

ing well clear of horses proven in a higher grade, but an overly strong gallop had much to do with that and helped **Arctic Sound** to come from last to first. Arctic Sound swept past **Bye Bye Hong Kong**, who was also held up, whereas **Prince Eiji** did really well to stay on the premises in third having been handy throughout, especially as it was 3¾l back to **Dunkerron** and **Cardini**, who fell away having gone too hard in front.

60 Shadwell Rockfel Stakes (Group 2) (Fillies) (7f)
Newmarket September 28 (Good To Firm)
1 **Just Wonderful** 2-9-0   Ryan Moore
2 **Dandhu** 2-9-0   Gerald Mosse
3 **Main Edition** 2-9-0   Frankie Dettori
7/2, 12/1, 15/8F. 1¾l, 1½l. 9 ran. 1m 25.30s
(A P O'Brien).

Another great act of redemption from **Just Wonderful**, who again put a poor performance behind her with a comfortable victory. Just Wonderful probably didn't even need to run to her best, hanging right as she surged clear of **Main Edition**, who had perhaps done enough for the year. **Dandhu** stayed on strongly to split the pair despite having to be switched, while **Model Guest** was fourth ahead of **Canton Queen** and **Dutch Treat**. **Yourtimeisnow** looked over the top and was too keen.

61 Juddmonte Cheveley Park Stakes (Group 1) (Fillies) (6f)
Newmarket September 29 (Good To Firm)
1 **Fairyland** 2-9-0   Donnacha O'Brien
2 **The Mackem Bullet** 2-9-0   Oisin Murphy
3 **So Perfect** 2-9-0   Seamie Heffernan
6/1, 25/1, 6/1. nk, ½l. 11 ran. 1m 10.13s

(A P O'Brien).

Pretty Pollyanna's below-par display threw this race wide-open, shown by the fact that less than 4l covered the first nine even in a strongly run race, and **Fairyland** made the most of her opportunity. Fairyland was among several previous front-runners unable to lead, but she took over before the furlong pole and stayed on strongly to beat **The Mackem Bullet** with a little more in hand than at York. **So Perfect** ran another solid race at the top level in third ahead of the disappointing Pretty Pollyanna, who raced too keenly when forced to drop into midfield and looked one-paced in fourth. **Gossamer Wings** was fifth ahead of **Lady Kaya** and **Queen Of Bermuda**, who may both have found the ground quicker than ideal, with **Angel's Hideaway** also in the main pack. **Signora Cabello** dropped out to finish a distant tenth.

62 Juddmonte Middle Park Stakes (Group 1) (6f)
Newmarket September 29 (Good To Firm)
1 **Ten Sovereigns** 2-9-0 Donnacha O'Brien
2 **Jash** 2-9-0   Jim Crowley
3 **Rumble Inthejungle** 2-9-0   James Doyle
8/13F, 4/1, 16/1. ½l, 3½l. 8 ran. 1m 10.04s
(A P O'Brien).

A great battle between two unbeaten colts, with **Ten Sovereigns** maintaining his flawless record at the expense of **Jash**. The pair both raced close to a strong gallop before Ten Sovereigns picked up just the best, both colts running huge races as they pulled 3½l clear of the rest. **Rumble Inthejungle** also did really well to take third as he stepped up in trip beyond 5f for the first time, finishing ahead of Richmond runner-up **Marie's Diamond** and Gimcrack winner **Emaraaty Ana**, who at least confirmed York form with **Legends Of War**. **Sergei Prokofiev** was again too keen and never got involved in seventh.

63 Juddmonte Royal Lodge Stakes (Group 2) (1m)
Newmarket September 29 (Good To Firm)
1 **Mohawk** 2-9-0   Donnacha O'Brien
2 **Sydney Opera House** 2-9-0   W Lordan
3 **Cape Of Good Hope** 2-9-0   S Heffernan
8/1, 20/1, 9/2. 1¼l, 1¾l. 7 ran. 1m 36.12s
(A P O'Brien).

A disappointing renewal with Aidan O'Brien able to dominate despite not sending over his best horses and seeing his first string, **Cape Of Good Hope**, run below-par. **Mohawk** came out on top despite not getting close in any of his three other runs at Group level, having too much speed for **Sydney Opera House**, who would come into his own over further. Cape Of Good Hope was only third on his first run in more than two months, while **Victory Command** repeated his Solario fourth but got much closer in this weaker race. **Arthur Kitt** was disappointing, failing to confirm that Sandown form, while **Beatboxer**, a strong favourite after impressive maiden and novice wins, flopped badly after a very awkward start.

64 Beresford Stakes (Group 2) (1m)
Naas (IRE) September 30 (Good)
1 **Japan** 2-9-3   Seamie Heffernan
2 **Mount Everest** 2-9-3   Ryan Moore
3 **Power Of Now** 2-9-3   Leigh Roche
11/2, 11/8F, 7/1. shd, 3l. 7 ran. 1m 38.68s
(A P O'Brien).

A race with a rich history but one hard to rate particularly highly at this stage, although **Japan** and **Mount Everest** may both prove better than the bare form. Japan did really well to overcome the loss of momentum when stuck in a pocket, albeit perhaps helped by Mount Everest idling slightly in front. The pair still pulled 3l clear of **Power Of Now**, but **Sovereign** got only marginally closer in a Group 3 won by **Guaranteed**, who was a disappointing last of seven in this race before producing the only other win outside maiden company by the entire field between them in 2018.

65 Weld Park Stakes (Group 3) (Fillies) (7f)
Naas (IRE) September 30 (Good)
1 **Hermosa** 2-9-0   Ryan Moore
2 **Foxtrot Liv** 2-9-0   W J Lee
3 **Chynna** 2-9-0   Ronan Whelan

5/4F, 7/2, 25/1. 2½l, 3l. 8 ran. 1m 26.52s
(A P O'Brien).

Hermosa had gone the right way when highly tried on her previous two starts and this marked a big step forward as the subsequent Fillies' Mile second ran away with a decent Group 3. Ridden far more prominently, Hermosa stayed on really well to beat **Foxtrot Liv**, who was in turn 3l clear of a solid yardstick in British raider **Chynna**. **Trethias** and **Servalan** were next.

66 iCopy Irish EBF Star Appeal Stakes (Listed) (7f)
Dundalk (AW) (IRE) October 5 (Standard)
1 **No Needs Never** 2-9-3 Seamie Heffernan
2 **Old Glory** 2-9-3   Donnacha O'Brien
3 **Inverleigh** 2-9-3   Colin Keane
8/1, 4/6F, 2/1. 1¾l, 1½l. 5 ran. 1m 24.31s
(Joseph Patrick O'Brien).

A good battle between two useful colts in **No Needs Never** and **Old Guard**, with No Needs Never picking up well to wear down the front-running second with a bit up his sleeve. Solid yardstick **Inverleigh** was third and, while there was a 100-1 shot, **Harriet's Force**, just ½l back in fourth to cast some doubt on the form, that filly at least won next time and even had her trainer talking of the Guineas after that success.

67 Racing UK Two-Year-Old Trophy (Listed) (5f217y)
Redcar October 6 (Good)
1 **Summer Daydream** 2-8-9 Connor Beasley
2 **Beat Le Bon** 2-9-2   Tom Marquand
3 **Kodyanna** 2-8-11   Jason Hart
8/1, 7/2F, 16/1. ¾l, 1¾l. 21 ran. 1m 13.75s
(Keith Dalgleish).

A sub-standard running of this valuable prize and **Summer Daydream** probably didn't even need to run to the level of her previous Group 3 fifth at Ayr to come out on top. Running on ground other than heavy for the first time, Summer Daydream coped well enough to see off **Beat Le Bon**, who was much the best horse at the weights but still well beaten off only 95 in a nursery next time.

68 Qatar Prix Marcel Boussac (Group 1) (1m)
Longchamp (FR) October 7 (Good)
1 **Lily's Candle** 2-8-11   P-C Boudot
2 **Matematica** 2-8-11   Maxime Guyon
3 **Star Terms** 2-8-11   Andrea Atzeni
28/1, 12/1, 6/1. snk, snk. 7 ran. 1m 38.98s
(F Vermeulen).

A messy race and a blanket finish led to a

surprise result as **Lily's Candle**, only fourth on her sole previous run in Group company and a big letdown at the Breeders' Cup, beat the maiden **Matematica**. The pair both challenged late and wide, benefiting from an overly strong gallop and a lack of room on the inside, as **Star Terms** and **Legrande-catherine** also finished within just ¾l. **Pink Dogwood**, highly touted after a seven-length maiden win, did too much in front and faded into fifth, with May Hill flop **Dubai Beauty** faring only marginally better in seventh.

69 Qatar Prix Jean-Luc Lagardere (Group 1) (1m)
Longchamp (FR) October 7 (Good)
1 **Royal Marine** 2-9-0   Oisin Murphy
2 **Broome** 2-9-0   Ryan Moore
3 **Anodor** 2-9-0   Aurelien Lemaitre
5/1, 9/1, 5/6F. nk, ¾l. 6 ran. 1m 39.10s
(Saeed bin Suroor).

Tactics seemed key in this race as Ryan Moore dictated a stop-start gallop on **Broome** and it proved hard to make up ground from off the pace, with only **Royal Marine**, ridden closest to the leader, able to get past him. The Godolphin colt was taking a big step up in class after winning a maiden and rose to the task, although Broome's near miss slightly holds down the form. Unbeaten French favourite **Anodor** was perhaps unsuited by the run of the race as he came up short in third, while **Boitron** was among those unable to land a blow from the rear in fourth.

70 bet365 Fillies' Mile (Group 1) (1m)
Newmarket October 12 (Good To Firm)
1 **Iridessa** 2-9-0   Wayne Lordan
2 **Hermosa** 2-9-0   Donnacha O'Brien
3 **Pretty Pollyanna** 2-9-0   Daniel Tudhope
14/1, 5/2F, 7/2. 1½l, ¾l. 8 ran. 1m 38.80s
(Joseph Patrick O'Brien).

A weak Group 1 with only one of the first four in the market having won above Group 3 level – **Pretty Pollyanna**, whose form was all over 6f – and **Iridessa** might just have dropped lucky. With a strong wind placing an even greater emphasis on stamina – so much so only four fillies finished within 14l of her – Iridessa proved in her element when hitting the rising ground as she outstayed **Hermosa**, leaving her previous form behind over the extra furlong and improving past the progressive runner-up. Pretty Pollyanna gave herself little chance of getting home by helping to force the pace but plugged on well enough to finish a clear third over **Shambolic**, with

another 8l back to **Zagitova** and **Layaleena**. **Beyond Reason** faded after making the running, while **Antonia De Vega** finished lame.

71 Newmarket Academy Godolphin Beacon Project Cornwallis Stakes (Group 3) (5f)
Newmarket October 12 (Good To Firm)
1 **Sergei Prokofiev** 2-9-1 Donnacha O'Brien
2 **Well Done Fox** 2-9-1   Jim Crowley
3 **Barbill** 2-9-1   J F Egan
3/1F, 6/1, 16/1. 1¼l, 2¼l. 14 ran. 59.46s
(A P O'Brien).

Connections finally found the key to **Sergei Prokofiev**, who had lost his way since a fine run in the Coventry but relished dropping back to the minimum trip. Finally able to settle better off a faster gallop and enjoying much quicker ground than he would get at the Breeders' Cup, Sergei Prokofiev produced a stunning turn of foot to come from last to first and see off **Well Done Fox**, who ran another fine race in second. The first two were much better than the rest, led home by **Barbill** and **The Cruising Lord**, although **Pocket Dynamo** may well have been involved with more luck in running. **True Mason** couldn't land a blow as he dropped back from 6f.

72 Godolphin Lifetime Care Oh So Sharp Stakes (Group 3) (Fillies) (7f)
Newmarket October 12 (Good To Firm)
1 **Mot Juste** 2-9-0   William Buick
2 **Angel's Hideaway** 2-9-3   Robert Havlin
3 **Sunday Star** 2-9-0   Gerald Mosse
12/1, 13/2, 11/2. ¾l, nk. 8 ran. 1m 26.36s
(Roger Varian).

A fair race for the grade and a good attempt to defy a 3lb penalty from **Angel's Hideaway**, who looked unlucky to lose out to **Mot Juste**. Back on track over an extra furlong having disappointed since her Princess Margaret win, Angel's Hideaway had been forced to switch just as Mot Juste made her decisive move and could never peg back the game winner. **Sunday Star** finished a close third, pulling 5l clear of subsequent Listed runner-up **Glance** with two highly regarded novice/maiden winners, **Hidden Message** and **Frosty**, behind. Subsequent Listed third **Mistress Of Love** was sixth.

73 Darley Dewhurst Stakes (Group 1) (7f)
Newmarket October 13 (Good To Firm)
1 **Too Darn Hot** 2-9-1   Frankie Dettori
2 **Advertise** 2-9-1   Oisin Murphy
3 **Anthony Van Dyck** 2-9-1   D O'Brien

EvensF, 7/1, 11/4. 2¾l, 1¼l. 7 ran. 1m 24.35s (John Gosden).

Too Darn Hot completed his brilliant unbeaten campaign, handing out another thrashing against the two best horses he had come up against in **Advertise** and **Anthony Van Dyck**. Briefly outpaced when asked to make his move, Too Darn Hot was imperious once getting into overdrive, storming clear of Advertise, who ran another excellent race in second. Anthony Van Dyck could perhaps have done with a stiffer test, but it bodes well for the form that he had managed to push Quorto much closer at the Curragh and still managed to beat **Christmas** and **Mohawk**, who finished in the last two places, by further than he had managed that day. **Sangarius** was another 4½l back, just pipping **Kuwait Currency** for fourth.

74 Masar Godolphin Autumn Stakes (Group 3) (1m)
Newmarket October 13 (Good To Firm)
1 **Persian King** 2-9-1 Pierre-Charles Boudot
2 **Magna Grecia** 2-9-1 Donnacha O'Brien
3 **Circus Maximus** 2-9-1 Seamie Heffernan
6/5F, 3/1, 8/1. nk, 3l. 7 ran. 1m 37.35s (A Fabre).

A red-hot Group 3, surely the strongest race of its type run all season, with French raider **Persian King** beating subsequent Vertem Futurity Trophy winner **Magna Grecia**. Persian King travelled really well and knuckled down when pressed by the high-class runner-up, the pair pulling clear of **Circus Maximus** with another 3¼l back to **Western Australia**. That pair also franked the form with big runs at Doncaster next time, with Western Australia beaten further than he had been behind Madhmoon previously as well, and there was another 10l gap back to the rest after **Boerhan** crossed the line in a good fifth.

75 Godolphin Flying Start Zetland Stakes (Listed) (1m2f)
Newmarket October 13 (Good To Firm)
1 **Norway** 2-9-2 Seamie Heffernan
2 **I'll Have Another** 2-8-13 S De Sousa
3 **Nate The Great** 2-9-2 Edward Greatrex
7/2, 12/1, 9/1. 1l, nk. 6 ran. 2m 7.87s (A P O'Brien).

This form would prove somewhat misleading over subsequent weeks, with the first two both disappointing, but **Norway** was much better under contrasting tactics to those used when a beaten favourite in France next time and produced a fine performance. Held up off a slow pace, Norway came through to

VINTAGE BRUT: resurgent on soft ground after a tough summer

win with a bit in hand from **I'll Have Another**, who was probably flattered to run him close in second. **Nate The Great** was third ahead of **Waldstern**, while nothing went right for **Sydney Opera House**, who would find the anticipated improvement over this trip when reversing the form with Norway in France but was badly short of room here.

76 coral.co.uk Rockingham Stakes (Listed) (6f)
York October 13 (Soft)
1 **Vintage Brut** 2-9-4 David Allan
2 **Dave Dexter** 2-9-4 Richard Kingscote
3 **Cosmic Law** 2-9-1 Paul Hanagan
8/1, 11/4F, 13/2. 4½l, 1l. 10 ran. 1m 12.64s (Tim Easterby).

A remarkably good performance from **Vintage Brut**, who had begun to look exposed on quicker ground through the summer but showed he could be a major force in these conditions by readily defying a penalty. Appearing to also benefit from an extra furlong, Vintage Brut comprehensively reversed recent Ayr form with **Dave Dexter**, who still ran a solid race in second ahead of **Cosmic Law**.

77 Killavullan Stakes (Group 3) (7f) Leopardstown (IRE) October 20 (Good To Yielding)
1 **Coral Beach** 2-9-0 Michael Hussey
2 **Guaranteed** 2-9-3 Ronan Whelan
3 **Old Glory** 2-9-3 Seamie Heffernan
16/1, 12/1, 2/1. 1l, hd. 10 ran. 1m 28.89s (A P O'Brien).

It doesn't say much for a Group 3 when it is won by an 87-rated filly boasting just one win in 12 races, but **Coral Beach** had long hinted at plenty of ability – she had even been sent off favourite five times – and finally fulfilled that potential by landing what otherwise looked a solid race for the grade. Coral Beach beat subsequent Eyrefield winner **Guaranteed** and **Old Guard**, who benefited from setting a stronger gallop than when beaten at Dundalk. **Could Be King** was fourth, pulling 3¾l clear of the below-par **No Needs Never**, with **Angelic Light** further back in seventh.

78 **ebfstallions.com Silver Tankard Stakes (Listed) (1m6y)**
Pontefract October 22 (Good To Soft)
1 **Manuela De Vega** 2-8-12   Harry Bentley
2 **Three Comets** 2-9-3   Andrea Atzeni
3 **I'll Have Another** 2-9-1   P J McDonald
10/11F, 3/1, 3/1. 2¾l, ¾l. 5 ran. 1m 46.85s
(Ralph Beckett).

Not a particularly competitive Listed race, but **Manuela De Vega** was much too good for her four rivals and won it well. Having won her sole start, Manuela De Vega still looked green but quickened up past **Three Comets** and **I'll Have Another**, who attempted to dominate as she dropped in trip after her Zetland second but was found wanting.

79 **Vertem Futurity Trophy (Group 1) (1m)**
Doncaster October 27 (Good To Soft)
1 **Magna Grecia** 2-9-1   Donnacha O'Brien
2 **Phoenix Of Spain** 2-9-1   Jamie Spencer
3 **Western Australia** 2-9-1   Michael Hussey
2/1F, 11/2, 50/1. hd, ¾l. 10 ran. 1m 37.72s
(A P O'Brien).

Somewhat bizarrely for a Group 1, the form shown by **Magna Grecia** in defeat in the Autumn Stakes proved good enough as he prevailed in a blanket finish from Champagne Stakes runner-up **Phoenix Of Spain** and a couple of stablemates he had beaten more comfortably at Newmarket. **Western Australia** and **Circus Maximus** perhaps benefited from being given plenty of rope in front this time and Magna Grecia did well to reel them in, though, with Phoenix Of Spain and **Great Scot** also running fine races to go close from off the pace. Those five were covered by just 1¼l before a 2l gap back to the rest, led by **Kick On** and **Turgenev**, while **Kuwait Currency** trailed home in last.

80 **Hilton Garden Inn Doncaster Stakes (Listed) (6f2y)**
Doncaster October 27 (Good To Soft)

1 **San Donato** 2-9-1   Andrea Atzeni
2 **Barbill** 2-9-1   J F Egan
3 **Breath Of Air** 2-9-1   Donnacha O'Brien
2/1F, 13/2, 5/1. ¾l, 3¾l. 9 ran. 1m 11.69s
(Roger Varian).

A cosy win for **San Donato**, who quickened through from the rear and completed a hat-trick in good style. **Barbill** produced another solid run in second to push him close, although it doesn't say much about the overall strength of the race that he was able to pull 3¾l clear of **Breath Of Air** in third, with **Canton Queen** below her best and **Dave Dexter** particularly disappointing.

81 **Molson Coors Stakes (registered as the Horris Hill Stakes) (Group 3) (7f)**
Newbury October 27 (Good To Soft)
1 **Mohaather** 2-9-0   Martin Dwyer
2 **Azano** 2-9-0   Kieran Shoemark
3 **Almufti** 2-9-0   Jason Watson
33/1, 7/1, 9/1. 1½l, 5l. 8 ran. 1m 27.56s
(Marcus Tregoning).

An eyecatching win from **Mohaather**, who was held up and quickened smartly to reel in the front-running **Azano**. It's hard to be confident about this form given none of the first six had ever competed in a Class 1 race before, but it bodes well that Azano pulled 5l clear of **Almufti** and **Fanaar**. It was another 4½l back to the disappointing **Dirty Rascal** and red-hot favourite **Chairmanoftheboard**.

82 **Byerley Stud Stakes (registered as the Radley Stakes) (Listed) (Fillies) (7f)**
Newbury October 27 (Good To Soft)
1 **Iconic Choice** 2-9-0   Franny Norton
2 **Glance** 2-9-0   Harry Bentley
3 **Ice Gala** 2-9-0   Martin Harley
7/1, 10/1, 5/1. 2½l, 2½l. 11 ran. 1m 28.21s
(Tom Dascombe).

Iconic Choice had been sharply progressive at a lower level and took another big step forward to land a comfortable victory. Having won three of her last four nurseries, Iconic Choice readily saw off **Glance**, who just about set the standard on her Oh So Sharp fourth, and **Ice Gala**. **Impulsion** was fourth with **Aim Power** and **Ajrar** among those further back.

83 **Criterium de Saint-Cloud (Group 1) (1m2f)**
Saint-Cloud (FR) October 27 (Good)
1 **Wonderment** 2-8-10   Stephane Pasquier
2 **Sydney Opera House** 2-9-0 M Barzalona

3 **Fox Tal** 2-9-0 Ioritz Mendizabal
129/10, 17/2, 33/1. nk, ¾l. 9 ran. 2m 10.91s
(N Clement).

A strong challenge from Aidan O'Brien was denied by French filly **Wonderment**, who produced a fine late run from the rear to get up close home. **Sydney Opera House** relished the longer trip and was just edged out in second, but favourite **Norway** seemed unsuited by a change in tactics from his Zetland win as he made the running, especially as the first two came from well off the pace. It was therefore a fine effort from **Fox Tal**, allowed to race more prominently having disappointed on his previous run at Salisbury, to very nearly last home in third, but **Shambolic** was well below her best in seventh.

84 thetote.com Eyrefield Stakes (Group 3) (1m1f)
Leopardstown (IRE) October 27 (Good)
1 **Guaranteed** 2-9-3 Kevin Manning
2 **Masaff** 2-9-3 Declan McDonogh
3 **Sovereign** 2-9-3 N G McCullagh
9/2, 13/8F, 3/1. ½l, 1¾l. 8 ran. 1m 54.94s
(J S Bolger).

Twice disappointing at a higher level earlier in the season, **Guaranteed** had shown his true colours when second in the Killavullan and stepped forward again over this extra quarter-mile. **Masaff** set the standard on his third behind Madhmoon at Leopardstown, but Guaranteed improved past him, racing prominently and grinding things out in the final furlong. **Sovereign** made the running but faded into third.

85 Criterium International (Group 1) (7f)
Chantilly (FR) October 28 (Good To Soft)
1 **Royal Meeting** 2-9-0 C Soumillon
2 **Hermosa** 2-8-10 Ryan Moore
3 **Graignes** 2-9-0 Cristian Demuro
4/1, 7/5F, 13/2. ¾l, nk. 6 ran. 1m 27.19s
(Saeed bin Suroor).

Royal Meeting was having only his second run after landing a Yarmouth maiden first time out, but he exposed the shortcomings in those with Group form by picking up well to run out a ready winner. Fillies' Mile runner-up **Hermosa** came up just short again and **Kessaar**, stepping up in trip after his Mill Reef win, faded in the final half-furlong to lose third to **Graignes**, who had finished no closer than third in lesser Group races beforehand, just like the only other home challenger **Ecolo**.

86 Irish Stallion Farms EBF "Bosra Sham" Fillies' Stakes (Listed) (6f)
Newmarket November 2 (Soft)
1 **Angelic Light** 2-9-0 Leigh Roche
2 **Chynna** 2-9-0 Franny Norton
3 **Gypsy Spirit** 2-9-0 Luke Morris
10/1, 9/2, 9/2. nse, hd. 7 ran. 1m 14.08s
(M D O'Callaghan).

Plenty of depth and **Angelic Light** beat two solid yardsticks, **Chynna** and **Gyspy Spirit**, in better fashion than the narrow margin suggests. Racing on soft ground for the first time – the key to her according to her rider – and benefiting from a change in tactics after being held up over 7f in the Killavullan, Angelic Light made all the running and only faltered late as she paid the price for racing too freely.

87 Breeders' Cup Juvenile Turf (Grade 1) (1m)
Churchill Downs (USA) November 2 (Yielding)
1 **Line Of Duty** 2-8-10 William Buick
2 **Uncle Benny** 2-8-10 Irad Ortiz Jr
3 **Somelikeithotbrown** 2-8-10 Jose L Ortiz
3/1J, 10/1, 16/1. ½l, nk. 12 ran. 1m 40.06s
(Charlie Appleby).

The European juveniles generally struggled at the Breeders' Cup – both other winners on turf made all the running, with the raiders largely losing too much ground at the start – but **Line Of Duty** bucked the trend for Godolphin. On a hat-trick after a Group 3 win at Chantilly, Line Of Duty stayed on well to run down the front-running **Somelikeithotbrown** and just held off **Uncle Benny**. **Arthur Kitt** ran well in fourth, but **Anthony Van Dyck** and **Marie's Diamond** were always too far behind.

88 British Stallion Studs EBF Montrose Fillies' Stakes (Listed) (1m)
Newmarket November 3 (Soft)
1 **Blue Gardenia** 2-9-0 Shane Gray
2 **Vivid Diamond** 2-9-0 Franny Norton
3 **Mistress Of Love** 2-9-0 Colin Keane
12/1, 14/1, 16/1. nk, 3¼l. 9 ran. 1m 42.32s
(David O'Meara).

A real test of stamina on soft ground and that seemed to play to the strengths of two of the least heralded fillies in the line-up, **Blue Gardenia** and **Vivid Diamond**, rather than some potentially classier types behind. Despite just a narrow maiden win from six previous outings between them, the pair pulled 3¼l clear of **Mistress Of Love**, but that one had been beaten 10l in the Oh So Sharp and the form seems moderate.

Two-year-old index

All horses placed or commented on in our two-year-old review section, with race numbers

ANGEL'S HIDEAWAY (left): close to a second Group win in the Oh So Sharp

HERMOSA: Group 3 winner but 0-4 at a higher level

Trainer Statistics

Mark
Johnston

By month - 2018

	Overall			Two-year-olds			Three-year-olds			Older horses		
	W-R	%	£1	W-R	%	£1	W-R	%	£1	W-R	%	£1
January	6-29	21	-5.65	0-0	-	+0.00	3-20	15	-10.90	3-9	33	+5.25
February	7-32	22	+4.88	0-0	-	+0.00	1-18	6	-14.75	6-14	43	+19.63
March	11-80	14	-27.13	0-3	-	-3.00	9-47	19	-3.63	2-30	7	-20.50
April	10-73	14	-19.15	3-13	23	-3.00	4-40	10	-16.15	3-20	15	+0.00
May	38-200	19	-18.78	13-41	32	+5.95	17-104	16	-13.47	8-55	15	-11.25
June	44-232	19	-53.57	18-63	29	-5.53	19-116	16	-24.77	7-53	13	-23.27
July	42-207	20	-16.81	16-61	26	-1.51	22-116	19	-14.05	4-30	13	-1.25
August	24-181	13	-50.15	12-66	18	-15.65	8-78	10	-40.50	4-37	11	+6.00
September	13-108	12	-34.72	7-55	13	-18.59	6-40	15	-3.13	0-13	-	-13.00
October	11-131	8	-40.47	4-71	6	-49.27	7-44	16	+24.80	0-16	-	-16.00
November	6-57	11	-17.50	2-33	6	-16.25	2-17	12	-5.00	2-7	29	+3.75
December	6-30	20	-12.18	3-12	25	-1.50	3-12	25	-4.68	0-6	-	-6.00

By month - 2017

	Overall			Two-year-olds			Three-year-olds			Older horses		
	W-R	%	£1	W-R	%	£1	W-R	%	£1	W-R	%	£1
January	8-51	16	-18.45	0-0	-	+0.00	4-34	12	-18.86	4-17	24	+0.41
February	8-47	17	-13.60	0-0	-	+0.00	4-28	14	-9.43	4-19	21	-4.17
March	12-44	27	+12.80	0-0	-	+0.00	5-21	24	+5.05	7-23	30	+7.75
April	12-81	15	-23.50	1-9	11	-7.56	7-45	16	-10.04	4-27	15	-5.90
May	24-172	14	-58.28	7-36	19	-15.36	14-92	15	-13.17	3-44	7	-29.75
June	37-213	17	-42.26	15-62	24	+15.14	17-119	14	-60.65	5-32	16	+3.25
July	38-203	19	-15.92	22-63	35	+40.16	13-112	12	-52.08	3-28	11	-4.00
August	33-196	17	-23.05	16-66	24	+18.58	13-103	13	-38.63	4-27	15	-3.00
September	17-156	11	-79.09	9-71	13	-41.97	7-64	11	-28.13	1-21	5	-9.00
October	19-133	14	+82.21	7-64	11	+28.83	10-52	19	+49.38	2-17	12	+4.00
November	6-46	13	-11.65	4-31	13	-16.65	1-9	11	+4.00	1-6	17	+1.00
December	0-21	-	-21.00	0-13	-	-13.00	0-2	-	-2.00	0-6	-	-6.00

By month - 2016

	Overall			Two-year-olds			Three-year-olds			Older horses		
	W-R	%	£1	W-R	%	£1	W-R	%	£1	W-R	%	£1
January	5-34	15	-13.70	0-0	-	+0.00	5-23	22	-2.70	0-11	-	-11.00
February	4-23	17	-12.40	0-0	-	+0.00	4-15	27	-4.40	0-8	-	-8.00
March	11-49	22	-10.64	3-3	100	+4.82	4-28	14	-18.45	4-18	22	+3.00
April	12-117	10	-75.76	3-24	13	-15.76	7-68	10	-41.88	2-25	8	-18.13
May	21-168	13	-62.71	11-52	21	+0.25	7-75	9	-38.79	3-41	7	-24.17
June	35-204	17	-33.23	23-74	31	+17.31	8-96	8	-48.04	4-34	12	-2.50
July	38-233	16	+24.03	15-84	18	-28.05	16-109	15	+42.58	7-40	18	+9.50
August	23-178	13	-98.89	12-82	15	-43.36	8-62	13	-36.94	3-34	9	-18.59
September	19-149	13	-4.29	10-67	15	+17.46	7-62	11	-10.00	2-20	10	-11.75
October	14-140	10	+10.41	10-82	12	+28.91	2-43	5	-17.00	2-15	13	-1.50
November	7-64	11	-32.53	5-41	12	-25.03	0-16	-	-16.00	2-7	29	+8.50
December	6-54	11	-7.25	2-31	6	-13.00	3-17	18	-3.25	1-6	17	+9.00

By race type - 2018

	Overall			Two-year-olds			Three-year-olds			Older horses		
	W-R	%	£1	W-R	%	£1	W-R	%	£1	W-R	%	£1
Handicap	123-858	14	-170.47	10-101	10	-55.54	77-495	16	-76.16	36-262	14	-38.77
Group	4-52	8	-30.92	4-19	21	+2.08	0-27	-	-27.00	0-6	-	-6.00
Maiden	15-89	17	-2.29	10-59	17	-1.59	5-29	17	+0.30	0-1	-	-1.00

By race type - 2017

	Overall			Two-year-olds			Three-year-olds			Older horses		
	W-R	%	£1	W-R	%	£1	W-R	%	£1	W-R	%	£1
Handicap	127-911	14	-230.55	17-107	16	+2.53	75-552	14	-185.17	35-252	14	-47.91
Group	7-49	14	-2.13	4-27	15	-7.13	3-20	15	+7.00	0-2	-	-2.00
Maiden	17-116	15	-28.59	9-44	20	+13.83	8-72	11	-42.42	0-0	-	+0.00

By race type - 2016

	Overall			Two-year-olds			Three-year-olds			Older horses		
	W-R	%	£1	W-R	%	£1	W-R	%	£1	W-R	%	£1
Handicap	101-854	12	-153.82	19-142	13	+21.22	55-485	11	-123.41	27-227	12	-51.63
Group	4-51	8	-7.63	4-31	13	+12.38	0-15	-	-15.00	0-5	-	-5.00
Maiden	41-277	15	-124.77	30-192	16	-78.22	11-83	13	-44.55	0-2	-	-2.00

By jockey - 2018

	Overall			Two-year-olds			Three-year-olds			Older horses		
	W-R	%	£1	W-R	%	£1	W-R	%	£1	W-R	%	£1
Joe Fanning	53-345	15	-105.68	11-74	15	-28.40	31-205	15	-68.41	11-66	17	-8.88
Franny Norton	47-295	16	-76.99	20-108	19	-24.94	21-139	15	-27.55	6-48	13	-24.50
P J McDonald	34-206	17	-45.99	13-74	18	-22.67	17-88	19	+4.68	4-44	9	-28.00
S De Sousa	24-121	20	-8.61	12-58	21	-1.53	11-52	21	+2.19	1-11	9	-9.27
James Doyle	8-32	25	-2.74	7-18	39	+7.51	1-12	8	-8.25	0-2	-	-2.00
O Stammers	6-45	13	+3.25	0-1	-	-1.00	0-11	-	-11.00	6-33	18	+15.25
Adam Kirby	5-20	25	+0.55	0-5	-	-5.00	2-4	50	+1.30	3-11	27	+4.25
William Buick	5-32	16	-14.00	3-14	21	-4.25	2-15	13	-6.75	0-3	-	-3.00
Andrew Breslin	5-38	13	-2.00	0-4	-	-4.00	3-20	15	+4.00	2-14	14	-2.00
Ryan Moore	4-17	24	-4.38	1-6	17	-3.00	2-7	29	-1.88	1-4	25	+0.50
R Kingscote	4-23	17	-6.75	2-8	25	-4.25	1-8	13	-2.50	1-7	14	+0.00
Jason Hart	3-24	13	+14.50	0-7	-	-7.00	3-14	21	+24.50	0-3	-	-3.00

By jockey - 2017

	Overall			Two-year-olds			Three-year-olds			Older horses		
	W-R	%	£1	W-R	%	£1	W-R	%	£1	W-R	%	£1
Joe Fanning	64-392	16	-50.66	17-96	18	-49.44	27-192	14	-7.21	20-104	19	+5.99
Franny Norton	41-294	14	-74.62	17-97	18	-6.03	19-147	13	-38.44	5-50	10	-30.15
P J McDonald	35-204	17	+25.44	16-74	22	+67.50	19-108	18	-20.06	0-22	-	-22.00
S De Sousa	21-79	27	+7.97	14-34	41	+23.28	6-32	19	-14.32	1-13	8	-1.00
Jim Crowley	9-32	28	+8.75	3-9	33	+0.25	4-17	24	+2.00	2-6	33	+6.50
James Doyle	6-51	12	-15.00	3-24	13	-6.50	2-23	9	-17.50	1-4	25	+9.00
Ryan Moore	4-13	31	-2.64	2-4	50	+0.62	2-7	29	-1.25	0-2	-	-2.00
Dane O'Neill	4-21	19	-4.09	1-4	25	-2.09	2-11	18	-2.50	1-6	17	+0.50
Richard Oliver	4-30	13	-10.25	0-0	-	+0.00	4-21	19	-1.25	0-9	-	-9.00

By jockey - 2016

	Overall			Two-year-olds			Three-year-olds			Older horses		
	W-R	%	£1	W-R	%	£1	W-R	%	£1	W-R	%	£1
Joe Fanning	73-491	15	-100.76	27-176	15	-19.01	34-221	15	-55.12	12-94	13	-26.63
Franny Norton	46-253	18	-3.72	23-103	22	-11.88	18-110	16	+15.92	5-40	13	-7.75
Silvestre De Sousa	15-91	16	-37.96	6-32	19	-8.65	6-35	17	-16.07	3-24	13	-13.25
James Doyle	12-67	18	-22.43	10-30	33	+10.43	1-33	3	-32.36	1-4	25	-0.50
P J McDonald	10-61	16	+21.25	7-32	22	+21.25	1-19	5	-15.00	2-10	20	+15.00
William Buick	8-57	14	-25.66	6-27	22	-9.66	2-27	7	-13.00	0-3	-	-3.00
Paul Mulrennan	5-61	8	-29.00	4-28	14	-9.00	1-27	4	-14.00	0-6	-	-6.00
Richard Kingscote	4-36	11	-8.00	2-12	17	+5.00	1-16	6	-12.50	1-8	13	-0.50
Andrew Mullen	3-34	9	+0.50	3-24	13	+10.50	0-8	-	-8.00	0-2	-	-2.00

By course - 2015-2018

	Overall			Two-year-olds			Three-year-olds			Older horses		
	W-R	%	£1	W-R	%	£1	W-R	%	£1	W-R	%	£1
Ascot	18-190	9	-74.88	9-56	16	-15.38	6-103	6	-52.00	3-31	10	-7.50
Ayr	10-108	9	-69.43	5-45	11	-31.77	4-43	9	-30.67	1-20	5	-7.00
Bath	13-63	21	-19.79	4-17	24	-0.52	8-36	22	-11.00	1-10	10	-8.27
Beverley	40-218	18	-39.64	19-74	26	-12.43	19-118	16	-8.21	2-26	8	-19.00
Brighton	12-74	16	-31.11	5-32	16	-19.45	7-32	22	-1.67	0-10	-	-10.00
Carlisle	20-101	20	-9.51	6-37	16	-15.50	9-45	20	-0.09	5-19	26	+6.08
Catterick	17-120	14	-57.76	13-62	21	-14.10	3-45	7	-34.40	1-13	8	-9.25
Chelmsf'd (AW)	58-355	16	-69.40	24-117	21	-10.67	23-161	14	-24.90	11-77	14	-33.83
Chepstow	5-39	13	-19.92	0-10	-	-10.00	5-24	21	-4.92	0-5	-	-5.00
Chester	33-196	17	-37.51	12-61	20	-9.39	15-98	15	-34.13	6-37	16	+6.00
Doncaster	23-149	15	-28.35	12-71	17	+2.26	11-60	18	-12.61	0-18	-	-18.00
Epsom	20-102	20	-15.58	12-26	46	+14.58	5-45	11	-18.75	3-31	10	-11.40
Ffos Las	0-14	-	-14.00	0-5	-	-5.00	0-8	-	-8.00	0-1	-	-1.00
Goodwood	39-251	16	+44.08	14-77	18	+4.83	17-123	14	+6.75	8-51	16	+32.50
Hamilton	27-165	16	-42.84	13-58	22	+5.77	12-85	14	-33.49	2-22	9	-15.13
Haydock	32-184	17	-2.22	15-65	23	-3.22	11-79	14	-10.00	6-40	15	+11.00
Kempton (AW)	24-209	11	-85.98	12-79	15	-36.35	6-80	8	-29.76	6-50	12	-19.88
Leicester	26-116	22	-1.61	8-52	15	-25.81	14-49	29	+13.57	4-15	27	+10.63
Lingfield	4-38	11	-22.75	1-11	9	-4.00	3-20	15	-11.75	0-7	-	-7.00
Lingfield (AW)	45-247	18	-23.69	9-41	22	+20.30	19-127	15	-53.54	17-79	22	+9.55
Musselburgh	37-189	20	-35.69	13-66	20	-30.71	19-91	21	+9.48	5-32	16	-14.47
Newbury	12-75	16	-0.53	6-32	19	+0.10	5-30	17	+6.38	1-13	8	-7.00
Newcastle	4-10	40	+9.75	2-6	33	+6.50	2-3	67	+4.25	0-1	-	-1.00
N'castle (AW)	24-227	11	-74.52	9-94	10	-63.54	10-88	11	+8.36	5-45	11	-19.34
Newmarket	25-211	12	-17.75	13-89	15	+10.03	8-82	10	-9.38	4-40	10	-18.40
Newmarket (J)	36-179	20	+1.51	11-60	18	-16.84	16-87	18	+5.85	9-32	28	+12.50
Nottingham	16-117	14	-46.43	11-62	18	-6.75	5-42	12	-26.68	0-13	-	-13.00
Pontefract	30-160	19	-50.68	13-55	24	-19.09	11-79	14	-29.50	6-26	23	-2.09
Redcar	17-103	17	-7.00	5-41	12	-23.80	7-47	15	-7.20	5-15	33	+24.00
Ripon	30-169	18	+26.62	13-50	26	-10.05	15-84	18	+62.92	2-35	6	-26.25
Salisbury	6-26	23	+11.10	4-14	29	+16.60	2-10	20	-3.50	0-2	-	-2.00
Sandown	13-92	14	-38.64	8-31	26	+4.52	5-47	11	-29.95	0-14	-	-14.00
S'well (AW)	11-79	14	-7.97	1-17	6	-13.25	7-38	18	+12.78	3-24	13	-7.50
Thirsk	5-63	8	-40.75	3-28	11	-13.25	2-27	7	-19.50	0-8	-	-8.00
Wetherby	3-15	20	+10.10	1-5	20	-2.90	2-9	22	+14.00	0-1	-	-1.00
Windsor	12-56	21	-8.36	8-23	35	+4.52	1-24	4	-21.13	3-9	33	+8.25
Wolves (AW)	50-365	14	-101.95	14-112	13	-36.81	25-181	14	-74.98	11-72	15	+9.83
Yarmouth	10-53	19	+44.45	5-15	33	+56.70	3-32	9	-20.75	2-6	33	+8.50
York	24-216	11	+16.76	12-89	13	+8.01	9-79	11	+15.75	3-48	6	-7.00

Ten-year summary

	Wins	Runs	%	Win prize-money	Total prize-money	£1
2018	218	1360	16	£2,279,823.24	£4,183,702.54	-291.23
2017	214	1363	16	£2,401,913.22	£3,506,059.94	-211.79
2016	195	1413	14	£1,553,727.94	£2,726,246.11	-316.95
2015	204	1208	17	£1,806,254.46	£2,749,132.37	-111.80
2014	207	1344	15	£1,985,940.54	£2,992,111.82	-283.07
2013	216	1557	14	£1,826,629.78	£2,743,581.49	-396.21
2012	215	1344	16	£1,545,130.29	£2,284,275.76	-148.88
2011	179	1311	14	£927,711.46	£1,550,631.62	-270.93
2010	211	1458	14	£1,657,512.68	£2,419,718.15	-377.04
2009	216	1227	18	£1,747,013.96	£2,843,943.25	-139.14

POET'S SOCIETY: Mark Johnston's record 4,194th career winner last August

Richard Fahey

By month - 2018

	Overall			Two-year-olds			Three-year-olds			Older horses		
	W-R	%	£1	W-R	%	£1	W-R	%	£1	W-R	%	£1
January	2-40	5	-31.75	0-0	-	+0.00	1-17	6	-12.50	1-23	4	-19.25
February	3-38	8	-10.00	0-0	-	+0.00	2-16	13	+3.00	1-22	5	-13.00
March	8-56	14	+7.00	0-2	-	-2.00	3-24	13	+1.00	5-30	17	+8.00
April	17-98	17	+13.75	2-14	14	-0.50	7-40	18	-1.50	8-44	18	+15.75
May	28-198	14	-39.70	9-44	20	+8.88	11-75	15	-18.37	8-79	10	-30.21
June	34-232	15	+40.41	8-60	13	-9.34	14-84	17	+49.63	12-88	14	+0.13
July	36-232	16	-25.13	12-82	15	-17.58	15-82	18	-1.80	9-68	13	-5.75
August	27-215	13	-26.88	12-90	13	-13.51	9-73	12	-25.59	6-52	12	+12.23
September	6-147	4	-67.25	1-55	2	-46.00	3-48	6	-7.00	2-44	5	-14.25
October	14-154	9	-30.38	6-60	10	-32.38	5-50	10	+21.00	3-44	7	-19.00
November	4-66	6	-34.50	1-30	3	-25.50	2-22	9	-6.00	1-14	7	-3.00
December	5-31	16	+1.50	2-17	12	-1.00	3-12	25	+4.50	0-2	-	-2.00

By month - 2017

	Overall			Two-year-olds			Three-year-olds			Older horses		
	W-R	%	£1	W-R	%	£1	W-R	%	£1	W-R	%	£1
January	6-61	10	-27.00	0-0	-	+0.00	4-25	16	-7.00	2-36	6	-20.00
February	8-38	21	+1.38	0-0	-	+0.00	1-14	7	-10.50	7-24	29	+11.88
March	5-35	14	-7.00	0-0	-	+0.00	0-10	-	-10.00	5-25	20	+3.00
April	19-122	16	+14.88	6-17	35	+13.00	4-34	12	+21.00	9-71	13	-19.13
May	27-198	14	-61.18	6-43	14	-22.88	6-70	9	-38.40	15-85	18	+0.10
June	29-232	13	-83.14	13-67	19	+8.16	7-64	11	-31.13	9-101	9	-60.17
July	21-259	8	-85.66	7-93	8	-57.74	10-77	13	-5.17	4-89	4	-22.75
August	18-235	8	-141.06	11-108	10	-37.56	5-53	9	-36.25	2-74	3	-67.25
September	29-233	12	-1.00	12-108	11	-33.08	10-44	23	+37.25	7-81	9	-5.17
October	20-188	11	-81.86	10-83	12	-31.02	6-45	13	-12.00	4-60	7	-38.84
November	5-61	8	-18.13	3-20	15	+8.38	0-15	-	-15.00	2-26	8	-11.50
December	6-43	14	-14.00	1-17	6	-12.50	1-9	11	-3.50	4-17	24	+2.00

By month - 2016

	Overall			Two-year-olds			Three-year-olds			Older horses		
	W-R	%	£1	W-R	%	£1	W-R	%	£1	W-R	%	£1
January	7-48	15	+0.25	0-0	-	+0.00	1-16	6	-9.50	6-32	19	+9.75
February	6-42	14	-13.25	0-0	-	+0.00	3-17	18	+0.50	3-25	12	-13.75
March	6-45	13	-13.30	0-1	-	-1.00	2-20	10	-12.39	4-24	17	+0.08
April	22-130	17	-13.13	3-11	27	+12.23	12-49	24	+2.89	7-70	10	-28.25
May	18-211	9	-67.50	5-38	13	+34.25	5-70	7	-40.13	8-103	8	-61.63
June	35-220	16	+25.23	6-51	12	-19.85	15-84	18	+10.08	14-85	16	+35.00
July	27-278	10	-84.00	10-91	11	-40.63	9-79	11	+7.75	8-108	7	-51.13
August	27-240	11	-46.73	11-90	12	-20.83	11-62	18	+16.60	5-88	6	-42.50
September	19-200	10	-77.85	9-66	14	-14.72	6-50	12	-6.75	4-84	5	-56.39
October	18-171	11	-62.80	10-61	16	-12.80	5-49	10	-8.00	3-61	5	-42.00
November	9-89	10	-28.75	4-30	13	-1.75	3-24	13	-3.00	2-35	6	-24.00
December	4-65	6	-16.00	0-17	-	-17.00	3-24	13	-1.00	1-24	4	+2.00

By race type - 2018

	Overall			Two-year-olds			Three-year-olds			Older horses		
	W-R	%	£1	W-R	%	£1	W-R	%	£1	W-R	%	£1
Handicap	115-1025	11	-156.76	10-126	8	-75.13	61-449	14	+0.07	44-450	10	-81.71
Group	5-40	13	+13.08	0-17	-	-17.00	2-7	29	+26.33	3-16	19	+3.75
Maiden	5-46	11	-23.95	2-31	6	-23.75	3-15	20	-0.20	0-0	-	+0.00

By race type - 2017

	Overall			Two-year-olds			Three-year-olds			Older horses		
	W-R	%	£1	W-R	%	£1	W-R	%	£1	W-R	%	£1
Handicap	106-1128	9	-350.03	13-150	9	-54.25	40-370	11	-93.71	53-608	9	-202.07
Group	3-52	6	-32.15	1-14	7	+1.00	0-10	-	-10.00	2-28	7	-23.15
Maiden	16-92	17	-10.73	6-36	17	+8.75	10-55	18	-18.48	0-1	-	-1.00

By race type - 2016

	Overall			Two-year-olds			Three-year-olds			Older horses		
	W-R	%	£1	W-R	%	£1	W-R	%	£1	W-R	%	£1
Handicap	125-1241	10	-334.48	17-137	12	-27.29	56-446	13	-42.03	52-658	8	-265.17
Group	2-51	4	-37.50	1-13	8	-7.50	1-16	6	-8.00	0-22	-	-22.00
Maiden	33-237	14	-84.87	21-177	12	-77.37	11-56	20	-8.00	1-4	25	+0.50

By jockey - 2018

	Overall			Two-year-olds			Three-year-olds			Older horses		
	W-R	%	£1	W-R	%	£1	W-R	%	£1	W-R	%	£1
Paul Hanagan	70-525	13	-25.61	18-146	12	-47.08	33-201	16	+47.20	19-178	11	-25.73
Tony Hamilton	28-299	9	-66.63	12-111	11	-31.25	8-103	8	-33.63	8-85	9	-1.75
David Nolan	12-52	23	+16.42	5-26	19	-0.71	2-11	18	+2.75	5-15	33	+14.38
C Murtagh	11-90	12	-24.25	2-18	11	-5.00	5-31	16	-1.00	4-41	10	-18.25
Barry McHugh	8-37	22	+36.25	3-18	17	+32.00	4-13	31	+7.00	1-6	17	-2.75
Jack Garritty	8-67	12	-7.84	2-23	9	-18.84	3-22	14	+17.50	3-22	14	-6.50
Paddy Mathers	8-120	7	-83.77	4-43	9	-28.18	4-48	8	-26.59	0-29	-	-29.00
S Woods	6-66	9	-13.50	0-5	-	-5.00	2-17	12	+5.00	4-44	9	-13.50
P J McDonald	4-20	20	+5.50	2-7	29	+7.00	2-12	17	-0.50	0-1	-	-1.00
Oisin Murphy	3-3	100	+12.00	1-1	100	+3.00	1-1	100	+6.00	1-1	100	+3.00
S De Sousa	3-11	27	+4.75	0-4	-	-4.00	2-5	40	+1.75	1-2	50	+7.00
Connor Beasley	3-12	25	+13.50	0-2	-	-2.00	1-6	17	-2.50	2-4	50	+18.00

By jockey - 2017

	Overall			Two-year-olds			Three-year-olds			Older horses		
	W-R	%	£1	W-R	%	£1	W-R	%	£1	W-R	%	£1
Paul Hanagan	68-453	15	-29.76	28-148	19	+3.59	10-123	8	-66.07	30-182	16	+32.72
Tony Hamilton	36-383	9	-155.58	16-144	11	-55.50	11-116	9	-28.58	9-123	7	-71.50
A McNamara	22-160	14	-34.50	7-49	14	-7.58	10-32	31	+22.83	5-79	6	-49.75
C Murtagh	12-104	12	-38.52	1-6	17	-3.50	6-35	17	-4.13	5-63	8	-30.90
Jack Garritty	10-114	9	-64.71	5-57	9	-33.13	3-28	11	-11.25	2-29	7	-20.33
Barry McHugh	9-61	15	+2.13	4-31	13	+4.38	3-21	14	-7.25	2-9	22	+5.00
S Woods	6-42	14	+0.50	0-1	-	-1.00	2-10	20	+1.00	4-31	13	+0.50
Sammy Jo Bell	6-77	8	-30.50	1-20	5	-16.00	3-21	14	+14.00	2-36	6	-28.50
William Buick	3-8	38	+0.85	1-1	100	+3.00	0-2	-	-2.00	2-5	40	-0.15

By jockey - 2016

	Overall			Two-year-olds			Three-year-olds			Older horses		
	W-R	%	£1	W-R	%	£1	W-R	%	£1	W-R	%	£1
Tony Hamilton	66-528	13	-151.07	31-195	16	-21.97	21-175	12	-37.29	14-158	9	-91.80
A McNamara	33-247	13	-61.28	6-32	19	+7.38	11-68	16	-14.53	16-147	11	-54.13
David Nolan	20-143	14	+0.17	3-38	8	-5.50	13-54	24	+30.17	4-51	8	-24.50
P Mathers	14-117	12	+15.25	5-36	14	+0.25	5-47	11	-10.50	4-34	12	+25.50
G Chaloner	14-137	10	-23.78	3-42	7	-20.00	6-30	20	+31.10	5-65	8	-34.88
Paul Hanagan	10-89	11	-4.50	3-24	13	-6.00	2-17	12	-6.00	5-48	10	+7.50
Sammy Jo Bell	7-57	12	-18.89	0-1	-	-1.00	1-17	6	-15.39	6-39	15	-2.50
Jack Garritty	7-117	6	-52.88	2-36	6	+0.88	4-37	11	-15.25	1-44	2	-38.50
Jamie Spencer	6-29	21	-2.04	3-9	33	-1.04	3-13	23	+6.00	0-7	-	-7.00

By course - 2015-2018

	Overall			Two-year-olds			Three-year-olds			Older horses		
	W-R	%	£1	W-R	%	£1	W-R	%	£1	W-R	%	£1
Ascot	7-148	5	-33.40	0-26	-	-26.00	2-31	6	+6.00	5-91	5	-13.40
Ayr	30-299	10	-94.37	9-72	13	-34.87	10-98	10	-21.25	11-129	9	-38.25
Bath	2-12	17	+0.00	0-0	-	+0.00	2-7	29	+5.00	0-5	-	-5.00
Beverley	42-295	14	-107.86	17-113	15	-45.24	17-97	18	-11.22	8-85	9	-51.40
Brighton	1-7	14	-3.00	0-2	-	-2.00	1-4	25	+0.00	0-1	-	-1.00
Carlisle	27-203	13	-68.01	10-75	13	-33.96	13-77	17	-22.55	4-51	8	-11.50
Catterick	31-179	17	-15.78	13-71	18	-24.50	5-51	10	-26.00	13-57	23	+34.73
Chelmsf'd (AW)	12-161	7	-59.08	3-30	10	-19.25	3-61	5	-35.33	6-70	9	-4.50
Chepstow	0-1	-	-1.00	0-1	-	-1.00	0-0	-	+0.00	0-0	-	+0.00
Chester	52-419	12	-61.55	10-73	14	-11.38	16-94	17	+22.08	26-252	10	-72.25
Doncaster	32-360	9	-96.12	9-94	10	-32.47	8-109	7	-22.90	15-157	10	-40.75
Epsom	10-92	11	-13.13	1-15	7	-4.00	2-25	8	-13.00	7-52	13	+3.88
Ffos Las	1-2	50	+0.50	1-2	50	+0.50	0-0	-	+0.00	0-0	-	+0.00
Goodwood	6-123	5	-71.50	2-23	9	-13.50	2-32	6	-18.00	2-68	3	-40.00
Hamilton	31-229	14	-71.13	8-72	11	-23.45	17-86	20	-6.79	6-71	8	-40.89
Haydock	26-292	9	-131.89	9-75	12	-22.93	12-92	13	-6.46	5-125	4	-102.50
Kempton (AW)	1-73	1	-62.00	0-22	-	-22.00	1-18	6	-7.00	0-33	-	-33.00
Leicester	28-143	20	+17.80	11-54	20	+6.60	12-55	22	+17.94	5-34	15	-6.75
Lingfield	2-11	18	-5.13	1-8	13	-5.38	1-3	33	+0.25	0-0	-	+0.00
Lingfield (AW)	23-197	12	-61.65	2-22	9	-14.25	9-67	13	-19.15	12-108	11	-28.25
Musselburgh	34-189	18	+30.83	10-48	21	+7.13	16-74	22	+30.70	8-67	12	-7.00
Newbury	8-61	13	+28.13	5-32	16	+37.63	0-10	-	-10.00	3-19	16	+0.50
Newcastle	5-50	10	-10.00	1-15	7	-11.00	2-17	12	-8.50	2-18	11	+9.50
N'castle (AW)	46-370	12	-40.38	15-115	13	-8.13	19-117	16	+26.75	12-138	9	-59.00
Newmarket	9-148	6	-72.75	1-36	3	-32.50	4-62	6	-31.00	4-50	8	-9.25
Newmarket (J)	15-126	12	+10.75	5-33	15	+11.00	8-53	15	+19.50	2-40	5	-19.75
Nottingham	32-177	18	+53.51	11-65	17	-8.04	12-70	17	+20.30	9-42	21	+41.25
Pontefract	42-262	16	-1.58	16-83	19	+21.25	14-95	15	-22.26	12-84	14	-0.57
Redcar	38-259	15	-40.85	17-120	14	-25.75	8-76	11	-46.26	13-63	21	+31.16
Ripon	37-278	13	-72.59	10-86	12	-39.46	18-89	20	+33.38	9-103	9	-66.51
Salisbury	1-7	14	-2.50	0-2	-	-2.00	0-3	-	-3.00	1-2	50	+2.50
Sandown	4-28	14	-14.38	2-5	40	+2.25	1-12	8	-8.50	1-11	9	-8.13
S'well (AW)	29-154	19	-5.54	6-36	17	-4.38	11-58	19	-1.83	12-60	20	+0.67
Thirsk	38-229	17	+8.42	13-86	15	+8.73	13-82	16	+9.57	12-61	20	-9.88
Wetherby	6-29	21	+16.25	2-8	25	-2.25	3-11	27	+20.50	1-10	10	-2.00
Windsor	7-46	15	-3.09	0-6	-	-6.00	3-20	15	-2.00	4-20	20	+4.91
Wolves (AW)	57-462	12	-123.41	11-138	8	-74.43	15-142	11	-34.53	31-182	17	-14.46
Yarmouth	2-21	10	-9.50	1-7	14	+0.00	0-7	-	-7.00	1-7	14	-2.50
York	36-500	7	-145.25	16-161	10	+9.25	7-116	6	-58.50	13-223	6	-96.00

Ten-year summary

	Wins	Runs	%	Win prize-money	Total prize-money	£1
2018	184	1507	12	£2,003,266.83	£3,242,071.77	-202.92
2017	193	1705	11	£2,439,577.60	£4,155,876.15	-503.77
2016	198	1739	11	£1,555,029.70	£3,162,107.98	-397.84
2015	235	1691	14	£2,394,305.99	£3,846,973.63	-227.69
2014	192	1502	13	£1,882,767.02	£2,882,652.01	-119.24
2013	164	1287	13	£1,588,826.54	£2,455,584.17	-236.90
2012	142	1294	11	£1,213,826.13	£1,982,267.62	-294.66
2011	151	1224	12	£980,328.63	£1,650,127.14	-260.88
2010	181	1356	13	£1,325,389.94	£2,075,925.44	-273.54
2009	165	1106	15	£1,123,057.39	£1,657,128.68	+25.22

RED BALLOONS: added nearly £150,000 to Richard Fahey's kitty at Doncaster

John Gosden

By month - 2018

	Overall			Two-year-olds			Three-year-olds			Older horses		
	W-R	%	£1	W-R	%	£1	W-R	%	£1	W-R	%	£1
January	6-25	24	-4.78	0-0	-	+0.00	6-24	25	-3.78	0-1	-	-1.00
February	5-13	38	+11.03	0-0	-	+0.00	4-11	36	+7.03	1-2	50	+4.00
March	3-22	14	-15.58	0-0	-	+0.00	3-17	18	-10.58	0-5	-	-5.00
April	20-55	36	+25.60	0-0	-	+0.00	17-50	34	+18.40	3-5	60	+7.20
May	28-96	29	-0.33	1-4	25	-1.00	20-72	28	+1.80	7-20	35	-1.13
June	18-85	21	-28.46	4-10	40	+1.23	11-57	19	-24.73	3-18	17	-4.96
July	17-68	25	-23.91	7-22	32	-2.02	9-39	23	-16.68	1-7	14	-5.20
August	17-62	27	-2.98	5-19	26	-3.59	10-37	27	-6.76	2-6	33	+7.36
September	11-54	20	+6.32	5-27	19	-0.80	6-23	26	+11.13	0-4	-	-4.00
October	17-85	20	-19.62	8-48	17	-17.30	7-28	25	+2.85	2-9	22	-5.17
November	13-58	22	+3.00	9-40	23	+0.28	3-15	20	-4.27	1-3	33	+7.00
December	10-31	32	+7.37	7-26	27	+5.82	3-5	60	+1.55	0-0	-	+0.00

By month - 2017

	Overall			Two-year-olds			Three-year-olds			Older horses		
	W-R	%	£1	W-R	%	£1	W-R	%	£1	W-R	%	£1
January	4-19	21	-5.14	0-0	-	+0.00	4-19	21	-5.14	0-0	-	+0.00
February	4-17	24	-9.18	0-0	-	+0.00	4-17	24	-9.18	0-0	-	+0.00
March	3-18	17	-8.25	0-0	-	+0.00	3-18	17	-8.25	0-0	-	+0.00
April	19-68	28	+30.42	0-0	-	+0.00	17-56	30	+34.04	2-12	17	-3.63
May	17-80	21	-24.70	1-7	14	-5.47	14-59	24	-13.73	2-14	14	-5.50
June	13-81	16	+0.21	0-11	-	-11.00	12-56	21	+23.41	1-14	7	-12.20
July	11-68	16	-37.99	1-14	7	-12.20	9-38	24	-13.79	1-16	6	-12.00
August	13-55	24	+4.42	5-27	19	-5.75	6-20	30	+4.67	2-8	25	+5.50
September	17-70	24	+9.07	10-30	33	+12.41	5-27	19	-4.58	2-13	15	+1.25
October	18-98	18	-3.76	10-48	21	+2.24	7-36	19	-1.00	1-14	7	-5.00
November	11-65	17	-13.52	9-49	18	-6.52	2-14	14	-5.00	0-2	-	-2.00
December	4-36	11	-24.56	4-30	13	-18.56	0-6	-	-6.00	0-0	-	+0.00

By month - 2016

	Overall			Two-year-olds			Three-year-olds			Older horses		
	W-R	%	£1	W-R	%	£1	W-R	%	£1	W-R	%	£1
January	5-17	29	-3.99	0-0	-	+0.00	4-14	29	-3.09	1-3	33	-0.90
February	1-11	9	-6.00	0-0	-	+0.00	0-6	-	-6.00	1-5	20	+0.00
March	2-8	25	-1.80	0-0	-	+0.00	2-6	33	+0.20	0-2	-	-2.00
April	16-61	26	-3.01	0-0	-	+0.00	14-53	26	-2.84	2-8	25	-0.17
May	14-79	18	-18.66	1-8	13	-3.50	11-56	20	-19.16	2-15	13	+4.00
June	12-89	13	-32.10	4-21	19	+8.42	8-56	14	-28.52	0-12	-	-12.00
July	18-75	24	+22.09	6-21	29	-1.52	10-39	26	+23.61	2-15	13	+0.00
August	16-45	36	+21.59	3-12	25	-5.70	12-29	41	+19.29	1-4	25	+8.00
September	14-69	20	-1.50	7-32	22	-5.90	5-24	21	-1.97	2-13	15	+6.38
October	26-93	28	+34.64	17-53	32	+40.42	8-26	31	+3.22	1-14	7	-9.00
November	11-49	22	-10.38	9-39	23	-5.13	1-5	20	-2.50	1-5	20	-2.75
December	6-17	35	+1.25	6-17	35	+1.25	0-0	-	+0.00	0-0	-	+0.00

By race type - 2018

	Overall			Two-year-olds			Three-year-olds			Older horses		
	W-R	%	£1	W-R	%	£1	W-R	%	£1	W-R	%	£1
Handicap	37-175	21	-23.57	4-17	24	+0.58	26-122	21	-29.94	7-36	19	+5.78
Group	21-80	26	-13.23	5-20	25	-5.55	7-35	20	-2.13	9-25	36	-5.55
Maiden	15-86	17	-19.50	5-38	13	-21.05	10-47	21	+2.55	0-1	-	-1.00

By race type - 2017

	Overall			Two-year-olds			Three-year-olds			Older horses		
	W-R	%	£1	W-R	%	£1	W-R	%	£1	W-R	%	£1
Handicap	32-191	17	-27.63	3-12	25	+6.63	26-147	18	-23.63	3-32	9	-10.63
Group	20-98	20	+6.41	2-8	25	+5.75	13-49	27	+16.86	5-41	12	-16.20
Maiden	40-168	24	-28.34	5-47	11	-34.30	35-121	29	+5.96	0-0	-	+0.00

By race type - 2016

	Overall			Two-year-olds			Three-year-olds			Older horses		
	W-R	%	£1	W-R	%	£1	W-R	%	£1	W-R	%	£1
Handicap	28-126	22	+35.44	3-14	21	-4.09	23-98	23	+27.03	2-14	14	+12.50
Group	12-84	14	-18.87	1-8	13	-2.00	6-28	21	+2.30	5-48	10	-19.17
Maiden	83-302	27	+10.64	41-148	28	+30.01	39-149	26	-38.47	3-5	60	+19.10

By jockey - 2018

	Overall			Two-year-olds			Three-year-olds			Older horses		
	W-R	%	£1	W-R	%	£1	W-R	%	£1	W-R	%	£1
Robert Havlin	84-286	29	+5.11	27-95	28	+1.51	52-169	31	+1.77	5-22	23	+1.83
Frankie Dettori	36-123	29	-5.46	6-28	21	-14.24	20-77	26	-2.79	10-18	56	+11.57
Nicky Mackay	12-78	15	-9.87	4-25	16	-5.92	8-50	16	-0.95	0-3	-	-3.00
Oisin Murphy	8-19	42	+7.17	3-8	38	+2.75	5-11	45	+4.42	0-0	-	+0.00
Kieran O'Neill	8-44	18	+8.00	3-16	19	+11.00	4-25	16	-4.00	1-3	33	+1.00
Jim Crowley	6-33	18	-9.25	1-12	8	-8.50	4-14	29	-5.75	1-7	14	+5.00
James Doyle	5-22	23	-6.99	0-1	-	-1.00	3-8	38	-0.90	2-13	15	-5.09
William Buick	2-12	17	-3.75	1-2	50	+3.00	1-5	20	-1.75	0-5	-	-5.00
Adam Kirby	1-1	100	+2.00	1-1	100	+2.00	0-0	-	+0.00	0-0	-	+0.00
Martin Harley	1-1	100	+2.00	0-0	-	+0.00	1-1	100	+2.00	0-0	-	+0.00
Andrea Atzeni	1-7	14	-5.20	0-0	-	+0.00	0-5	-	-5.00	1-2	50	-0.20
Dane O'Neill	1-13	8	-11.09	0-0	-	+0.00	1-10	10	-8.09	0-3	-	-3.00

By jockey - 2017

	Overall			Two-year-olds			Three-year-olds			Older horses		
	W-R	%	£1	W-R	%	£1	W-R	%	£1	W-R	%	£1
Frankie Dettori	37-131	28	+44.96	8-25	32	+14.70	27-84	32	+38.76	2-22	9	-8.50
Robert Tart	19-80	24	+7.30	4-28	14	-12.20	13-48	27	+12.00	2-4	50	+7.50
Robert Havlin	15-106	14	-47.14	12-66	18	-19.14	3-31	10	-19.00	0-9	-	-9.00
James Doyle	10-43	23	-7.27	1-9	11	-7.71	7-22	32	+4.65	2-12	17	-4.20
Nicky Mackay	10-55	18	-17.56	2-24	8	-8.50	8-31	26	-9.06	0-0	-	+0.00
Jim Crowley	9-41	22	-12.40	3-10	30	-2.06	4-19	21	-7.09	2-12	17	-3.25
K Shoemark	7-32	22	-0.09	2-12	17	-1.50	4-16	25	-5.59	1-4	25	+7.00
Andrea Atzeni	5-27	19	-6.72	1-3	33	-0.50	4-20	20	-2.22	0-4	-	-4.00
Jimmy Fortune	4-12	33	+7.38	1-1	100	+7.00	2-8	25	-0.63	1-3	33	+1.00

By jockey - 2016

	Overall			Two-year-olds			Three-year-olds			Older horses		
	W-R	%	£1	W-R	%	£1	W-R	%	£1	W-R	%	£1
Robert Havlin	55-211	26	+48.38	22-71	31	+14.40	25-105	24	-1.38	8-35	23	+35.35
Frankie Dettori	38-144	26	-2.57	13-43	30	+8.60	22-76	29	+4.46	3-25	12	-15.63
Nicky Mackay	13-63	21	-9.68	3-24	13	-13.02	10-36	28	+6.35	0-3	-	-3.00
James Doyle	11-42	26	+1.45	8-20	40	+5.36	3-19	16	-0.91	0-3	-	-3.00
Paul Hanagan	7-32	22	-12.56	1-6	17	-2.25	5-15	33	-3.65	1-11	9	-6.67
Tom Queally	5-11	45	+6.41	0-0	-	+0.00	5-11	45	+6.41	0-0	-	+0.00
Robert Tart	3-22	14	+12.75	3-12	25	+22.75	0-8	-	-8.00	0-2	-	-2.00
Graham Lee	2-7	29	-2.29	0-3	-	-3.00	2-3	67	+1.71	0-1	-	-1.00
William Buick	2-36	6	-28.75	0-9	-	-9.00	2-21	10	-13.75	0-6	-	-6.00

By course - 2015-2018

	Overall			Two-year-olds			Three-year-olds			Older horses		
	W-R	%	£1	W-R	%	£1	W-R	%	£1	W-R	%	£1
Ascot	33-212	16	-28.88	5-19	26	+15.50	15-112	13	-37.63	13-81	16	-6.76
Ayr	1-2	50	-0.92	0-0	-	+0.00	1-1	100	+0.08	0-1	-	-1.00
Bath	0-4	-	-4.00	0-1	-	-1.00	0-3	-	-3.00	0-0	-	+0.00
Beverley	1-7	14	-3.75	0-0	-	+0.00	1-7	14	-3.75	0-0	-	+0.00
Brighton	1-5	20	-2.13	0-2	-	-2.00	0-2	-	-2.00	1-1	100	+1.88
Carlisle	0-2	-	-2.00	0-0	-	+0.00	0-2	-	-2.00	0-0	-	+0.00
Catterick	1-1	100	+0.83	0-0	-	+0.00	1-1	100	+0.83	0-0	-	+0.00
Chelmsf'd (AW)	39-168	23	-37.43	9-59	15	-22.02	25-100	25	-22.90	5-9	56	+7.49
Chepstow	4-7	57	+3.82	0-0	-	+0.00	4-7	57	+3.82	0-0	-	+0.00
Chester	6-27	22	-4.92	0-1	-	-1.00	4-20	20	-7.42	2-6	33	+3.50
Doncaster	22-117	19	-30.70	9-37	24	-5.89	12-61	20	-15.81	1-19	5	-9.00
Epsom	11-40	28	-3.96	0-5	-	-5.00	8-29	28	-2.04	3-6	50	+3.09
Goodwood	16-91	18	-37.64	4-16	25	-8.99	8-51	16	-23.45	4-24	17	-5.20
Hamilton	0-1	-	-1.00	0-0	-	+0.00	0-1	-	-1.00	0-0	-	+0.00
Haydock	21-76	28	+4.19	10-26	38	+9.91	9-36	25	+2.28	2-14	14	-8.00
Kempton (AW)	56-215	26	+28.63	24-109	22	+1.38	30-90	33	+39.39	2-16	13	-12.14
Leicester	7-51	14	-16.62	4-20	20	-8.62	1-28	4	-25.25	2-3	67	+17.25
Lingfield	4-18	22	+0.00	0-2	-	-2.00	4-16	25	+2.00	0-0	-	+0.00
Lingfield (AW)	35-174	20	-31.17	9-48	19	-3.81	23-106	22	-22.12	3-20	15	-5.25
Newbury	37-159	23	+17.42	15-56	27	+2.96	17-77	22	+9.96	5-26	19	+4.50
Newcastle	0-4	-	-4.00	0-0	-	+0.00	0-3	-	-3.00	0-1	-	-1.00
N'castle (AW)	26-75	35	-3.77	12-28	43	+7.70	14-43	33	-7.47	0-4	-	-4.00
Newmarket	52-261	20	+21.59	20-93	22	+21.38	28-133	21	+19.33	4-35	11	-19.13
Newmarket (J)	32-173	18	-31.42	11-69	16	-16.84	20-87	23	-3.58	1-17	6	-11.00
Nottingham	16-104	15	-11.23	8-45	18	+1.60	7-50	14	-20.83	1-9	11	+8.00
Pontefract	0-6	-	-6.00	0-0	-	+0.00	0-5	-	-5.00	0-1	-	-1.00
Redcar	1-4	25	+0.50	1-4	25	+0.50	0-0	-	+0.00	0-0	-	+0.00
Ripon	1-3	33	-1.50	0-1	-	-1.00	1-2	50	-0.50	0-0	-	+0.00
Salisbury	11-38	29	+36.36	2-9	22	+0.50	8-25	32	+38.13	1-4	25	-2.27
Sandown	25-111	23	-9.92	7-29	24	-7.69	15-62	24	-7.48	3-20	15	+5.25
S'well (AW)	7-18	39	-3.22	0-2	-	-2.00	5-13	38	-1.65	2-3	67	+0.43
Thirsk	1-6	17	-4.20	1-3	33	-1.20	0-3	-	-3.00	0-0	-	+0.00
Wetherby	3-4	75	+8.00	0-0	-	+0.00	3-4	75	+8.00	0-0	-	+0.00
Windsor	19-63	30	-10.22	4-11	36	+5.10	15-48	31	-11.32	0-4	-	-4.00
Wolves (AW)	44-139	32	-5.12	18-60	30	-0.54	25-76	33	-2.79	1-3	33	-1.80
Yarmouth	20-60	33	+26.52	9-35	26	+1.27	11-24	46	+26.25	0-1	-	-1.00
York	21-73	29	+12.65	0-5	-	-5.00	15-43	35	+17.12	6-24	24	+0.53

Ten-year summary

	Wins	Runs	%	Win prize-money	Total prize-money	£1
2018	165	654	25	£6,422,781.63	£8,262,497.30	-42.34
2017	134	675	20	£4,541,824.95	£6,163,758.83	-82.98
2016	142	613	23	£1,997,426.28	£3,487,430.77	+7.64
2015	133	577	23	£3,094,711.38	£5,277,650.54	-17.52
2014	132	613	22	£2,876,012.06	£4,241,990.89	-24.63
2013	108	525	21	£1,263,914.58	£2,033,077.64	-24.83
2012	119	629	19	£2,150,284.26	£3,739,407.23	-60.64
2011	99	553	18	£1,828,265.33	£2,529,369.21	-14.31
2010	105	518	20	£1,101,277.72	£1,714,237.43	-28.71
2009	88	516	17	£1,447,841.46	£2,308,709.36	-97.55

STRADIVARIUS: superstar stayer won five out of five for John Gosden last year

Richard Hannon

By month - 2018

	Overall			Two-year-olds			Three-year-olds			Older horses		
	W-R	%	£1	W-R	%	£1	W-R	%	£1	W-R	%	£1
January	1-28	4	-24.50	0-0	-	+0.00	1-18	6	-14.50	0-10	-	-10.00
February	3-16	19	-7.25	0-0	-	+0.00	2-11	18	-6.00	1-5	20	-1.25
March	6-23	26	+1.83	0-0	-	+0.00	2-12	17	-6.50	4-11	36	+8.33
April	14-84	17	+47.88	2-8	25	-2.13	8-53	15	+38.50	4-23	17	+11.50
May	25-187	13	-7.66	7-42	17	-8.80	13-107	12	+14.31	5-38	13	-13.17
June	19-202	9	-74.22	9-72	13	-12.84	8-96	8	-57.38	2-34	6	-4.00
July	29-176	16	-17.27	14-88	16	-13.69	13-66	20	+8.92	2-22	9	-12.50
August	35-234	15	-55.23	18-122	15	-41.69	14-85	16	-14.53	3-27	11	+1.00
September	9-108	8	-67.92	7-73	10	-37.03	0-24	-	-24.00	2-11	18	-6.90
October	12-148	8	-82.27	9-104	9	-55.77	0-28	-	-28.00	3-16	19	+1.50
November	5-51	10	-19.75	5-35	14	-3.75	0-11	-	-11.00	0-5	-	-5.00
December	2-43	5	-15.00	2-31	6	-3.00	0-9	-	-9.00	0-3	-	-3.00

By month - 2017

	Overall			Two-year-olds			Three-year-olds			Older horses		
	W-R	%	£1	W-R	%	£1	W-R	%	£1	W-R	%	£1
January	4-28	14	+19.88	0-0	-	+0.00	2-20	10	-13.13	2-8	25	+33.00
February	4-17	24	+6.57	0-0	-	+0.00	4-14	29	+9.57	0-3	-	-3.00
March	5-31	16	+13.98	0-0	-	+0.00	5-29	17	+15.98	0-2	-	-2.00
April	20-125	16	-7.84	1-12	8	-9.25	14-87	16	-14.59	5-26	19	+16.00
May	30-173	17	-29.49	10-38	26	-1.32	12-113	11	-45.13	8-22	36	+16.95
June	19-167	11	-56.47	8-58	14	-23.97	10-89	11	-17.50	1-20	5	-15.00
July	27-206	13	+20.63	15-101	15	+38.63	11-91	12	-15.00	1-14	7	-3.00
August	32-198	16	-32.41	18-101	18	-6.72	13-82	16	-14.69	1-15	7	-11.00
September	18-160	11	+2.99	9-88	10	+22.91	7-57	12	-15.92	2-15	13	-4.00
October	17-152	11	-5.98	10-98	10	-9.90	5-41	12	+5.55	2-13	15	-1.63
November	7-49	14	-20.09	6-38	16	-11.97	1-10	10	-7.13	0-1	-	-1.00
December	6-29	21	-1.13	6-21	29	+6.88	0-7	-	-7.00	0-1	-	-1.00

By month - 2016

	Overall			Two-year-olds			Three-year-olds			Older horses		
	W-R	%	£1	W-R	%	£1	W-R	%	£1	W-R	%	£1
January	8-28	29	+13.82	0-0	-	+0.00	7-23	30	+13.82	1-5	20	+0.00
February	2-18	11	-7.00	0-0	-	+0.00	2-17	12	-6.00	0-1	-	-1.00
March	2-19	11	-11.63	0-1	-	-1.00	1-12	8	-9.13	1-6	17	-1.50
April	13-110	12	-41.26	4-18	22	-9.31	8-73	11	-17.46	1-19	5	-14.50
May	36-196	18	+68.61	15-56	27	+17.08	20-118	17	+60.53	1-22	5	-9.00
June	20-191	10	-71.97	9-75	12	-28.63	11-97	11	-24.34	0-19	-	-19.00
July	31-223	14	-9.35	15-103	15	-13.50	15-91	16	+31.15	1-29	3	-27.00
August	24-170	14	-47.07	19-102	19	-4.40	5-56	9	-30.67	0-12	-	-12.00
September	9-118	5	-119.92	7-112	6	-64.25	2-50	4	-39.67	0-16	-	-16.00
October	17-145	12	+3.75	10-101	10	+0.00	6-34	18	+9.25	1-10	10	-5.50
November	7-44	16	+26.00	4-31	13	+16.00	3-10	30	+13.00	0-3	-	-3.00
December	4-35	11	-7.92	4-23	17	+4.08	0-12	-	-12.00	0-0	-	+0.00

By race type - 2018

	Overall			Two-year-olds			Three-year-olds			Older horses		
	W-R	%	£1	W-R	%	£1	W-R	%	£1	W-R	%	£1
Handicap	71-643	11	-212.18	15-135	11	-46.99	39-361	11	-134.27	17-147	12	-30.92
Group	4-65	6	+25.50	0-22	-	-22.00	3-23	13	+60.00	1-20	5	-12.50
Maiden	13-96	14	-13.17	9-75	12	-18.67	4-20	20	+6.50	0-1	-	-1.00

By race type - 2017

	Overall			Two-year-olds			Three-year-olds			Older horses		
	W-R	%	£1	W-R	%	£1	W-R	%	£1	W-R	%	£1
Handicap	83-700	12	-129.34	16-124	13	-14.04	53-474	11	-125.50	14-102	14	+10.20
Group	7-54	13	+30.00	3-24	13	+33.00	2-13	15	-6.00	2-17	12	+3.00
Maiden	22-178	12	-24.44	8-73	11	+15.41	14-105	13	-39.85	0-0	-	+0.00

By race type - 2016

	Overall			Two-year-olds			Three-year-olds			Older horses		
	W-R	%	£1	W-R	%	£1	W-R	%	£1	W-R	%	£1
Handicap	66-636	10	-116.18	13-140	9	-41.00	51-408	13	-4.68	2-88	2	-70.50
Group	6-74	8	-43.75	4-29	14	-6.75	1-26	4	-22.50	1-19	5	-14.50
Maiden	52-381	14	-40.77	40-275	15	+6.68	12-106	11	-47.45	0-0	-	+0.00

By jockey - 2018

	Overall			Two-year-olds			Three-year-olds			Older horses		
	W-R	%	£1	W-R	%	£1	W-R	%	£1	W-R	%	£1
Tom Marquand	47-367	13	-101.43	23-175	13	-48.57	20-151	13	-41.86	4-41	10	-11.00
Sean Levey	17-180	9	+7.49	7-67	10	-17.14	8-84	10	+40.13	2-29	7	-15.50
Rossa Ryan	15-139	11	-65.42	9-64	14	-15.15	3-41	7	-32.50	3-34	9	-17.77
S De Sousa	11-30	37	+17.49	5-17	29	+1.62	5-10	50	+15.37	1-3	33	+0.50
T H Hansen	7-40	18	+6.85	1-16	6	-9.00	5-23	22	+9.85	1-1	100	+6.00
Jim Crowley	7-43	16	-14.61	4-18	22	-3.56	2-17	12	-7.39	1-8	13	-3.67
Pat Dobbs	6-43	14	+2.88	2-20	10	-10.63	4-18	22	+18.50	0-5	-	-5.00
Ryan Moore	6-58	10	-31.93	4-29	14	-13.31	0-17	-	-17.00	2-12	17	-1.63
Hollie Doyle	6-83	7	-28.00	1-22	5	-1.00	0-39	-	-39.00	5-22	23	+12.00
Harry Bentley	4-16	25	+18.75	2-10	20	+9.25	2-4	50	+11.50	0-2	-	-2.00
Andrea Atzeni	4-17	24	-6.09	3-7	43	+1.41	1-4	25	-1.50	0-6	-	-6.00
Oisin Murphy	4-17	24	+0.75	4-13	31	+4.75	0-4	-	-4.00	0-0	-	+0.00

By jockey - 2017

	Overall			Two-year-olds			Three-year-olds			Older horses		
	W-R	%	£1	W-R	%	£1	W-R	%	£1	W-R	%	£1
Sean Levey	54-368	15	-23.19	26-174	15	-8.51	24-157	15	-2.18	4-37	11	-12.50
Tom Marquand	33-275	12	-18.55	18-130	14	+28.60	13-125	10	-32.77	2-20	10	-14.38
Hollie Doyle	20-124	16	+12.04	6-47	13	-12.29	11-64	17	+12.33	3-13	23	+12.00
Jim Crowley	12-46	26	+3.39	4-15	27	+4.67	6-24	25	-4.78	2-7	29	+3.50
Dane O'Neill	10-35	29	+53.43	7-21	33	+35.92	3-14	21	+17.50	0-0	-	+0.00
Ryan Moore	10-73	14	-30.81	4-38	11	-27.81	4-25	16	-9.00	2-10	20	+6.00
Rossa Ryan	9-61	15	+14.33	2-16	13	-5.00	4-36	11	+8.63	3-9	33	+10.70
Pat Dobbs	7-79	9	-42.80	1-14	7	-12.39	4-53	8	-33.42	2-12	17	+3.00
S De Sousa	6-17	35	+3.22	2-6	33	+2.30	4-10	40	+1.92	0-1	-	-1.00

By jockey - 2016

	Overall			Two-year-olds			Three-year-olds			Older horses		
	W-R	%	£1	W-R	%	£1	W-R	%	£1	W-R	%	£1
Sean Levey	44-371	12	-96.99	21-185	11	-44.76	22-154	14	-25.23	1-32	3	-27.00
Tom Marquand	26-209	12	+11.53	15-100	15	+27.28	10-95	11	-14.75	1-14	7	-1.00
Pat Dobbs	20-233	9	-91.95	14-109	13	-39.95	6-95	6	-23.00	0-29	-	-29.00
Kieran O'Neill	18-152	12	-34.22	6-62	10	-16.00	11-69	16	-1.72	1-21	5	-16.50
Hollie Doyle	10-60	17	+2.50	3-19	16	+3.00	7-35	20	+5.50	0-6	-	-6.00
Frankie Dettori	9-43	21	-2.67	6-24	25	+3.58	3-14	21	-1.25	0-5	-	-5.00
Timmy Murphy	7-22	32	+16.67	5-15	33	+6.83	2-7	29	+9.83	0-0	-	+0.00
Megan Nicholls	5-23	22	+39.50	1-3	33	+10.00	4-19	21	+30.50	0-1	-	-1.00
Gary Mahon	5-31	16	-15.19	3-12	25	-2.60	2-13	15	-6.59	0-6	-	-6.00

By course - 2015-2018

	Overall			Two-year-olds			Three-year-olds			Older horses		
	W-R	%	£1	W-R	%	£1	W-R	%	£1	W-R	%	£1
Ascot	20-254	8	-108.00	12-89	13	+5.00	6-104	6	-65.50	2-61	3	-47.50
Ayr	1-15	7	-7.00	0-9	-	-9.00	1-4	25	+4.00	0-2	-	-2.00
Bath	23-136	17	-26.24	11-63	17	-15.47	11-67	16	-8.77	1-6	17	-2.00
Beverley	3-10	30	+2.17	3-7	43	+5.17	0-3	-	-3.00	0-0	-	+0.00
Brighton	28-118	24	+45.81	12-50	24	+27.99	16-65	25	+20.82	0-3	-	-3.00
Catterick	0-7	-	-7.00	0-4	-	-4.00	0-3	-	-3.00	0-0	-	+0.00
Chelmsf'd (AW)	31-263	12	-92.36	15-118	13	-25.68	16-121	13	-42.67	0-24	-	-24.00
Chepstow	20-123	16	-36.94	12-47	26	-3.44	7-66	11	-35.50	1-10	10	+2.00
Chester	9-71	13	-18.50	6-31	19	+0.00	2-30	7	-12.50	1-10	10	-6.00
Doncaster	29-243	12	-19.77	13-117	11	-48.65	10-86	12	+27.63	6-40	15	+1.25
Epsom	7-71	10	-30.75	5-28	18	-3.00	1-34	3	-30.75	1-9	11	+3.00
Ffos Las	4-34	12	-20.50	3-24	13	-14.50	1-10	10	-6.00	0-0	-	+0.00
Goodwood	33-298	11	-94.97	18-131	14	-31.47	13-118	11	-25.75	2-49	4	-37.75
Hamilton	2-3	67	+8.75	0-1	-	-1.00	2-2	100	+9.75	0-0	-	+0.00
Haydock	20-177	11	-37.44	8-73	11	-11.52	8-72	11	-31.00	4-32	13	+5.08
Kempton (AW)	57-483	12	-138.08	28-227	12	-52.82	22-209	11	-108.85	7-47	15	+23.58
Leicester	25-174	14	-48.35	16-86	19	-7.90	8-72	11	-28.95	1-16	6	-11.50
Lingfield	20-126	16	-17.76	6-46	13	-6.27	11-69	16	-12.99	3-11	27	+1.50
Lingfield (AW)	52-320	16	+17.81	17-93	18	-6.15	28-178	16	+34.98	7-49	14	-11.02
Musselburgh	1-3	33	+18.00	0-1	-	-1.00	0-1	-	-1.00	1-1	100	+20.00
Newbury	43-414	10	-96.80	24-231	10	-79.40	16-132	12	+17.35	3-51	6	-34.75
N'castle (AW)	1-10	10	-8.67	1-4	25	-2.67	0-6	-	-6.00	0-0	-	+0.00
Newmarket	26-267	10	-3.13	8-123	7	-72.75	14-113	12	+71.13	4-31	13	-1.50
Newmarket (J)	40-308	13	-60.65	23-159	14	-32.08	14-125	11	-23.07	3-24	13	-5.50
Nottingham	20-139	14	-35.49	9-70	13	-19.44	10-56	18	-8.05	1-13	8	-8.00
Pontefract	4-15	27	-2.25	1-6	17	-3.38	3-6	50	+4.13	0-3	-	-3.00
Redcar	8-26	31	+35.58	3-13	23	+20.58	3-10	30	+8.00	2-3	67	+7.00
Ripon	6-18	33	+2.94	2-5	40	+4.50	4-11	36	+0.44	0-2	-	-2.00
Salisbury	45-307	15	-28.24	26-148	18	+18.54	16-137	12	-37.40	3-22	14	-9.38
Sandown	30-220	14	-11.22	14-89	16	+0.28	14-106	13	+1.00	2-25	8	-12.50
S'well (AW)	7-32	22	-0.75	2-13	15	-2.50	4-15	27	+0.75	1-4	25	+1.00
Thirsk	3-6	50	+3.41	2-4	50	+3.41	0-0	-	+0.00	1-2	50	+0.00
Wetherby	1-6	17	-2.50	0-0	-	+0.00	0-3	-	-3.00	1-3	33	+0.50
Windsor	49-304	16	-43.78	26-134	19	-38.06	19-136	14	+4.17	4-34	12	-9.89
Wolves (AW)	38-241	16	-53.86	17-114	15	-5.68	19-114	17	-51.69	2-13	15	+3.50
Yarmouth	1-15	7	-10.50	1-10	10	-5.50	0-4	-	-4.00	0-1	-	-1.00
York	9-117	8	-44.00	7-59	12	-5.00	1-39	3	-33.00	1-19	5	-6.00

Ten-year summary

	Wins	Runs	%	Win prize-money	Total prize-money	£1
2018	160	1300	12	£1,720,758.16	£2,966,797.13	-321.36
2017	189	1335	14	£1,820,484.01	£2,957,106.43	-89.36
2016	172	1357	13	£1,562,891.35	£2,809,779.05	-211.92
2015	195	1382	14	£2,050,242.78	£3,606,069.97	-348.38
2014	206	1404	15	£2,729,648.95	£4,749,469.60	-366.41
2013*	235	1412	17	£3,137,720.00	£4,532,464.69	-306.32
2012*	218	1367	16	£1,767,369.39	£2,821,469.49	-165.90
2011*	218	1408	15	£2,283,589.58	£3,726,396.80	-46.12
2010*	210	1341	16	£2,054,058.90	£3,218,574.92	-203.61
2009*	188	1371	14	£1,751,642.04	£2,814,384.49	-193.61

*Richard Hannon Sr training

BILLESDON BROOK: a second Classic winner for Richard Hannon at 66-1

William Haggas

By month - 2018

	Overall			Two-year-olds			Three-year-olds			Older horses		
	W-R	%	£1	W-R	%	£1	W-R	%	£1	W-R	%	£1
January	3-16	19	-9.60	0-0	-	+0.00	2-13	15	-8.00	1-3	33	-1.60
February	1-7	14	-3.50	0-0	-	+0.00	1-6	17	-2.50	0-1	-	-1.00
March	7-14	50	+7.43	0-0	-	+0.00	2-6	33	-2.33	5-8	63	+9.76
April	8-29	28	-8.93	1-3	33	+0.25	6-23	26	-8.68	1-3	33	-0.50
May	22-84	26	+4.02	2-9	22	-5.23	14-46	30	+8.88	6-29	21	+0.38
June	13-92	14	-49.40	2-11	18	-5.15	6-56	11	-40.00	5-25	20	-4.25
July	23-87	26	-1.51	2-16	13	-9.13	18-51	35	+11.62	3-20	15	-4.00
August	17-91	19	-31.80	3-23	13	-14.84	10-43	23	-11.96	4-25	16	-5.00
September	16-62	26	+32.95	6-30	20	+21.95	8-20	40	+14.50	2-12	17	-3.50
October	15-80	19	-29.42	10-43	23	-10.42	5-25	20	-7.00	0-12	-	-12.00
November	9-35	26	-7.46	5-20	25	-6.34	3-9	33	+2.00	1-6	17	-3.13
December	4-11	36	+8.00	2-6	33	+2.50	0-3	-	-3.00	2-2	100	+8.50

By month - 2017

	Overall			Two-year-olds			Three-year-olds			Older horses		
	W-R	%	£1	W-R	%	£1	W-R	%	£1	W-R	%	£1
January	6-10	60	+8.24	0-0	-	+0.00	6-10	60	+8.24	0-0	-	+0.00
February	2-3	67	+7.44	0-0	-	+0.00	1-1	100	+8.00	1-2	50	-0.56
March	4-7	57	+1.56	0-0	-	+0.00	3-5	60	+2.23	1-2	50	-0.67
April	10-32	31	+5.95	0-1	-	-1.00	5-21	24	+2.54	5-10	50	+4.41
May	18-70	26	+5.89	3-9	33	+3.80	9-42	21	-13.84	6-19	32	+15.93
June	18-85	21	-24.10	4-16	25	-4.49	11-53	21	-16.44	3-16	19	-3.17
July	29-92	32	+36.89	7-15	47	+2.59	16-55	29	+33.13	6-22	27	+1.17
August	17-86	20	+0.73	2-30	7	-8.50	13-41	32	+14.66	2-15	13	-5.43
September	18-80	23	-19.39	7-29	24	-5.04	8-34	24	-15.60	3-17	18	+1.25
October	19-72	26	+16.10	10-40	25	-6.50	6-20	30	+23.60	3-12	25	-1.00
November	12-35	34	+2.38	8-22	36	+1.06	2-8	25	-0.56	2-5	40	+1.88
December	3-10	30	+4.73	3-9	33	+5.73	0-1	-	-1.00	0-0	-	+0.00

By month - 2016

	Overall			Two-year-olds			Three-year-olds			Older horses		
	W-R	%	£1	W-R	%	£1	W-R	%	£1	W-R	%	£1
January	3-15	20	+0.20	0-0	-	+0.00	1-12	8	-10.80	2-3	67	+11.00
February	0-3	-	-3.00	0-0	-	+0.00	0-0	-	+0.00	0-3	-	-3.00
March	4-8	50	+8.25	0-0	-	+0.00	2-5	40	+0.50	2-3	67	+7.75
April	7-30	23	-10.36	0-0	-	+0.00	6-25	24	-10.36	1-5	20	+0.00
May	10-60	17	-15.97	0-4	-	-4.00	9-44	20	-11.97	1-12	8	+0.00
June	15-71	21	-15.72	2-11	18	-3.75	11-51	22	-10.72	2-9	22	-1.25
July	21-102	21	-25.32	6-25	24	-9.89	13-62	21	-21.93	2-15	13	+6.50
August	20-86	23	-30.63	6-28	21	-10.22	14-48	29	-10.41	0-10	-	-10.00
September	36-104	35	+42.88	12-39	31	+18.95	21-54	39	+18.43	3-11	27	+5.50
October	13-80	16	-25.40	8-47	17	-20.65	2-21	10	-10.50	3-12	25	+5.75
November	6-24	25	-0.33	4-19	21	-2.00	2-4	50	+2.67	0-1	-	-1.00
December	2-13	15	-7.89	2-10	20	-4.89	0-1	-	-1.00	0-2	-	-2.00

By race type - 2018

	Overall			Two-year-olds			Three-year-olds			Older horses		
	W-R	%	£1	W-R	%	£1	W-R	%	£1	W-R	%	£1
Handicap	50-231	22	-16.62	3-25	12	-10.20	27-122	22	-20.67	20-84	24	+14.25
Group	8-48	17	-19.92	1-8	13	-2.50	6-14	43	+6.08	1-26	4	-23.50
Maiden	21-87	24	+4.54	11-43	26	+17.22	10-43	23	-11.68	0-1	-	-1.00

By race type - 2017

	Overall			Two-year-olds			Three-year-olds			Older horses		
	W-R	%	£1	W-R	%	£1	W-R	%	£1	W-R	%	£1
Handicap	59-238	25	+26.72	5-15	33	+20.70	35-152	23	+0.10	19-71	27	+5.92
Group	2-57	4	-40.43	0-12	-	-12.00	0-19	-	-19.00	2-26	8	-9.43
Maiden	44-122	36	+30.19	7-29	24	-10.49	35-91	38	+39.14	2-2	100	+1.54

By race type - 2016

	Overall			Two-year-olds			Three-year-olds			Older horses		
	W-R	%	£1	W-R	%	£1	W-R	%	£1	W-R	%	£1
Handicap	54-241	22	-16.18	4-30	13	-15.59	41-158	26	-6.09	9-53	17	+5.50
Group	6-45	13	-16.93	2-12	17	-5.50	1-16	6	-14.43	3-17	18	+3.00
Maiden	63-244	26	-45.34	26-118	22	-19.52	37-126	29	-25.82	0-0	-	+0.00

By jockey - 2018

	Overall			Two-year-olds			Three-year-olds			Older horses		
	W-R	%	£1	W-R	%	£1	W-R	%	£1	W-R	%	£1
James Doyle	49-164	30	+13.19	9-43	21	-18.04	31-78	40	+38.36	9-43	21	-7.13
Jim Crowley	13-47	28	+1.46	3-21	14	-13.79	5-11	45	+4.00	5-15	33	+11.25
Daniel Tudhope	10-51	20	-19.70	0-5	-	-5.00	8-31	26	-8.07	2-15	13	-6.63
Tom Marquand	9-38	24	-3.02	2-13	15	-4.50	5-19	26	-3.02	2-6	33	+4.50
Oisin Murphy	7-18	39	+9.28	3-8	38	+2.88	2-6	33	+5.50	2-4	50	+0.90
Ryan Moore	6-20	30	-2.50	2-6	33	-2.76	1-5	20	-3.96	3-9	33	+4.23
Liam Jones	5-29	17	-14.01	1-7	14	-5.64	4-22	18	-8.38	0-0	-	+0.00
Ben Curtis	4-11	36	+3.17	1-4	25	-2.33	1-5	20	-2.00	2-2	100	+7.50
Joe Fanning	4-13	31	+2.00	1-2	50	+3.50	3-10	30	-0.50	0-1	-	-1.00
Tom Queally	3-5	60	+3.25	1-2	50	+1.50	1-1	100	+1.25	1-2	50	+0.50
Paul Hanagan	3-10	30	-4.76	1-3	33	-1.20	1-4	25	-2.09	1-3	33	-1.47
Martin Harley	3-16	19	+29.00	3-9	33	+36.00	0-7	-	-7.00	0-0	-	+0.00

By jockey - 2017

	Overall			Two-year-olds			Three-year-olds			Older horses		
	W-R	%	£1	W-R	%	£1	W-R	%	£1	W-R	%	£1
Pat Cosgrave	26-134	19	-36.76	8-36	22	-9.72	14-71	20	-17.78	4-27	15	-9.25
Ryan Moore	17-46	37	+16.70	4-13	31	-5.63	10-24	42	+16.08	3-9	33	+6.25
Jim Crowley	13-58	22	-8.16	5-18	28	-4.61	4-20	20	-8.40	4-20	20	+4.85
Georgia Cox	11-50	22	+6.28	2-13	15	-2.30	4-18	22	+2.75	5-19	26	+5.83
Daniel Tudhope	10-27	37	+0.36	6-16	38	+2.38	3-9	33	-1.58	1-2	50	-0.43
James Doyle	9-17	53	+9.45	3-7	43	+0.05	4-7	57	+6.78	2-3	67	+2.63
Martin Harley	8-25	32	+19.54	3-12	25	-3.55	4-11	36	+20.58	1-2	50	+2.50
Paul Hanagan	6-14	43	+8.78	0-0	-	+0.00	2-8	25	+0.00	4-6	67	+8.78
Joe Fanning	5-16	31	+3.38	1-5	20	-1.25	4-8	50	+7.63	0-3	-	-3.00

By jockey - 2016

	Overall			Two-year-olds			Three-year-olds			Older horses		
	W-R	%	£1	W-R	%	£1	W-R	%	£1	W-R	%	£1
Pat Cosgrave	57-218	26	+20.37	17-75	23	-0.07	30-107	28	+2.19	10-36	28	+18.25
Ben Curtis	13-32	41	+14.23	7-16	44	+2.78	5-13	38	+2.45	1-3	33	+9.00
Frankie Dettori	12-28	43	+7.72	5-8	63	+7.91	6-15	40	-1.69	1-5	20	+1.50
G Gibbons	7-30	23	-6.26	0-4	-	-4.00	7-25	28	-1.26	0-1	-	-1.00
Ryan Moore	7-32	22	-10.29	3-9	33	+1.13	4-17	24	-5.42	0-6	-	-6.00
Georgia Cox	7-37	19	-11.26	0-8	-	-8.00	6-22	27	-3.26	1-7	14	+0.00
Paul Hanagan	6-43	14	-30.00	1-14	7	-12.39	5-20	25	-8.61	0-9	-	-9.00
Jim Crowley	4-18	22	-5.63	0-6	-	-6.00	4-12	33	+0.38	0-0	-	+0.00
Dane O'Neill	3-17	18	+7.50	0-5	-	-5.00	1-8	13	-5.00	2-4	50	+17.50

By course - 2015-2018

	Overall			Two-year-olds			Three-year-olds			Older horses		
	W-R	%	£1	W-R	%	£1	W-R	%	£1	W-R	%	£1
Ascot	19-142	13	-26.56	3-21	14	+7.88	10-67	15	-6.26	6-54	11	-28.18
Ayr	2-5	40	+2.07	1-1	100	+4.50	1-2	50	-0.43	0-2	-	-2.00
Bath	6-28	21	-14.73	2-6	33	-1.22	3-19	16	-12.42	1-3	33	-1.09
Beverley	8-22	36	+3.19	3-5	60	+8.44	5-16	31	-4.25	0-1	-	-1.00
Brighton	5-19	26	-4.68	1-6	17	-4.64	4-12	33	+0.96	0-1	-	-1.00
Carlisle	4-15	27	-1.00	0-0	-	+0.00	4-15	27	-1.00	0-0	-	+0.00
Catterick	5-11	45	-2.57	3-7	43	-2.01	2-4	50	-0.56	0-0	-	+0.00
Chelmsf'd (AW)	40-150	27	-4.08	11-45	24	-11.76	20-81	25	-3.36	9-24	38	+11.03
Chepstow	8-24	33	-2.65	1-7	14	-5.47	7-14	50	+5.81	0-3	-	-3.00
Chester	8-29	28	-4.68	3-5	60	+5.80	4-18	22	-6.32	1-6	17	-4.17
Doncaster	17-91	19	-29.54	9-26	35	+9.44	6-48	13	-30.08	2-17	12	-8.90
Epsom	2-15	13	-10.13	1-3	33	-0.63	1-9	11	-6.50	0-3	-	-3.00
Ffos Las	2-5	40	-0.54	0-0	-	+0.00	1-3	33	-1.17	1-2	50	+0.63
Goodwood	21-98	21	-6.18	3-17	18	-11.43	14-49	29	+17.00	4-32	13	-11.75
Hamilton	3-9	33	-2.10	0-0	-	+0.00	3-9	33	-2.10	0-0	-	+0.00
Haydock	30-105	29	+0.86	4-20	20	-8.22	18-56	32	+3.26	8-29	28	+5.82
Kempton (AW)	27-135	20	-33.91	9-52	17	-26.57	13-65	20	-14.59	5-18	28	+7.25
Leicester	6-47	13	-29.26	3-17	18	-8.26	3-27	11	-18.00	0-3	-	-3.00
Lingfield	21-47	45	+34.70	10-16	63	+33.33	11-27	41	+5.37	0-4	-	-4.00
Lingfield (AW)	31-120	26	+1.53	10-36	28	+8.53	14-60	23	-7.63	7-24	29	+0.63
Musselburgh	7-22	32	+5.58	3-3	100	+2.96	3-16	19	+3.13	1-3	33	-0.50
Newbury	36-149	24	+15.25	10-63	16	-30.58	18-63	29	+19.33	8-23	35	+26.50
Newcastle	1-3	33	-0.75	0-0	-	+0.00	1-2	50	+0.25	0-1	-	-1.00
N'castle (AW)	19-49	39	+9.23	6-18	33	+3.42	10-24	42	+7.17	3-7	43	-1.35
Newmarket	15-145	10	-40.71	4-60	7	-13.46	8-63	13	-26.75	3-22	14	-0.50
Newmarket (J)	16-108	15	-26.61	3-30	10	-13.88	9-54	17	-14.49	4-24	17	+1.75
Nottingham	12-66	18	-17.21	3-24	13	-11.90	9-35	26	+1.69	0-7	-	-7.00
Pontefract	6-30	20	-14.86	2-10	20	-4.84	4-17	24	-7.02	0-3	-	-3.00
Redcar	12-31	39	+2.67	5-16	31	-1.05	7-15	47	+3.72	0-0	-	+0.00
Ripon	15-35	43	+10.82	2-9	22	-2.83	13-26	50	+13.65	0-0	-	+0.00
Salisbury	9-35	26	-5.82	2-16	13	-9.42	7-17	41	+5.59	0-2	-	-2.00
Sandown	14-56	25	-2.74	5-13	38	+3.68	6-28	21	-2.25	3-15	20	-4.17
S'well (AW)	3-7	43	+5.17	1-1	100	+0.67	1-4	25	+2.00	1-2	50	+2.50
Thirsk	10-35	29	-10.63	4-13	31	-2.08	5-21	24	-10.05	1-1	100	+1.50
Wetherby	2-8	25	+0.67	0-0	-	+0.00	1-6	17	-4.33	1-2	50	+5.00
Windsor	14-56	25	-18.21	3-19	16	-12.85	11-30	37	+1.64	0-7	-	-7.00
Wolves (AW)	33-105	31	-3.46	13-38	34	+8.22	14-52	27	-18.05	6-15	40	+6.38
Yarmouth	27-112	24	-10.38	12-53	23	-9.60	13-51	25	-0.28	2-8	25	-0.50
York	28-150	19	-20.95	10-39	26	-6.63	8-54	15	-21.00	10-57	18	+6.68

Ten-year summary

	Wins	Runs	%	Win prize-money	Total prize-money	£1
2018	138	608	23	£2,099,924.29	£2,945,711.80	-89.22
2017	156	582	27	£1,581,585.23	£2,689,295.73	+46.43
2016	137	596	23	£1,423,781.23	£2,127,308.68	-83.29
2015	113	533	21	£1,583,672.69	£2,364,888.31	-127.11
2014	113	520	22	£1,478,038.78	£2,281,869.22	+17.06
2013	107	503	21	£1,133,364.77	£1,896,067.18	-12.27
2012	83	448	19	£748,501.35	£1,257,840.26	-65.35
2011	76	423	18	£848,955.18	£1,228,089.25	-96.35
2010	59	361	16	£942,548.43	£1,181,417.91	-91.16
2009	69	346	20	£793,312.00	£1,320,567.05	-53.39

ADDEYBB: got William Haggas's year off to a flyer by winning the Lincoln

Andrew Balding

By month - 2018

	Overall			Two-year-olds			Three-year-olds			Older horses		
	W-R	%	£1	W-R	%	£1	W-R	%	£1	W-R	%	£1
January	7-31	23	-10.74	0-0	-	+0.00	5-12	42	+3.96	2-19	11	-14.70
February	6-24	25	-3.68	0-0	-	+0.00	5-12	42	-1.68	1-12	8	-2.00
March	4-19	21	-9.04	0-0	-	+0.00	4-9	44	+0.96	0-10	-	-10.00
April	6-56	11	-31.25	0-0	-	+0.00	5-44	11	-20.75	1-12	8	-10.50
May	4-94	4	-74.25	0-8	-	-8.00	4-49	8	-29.25	0-37	-	-37.00
June	20-106	19	+13.10	1-14	7	-11.00	12-57	21	+20.73	7-35	20	+3.38
July	15-92	16	-32.79	5-20	25	+0.42	5-42	12	-20.88	5-30	17	-12.33
August	27-120	23	+59.45	8-44	18	+34.63	11-44	25	+18.66	8-32	25	+6.16
September	13-66	20	-6.56	3-24	13	-12.08	4-22	18	-6.10	6-20	30	+11.63
October	7-69	10	+48.25	5-32	16	+75.75	1-23	4	-18.00	1-14	7	-9.50
November	3-29	10	+13.50	1-12	8	+22.00	1-11	9	-5.50	1-6	17	-3.00
December	1-19	5	-15.25	0-7	-	-7.00	1-11	9	-7.25	0-1	-	-1.00

By month - 2017

	Overall			Two-year-olds			Three-year-olds			Older horses		
	W-R	%	£1	W-R	%	£1	W-R	%	£1	W-R	%	£1
January	4-31	13	-1.88	0-0	-	+0.00	0-8	-	-8.00	4-23	17	+6.13
February	7-35	20	-0.97	0-0	-	+0.00	2-10	20	-5.84	5-25	20	+4.88
March	5-25	20	-11.37	0-0	-	+0.00	3-8	38	-2.62	2-17	12	-8.75
April	6-52	12	-19.63	0-0	-	+0.00	4-27	15	-9.63	2-25	8	-10.00
May	13-85	15	+15.88	0-5	-	-5.00	8-45	18	-3.13	5-35	14	+24.00
June	10-74	14	-13.25	0-10	-	-10.00	6-46	13	-12.63	4-18	22	+9.38
July	10-83	12	+22.35	4-16	25	+5.75	4-48	8	-26.40	2-19	11	+43.00
August	13-89	15	+3.81	3-22	14	+2.06	8-43	19	-12.25	2-24	8	+14.00
September	16-87	18	-6.18	1-28	4	-23.00	7-33	21	-7.88	8-26	31	+24.70
October	6-66	9	-19.50	1-24	4	-11.00	4-28	14	-3.50	1-14	7	-5.00
November	3-35	9	-21.67	1-17	6	-13.00	1-10	10	-5.00	1-8	13	-3.67
December	0-10	-	-10.00	0-4	-	-4.00	0-4	-	-4.00	0-2	-	-2.00

By month - 2016

	Overall			Two-year-olds			Three-year-olds			Older horses		
	W-R	%	£1	W-R	%	£1	W-R	%	£1	W-R	%	£1
January	4-35	11	-18.25	0-0	-	+0.00	1-6	17	-1.50	3-29	10	-16.75
February	1-20	5	-15.00	0-0	-	+0.00	0-7	-	-7.00	1-13	8	-8.00
March	7-33	21	-7.38	0-0	-	+0.00	3-11	27	-2.25	4-22	18	-5.13
April	5-50	10	-25.50	0-0	-	+0.00	2-28	7	-18.00	3-22	14	-7.50
May	9-104	9	-42.00	2-12	17	+14.00	5-60	8	-35.00	2-32	6	-21.00
June	21-109	19	+4.98	2-14	14	-4.25	14-57	25	+18.32	5-38	13	-9.09
July	21-119	18	+5.53	6-30	20	-0.10	15-66	23	+28.63	0-23	-	-23.00
August	13-79	16	-1.50	6-18	33	+8.25	7-38	18	+13.25	0-23	-	-23.00
September	14-85	16	-18.75	6-27	22	+1.75	7-42	17	-7.25	1-16	6	-13.25
October	8-65	12	+29.38	4-27	15	+12.38	2-20	10	-9.00	2-18	11	+26.00
November	4-24	17	-6.25	2-10	20	+0.75	1-6	17	-2.75	1-8	13	-4.25
December	0-8	-	-8.00	0-4	-	-4.00	0-3	-	-3.00	0-1	-	-1.00

By race type - 2018

	Overall			Two-year-olds			Three-year-olds			Older horses		
	W-R	%	£1	W-R	%	£1	W-R	%	£1	W-R	%	£1
Handicap	62-370	17	-42.35	1-19	5	-15.25	38-196	19	+8.45	23-155	15	-35.55
Group	6-56	11	-34.88	0-12	-	-12.00	1-9	11	-6.75	5-35	14	-16.13
Maiden	9-71	13	-5.38	4-34	12	+5.63	5-37	14	-11.00	0-0	-	+0.00

By race type - 2017

	Overall			Two-year-olds			Three-year-olds			Older horses		
	W-R	%	£1	W-R	%	£1	W-R	%	£1	W-R	%	£1
Handicap	50-376	13	-18.59	1-13	8	-8.00	24-184	13	-68.28	25-179	14	+57.68
Group	6-48	13	+14.13	0-7	-	-7.00	2-21	10	-15.88	4-20	20	+37.00
Maiden	21-125	17	-61.77	2-28	7	-21.94	16-84	19	-36.21	3-13	23	-3.63

By race type - 2016

	Overall			Two-year-olds			Three-year-olds			Older horses		
	W-R	%	£1	W-R	%	£1	W-R	%	£1	W-R	%	£1
Handicap	59-410	14	-82.87	0-13	-	-13.00	43-205	21	+29.85	16-192	8	-99.72
Group	4-28	14	+7.25	2-9	22	+1.75	0-5	-	-5.00	2-14	14	+10.50
Maiden	34-204	17	-21.58	20-81	25	+17.83	14-120	12	-36.40	0-3	-	-3.00

By jockey - 2018

	Overall			Two-year-olds			Three-year-olds			Older horses		
	W-R	%	£1	W-R	%	£1	W-R	%	£1	W-R	%	£1
Oisin Murphy	31-181	17	-33.50	5-39	13	+12.50	17-77	22	-11.51	9-65	14	-34.49
David Probert	22-157	14	+17.46	8-58	14	+51.67	9-69	13	-25.00	5-30	17	-9.21
Jason Watson	20-84	24	-12.94	1-10	10	-6.75	12-47	26	-7.89	7-27	26	+1.70
Rob Hornby	10-70	14	+7.85	2-18	11	+17.50	6-34	18	-4.15	2-18	11	-5.50
Joshua Bryan	8-52	15	-9.00	2-12	17	-6.25	4-23	17	+0.75	2-17	12	-3.50
William Cox	5-42	12	+1.45	1-3	33	+31.00	3-14	21	-8.30	1-25	4	-21.25
Graham Lee	3-10	30	+2.63	1-3	33	-0.38	2-3	67	+7.00	0-4	-	-4.00
Martin Dwyer	3-33	9	-18.33	1-5	20	-3.33	1-24	4	-21.00	1-4	25	+6.00
Franny Norton	2-6	33	+2.38	0-1	-	-1.00	1-2	50	+3.50	1-3	33	-0.13
James Doyle	2-6	33	+5.00	1-2	50	+6.00	0-1	-	-1.00	1-3	33	+0.00
Andrasch Starke	1-1	100	+9.00	0-0	-	+0.00	0-0	-	+0.00	1-1	100	+9.00
Jason Hart	1-1	100	+2.75	1-1	100	+2.75	0-0	-	+0.00	0-0	-	+0.00

By jockey - 2017

	Overall			Two-year-olds			Three-year-olds			Older horses		
	W-R	%	£1	W-R	%	£1	W-R	%	£1	W-R	%	£1
David Probert	30-213	14	-54.91	5-57	9	-33.94	15-86	17	-16.48	10-70	14	-4.50
Oisin Murphy	27-145	19	+8.59	3-25	12	+7.50	18-71	25	+0.24	6-49	12	+0.85
Joshua Bryan	8-41	20	-2.63	0-3	-	-3.00	3-15	20	+0.00	5-23	22	+0.38
Rob Hornby	8-75	11	-6.50	0-21	-	-21.00	5-38	13	-17.50	3-16	19	+32.00
William Cox	5-31	16	+0.58	1-4	25	-1.75	0-7	-	-7.00	4-20	20	+9.33
P J McDonald	3-8	38	+21.50	0-0	-	+0.00	0-3	-	-3.00	3-5	60	+24.50
Liam Keniry	3-40	8	-22.88	0-5	-	-5.00	3-23	13	-5.88	0-12	-	-12.00
Jim Crowley	2-5	40	+24.00	0-1	-	-1.00	1-2	50	+6.00	1-2	50	+19.00
Jimmy Quinn	2-23	9	-5.00	1-3	33	+7.00	0-13	-	-13.00	1-7	14	+1.00

By jockey - 2016

	Overall			Two-year-olds			Three-year-olds			Older horses		
	W-R	%	£1	W-R	%	£1	W-R	%	£1	W-R	%	£1
Oisin Murphy	31-201	15	-40.33	12-49	24	+27.08	12-86	14	-36.65	7-66	11	-30.75
David Probert	28-191	15	-57.45	7-38	18	+2.45	18-102	18	-25.90	3-51	6	-34.00
Rob Hornby	17-74	23	+16.75	6-11	55	+28.25	9-37	24	+5.50	2-26	8	-17.00
E Greatrex	9-57	16	+27.00	0-6	-	-6.00	8-32	25	+43.00	1-19	5	-10.00
Liam Keniry	7-51	14	+11.41	1-15	7	-10.50	3-22	14	+7.25	3-14	21	+14.66
Jimmy Quinn	5-14	36	+25.75	0-0	-	+0.00	5-12	42	+27.75	0-2	-	-2.00
Jim Crowley	4-15	27	+5.38	1-1	100	+7.00	1-3	33	+1.50	2-11	18	-3.13
Graham Lee	2-3	67	+20.75	0-0	-	+0.00	0-0	-	+0.00	2-3	67	+20.75
Luke Morris	1-1	100	+1.00	0-0	-	+0.00	1-1	100	+1.00	0-0	-	+0.00

By course - 2015-2018

	Overall			Two-year-olds			Three-year-olds			Older horses		
	W-R	%	£1	W-R	%	£1	W-R	%	£1	W-R	%	£1
Ascot	10-135	7	-84.00	0-13	-	-13.00	6-53	11	-27.75	4-69	6	-43.25
Ayr	3-16	19	+0.00	2-3	67	+7.50	1-3	33	+2.50	0-10	-	-10.00
Bath	10-71	14	-8.59	2-12	17	+11.25	4-41	10	-15.50	4-18	22	-4.34
Beverley	2-8	25	-2.13	0-1	-	-1.00	2-6	33	-0.13	0-1	-	-1.00
Brighton	9-49	18	-13.99	2-11	18	-5.44	3-23	13	-12.47	4-15	27	+3.92
Carlisle	4-10	40	+2.75	0-1	-	-1.00	4-8	50	+4.75	0-1	-	-1.00
Catterick	0-2	-	-2.00	0-0	-	+0.00	0-2	-	-2.00	0-0	-	+0.00
Chelmsf'd (AW)	25-169	15	-72.19	0-20	-	-20.00	17-76	22	-12.30	8-73	11	-39.89
Chepstow	17-92	18	-7.70	2-16	13	-7.30	7-56	13	-9.88	8-20	40	+9.48
Chester	33-150	22	+53.10	6-24	25	+7.67	15-68	22	+7.50	12-58	21	+37.93
Doncaster	9-65	14	+18.25	3-18	17	+13.75	3-20	15	+22.50	3-27	11	-18.00
Epsom	11-77	14	+19.21	1-9	11	+20.00	4-33	12	-15.63	6-35	17	+14.83
Ffos Las	15-51	29	+32.52	3-13	23	+1.67	9-28	32	+28.85	3-10	30	+2.00
Goodwood	15-139	11	-54.76	1-32	3	-23.00	11-52	21	-5.14	3-55	5	-26.63
Hamilton	3-9	33	+0.63	2-3	67	+2.13	1-5	20	-0.50	0-1	-	-1.00
Haydock	11-81	14	-31.55	4-9	44	+4.20	2-42	5	-33.50	5-30	17	-2.25
Kempton (AW)	28-255	11	-75.62	6-55	11	+9.75	14-116	12	-52.17	8-84	10	-33.20
Leicester	6-57	11	-27.13	0-6	-	-6.00	6-34	18	-4.13	0-17	-	-17.00
Lingfield	11-45	24	+5.50	1-6	17	+0.00	6-22	27	-4.50	4-17	24	+10.00
Lingfield (AW)	30-203	15	-56.56	2-19	11	-10.20	15-89	17	-34.61	13-95	14	-11.75
Musselburgh	0-3	-	-3.00	0-0	-	+0.00	0-2	-	+0.00	0-1	-	-1.00
Newbury	16-151	11	+3.42	3-50	6	+16.50	9-75	12	-34.58	4-26	15	+21.50
N'castle (AW)	3-24	13	-7.38	1-4	25	+0.00	0-9	-	-9.00	2-11	18	+1.63
Newmarket	9-127	7	-55.03	2-41	5	+0.50	5-42	12	-17.38	2-44	5	-38.15
Newmarket (J)	15-91	16	+12.29	3-23	13	+3.25	11-38	29	+31.04	1-30	3	-22.00
Nottingham	8-44	18	-2.81	4-18	22	+4.13	1-16	6	-14.27	3-10	30	+7.33
Pontefract	2-17	12	-6.25	2-5	40	+5.75	0-7	-	-7.00	0-5	-	-5.00
Redcar	1-15	7	-12.50	0-7	-	-7.00	1-7	14	-4.50	0-1	-	-1.00
Ripon	1-4	25	-1.50	0-0	-	+0.00	1-2	50	+0.50	0-2	-	-2.00
Salisbury	25-144	11	-8.71	9-44	20	+27.20	11-70	16	-24.60	5-30	17	-11.32
Sandown	14-132	11	-8.73	3-33	9	-10.75	6-65	9	-24.68	5-34	15	+26.70
S'well (AW)	18-78	23	-16.92	0-5	-	-5.00	11-38	29	-2.24	7-35	20	-9.68
Thirsk	1-9	11	+8.00	0-0	-	+0.00	1-9	11	+8.00	0-0	-	+0.00
Wetherby	1-9	11	-7.50	0-0	-	+0.00	1-5	20	-3.50	0-4	-	-4.00
Windsor	13-122	11	-55.90	5-23	22	-5.00	7-63	11	-17.78	1-36	3	-33.13
Wolves (AW)	16-115	14	-33.30	1-19	5	+7.00	11-52	21	-21.05	4-44	9	-19.25
Yarmouth	3-21	14	-10.25	1-2	50	+3.00	2-14	14	-8.25	0-5	-	-5.00
York	10-93	11	+23.00	1-19	5	-17.00	2-24	8	-3.00	7-50	14	+43.00

Ten-year summary

	Wins	Runs	%	Win prize-money	Total prize-money	£1
2018	113	725	16	£1,300,724.27	£2,382,134.93	-49.26
2017	93	672	14	£1,702,065.55	£2,565,904.52	-62.39
2016	107	731	15	£1,038,999.35	£1,672,623.97	-102.74
2015	95	755	13	£837,267.45	£1,548,715.65	-272.93
2014	119	659	18	£1,335,198.23	£2,035,497.26	-35.60
2013	99	713	14	£873,940.78	£1,356,742.43	-13.36
2012	93	712	13	£779,847.73	£1,365,377.42	-155.54
2011	70	543	13	£620,393.39	£971,676.62	-59.07
2010	78	511	15	£707,996.22	£1,116,809.38	-11.81
2009	68	498	14	£460,056.19	£783,172.54	-38.44

BEAT THE BANK: a dual Group 2 winner for Andrew Balding last season

Tim Easterby

By month - 2018

	Overall			Two-year-olds			Three-year-olds			Older horses		
	W-R	%	£1	W-R	%	£1	W-R	%	£1	W-R	%	£1
January	2-6	33	+11.00	0-0	-	+0.00	0-0	-	+0.00	2-6	33	+11.00
February	0-2	-	-2.00	0-0	-	+0.00	0-0	-	+0.00	0-2	-	-2.00
March	0-2	-	-2.00	0-0	-	+0.00	0-2	-	-2.00	0-0	-	+0.00
April	2-71	3	-40.50	1-5	20	+21.00	1-29	3	-24.50	0-37	-	-37.00
May	17-130	13	-34.42	2-12	17	-4.75	7-48	15	-8.17	8-70	11	-21.50
June	27-153	18	+48.85	1-28	4	-23.00	5-39	13	-4.90	21-86	24	+76.75
July	22-172	13	+24.83	0-27	-	-27.00	10-67	15	+37.67	12-78	15	+14.16
August	17-161	11	-55.82	3-38	8	-27.00	8-51	16	+4.10	6-72	8	-32.92
September	9-116	8	-54.00	1-31	3	-27.60	3-25	12	-2.50	5-60	8	-23.90
October	13-133	10	-4.50	3-36	8	-8.00	4-24	17	+1.50	6-73	8	+2.00
November	3-33	9	-8.92	1-8	13	+9.00	0-3	-	-3.00	2-22	9	-14.92
December	0-2	-	-2.00	0-0	-	+0.00	0-0	-	+0.00	0-2	-	-2.00

By month - 2017

	Overall			Two-year-olds			Three-year-olds			Older horses		
	W-R	%	£1	W-R	%	£1	W-R	%	£1	W-R	%	£1
January	0-5	-	-5.00	0-0	-	+0.00	0-2	-	-2.00	0-3	-	-3.00
February	0-2	-	-2.00	0-0	-	+0.00	0-1	-	-1.00	0-1	-	-1.00
March	1-8	13	-4.75	0-0	-	+0.00	0-1	-	-1.00	1-7	14	-3.75
April	2-66	3	-54.00	0-6	-	-6.00	1-28	4	-22.00	1-32	3	-26.00
May	6-111	5	-74.50	0-13	-	-13.00	4-47	9	-20.50	2-51	4	-41.00
June	12-131	9	-18.05	1-18	6	-8.00	7-42	17	+14.45	4-71	6	-24.50
July	24-138	17	+88.00	3-26	12	+47.00	14-53	26	+21.00	7-59	12	+20.00
August	16-161	10	-35.50	2-45	4	-30.75	5-49	10	-26.75	9-67	13	+22.00
September	13-138	9	-46.00	2-46	4	-33.50	5-33	15	+0.00	6-59	10	-12.50
October	6-98	6	-60.25	2-28	7	-21.25	2-25	8	-12.50	2-45	4	-26.50
November	1-28	4	-17.00	0-10	-	-10.00	0-7	-	-7.00	1-11	9	+0.00
December	2-5	40	+2.50	0-0	-	+0.00	2-3	67	+4.50	0-2	-	-2.00

By month - 2016

	Overall			Two-year-olds			Three-year-olds			Older horses		
	W-R	%	£1	W-R	%	£1	W-R	%	£1	W-R	%	£1
January	0-3	-	-3.00	0-0	-	+0.00	0-0	-	+0.00	0-3	-	-3.00
February	0-3	-	-3.00	0-0	-	+0.00	0-2	-	-2.00	0-1	-	-1.00
March	0-11	-	-11.00	0-0	-	+0.00	0-4	-	-4.00	0-7	-	-7.00
April	4-70	6	-5.00	0-5	-	-5.00	2-23	9	+13.00	2-42	5	-13.00
May	13-110	12	-4.00	1-18	6	-9.00	4-34	12	+1.00	8-58	14	+4.00
June	12-113	11	-18.63	1-26	4	-19.50	5-31	16	+12.50	6-56	11	-11.63
July	14-149	9	-58.63	1-37	3	-32.00	6-46	13	-6.00	7-66	11	-20.63
August	15-138	11	-16.93	2-39	5	-18.25	7-45	16	+0.82	6-54	11	+0.50
September	14-116	12	-26.40	1-37	3	-34.90	5-32	16	+2.50	8-47	17	+6.00
October	2-67	3	-58.50	1-19	5	-15.50	0-14	-	-14.00	1-34	3	-29.00
November	2-23	9	-4.00	1-10	10	+0.00	0-2	-	-2.00	1-11	9	-2.00
December	0-4	-	-4.00	0-2	-	-2.00	0-0	-	+0.00	0-2	-	-2.00

By race type - 2018

	Overall			Two-year-olds			Three-year-olds			Older horses		
	W-R	%	£1	W-R	%	£1	W-R	%	£1	W-R	%	£1
Handicap	96-787	12	-41.96	2-44	5	-25.00	33-245	13	+9.87	61-498	12	-26.83
Group	1-8	13	+0.00	0-3	-	-3.00	1-4	25	+4.00	0-1	-	-1.00
Maiden	4-35	11	+4.50	1-14	7	+12.00	3-18	17	-4.50	0-3	-	-3.00

By race type - 2017

	Overall			Two-year-olds			Three-year-olds			Older horses		
	W-R	%	£1	W-R	%	£1	W-R	%	£1	W-R	%	£1
Handicap	73-670	11	-121.55	3-49	6	-35.50	38-232	16	-0.80	32-389	8	-85.25
Group	1-10	10	+1.00	1-3	33	+8.00	0-0	-	+0.00	0-7	-	-7.00
Maiden	2-78	3	-71.00	0-14	-	-14.00	2-58	3	-51.00	0-6	-	-6.00

By race type - 2016

	Overall			Two-year-olds			Three-year-olds			Older horses		
	W-R	%	£1	W-R	%	£1	W-R	%	£1	W-R	%	£1
Handicap	68-610	11	-99.18	2-50	4	-36.25	27-190	14	+4.82	39-370	11	-67.75
Group	0-3	-	-3.00	0-0	-	+0.00	0-0	-	+0.00	0-3	-	-3.00
Maiden	7-130	5	-47.00	4-79	5	-47.00	3-46	7	+5.00	0-5	-	-5.00

By jockey - 2018

	Overall			Two-year-olds			Three-year-olds			Older horses		
	W-R	%	£1	W-R	%	£1	W-R	%	£1	W-R	%	£1
David Allan	46-362	13	-61.26	8-92	9	-20.35	14-99	14	-16.67	24-171	14	-24.24
R Richardson	17-221	8	-58.92	1-30	3	-24.00	5-63	8	-16.00	11-128	9	-18.92
Miss E Easterby	7-28	25	+2.42	0-0	-	+0.00	3-6	50	+3.92	4-22	18	-1.50
James Sullivan	7-48	15	+15.25	2-14	14	+2.75	3-21	14	-1.00	2-13	15	+13.50
Jason Hart	6-37	16	-10.50	0-3	-	-3.00	2-17	12	-8.00	4-17	24	+0.50
Duran Fentiman	6-100	6	-20.00	0-30	-	-30.00	2-33	6	+5.50	4-37	11	+4.50
R Dodsworth	4-30	13	+25.50	0-2	-	-2.00	2-12	17	+31.00	2-16	13	-3.50
Jamie Gormley	3-12	25	+6.00	0-0	-	+0.00	1-2	50	+6.00	2-10	20	+0.00
Nathan Evans	3-14	21	+18.00	0-4	-	-4.00	1-1	100	+4.00	2-9	22	+18.00
Rob Hornby	2-8	25	+20.00	0-0	-	+0.00	1-1	100	+8.00	1-7	14	+12.00
Jack Garritty	2-13	15	-0.13	0-1	-	-1.00	1-3	33	-0.13	1-9	11	+1.00
Tony Hamilton	2-13	15	-0.50	0-0	-	+0.00	1-5	20	+2.00	1-8	13	-2.50

By jockey - 2017

	Overall			Two-year-olds			Three-year-olds			Older horses		
	W-R	%	£1	W-R	%	£1	W-R	%	£1	W-R	%	£1
David Allan	39-315	12	+34.58	6-79	8	+13.50	16-109	15	-12.43	17-127	13	+33.50
R Richardson	14-217	6	-93.25	0-40	-	-40.00	6-53	11	-18.00	8-124	6	-35.25
James Sullivan	7-45	16	-1.25	1-12	8	-8.75	6-26	23	+14.50	0-7	-	-7.00
Andrew Mullen	3-24	13	-7.13	1-4	25	+6.00	2-13	15	-6.13	0-7	-	-7.00
Duran Fentiman	3-88	3	-65.50	0-29	-	-29.00	2-30	7	-20.50	1-29	3	-16.00
Sammy Jo Bell	2-3	67	+11.50	0-0	-	+0.00	1-2	50	+8.00	1-1	100	+3.50
P J McDonald	2-4	50	+2.50	0-1	-	-1.00	1-1	100	+2.00	1-2	50	+1.50
Cam Hardie	2-27	7	-13.25	0-5	-	-5.00	2-11	18	+2.75	0-11	-	-11.00
Jason Hart	2-40	5	-32.75	1-7	14	-4.25	1-13	8	-8.50	0-20	-	-20.00

By jockey - 2016

	Overall			Two-year-olds			Three-year-olds			Older horses		
	W-R	%	£1	W-R	%	£1	W-R	%	£1	W-R	%	£1
David Allan	27-294	9	-116.28	6-86	7	-49.90	11-96	11	-30.88	10-112	9	-35.50
R Richardson	21-178	12	-14.80	1-20	5	-3.00	5-33	15	+7.95	15-125	12	-19.75
Miss E Easterby	4-19	21	+11.00	0-0	-	+0.00	0-0	-	+0.00	4-19	21	+11.00
James Sullivan	4-34	12	+6.50	1-12	8	-8.25	2-13	15	+13.75	1-9	11	+1.00
Jason Hart	4-63	6	-27.50	0-9	-	-9.00	3-23	13	+6.50	1-31	3	-25.00
Duran Fentiman	4-74	5	-35.00	0-36	-	-36.00	3-22	14	+9.50	1-16	6	-8.50
Rob Hornby	2-5	40	+13.00	0-0	-	+0.00	2-3	67	+15.00	0-2	-	-2.00
Jack Garritty	2-14	14	-4.50	0-1	-	-1.00	0-2	-	-2.00	2-11	18	-1.50
Cam Hardie	2-23	9	+3.50	0-4	-	-4.00	1-6	17	-0.50	1-13	8	+8.00

By course - 2015-2018

	Overall			Two-year-olds			Three-year-olds			Older horses		
	W-R	%	£1	W-R	%	£1	W-R	%	£1	W-R	%	£1
Ascot	3-22	14	+15.50	0-1	-	-1.00	2-6	33	+5.50	1-15	7	+11.00
Ayr	11-114	10	-19.09	0-12	-	-12.00	5-27	19	+30.00	6-75	8	-37.09
Beverley	31-263	12	-97.08	3-70	4	-54.50	13-103	13	-25.21	15-90	17	-17.38
Carlisle	21-188	11	-58.03	2-47	4	-40.90	7-58	12	-18.50	12-83	14	+1.38
Catterick	22-193	11	-44.15	3-40	8	-13.25	8-68	12	-21.27	11-85	13	-9.63
Chelmsf'd (AW)	1-25	4	-22.00	0-2	-	-2.00	1-5	20	-2.00	0-18	-	-18.00
Chester	15-103	15	+2.25	1-14	7	-9.00	3-20	15	+0.75	11-69	16	+10.50
Doncaster	8-188	4	-103.00	2-42	5	-25.00	2-37	5	-15.00	4-109	4	-63.00
Epsom	1-7	14	-2.50	0-0	-	+0.00	0-0	-	+0.00	1-7	14	-2.50
Goodwood	1-16	6	-11.00	0-2	-	-2.00	0-0	-	+0.00	1-14	7	-9.00
Hamilton	18-77	23	+27.15	3-9	33	+2.15	7-28	25	+12.25	8-40	20	+12.75
Haydock	17-178	10	-14.00	3-38	8	+22.75	5-51	10	-18.25	9-89	10	-18.50
Kempton (AW)	0-3	-	-3.00	0-1	-	-1.00	0-0	-	+0.00	0-2	-	-2.00
Leicester	4-36	11	-7.50	1-9	11	-3.00	2-12	17	+1.00	1-15	7	-5.50
Lingfield (AW)	0-2	-	-2.00	0-0	-	+0.00	0-0	-	+0.00	0-2	-	-2.00
Musselburgh	15-120	13	-34.30	4-19	21	-1.50	7-40	18	-2.55	4-61	7	-30.25
Newbury	0-11	-	-11.00	0-6	-	-6.00	0-0	-	+0.00	0-5	-	-5.00
Newcastle	2-27	7	-3.13	0-6	-	-6.00	1-9	11	-6.13	1-12	8	+9.00
N'castle (AW)	6-150	4	-107.00	0-38	-	-38.00	2-45	4	-35.50	4-67	6	-33.50
Newmarket	0-14	-	-14.00	0-3	-	-3.00	0-3	-	-3.00	0-8	-	-8.00
Newmarket (J)	3-16	19	-0.25	0-2	-	-2.00	3-11	27	+4.75	0-3	-	-3.00
Nottingham	6-60	10	-21.17	1-15	7	-8.50	2-11	18	+10.00	3-34	9	-22.67
Pontefract	20-162	12	-30.67	1-38	3	-31.00	8-47	17	+0.33	11-77	14	+0.00
Redcar	26-324	8	-121.19	2-92	2	-76.00	15-124	12	-8.44	9-108	8	-36.75
Ripon	39-341	11	-62.16	7-82	9	-37.92	14-106	13	-6.18	18-153	12	-18.07
Salisbury	1-1	100	+5.50	0-0	-	+0.00	0-0	-	+0.00	1-1	100	+5.50
Sandown	1-3	33	+1.50	1-1	100	+3.50	0-1	-	-1.00	0-1	-	-1.00
S'well (AW)	3-31	10	+5.50	1-2	50	+15.00	0-4	-	-4.00	2-25	8	-5.50
Thirsk	24-285	8	-29.38	5-83	6	-3.00	7-96	7	-40.38	12-106	11	+14.00
Wetherby	5-32	16	+11.80	0-5	-	-5.00	3-16	19	+8.80	2-11	18	+8.00
Windsor	0-1	-	-1.00	0-0	-	+0.00	0-0	-	+0.00	0-1	-	-1.00
Wolves (AW)	13-90	14	+25.63	0-12	-	-12.00	5-33	15	-7.63	8-45	18	+45.25
Yarmouth	0-1	-	-1.00	0-0	-	+0.00	0-0	-	+0.00	0-1	-	-1.00
York	24-286	8	-36.50	3-51	6	-14.00	6-48	13	-13.00	15-187	8	-9.50

Ten-year summary

	Wins	Runs	%	Win prize-money	Total prize-money	£1
2018	112	981	11	£900,076.36	£1,426,706.09	-119.47
2017	83	891	9	£776,394.66	£1,192,158.24	-226.55
2016	76	807	9	£472,565.89	£781,938.87	-213.08
2015	70	691	10	£354,477.64	£791,794.20	-202.16
2014	53	769	7	£346,857.09	£740,473.45	-293.98
2013	68	868	8	£470,015.75	£786,997.71	-381.88
2012	88	972	9	£687,967.28	£1,042,964.97	-344.13
2011	90	902	10	£481,298.69	£882,568.01	-81.31
2010	98	846	12	£551,995.88	£902,812.12	-200.59
2009	54	628	9	£423,561.62	£691,718.70	-229.88

EEH BAH GUM: Tim Easterby's most prolific horse in 2018, winning five times

David O'Meara

By month - 2018

	Overall			Two-year-olds			Three-year-olds			Older horses		
	W-R	%	£1	W-R	%	£1	W-R	%	£1	W-R	%	£1
January	0-34	-	-34.00	0-0	-	+0.00	0-1	-	-1.00	0-33	-	-33.00
February	0-23	-	-23.00	0-0	-	+0.00	0-2	-	-2.00	0-21	-	-21.00
March	1-31	3	-27.00	1-2	50	+2.00	0-7	-	-7.00	0-22	-	-22.00
April	9-56	16	+7.28	0-5	-	-5.00	3-16	19	+2.25	6-35	17	+10.03
May	14-130	11	-52.42	1-10	10	-2.00	3-34	9	-20.00	10-86	12	-30.42
June	16-158	10	-57.79	1-12	8	+5.00	4-39	10	-16.13	11-107	10	-46.67
July	29-146	20	+15.13	4-18	22	+10.88	6-37	16	-10.42	19-91	21	+14.67
August	15-126	12	-47.08	3-21	14	-9.50	5-34	15	+4.38	7-71	10	-41.96
September	9-87	10	+6.38	1-12	8	-9.63	2-22	9	-9.00	6-53	11	+25.00
October	7-102	7	-16.50	2-20	10	+0.00	4-24	17	+30.50	1-58	2	-47.00
November	5-71	7	-23.02	2-18	11	-3.47	0-8	-	-8.00	3-45	7	-11.56
December	1-51	2	-36.00	0-12	-	-12.00	1-6	17	+9.00	0-33	-	-33.00

By month - 2017

	Overall			Two-year-olds			Three-year-olds			Older horses		
	W-R	%	£1	W-R	%	£1	W-R	%	£1	W-R	%	£1
January	4-21	19	+9.25	0-0	-	+0.00	0-3	-	-3.00	4-18	22	+12.25
February	1-25	4	-20.50	0-0	-	+0.00	1-7	14	-2.50	0-18	-	-18.00
March	2-18	11	+10.10	0-0	-	+0.00	1-8	13	-5.90	1-10	10	+16.00
April	6-65	9	-7.63	0-1	-	-1.00	2-21	10	-12.13	4-43	9	+5.50
May	15-137	11	+23.91	1-10	10	-5.50	8-48	17	+62.41	6-79	8	-33.00
June	18-147	12	-5.24	4-19	21	+8.93	9-46	20	+10.58	5-82	6	-24.75
July	9-146	6	-77.48	1-16	6	-14.33	4-46	9	-29.15	4-84	5	-34.00
August	20-165	12	-61.05	1-21	5	-19.43	10-49	20	+5.88	9-95	9	-47.50
September	11-116	9	-40.13	2-21	10	-4.00	5-36	14	+6.75	4-59	7	-42.88
October	9-106	8	-46.88	1-13	8	+0.00	3-33	9	-17.00	5-60	8	-29.88
November	8-71	11	-27.50	1-7	14	-4.00	4-16	25	+8.00	3-48	6	-31.50
December	5-52	10	+0.00	0-9	-	-9.00	1-11	9	-6.00	4-32	13	+15.00

By month - 2016

	Overall			Two-year-olds			Three-year-olds			Older horses		
	W-R	%	£1	W-R	%	£1	W-R	%	£1	W-R	%	£1
January	2-17	12	-2.00	0-0	-	+0.00	0-3	-	-3.00	2-14	14	+1.00
February	0-10	-	-10.00	0-0	-	+0.00	0-2	-	-2.00	0-8	-	-8.00
March	1-10	10	-7.63	0-0	-	+0.00	0-2	-	-2.00	1-8	13	-5.63
April	7-77	9	-24.13	2-3	67	+4.88	0-13	-	-13.00	5-61	8	-16.00
May	15-125	12	-20.42	2-9	22	-2.13	3-20	15	+6.13	10-96	10	-24.42
June	12-151	8	-68.50	3-21	14	+9.75	3-28	11	-15.00	6-102	6	-63.25
July	14-141	10	-65.71	3-22	14	-10.46	2-23	9	-11.00	9-96	9	-44.25
August	14-125	11	-33.17	2-15	13	-3.50	2-26	8	-12.50	10-84	12	-17.17
September	8-125	6	-76.38	0-19	-	-19.00	3-22	14	-4.63	5-84	6	-52.75
October	16-114	14	-22.18	0-13	-	-13.00	5-23	22	+9.00	11-78	14	-18.18
November	7-53	13	-7.02	0-5	-	-5.00	2-16	13	+1.00	5-32	16	-3.02
December	7-27	26	+0.50	0-3	-	-3.00	2-9	22	+0.00	5-15	33	+3.50

By race type - 2018

	Overall			Two-year-olds			Three-year-olds			Older horses		
	W-R	%	£1	W-R	%	£1	W-R	%	£1	W-R	%	£1
Handicap	74-768	10	-212.33	2-32	6	-9.00	21-177	12	-11.54	51-559	9	-191.79
Group	1-25	4	-22.00	0-1	-	-1.00	0-1	-	-1.00	1-23	4	-20.00
Maiden	1-28	4	-26.00	0-15	-	-15.00	1-13	8	-11.00	0-0	-	+0.00

By race type - 2017

	Overall			Two-year-olds			Three-year-olds			Older horses		
	W-R	%	£1	W-R	%	£1	W-R	%	£1	W-R	%	£1
Handicap	78-795	10	-197.17	1-28	4	-17.00	33-225	15	-1.17	44-542	8	-179.00
Group	0-26	-	-26.00	0-2	-	-2.00	0-1	-	-1.00	0-23	-	-23.00
Maiden	13-97	13	+0.88	1-10	10	-4.00	12-84	14	+7.88	0-3	-	-3.00

By race type - 2016

	Overall			Two-year-olds			Three-year-olds			Older horses		
	W-R	%	£1	W-R	%	£1	W-R	%	£1	W-R	%	£1
Handicap	74-749	10	-230.79	2-25	8	-10.00	14-139	10	-26.50	58-585	10	-194.29
Group	0-37	-	-37.00	0-2	-	-2.00	0-0	-	+0.00	0-35	-	-35.00
Maiden	11-88	13	-47.33	2-39	5	-31.83	6-41	15	-20.50	3-8	38	+5.00

By jockey - 2018

	Overall			Two-year-olds			Three-year-olds			Older horses		
	W-R	%	£1	W-R	%	£1	W-R	%	£1	W-R	%	£1
D Tudhope	36-274	13	-68.40	3-25	12	-10.00	9-57	16	-0.50	24-192	13	-57.90
David Nolan	27-172	16	-15.13	4-26	15	-16.72	7-42	17	+6.63	16-104	15	-5.04
C McGovern	11-119	9	-63.25	0-15	-	-15.00	5-37	14	-12.42	6-67	9	-35.83
Martin Harley	8-63	13	-6.38	1-6	17	+0.00	3-15	20	+0.88	4-42	10	-7.25
Shane Gray	5-59	8	+8.50	1-14	7	-1.00	2-18	11	+19.00	2-27	7	-9.50
Phillip Makin	3-30	10	-1.50	2-4	50	+15.50	0-3	-	-3.00	1-23	4	-14.00
Adam Kirby	3-37	8	+4.00	0-1	-	-1.00	1-3	33	+12.00	2-33	6	-7.00
Harry Bentley	2-21	10	-15.75	0-1	-	-1.00	0-4	-	-4.00	2-16	13	-10.75
Sam James	2-47	4	-23.50	1-11	9	+10.00	0-18	-	-18.00	1-18	6	-15.50
Ben Curtis	1-2	50	+1.00	1-1	100	+2.00	0-0	-	+0.00	0-1	-	-1.00
Scott McCullagh	1-2	50	+24.00	0-0	-	+0.00	0-0	-	+0.00	1-2	50	+24.00
S De Sousa	1-4	25	-1.50	1-1	100	+1.50	0-1	-	-1.00	0-2	-	-2.00

By jockey - 2017

	Overall			Two-year-olds			Three-year-olds			Older horses		
	W-R	%	£1	W-R	%	£1	W-R	%	£1	W-R	%	£1
D Tudhope	54-389	14	+18.69	4-41	10	-20.15	26-115	23	+96.34	24-233	10	-57.50
Phillip Makin	11-108	10	-15.68	2-29	7	-16.43	7-43	16	-1.25	2-36	6	+2.00
David Nolan	6-73	8	-19.50	1-12	8	+1.00	1-18	6	-12.50	4-43	9	-8.00
Josh Doyle	5-99	5	-38.75	0-4	-	-4.00	2-36	6	-11.00	3-59	5	-23.75
K Shoemark	4-19	21	+4.00	0-1	-	-1.00	1-6	17	-2.00	3-12	25	+7.00
Martin Harley	4-34	12	-12.25	0-3	-	-3.00	1-8	13	-3.00	3-23	13	-6.25
Shelley Birkett	4-64	6	-25.50	0-0	-	+0.00	2-30	7	-9.00	2-34	6	-16.50
Patrick Vaughan	4-72	6	-19.75	0-1	-	-1.00	1-11	9	-8.25	3-60	5	-10.50
Adam Kirby	3-25	12	-11.25	0-0	-	+0.00	1-4	25	+0.50	2-21	10	-11.75

By jockey - 2016

	Overall			Two-year-olds			Three-year-olds			Older horses		
	W-R	%	£1	W-R	%	£1	W-R	%	£1	W-R	%	£1
D Tudhope	47-343	14	-85.09	5-39	13	-18.58	11-62	18	+13.88	31-242	13	-80.38
Josh Doyle	9-119	8	-68.52	1-8	13	-4.00	2-21	10	-8.00	6-90	7	-56.52
Phillip Makin	8-79	10	-24.13	1-15	7	-12.13	1-17	6	-13.50	6-47	13	+1.50
G Gibbons	7-44	16	-5.25	1-5	20	-1.50	3-16	19	+7.00	3-23	13	-10.75
Shelley Birkett	7-57	12	+14.25	0-2	-	-2.00	0-9	-	-9.00	7-46	15	+25.25
David Nolan	5-77	6	-38.38	0-2	-	-2.00	1-7	14	-4.38	4-68	6	-32.00
Sam James	4-83	5	-50.25	3-21	14	+1.75	0-19	-	-19.00	1-43	2	-33.00
Martin Harley	3-9	33	+3.00	0-0	-	+0.00	0-0	-	+0.00	3-9	33	+3.00
Harry Bentley	3-14	21	+19.00	1-4	25	+11.00	0-3	-	-3.00	2-7	29	+11.00

By course - 2015-2018

	Overall			Two-year-olds			Three-year-olds			Older horses		
	W-R	%	£1	W-R	%	£1	W-R	%	£1	W-R	%	£1
Ascot	3-120	3	-64.00	0-9	-	-9.00	0-12	-	-12.00	3-99	3	-43.00
Ayr	26-172	15	-25.75	0-14	-	-14.00	8-38	21	+1.33	18-120	15	-13.08
Bath	0-2	-	-2.00	0-0	-	+0.00	0-0	-	+0.00	0-2	-	-2.00
Beverley	35-215	16	-4.54	2-39	5	-11.00	14-61	23	+15.21	19-115	17	-8.75
Carlisle	6-67	9	-25.17	1-8	13	-1.00	2-29	7	-20.17	3-30	10	-4.00
Catterick	16-149	11	-61.07	6-34	18	-17.69	3-47	6	-12.63	7-68	10	-30.75
Chelmsf'd (AW)	14-164	9	-61.36	1-14	7	-11.50	2-35	6	-24.50	11-115	10	-25.36
Chester	2-52	4	-27.00	0-5	-	-5.00	0-15	-	-15.00	2-32	6	-7.00
Doncaster	20-211	9	-66.09	4-11	36	+13.13	3-43	7	-27.38	13-157	8	-51.84
Epsom	5-40	13	-5.00	0-0	-	+0.00	0-3	-	-3.00	5-37	14	-2.00
Goodwood	1-40	3	-36.50	0-1	-	-1.00	0-3	-	-3.00	1-36	3	-32.50
Hamilton	24-119	20	-18.65	1-13	8	-1.00	11-43	26	-2.10	12-63	19	-15.56
Haydock	21-187	11	-17.53	0-5	-	-5.00	6-39	15	+22.50	15-143	10	-35.03
Kempton (AW)	6-64	9	-8.50	0-3	-	-3.00	1-17	6	+0.00	5-44	11	-5.50
Leicester	10-73	14	-28.00	0-7	-	-7.00	5-28	18	-5.00	5-38	13	-16.00
Lingfield	4-11	36	-0.83	0-3	-	-3.00	0-3	-	-3.00	4-5	80	+5.17
Lingfield (AW)	11-108	10	-43.25	0-3	-	-3.00	2-17	12	-2.25	9-88	10	-38.00
Musselburgh	12-109	11	-50.60	4-26	15	-9.43	3-33	9	-16.00	5-50	10	-25.17
Newbury	0-19	-	-19.00	0-2	-	-2.00	0-7	-	-7.00	0-10	-	-10.00
Newcastle	4-32	13	-16.92	0-2	-	-2.00	4-17	24	-1.92	0-13	-	-13.00
N'castle (AW)	20-247	8	-75.65	3-32	9	+8.00	9-81	11	-7.02	8-134	6	-76.63
Newmarket	4-59	7	-29.00	2-2	100	+14.00	1-9	11	-5.00	1-48	2	-38.00
Newmarket (J)	2-35	6	-22.88	0-2	-	-2.00	0-6	-	-6.00	2-27	7	-14.88
Nottingham	5-47	11	-22.38	1-5	20	-2.63	0-14	-	-14.00	4-28	14	-5.75
Pontefract	16-146	11	-51.00	0-15	-	-15.00	6-37	16	-1.13	10-94	11	-34.88
Redcar	32-212	15	-15.36	6-37	16	+3.00	11-73	15	+4.25	15-102	15	-22.61
Ripon	35-235	15	+16.38	5-27	19	+12.75	11-63	17	+10.25	19-145	13	-6.63
Salisbury	0-6	-	-6.00	0-0	-	+0.00	0-1	-	-1.00	0-5	-	-5.00
Sandown	1-15	7	-10.00	0-1	-	-1.00	0-5	-	-5.00	1-9	11	-4.00
S'well (AW)	10-83	12	-13.02	0-7	-	-7.00	3-19	16	+6.50	7-57	12	-12.52
Thirsk	25-197	13	-31.05	4-28	14	-13.08	8-57	14	-2.59	13-112	12	-15.38
Wetherby	5-28	18	+45.75	0-3	-	-3.00	2-9	22	+48.00	3-16	19	+0.75
Windsor	0-14	-	-14.00	0-0	-	+0.00	0-4	-	-4.00	0-10	-	-10.00
Wolves (AW)	39-358	11	-106.27	2-47	4	-39.47	19-112	17	-2.67	18-199	9	-64.14
Yarmouth	4-24	17	-8.86	1-3	33	-1.33	2-9	22	-4.52	1-12	8	-3.00
York	21-330	6	-119.00	0-25	-	-25.00	2-42	5	-4.00	19-263	7	-90.00

Ten-year summary

	Wins	Runs	%	Win prize-money	Total prize-money	£1
2018	106	1015	10	£700,533.39	£1,834,808.38	-288.03
2017	108	1069	10	£1,007,942.19	£1,689,956.18	-243.14
2016	103	975	11	£767,371.55	£1,680,593.79	-336.62
2015	122	931	13	£1,024,052.53	£1,580,833.33	-176.30
2014	112	830	13	£1,257,328.64	£1,772,806.65	-102.16
2013	136	905	15	£777,659.87	£1,159,386.21	-121.29
2012	69	542	13	£517,175.66	£709,691.68	-34.43
2011	48	423	11	£297,865.68	£479,370.95	-149.06
2010	25	153	16	£87,754.32	£122,742.04	-29.60

*first runners in 2010

LORD GLITTERS: earned more than £300,000 in prize-money last year

Roger Varian

By month - 2018

	Overall			Two-year-olds			Three-year-olds			Older horses		
	W-R	%	£1	W-R	%	£1	W-R	%	£1	W-R	%	£1
January	0-5	-	-5.00	0-0	-	+0.00	0-3	-	-3.00	0-2	-	-2.00
February	0-4	-	-4.00	0-0	-	+0.00	0-1	-	-1.00	0-3	-	-3.00
March	1-8	13	-6.09	0-0	-	+0.00	0-3	-	-3.00	1-5	20	-3.09
April	6-62	10	-44.75	0-0	-	+0.00	2-49	4	-44.25	4-13	31	-0.50
May	15-84	18	-3.30	0-1	-	-1.00	7-57	12	-4.38	8-26	31	+2.08
June	16-73	22	+0.90	1-7	14	-1.50	11-50	22	+10.56	4-16	25	-8.17
July	11-61	18	-24.29	2-8	25	-3.42	9-38	24	-5.87	0-15	-	-15.00
August	11-65	17	-32.42	1-16	6	-11.00	8-33	24	-11.43	2-16	13	-10.00
September	10-58	17	-12.99	3-20	15	-11.06	6-25	24	+7.57	1-13	8	-9.50
October	14-77	18	+14.03	8-39	21	+22.78	5-28	18	-7.75	1-10	10	-1.00
November	10-46	22	+4.91	6-34	18	-10.34	4-9	44	+18.25	0-3	-	-3.00
December	3-19	16	-7.93	2-15	13	-8.43	1-4	25	+0.50	0-0	-	+0.00

By month - 2017

	Overall			Two-year-olds			Three-year-olds			Older horses		
	W-R	%	£1	W-R	%	£1	W-R	%	£1	W-R	%	£1
January	0-7	-	-7.00	0-0	-	+0.00	0-1	-	-1.00	0-6	-	-6.00
February	0-0	-	+0.00	0-0	-	+0.00	0-0	-	+0.00	0-0	-	+0.00
March	1-1	100	+0.05	0-0	-	+0.00	0-0	-	+0.00	1-1	100	+0.05
April	15-41	37	+3.17	0-1	-	-1.00	11-27	41	+0.80	4-13	31	+3.38
May	17-68	25	-3.48	2-6	33	+1.13	9-37	24	-1.40	6-25	24	-3.20
June	14-78	18	-34.38	2-6	33	-0.75	9-50	18	-19.88	3-22	14	-13.75
July	19-83	23	-22.38	2-13	15	-6.04	10-45	22	-13.83	7-25	28	-2.51
August	10-94	11	-46.38	1-25	4	-22.25	7-49	14	-11.71	2-20	10	-12.42
September	12-74	16	-16.40	2-24	8	-7.25	8-37	22	-0.88	2-13	15	-8.27
October	13-72	18	+16.09	4-36	11	+2.73	8-27	30	+19.48	1-9	11	-6.13
November	6-30	20	-2.19	4-20	20	-4.94	0-4	-	-4.00	2-6	33	+6.75
December	2-7	29	-1.67	1-5	20	-1.50	1-1	100	+0.83	0-1	-	-1.00

By month - 2016

	Overall			Two-year-olds			Three-year-olds			Older horses		
	W-R	%	£1	W-R	%	£1	W-R	%	£1	W-R	%	£1
January	3-11	27	-3.44	0-0	-	+0.00	3-5	60	+2.56	0-6	-	-6.00
February	6-15	40	-4.11	0-0	-	+0.00	3-6	50	-0.04	3-9	33	-4.07
March	2-10	20	+3.50	0-0	-	+0.00	1-6	17	+3.00	1-4	25	+0.50
April	7-41	17	-22.64	0-0	-	+0.00	5-30	17	-15.08	2-11	18	-7.55
May	15-99	15	-37.00	1-6	18	-4.43	7-62	11	-32.92	7-31	23	+0.35
June	17-93	18	-20.22	2-11	18	-3.83	11-58	19	-1.85	4-24	17	-14.54
July	7-42	17	-16.13	1-9	11	-5.25	5-18	28	+0.62	1-15	7	-11.50
August	5-21	24	+2.38	0-0	-	+0.00	1-10	10	-8.00	4-11	36	+10.38
September	17-78	22	+10.29	7-26	27	+16.93	6-36	17	-18.51	4-16	25	+11.88
October	11-98	11	-44.97	4-57	7	-31.20	7-33	21	-5.77	0-8	-	-8.00
November	5-32	16	+0.63	3-20	15	+6.88	2-10	20	-4.25	0-2	-	-2.00
December	2-14	14	-9.63	0-6	-	-6.00	2-7	29	-2.63	0-1	-	-1.00

By race type - 2018

	Overall			Two-year-olds			Three-year-olds			Older horses		
	W-R	%	£1	W-R	%	£1	W-R	%	£1	W-R	%	£1
Handicap	35-215	16	-73.42	2-7	29	+2.00	20-120	17	-37.17	13-88	15	-38.25
Group	5-31	16	-5.00	1-4	25	+9.00	1-15	7	-11.25	3-12	25	-2.75
Maiden	10-69	14	-13.01	5-36	14	+2.24	5-32	16	-14.25	0-1	-	-1.00

By race type - 2017

	Overall			Two-year-olds			Three-year-olds			Older horses		
	W-R	%	£1	W-R	%	£1	W-R	%	£1	W-R	%	£1
Handicap	49-228	21	-12.32	0-7	-	-7.00	29-132	22	+15.79	20-89	22	-21.11
Group	2-34	6	-5.38	1-6	17	+20.00	1-13	8	-10.38	0-15	-	-15.00
Maiden	30-145	21	-70.62	2-35	6	-29.13	26-104	25	-38.92	2-6	33	-2.58

By race type - 2016

	Overall			Two-year-olds			Three-year-olds			Older horses		
	W-R	%	£1	W-R	%	£1	W-R	%	£1	W-R	%	£1
Handicap	37-228	16	-75.33	2-11	18	+7.75	21-131	16	-56.04	14-86	16	-27.04
Group	4-34	12	-5.40	0-3	-	-3.00	0-7	-	-7.00	4-24	17	+4.60
Maiden	41-229	18	-42.23	13-102	13	-21.40	25-123	20	-24.59	3-4	75	+3.77

By jockey - 2018

	Overall			Two-year-olds			Three-year-olds			Older horses		
	W-R	%	£1	W-R	%	£1	W-R	%	£1	W-R	%	£1
Andrea Atzeni	38-217	18	-88.93	5-41	12	-27.15	21-120	18	-39.10	12-56	21	-22.68
David Egan	22-121	18	+19.98	7-31	23	+21.53	14-69	20	+14.45	1-21	5	-16.00
Jack Mitchell	20-114	18	-15.44	6-43	14	-18.17	9-53	17	+8.48	5-18	28	-5.75
Jim Crowley	8-31	26	-8.71	2-7	29	-1.68	5-17	29	-3.78	1-7	14	-3.25
Tony Hamilton	1-1	100	+3.00	0-0	-	+0.00	1-1	100	+3.00	0-0	-	+0.00
James Doyle	1-2	50	+7.00	0-0	-	+0.00	0-0	-	+0.00	1-2	50	+7.00
Kieran Shoemark	1-2	50	+5.00	0-1	-	-1.00	1-1	100	+6.00	0-0	-	+0.00
William Buick	1-2	50	+11.00	1-2	50	+11.00	0-0	-	+0.00	0-0	-	+0.00
Daniel Tudhope	1-3	33	+0.75	1-2	50	+1.75	0-1	-	-1.00	0-0	-	+0.00
Luke Morris	1-3	33	-0.25	1-1	100	+1.75	0-2	-	-2.00	0-0	-	+0.00
Frankie Dettori	1-4	25	+1.50	0-0	-	+0.00	0-3	-	-3.00	1-1	100	+4.50
Yuga Kawada	1-8	13	-6.17	0-1	-	-1.00	1-5	20	-3.17	0-2	-	-2.00

By jockey - 2017

	Overall			Two-year-olds			Three-year-olds			Older horses		
	W-R	%	£1	W-R	%	£1	W-R	%	£1	W-R	%	£1
Andrea Atzeni	51-218	23	-3.60	9-54	17	+12.44	29-101	29	+4.75	13-63	21	-20.79
S De Sousa	21-78	27	-5.03	2-16	13	-10.63	15-46	33	+10.74	4-16	25	-5.15
Jack Mitchell	18-93	19	-6.93	5-35	14	-16.44	10-37	27	+19.63	3-21	14	-10.13
Harry Bentley	6-52	12	-37.51	0-11	-	-11.00	4-29	14	-19.81	2-12	17	-6.70
Cameron Noble	3-12	25	-1.50	0-0	-	+0.00	1-5	20	-1.50	2-7	29	+0.00
Jim Crowley	3-25	12	-4.75	1-7	14	-3.25	1-15	7	-7.50	1-3	33	+6.00
Dane O'Neill	2-9	22	-4.90	1-5	20	-3.00	1-3	33	-0.90	0-1	-	-1.00
Daniel Tudhope	1-3	33	+0.75	0-0	-	+0.00	0-2	-	-2.00	1-1	100	+2.75
Ryan Moore	1-3	33	-1.09	0-0	-	+0.00	0-0	-	+0.00	1-3	33	-1.09

By jockey - 2016

	Overall			Two-year-olds			Three-year-olds			Older horses		
	W-R	%	£1	W-R	%	£1	W-R	%	£1	W-R	%	£1
Andrea Atzeni	52-242	21	-5.88	12-70	17	+4.75	21-107	20	-29.29	19-65	29	+18.66
Harry Bentley	16-95	17	-22.07	1-12	8	+3.00	13-64	20	-11.40	2-19	11	-13.67
Jack Mitchell	16-103	16	-41.93	3-24	13	-12.46	11-53	21	-15.97	2-26	8	-13.50
Paul Hanagan	3-25	12	-10.25	1-6	17	-0.50	2-13	15	-3.75	0-6	-	-6.00
Joe Fanning	2-4	50	+0.71	0-1	-	-1.00	2-3	67	+1.71	0-0	-	+0.00
Frederik Tylicki	2-10	20	+1.50	0-2	-	-2.00	2-8	25	+3.50	0-0	-	+0.00
Dane O'Neill	2-14	14	-9.20	1-5	20	-3.70	1-7	14	-3.50	0-2	-	-2.00
William Buick	1-3	33	-1.17	0-1	-	-1.00	1-1	100	+0.83	0-1	-	-1.00
Jim Crowley	1-5	20	-3.50	0-2	-	-2.00	0-1	-	-1.00	1-2	50	-0.50

By course - 2015-2018

	Overall			Two-year-olds			Three-year-olds			Older horses		
	W-R	%	£1	W-R	%	£1	W-R	%	£1	W-R	%	£1
Ascot	12-102	12	-50.27	1-14	7	-12.00	5-41	12	-24.43	6-47	13	-13.84
Ayr	3-8	38	-0.67	0-1	-	-1.00	1-2	50	+2.00	2-5	40	-1.67
Bath	8-23	35	-4.90	1-4	25	-2.00	5-16	31	-6.65	2-3	67	+3.75
Beverley	6-14	43	+5.56	4-6	67	+9.08	2-7	29	-2.52	0-1	-	-1.00
Brighton	3-21	14	-11.92	0-4	-	-4.00	3-16	19	-6.92	0-1	-	-1.00
Carlisle	1-8	13	-6.92	0-1	-	-1.00	0-5	-	-5.00	1-2	50	-0.92
Catterick	1-10	10	-7.13	0-1	-	-1.00	1-9	11	-6.13	0-0	-	+0.00
Chelmsf'd (AW)	18-113	16	-31.72	3-22	14	-3.75	12-65	18	-11.41	3-26	12	-16.57
Chepstow	2-10	20	-5.00	1-2	50	+0.75	1-6	17	-3.75	0-2	-	-2.00
Chester	6-34	18	-15.59	1-3	33	-1.09	4-20	20	-7.00	1-11	9	-7.50
Doncaster	33-128	26	+41.48	3-26	12	-7.00	18-62	29	+20.08	12-40	30	+28.40
Epsom	8-25	32	+7.38	0-3	-	-3.00	5-11	45	+14.15	3-11	27	-3.77
Ffos Las	2-5	40	-0.45	1-1	100	+0.30	0-3	-	-3.00	1-1	100	+2.25
Goodwood	11-69	16	-17.00	3-13	23	-0.75	4-29	14	-8.25	4-27	15	-8.00
Hamilton	2-8	25	-4.18	0-0	-	+0.00	2-7	29	-3.18	0-1	-	-1.00
Haydock	11-79	14	-35.58	1-18	6	-14.00	9-44	20	-6.15	1-17	6	-15.43
Kempton (AW)	37-170	22	-13.45	16-77	21	+7.60	16-73	22	-20.09	5-20	25	-0.96
Leicester	12-68	18	-28.57	2-19	11	-14.55	8-41	20	-11.65	2-8	25	-2.38
Lingfield	9-36	25	-5.97	2-10	20	-0.75	6-19	32	-3.72	1-7	14	-1.50
Lingfield (AW)	22-95	23	+17.02	4-15	27	-4.75	13-56	23	+17.72	5-24	21	+4.05
Musselburgh	0-5	-	-5.00	0-0	-	+0.00	0-3	-	-3.00	0-2	-	-2.00
Newbury	12-90	13	-21.00	3-29	10	-17.63	6-46	13	-4.13	3-15	20	+0.75
Newcastle	0-2	-	-2.00	0-1	-	-1.00	0-0	-	+0.00	0-1	-	-1.00
N'castle (AW)	16-78	21	-23.87	2-27	7	-22.40	11-36	31	+4.28	3-15	20	-5.75
Newmarket	19-162	12	-22.50	6-51	12	+32.00	10-79	13	-30.75	3-32	9	-23.75
Newmarket (J)	9-80	11	-37.34	1-23	4	-19.50	4-38	11	-13.00	4-19	21	-4.84
Nottingham	17-92	18	-18.87	4-35	11	-8.59	6-40	15	-19.00	7-17	41	+8.73
Pontefract	2-21	10	-13.00	0-1	-	-1.00	2-14	14	-6.00	0-6	-	-6.00
Redcar	5-24	21	-5.79	2-5	40	+4.00	3-14	21	-4.79	0-5	-	-5.00
Ripon	9-36	25	-12.26	1-5	20	-2.25	6-21	29	-5.26	2-10	20	-4.75
Salisbury	9-51	18	+0.73	2-11	18	-4.27	7-36	19	+9.00	0-4	-	-4.00
Sandown	16-66	24	-5.63	1-12	8	-9.25	12-40	30	+9.38	3-14	21	-5.75
S'well (AW)	2-12	17	-8.25	0-0	-	+0.00	2-9	22	-5.25	0-3	-	-3.00
Thirsk	3-24	13	-12.00	0-2	-	-2.00	3-21	14	-9.00	0-1	-	-1.00
Wetherby	1-3	33	-1.33	0-0	-	+0.00	0-2	-	-2.00	1-1	100	+0.67
Windsor	22-76	29	-5.45	1-8	13	-5.50	14-51	27	-7.86	7-17	41	+7.91
Wolves (AW)	29-138	21	+23.09	5-36	14	-4.18	17-81	21	+28.21	7-21	33	-0.94
Yarmouth	18-80	23	-11.22	6-32	19	-10.19	9-37	24	+1.50	3-11	27	-2.52
York	7-79	9	-48.88	0-11	-	-11.00	2-21	10	-11.50	5-47	11	-26.38

Ten-year summary

	Wins	Runs	%	Win prize-money	Total prize-money	£1
2018	97	562	17	£1,227,272.13	£1,905,728.79	-120.93
2017	109	555	20	£1,217,847.83	£1,897,248.44	-114.57
2016	97	554	18	£1,788,831.62	£2,394,852.99	-141.34
2015	100	474	21	£887,554.86	£1,541,464.56	-21.60
2014	78	471	17	£1,374,851.71	£2,252,219.09	-80.70
2013	89	402	22	£921,239.74	£1,332,296.98	+19.63
2012	72	398	18	£532,154.46	£877,983.27	-55.48
2011	53	272	19	£387,237.31	£702,386.72	+56.94

*first runners in 2011

DEFOE: won twice in Britain last year before Roger Varian sent him travelling

Archie Watson

By month - 2018

	Overall			Two-year-olds			Three-year-olds			Older horses		
	W-R	%	£1	W-R	%	£1	W-R	%	£1	W-R	%	£1
January	8-25	32	+34.13	0-0	-	+0.00	2-6	33	+17.00	6-19	32	+17.13
February	7-29	24	-5.18	0-0	-	+0.00	3-9	33	+0.35	4-20	20	-5.53
March	10-40	25	+4.98	0-1	-	-1.00	4-15	27	+0.85	6-24	25	+5.13
April	3-34	9	-27.71	0-7	-	-7.00	3-19	16	-12.71	0-8	-	-8.00
May	7-49	14	-23.24	3-15	20	-4.90	1-16	6	-12.50	3-18	17	-5.84
June	9-47	19	+3.78	8-22	36	+25.28	0-11	-	-11.00	1-14	7	-10.50
July	15-53	28	-8.55	10-25	40	+3.38	4-15	27	-1.43	1-13	8	-10.50
August	15-62	24	-14.28	15-43	35	+4.72	0-14	-	-14.00	0-5	-	-5.00
September	8-38	21	-8.76	6-23	26	-0.14	0-11	-	-11.00	2-4	50	+2.38
October	6-49	12	-10.50	3-35	9	-13.50	3-9	33	+8.00	0-5	-	-5.00
November	4-36	11	-16.25	2-18	11	-9.00	1-9	11	-5.25	1-9	11	-2.00
December	5-35	14	-4.00	1-15	7	-11.50	3-10	30	+10.00	1-10	10	-2.50

By month - 2017

	Overall			Two-year-olds			Three-year-olds			Older horses		
	W-R	%	£1	W-R	%	£1	W-R	%	£1	W-R	%	£1
January	3-11	27	+5.50	0-0	-	+0.00	0-3	-	-3.00	3-8	38	+8.50
February	2-12	17	-3.25	0-0	-	+0.00	1-2	50	+1.25	1-10	10	-4.50
March	2-15	13	-8.75	0-0	-	+0.00	0-2	-	-2.00	2-13	15	-6.75
April	2-10	20	-3.56	1-4	25	-2.56	0-2	-	-2.00	1-4	25	+1.00
May	3-23	13	-10.06	0-11	-	-11.00	2-8	25	+0.94	1-4	25	+0.00
June	4-34	12	-9.67	4-18	22	+6.33	0-10	-	-10.00	0-6	-	-6.00
July	7-29	24	+8.83	3-15	20	-0.17	3-9	33	+10.75	1-5	20	-1.75
August	10-33	30	+15.49	5-10	50	+13.61	2-15	13	-3.50	3-8	38	+5.38
September	7-27	26	+13.33	1-8	13	+4.00	2-9	22	+5.75	4-10	40	+3.58
October	4-22	18	-5.38	0-8	-	-8.00	3-11	27	+3.13	1-3	33	-0.50
November	4-25	16	-11.13	0-7	-	-7.00	3-12	25	-0.75	1-6	17	-3.38
December	7-32	22	+0.96	0-4	-	-4.00	5-18	28	+1.47	2-10	20	+3.50

By month - 2016

	Overall			Two-year-olds			Three-year-olds			Older horses		
	W-R	%	£1	W-R	%	£1	W-R	%	£1	W-R	%	£1
January	0-0	-	+0.00	0-0	-	+0.00	0-0	-	+0.00	0-0	-	+0.00
February	0-0	-	+0.00	0-0	-	+0.00	0-0	-	+0.00	0-0	-	+0.00
March	0-0	-	+0.00	0-0	-	+0.00	0-0	-	+0.00	0-0	-	+0.00
April	0-0	-	+0.00	0-0	-	+0.00	0-0	-	+0.00	0-0	-	+0.00
May	0-0	-	+0.00	0-0	-	+0.00	0-0	-	+0.00	0-0	-	+0.00
June	0-0	-	+0.00	0-0	-	+0.00	0-0	-	+0.00	0-0	-	+0.00
July	0-0	-	+0.00	0-0	-	+0.00	0-0	-	+0.00	0-0	-	+0.00
August	0-3	-	-3.00	0-0	-	+0.00	0-2	-	-2.00	0-1	-	-1.00
September	0-5	-	-5.00	0-0	-	+0.00	0-3	-	-3.00	0-2	-	-2.00
October	1-6	17	-2.75	0-4	-	-4.00	1-2	50	+1.25	0-0	-	+0.00
November	0-6	-	-6.00	0-3	-	-3.00	0-2	-	-2.00	0-1	-	-1.00
December	3-9	33	+10.75	2-4	50	+13.00	1-3	33	-0.25	0-2	-	-2.00

By race type - 2018

	Overall			Two-year-olds			Three-year-olds			Older horses		
	W-R	%	£1	W-R	%	£1	W-R	%	£1	W-R	%	£1
Handicap	42-252	17	-40.01	12-44	27	+9.39	13-88	15	-20.38	17-120	14	-29.03
Group	1-13	8	-8.00	1-8	13	-3.00	0-1	-	-1.00	0-4	-	-4.00
Maiden	6-35	17	+6.25	5-25	20	-4.75	1-9	11	+12.00	0-1	-	-1.00

By race type - 2017

	Overall			Two-year-olds			Three-year-olds			Older horses		
	W-R	%	£1	W-R	%	£1	W-R	%	£1	W-R	%	£1
Handicap	31-164	19	-14.05	1-14	7	-6.00	13-74	18	-6.00	17-76	22	-2.05
Group	0-6	-	-6.00	0-4	-	-4.00	0-0	-	+0.00	0-2	-	-2.00
Maiden	9-26	35	+30.41	2-4	50	+20.00	7-22	32	+10.41	0-0	-	+0.00

By race type - 2016

	Overall			Two-year-olds			Three-year-olds			Older horses		
	W-R	%	£1	W-R	%	£1	W-R	%	£1	W-R	%	£1
Handicap	2-24	8	-18.00	0-6	-	-6.00	2-12	17	-6.00	0-6	-	-6.00
Group	0-0	-	+0.00	0-0	-	+0.00	0-0	-	+0.00	0-0	-	+0.00
Maiden	2-5	40	+12.00	2-5	40	+12.00	0-0	-	+0.00	0-0	-	+0.00

By jockey - 2018

	Overall			Two-year-olds			Three-year-olds			Older horses		
	W-R	%	£1	W-R	%	£1	W-R	%	£1	W-R	%	£1
E Greatrex	31-183	17	-37.27	14-79	18	-19.33	10-55	18	+1.83	7-49	14	-19.77
Oisin Murphy	18-76	24	-15.05	8-33	24	-4.83	4-20	20	-3.75	6-23	26	-6.46
Hollie Doyle	18-85	21	-21.07	15-49	31	+6.11	3-29	10	-20.18	0-7	-	-7.00
Daniel Tudhope	9-31	29	+11.43	7-19	37	+17.64	2-8	25	-2.21	0-4	-	-4.00
T Greatrex	4-13	31	+9.75	0-6	-	-6.00	3-4	75	+11.75	1-3	33	+4.00
Luke Morris	4-30	13	-0.38	0-2	-	-2.00	0-7	-	-7.00	4-21	19	+8.63
P-L Jamin	4-31	13	-8.25	0-1	-	-1.00	1-7	14	-0.50	3-23	13	-6.75
Mr S Walker	3-8	38	+1.13	0-0	-	+0.00	0-1	-	-1.00	3-7	43	+2.13
Ben Curtis	2-5	40	+1.41	2-5	40	+1.41	0-0	-	+0.00	0-0	-	+0.00
Andrew Mullen	2-13	15	+0.38	0-3	-	-3.00	1-5	20	-2.63	1-5	20	+6.00
James Doyle	1-1	100	+2.00	1-1	100	+2.00	0-0	-	+0.00	0-0	-	+0.00
David Probert	1-2	50	-0.67	1-1	100	+0.33	0-1	-	-1.00	0-0	-	+0.00

By jockey - 2017

	Overall			Two-year-olds			Three-year-olds			Older horses		
	W-R	%	£1	W-R	%	£1	W-R	%	£1	W-R	%	£1
E Greatrex	18-83	22	+4.54	4-20	20	+11.00	9-38	24	-4.96	5-25	20	-1.50
Luke Morris	11-52	21	-8.56	3-17	18	-8.80	1-8	13	-6.39	7-27	26	+6.63
Oisin Murphy	9-32	28	+5.07	3-14	21	-1.81	4-13	31	+3.63	2-5	40	+3.25
Andrew Mullen	5-9	56	+15.45	0-0	-	+0.00	2-5	40	+11.00	3-4	75	+4.45
Mr S Walker	3-8	38	+6.25	0-0	-	+0.00	2-3	67	+5.25	1-5	20	+1.00
Ben Curtis	3-14	21	-5.92	1-4	25	-2.17	0-6	-	-6.00	2-4	50	+2.25
Daniel Tudhope	2-6	33	+12.50	0-3	-	-3.00	2-3	67	+15.50	0-0	-	+0.00
Jimmy Quinn	1-2	50	+6.00	1-2	50	+6.00	0-0	-	+0.00	0-0	-	+0.00
Paul Mulrennan	1-3	33	+6.00	0-0	-	+0.00	1-3	33	+6.00	0-0	-	+0.00

By jockey - 2016

	Overall			Two-year-olds			Three-year-olds			Older horses		
	W-R	%	£1	W-R	%	£1	W-R	%	£1	W-R	%	£1
Jack Mitchell	1-1	100	+8.00	1-1	100	+8.00	0-0	-	+0.00	0-0	-	+0.00
Jim Crowley	1-1	100	+2.25	0-0	-	+0.00	1-1	100	+2.25	0-0	-	+0.00
David Probert	1-5	20	+3.00	1-4	25	+4.00	0-1	-	-1.00	0-0	-	+0.00
Luke Morris	1-8	13	-5.25	0-3	-	-3.00	1-2	50	+0.75	0-3	-	-3.00
Ben Curtis	0-1	-	-1.00	0-1	-	-1.00	0-0	-	+0.00	0-0	-	+0.00
Frankie Dettori	0-1	-	-1.00	0-0	-	+0.00	0-0	-	+0.00	0-1	-	-1.00
Georgia Cox	0-1	-	-1.00	0-0	-	+0.00	0-1	-	-1.00	0-0	-	+0.00
J Gordon	0-1	-	-1.00	0-0	-	+0.00	0-1	-	-1.00	0-0	-	+0.00
Joshua Bryan	0-1	-	-1.00	0-0	-	+0.00	0-1	-	-1.00	0-0	-	+0.00

By course - 2016-2018

	Overall			Two-year-olds			Three-year-olds			Older horses		
	W-R	%	£1	W-R	%	£1	W-R	%	£1	W-R	%	£1
Ascot	1-16	6	-3.00	1-10	10	+3.00	0-3	-	-3.00	0-3	-	-3.00
Ayr	1-7	14	-4.50	0-4	-	-4.00	0-0	-	+0.00	1-3	33	-0.50
Bath	2-19	11	-12.00	1-5	20	-2.00	0-5	-	-5.00	1-9	11	-5.00
Beverley	2-9	22	-2.38	2-6	33	+0.63	0-3	-	-3.00	0-0	-	+0.00
Brighton	2-13	15	-8.56	1-5	20	-2.00	1-5	20	-3.56	0-3	-	-3.00
Carlisle	2-8	25	-0.67	2-6	33	+1.33	0-0	-	+0.00	0-2	-	-2.00
Catterick	5-11	45	+1.08	3-5	60	+1.76	0-3	-	-3.00	2-3	67	+2.33
Chelmsf'd (AW)	14-100	14	-28.65	5-36	14	-8.50	6-34	18	-0.90	3-30	10	-19.25
Chepstow	3-14	21	-2.75	2-5	40	+2.50	1-7	14	-3.25	0-2	-	-2.00
Chester	2-10	20	-4.05	1-5	20	-2.80	0-1	-	-1.00	1-4	25	-0.25
Doncaster	2-10	20	+3.00	2-8	25	+5.00	0-2	-	-2.00	0-0	-	+0.00
Epsom	1-9	11	-5.25	0-3	-	-3.00	1-2	50	+1.75	0-4	-	-4.00
Ffos Las	2-10	20	-0.75	1-4	25	+2.00	1-6	17	-2.75	0-0	-	+0.00
Goodwood	1-10	10	-6.75	0-6	-	-6.00	0-1	-	-1.00	1-3	33	+0.25
Hamilton	3-6	50	+5.90	1-1	100	+0.33	2-4	50	+6.57	0-1	-	-1.00
Haydock	2-13	15	-4.97	2-6	33	+2.03	0-3	-	-3.00	0-4	-	-4.00
Kempton (AW)	19-83	23	+5.80	6-36	17	-13.52	8-29	28	+15.85	5-18	28	+3.47
Leicester	2-13	15	-4.50	1-8	13	-3.00	1-3	33	+0.50	0-2	-	-2.00
Lingfield	4-22	18	-6.13	2-10	20	+0.13	1-7	14	-3.75	1-5	20	-2.50
Lingfield (AW)	27-114	24	+23.63	5-21	24	+2.00	7-27	26	-1.46	15-66	23	+23.09
Musselburgh	5-9	56	+13.11	1-1	100	+0.11	1-3	33	+1.50	3-5	60	+11.50
Newbury	1-13	8	-4.50	1-7	14	+1.50	0-4	-	-4.00	0-2	-	-2.00
N'castle (AW)	4-33	12	-18.15	0-6	-	-6.00	3-17	18	-5.65	1-10	10	-6.50
Newmarket	0-10	-	-10.00	0-8	-	-8.00	0-0	-	+0.00	0-2	-	-2.00
Newmarket (J)	0-7	-	-7.00	0-5	-	-5.00	0-1	-	-1.00	0-1	-	-1.00
Nottingham	2-14	14	-1.50	1-8	13	-2.50	0-3	-	-3.00	1-3	33	+4.00
Pontefract	0-1	-	-1.00	0-1	-	-1.00	0-0	-	+0.00	0-0	-	+0.00
Redcar	3-12	25	+0.50	2-7	29	-2.00	1-4	25	+3.50	0-1	-	-1.00
Ripon	1-10	10	-7.63	0-2	-	-2.00	1-5	20	-2.63	0-3	-	-3.00
Salisbury	5-15	33	+12.75	3-6	50	+11.25	0-4	-	-4.00	2-5	40	+5.50
Sandown	2-8	25	+5.00	1-2	50	+6.00	1-4	25	+1.00	0-2	-	-2.00
S'well (AW)	6-37	16	-9.81	1-4	25	+2.00	4-23	17	-3.39	1-10	10	-8.43
Thirsk	2-3	67	+4.40	2-2	100	+5.40	0-1	-	-1.00	0-0	-	+0.00
Wetherby	1-4	25	+0.50	1-2	50	+2.50	0-2	-	-2.00	0-0	-	+0.00
Windsor	3-14	21	+3.17	3-8	38	+9.17	0-6	-	-6.00	0-0	-	+0.00
Wolves (AW)	22-91	24	-0.13	8-29	28	+0.75	7-32	22	+6.00	7-30	23	-6.88
Yarmouth	2-12	17	-4.50	2-6	33	+1.50	0-3	-	-3.00	0-3	-	-3.00
York	0-9	-	-9.00	0-6	-	-6.00	0-0	-	+0.00	0-3	-	-3.00

Ten-year summary

	Wins	Runs	%	Win prize-money	Total prize-money	£1
2018	97	497	20	£701,880.72	£1,056,809.05	-75.59
2017	55	273	20	£265,960.65	£455,593.24	-7.67
2016	4	29	14	£13,261.45	£32,685.67	-6.00

*first runners in 2016

SOLDIER'S CALL: provided Archie Watson with his first Group victories

Top trainers by winners (Turf)

All runs				First time out			Horses		
Won	Ran	%	Trainer	Won	Ran	%	Won	Ran	%
161	963	17	**Mark Johnston**	32	227	14	112	227	49
148	1179	13	**Richard Fahey**	32	256	13	131	256	51
117	952	12	**Richard Hannon**	32	289	11	112	289	39
104	907	11	**Tim Easterby**	6	157	4	67	157	43
96	420	23	**John Gosden**	56	218	26	116	218	53
93	437	21	**William Haggas**	31	175	18	95	175	54
85	713	12	**David O'Meara**	13	148	9	64	148	43
79	519	15	**Andrew Balding**	16	182	9	75	182	41
74	499	15	**Mick Channon**	18	106	17	56	106	53
65	386	17	**Roger Varian**	27	174	16	71	174	41
56	337	17	**Ralph Beckett**	21	129	16	59	129	46
54	536	10	**Keith Dalgleish**	7	125	6	51	125	41
50	274	18	**Sir Michael Stoute**	16	118	14	52	118	44
50	219	23	**Charlie Appleby**	43	119	36	59	119	50
49	423	12	**Kevin Ryan**	16	123	13	45	123	37
48	283	17	**Ian Williams**	7	83	8	36	83	43
48	333	14	**Tom Dascombe**	14	87	16	42	87	48
45	220	20	**Saeed bin Suroor**	21	125	17	52	125	42
43	214	20	**Archie Watson**	23	115	20	54	115	47
43	328	13	**Michael Appleby**	16	143	11	60	143	42
42	279	15	**Hugo Palmer**	16	116	14	52	116	45
40	352	11	**Charles Hills**	12	135	9	42	135	31
40	317	13	**Clive Cox**	15	123	12	46	123	37
40	310	13	**Roger Fell**	3	61	5	25	61	41
39	261	15	**Michael Bell**	11	93	12	36	93	39
38	354	11	**Michael Dods**	11	88	13	36	88	41
36	383	9	**K R Burke**	9	131	7	45	131	34
35	290	12	**John Quinn**	4	75	5	26	75	35
33	318	10	**Paul Midgley**	1	52	2	20	52	38
32	291	11	**Ed Walker**	9	106	8	39	106	37
31	244	13	**Nigel Tinkler**	3	42	7	19	42	45
30	153	20	**Simon Crisford**	20	99	20	46	99	46
30	213	14	**Stuart Williams**	5	64	8	36	64	56
28	237	12	**Hughie Morrison**	2	72	3	29	72	40
28	392	7	**Ruth Carr**	6	59	10	29	59	49
28	303	9	**Michael Easterby**	9	89	10	30	89	34
27	232	12	**Richard Hughes**	9	87	10	38	87	44
27	97	28	**Sir Mark Prescott**	11	64	17	24	64	38
26	240	11	**Tony Carroll**	7	87	8	30	87	34
25	165	15	**Roger Charlton**	11	102	11	33	102	32
24	225	11	**A P O'Brien**	11	96	11	21	96	22
24	326	7	**Iain Jardine**	1	72	1	20	72	28
23	112	21	**Owen Burrows**	11	64	17	30	64	47
23	181	13	**Declan Carroll**	3	36	8	21	36	58
22	233	9	**David Simcock**	11	122	9	43	122	35
22	235	9	**Eve Johnson Houghton**	9	75	12	25	75	33
22	251	9	**Jim Goldie**	4	40	10	19	40	48

Top trainers by prize-money (Turf)

Total prize-money	Trainer	Win prize-money	Wins	Class 1-3 Won	Ran	%	Class 4-6 Won	Ran	%
£7,732,366	John Gosden	£6,018,088	96	49	231	21	47	189	25
£6,196,267	A P O'Brien	£3,495,007	24	24	222	11	0	3	—
£4,121,984	Sir Michael Stoute	£2,435,182	50	25	141	18	25	133	19
£3,480,308	Mark Johnston	£1,875,574	161	66	431	15	95	532	18
£3,450,557	Charlie Appleby	£2,605,700	50	31	151	21	19	68	28
£2,860,345	Richard Fahey	£1,822,493	148	47	474	10	101	705	14
£2,532,308	Richard Hannon	£1,483,596	117	41	370	11	76	582	13
£2,194,258	William Haggas	£1,498,176	93	38	200	19	55	237	23
£2,051,038	Andrew Balding	£1,082,701	79	31	251	12	48	268	18
£1,589,918	Roger Varian	£1,039,366	65	26	180	14	39	206	19
£1,536,591	David O'Meara	£594,351	85	18	262	7	67	451	15
£1,339,436	Tim Easterby	£834,501	104	19	266	7	85	641	13
£1,279,219	Kevin Ryan	£698,084	49	19	158	12	30	265	11
£1,249,461	David Simcock	£742,648	22	9	135	7	13	98	13
£1,044,671	Charles Hills	£578,879	40	14	141	10	26	211	12
£1,000,381	Ralph Beckett	£707,689	56	26	135	19	30	202	15
£891,862	Clive Cox	£475,155	40	14	131	11	26	186	14
£863,677	Mick Channon	£530,821	74	18	165	11	56	334	17
£826,658	K R Burke	£419,366	36	10	127	8	26	256	10
£824,778	David Elsworth	£519,941	14	9	58	16	5	34	15
£802,154	W P Mullins	£525,902	6	6	28	21	0	0	—
£783,875	Ian Williams	£519,219	48	17	143	12	31	140	22
£757,021	Hugo Palmer	£498,543	42	8	110	7	34	169	20
£704,757	Michael Dods	£344,074	38	15	92	16	23	262	9
£700,843	Simon Crisford	£340,455	30	8	50	16	22	103	21
£682,579	Eve Johnson Houghton	£529,763	22	7	69	10	15	166	9
£680,001	Tom Dascombe	£417,658	48	15	121	12	33	212	16
£649,663	Keith Dalgleish	£391,128	54	6	111	5	48	425	11
£620,670	Mrs John Harrington	£452,971	3	3	15	20	0	0	—
£555,852	Ed Walker	£228,777	32	5	95	5	27	196	14
£554,022	Archie Watson	£342,012	43	5	59	8	38	155	25
£537,620	Roger Fell	£396,528	40	7	79	9	33	231	14
£533,576	Saeed bin Suroor	£340,892	45	14	107	13	31	113	27
£532,244	Hughie Morrison	£304,937	28	11	80	14	17	156	11
£525,760	John Quinn	£375,284	35	10	76	13	25	214	12
£521,504	Jim Goldie	£351,502	22	5	62	8	17	189	9
£518,612	Michael Bell	£305,490	39	7	73	10	32	188	17
£495,762	Paul Midgley	£296,802	33	12	99	12	21	219	10
£452,002	Bryan Smart	£295,310	18	3	47	6	15	135	11
£451,809	Roger Charlton	£235,732	25	9	66	14	16	99	16
£431,833	Michael Appleby	£301,077	43	5	65	8	38	263	14
£422,151	Martyn Meade	£143,603	9	3	35	9	6	46	13
£369,793	Stuart Williams	£229,699	30	7	70	10	23	143	16
£365,506	David Menuisier	£176,799	10	6	30	20	4	66	6
£336,483	Ruth Carr	£163,798	28	7	64	11	21	327	6
£334,602	Ed Dunlop	£91,650	14	2	51	4	12	178	7
£331,716	Brian Ellison	£139,733	19	4	30	13	15	161	9

Top trainers by winners (AW)

All runs				First time out			Horses		
Won	Ran	%	Trainer	Won	Ran	%	Won	Ran	%
73	253	29	**John Gosden**	56	218	26	116	218	53
60	414	14	**Mark Johnston**	32	227	14	112	227	49
56	292	19	**Archie Watson**	23	115	20	54	115	47
51	448	11	**Michael Appleby**	16	143	11	60	143	42
47	181	26	**William Haggas**	31	175	18	95	175	54
43	366	12	**Richard Hannon**	32	289	11	112	289	39
39	164	24	**Simon Crisford**	20	99	20	46	99	46
36	337	11	**Richard Fahey**	32	256	13	131	256	51
35	84	42	**Charlie Appleby**	43	119	36	59	119	50
34	213	16	**Andrew Balding**	16	182	9	75	182	41
34	183	19	**Roger Varian**	27	174	16	71	174	41
34	141	24	**Saeed bin Suroor**	21	125	17	52	125	42
33	197	17	**Hugo Palmer**	16	116	14	52	116	45
32	230	14	**David Simcock**	11	122	9	43	122	35
32	226	14	**Dean Ivory**	6	63	10	18	63	29
32	199	16	**Richard Hughes**	9	87	10	38	87	44
30	277	11	**Jamie Osborne**	7	90	8	34	90	38
28	264	11	**Tony Carroll**	7	87	8	30	87	34
27	193	14	**Stuart Williams**	5	64	8	36	64	56
27	155	17	**Ralph Beckett**	21	129	16	59	129	46
26	216	12	**K R Burke**	9	131	7	45	131	34
25	130	19	**Tom Dascombe**	14	87	16	42	87	48
25	134	19	**James Tate**	10	77	13	28	77	36
24	257	9	**Marco Botti**	6	97	6	26	97	27
23	142	16	**Clive Cox**	15	123	12	46	123	37
22	243	9	**John Butler**	5	68	7	25	68	37
21	310	7	**David O'Meara**	13	148	9	64	148	43
21	121	17	**Sir Michael Stoute**	16	118	14	52	118	44
21	290	7	**David Evans**	6	93	6	31	93	33
21	160	13	**Kevin Ryan**	16	123	13	45	123	37
21	198	11	**Phil McEntee**	4	30	13	14	30	47
20	124	16	**Roger Charlton**	11	102	11	33	102	32
20	170	12	**Ed Walker**	9	106	8	39	106	37
20	184	11	**Derek Shaw**	0	40	—	12	40	30
20	158	13	**Sir Mark Prescott**	11	64	17	24	64	38
20	211	9	**Daniel Mark Loughnane**	5	58	9	17	58	29
19	145	13	**James Fanshawe**	7	72	10	25	72	35
19	106	18	**Alan King**	5	67	7	22	67	33
19	161	12	**Michael Easterby**	9	89	10	30	89	34
18	164	11	**Keith Dalgleish**	7	125	6	51	125	41
18	144	13	**Charlie Wallis**	1	21	5	9	21	43
18	165	11	**Ivan Furtado**	4	71	6	23	71	32
17	127	13	**Jim Goldie**	4	40	10	19	40	48
17	157	11	**Charles Hills**	12	135	9	42	135	31
17	153	11	**Richard Guest**	2	28	7	10	28	36
17	167	10	**Antony Brittain**	2	33	6	10	33	30
16	146	11	**Robert Cowell**	6	78	8	24	78	31

Top trainers by prize-money (AW)

Total prize-money	Trainer	Win prize-money	Wins	Class 1-3			Class 4-6		
				Won	Ran	%	Won	Ran	%
£765,695	William Haggas	£611,031	47	17	49	35	30	132	23
£714,483	Mark Johnston	£411,882	60	11	98	11	49	316	16
£558,424	John Gosden	£422,419	73	12	46	26	61	207	29
£514,444	Archie Watson	£367,762	56	7	49	14	49	243	20
£476,159	Michael Appleby	£254,466	51	4	52	8	45	384	12
£435,878	Richard Hannon	£237,162	43	6	54	11	37	312	12
£393,071	Richard Fahey	£180,774	36	3	70	4	33	266	12
£389,002	David Simcock	£219,074	32	9	84	11	23	146	16
£387,247	Dean Ivory	£278,253	32	12	43	28	20	181	11
£333,539	Andrew Balding	£218,023	34	5	58	9	28	151	19
£333,332	Stuart Williams	£178,458	27	6	80	8	20	111	18
£331,023	Roger Varian	£199,162	34	7	28	25	27	155	17
£317,676	Marco Botti	£166,746	24	4	47	9	20	210	10
£313,081	Saeed bin Suroor	£220,251	34	8	39	21	26	102	25
£302,259	Simon Crisford	£198,381	39	3	32	9	36	132	27
£299,748	David O'Meara	£106,183	21	2	91	2	19	217	9
£289,480	Hugo Palmer	£202,517	33	5	32	16	28	165	17
£283,215	James Fanshawe	£168,734	19	6	37	16	13	108	12
£276,927	Sir Michael Stoute	£192,441	21	6	25	24	15	96	16
£275,503	Tom Dascombe	£185,926	25	11	27	41	14	103	14
£263,569	Jamie Osborne	£138,132	30	3	37	8	27	237	11
£255,641	Richard Hughes	£166,481	32	3	20	15	29	179	16
£239,768	K R Burke	£128,682	26	2	23	9	24	192	13
£233,239	Roger Charlton	£194,327	20	4	19	21	16	105	15
£227,269	Charlie Appleby	£185,883	35	5	15	33	30	69	43
£223,302	Ralph Beckett	£138,329	27	2	18	11	25	137	18
£215,345	David Evans	£98,910	21	1	29	3	20	257	8
£205,119	Tony Carroll	£111,620	28	1	17	6	25	215	12
£200,038	Robert Cowell	£108,522	16	3	38	8	13	108	12
£195,716	Jeremy Noseda	£156,149	12	5	15	33	7	33	21
£186,370	Charlie Fellowes	£91,468	9	3	17	18	6	78	8
£183,672	David Elsworth	£127,334	11	3	12	25	8	50	16
£177,745	James Tate	£104,604	25	0	2	—	25	132	19
£174,487	Kevin Ryan	£89,757	21	2	23	9	19	137	14
£172,920	Ed Walker	£89,586	20	2	14	14	18	156	12
£170,894	Alan King	£124,550	19	6	30	20	13	76	17
£169,765	Clive Cox	£120,961	23	2	10	20	21	132	16
£169,577	William Knight	£112,107	16	2	28	7	14	104	13
£164,670	Gay Kelleway	£116,972	16	3	13	23	13	114	11
£162,412	Mick Channon	£78,516	15	3	28	11	12	110	11
£162,332	Ian Williams	£86,749	16	1	27	4	15	116	13
£158,571	Eve Johnson Houghton	£103,664	15	4	17	24	11	101	11
£156,063	John Butler	£79,084	22	1	14	7	20	215	9
£151,892	Keith Dalgleish	£80,799	18	2	26	8	16	138	12
£151,002	Jim Goldie	£80,363	17	0	13	—	17	111	15
£149,487	Derek Shaw	£98,345	20	2	27	7	17	156	11
£146,999	Charles Hills	£90,011	17	3	14	21	14	143	10

Top jockeys (Turf)

Won	Ran	%	Jockey	Best Trainer	Won	Ran
133	672	20	**Silvestre De Sousa**	Mark Johnston	24	121
97	545	18	**Daniel Tudhope**	David O'Meara	36	274
88	421	21	**James Doyle**	William Haggas	49	164
87	604	14	**Oisin Murphy**	Andrew Balding	31	181
80	625	13	**Paul Hanagan**	Richard Fahey	70	525
77	496	16	**Jim Crowley**	Owen Burrows	16	75
76	520	15	**Joe Fanning**	Mark Johnston	53	345
75	454	17	**Andrea Atzeni**	Roger Varian	38	217
68	439	15	**Ben Curtis**	K R Burke	23	120
67	443	15	**Franny Norton**	Mark Johnston	47	295
66	346	19	**William Buick**	Charlie Appleby	46	157
66	478	14	**P J McDonald**	Mark Johnston	34	206
64	408	16	**Richard Kingscote**	Tom Dascombe	39	252
63	375	17	**Ryan Moore**	Sir Michael Stoute	19	82
63	528	12	**David Allan**	Tim Easterby	46	362
57	399	14	**Harry Bentley**	Ralph Beckett	37	185
57	326	17	**Jason Watson**	Andrew Balding	20	84
55	479	11	**Luke Morris**	Sir Mark Prescott	34	173
51	405	13	**Jason Hart**	John Quinn	29	216
48	209	23	**Frankie Dettori**	John Gosden	36	123
47	398	12	**David Egan**	Roger Varian	22	121
47	273	17	**Robert Havlin**	John Gosden	84	286
46	349	13	**Adam Kirby**	Clive Cox	37	218
46	366	13	**Jamie Spencer**	David Simcock	18	117
46	444	10	**David Probert**	Andrew Balding	22	157
44	323	14	**Charles Bishop**	Mick Channon	23	126
42	448	9	**Tom Marquand**	Richard Hannon	47	367
40	310	13	**Kevin Stott**	Kevin Ryan	25	162
39	487	8	**Graham Lee**	Bryan Smart	16	149
39	503	8	**James Sullivan**	Ruth Carr	18	318
39	285	14	**Kieran O'Neill**	John Bridger	11	85
39	270	14	**David Nolan**	David O'Meara	27	172
36	440	8	**Andrew Mullen**	Mark Walford	6	12
36	417	9	**Tony Hamilton**	Richard Fahey	28	299
35	378	9	**Fran Berry**	Henry Candy	11	90
35	313	11	**Callum Rodriguez**	Michael Dods	22	175
35	229	15	**Jack Mitchell**	Roger Varian	20	114
34	330	10	**Martin Harley**	Alan King	22	140
34	250	14	**Rob Hornby**	Jonathan Portman	23	141
34	323	11	**Jamie Gormley**	Iain Jardine	13	159
33	324	10	**Nicola Currie**	Phil McEntee	14	105
31	252	12	**Pat Cosgrave**	Ed Walker	8	66
30	239	13	**Paul Mulrennan**	Julie Camacho	9	40
30	273	11	**Connor Beasley**	Keith Dalgleish	15	122
30	286	10	**Rossa Ryan**	Richard Hannon	15	139
29	224	13	**Hayley Turner**	Michael Bell	10	82
29	293	10	**Josephine Gordon**	Hugo Palmer	21	133
29	202	14	**Edward Greatrex**	Archie Watson	31	183

Top jockeys (AW)

Won	Ran	%	Jockey	Best Trainer	Won	Ran
100	482	21	Oisin Murphy	Andrew Balding	31	181
90	988	9	Luke Morris	Sir Mark Prescott Bt	34	173
75	380	20	Robert Havlin	John Gosden	84	286
72	423	17	Adam Kirby	Clive Cox	37	218
59	495	12	Tom Marquand	Richard Hannon	47	367
57	172	33	James Doyle	William Haggas	49	164
56	371	15	Joe Fanning	Mark Johnston	53	345
53	307	17	Martin Harley	Alan King	22	140
50	394	13	P J McDonald	Mark Johnston	34	206
48	411	12	David Probert	Andrew Balding	22	157
46	439	10	Nicola Currie	Phil McEntee	14	105
45	335	13	Jason Watson	Andrew Balding	20	84
44	259	17	Rossa Ryan	Richard Hannon	15	139
43	355	12	Franny Norton	Mark Johnston	47	295
43	271	16	Richard Kingscote	Tom Dascombe	39	252
43	173	25	Jim Crowley	Owen Burrows	16	75
42	284	15	Robert Winston	Dean Ivory	20	105
39	337	12	Stevie Donohoe	Charlie Fellowes	13	139
39	296	13	Edward Greatrex	Archie Watson	31	183
38	284	13	Charles Bishop	Mick Channon	23	126
36	343	10	Fran Berry	Henry Candy	11	90
35	203	17	Ben Curtis	K R Burke	23	120
33	407	8	Liam Keniry	Ed Walker	19	186
32	370	9	Shane Kelly	Richard Hughes	35	265
31	201	15	Silvestre De Sousa	Mark Johnston	24	121
29	341	9	Kieran O'Neill	John Bridger	11	85
28	143	20	Andrea Atzeni	Roger Varian	38	217
28	126	22	Callum Rodriguez	Michael Dods	22	175
27	301	9	Hollie Doyle	Archie Watson	18	85
25	126	20	Jamie Spencer	David Simcock	18	117
25	302	8	Dougie Costello	Jamie Osborne	15	181
25	307	8	Paddy Mathers	Derek Shaw	18	173
25	228	11	Jack Mitchell	Roger Varian	20	114
24	215	11	David Egan	Roger Varian	22	121
23	292	8	Josephine Gordon	Hugo Palmer	21	133
23	328	7	Andrew Mullen	Mark Walford	6	12
23	151	15	Alistair Rawlinson	Michael Appleby	26	194
23	259	9	Callum Shepherd	Charles Hills	13	115
23	245	9	Rob Hornby	Jonathan Portman	23	141
21	215	10	Gabriele Malune	Ivan Furtado	8	65
21	163	13	George Wood	James Fanshawe	14	107
19	203	9	Jason Hart	John Quinn	29	216
19	278	7	Cam Hardie	Antony Brittain	17	215
17	59	29	Ryan Moore	Sir Michael Stoute	19	82
17	174	10	Martin Dwyer	William Muir	6	75
16	183	9	Sean Levey	Richard Hannon	17	180
16	131	12	Paul Hanagan	Richard Fahey	70	525
16	243	7	William Cox	John Flint	6	55

RACING & FOOTBALL outlook

Group 1 records

Year	Winner	Age (if appropriate)	Trainer	Jockey	SP	draw/ran

2008 Henry The Navigator

2,000 Guineas (1m) Newmarket

Year	Winner	Trainer	Jockey	SP	draw/ran
2009	**Sea The Stars**	J Oxx	M Kinane	8-1	15/15
2010	**Makfi**	M Delzangles	C-P Lemaire	33-1	5/19
2011	**Frankel**	Sir H Cecil	T Queally	1-2f	1/13
2012	**Camelot**	A O'Brien	J O'Brien	15-8f	12/18
2013	**Dawn Approach**	J Bolger	K Manning	11-8f	6/13
2014	**Night Of Thunder**	R Hannon	K Fallon	40-1	3/14
2015	**Gleneagles**	A O'Brien	R Moore	4-1f	16/18
2016	**Galileo Gold**	H Palmer	F Dettori	14-1	1/13
2017	**Churchill**	A O'Brien	R Moore	6-4f	3/10
2018	**Saxon Warrior**	A O'Brien	D O'Brien	3-1	9/14

THIS IS a specialist miler's race rather than a stepping stone to the Derby despite the recent success of Camelot and Sea The Stars – prior to the latter's 2009 win there had been a 20-year wait for a horse to do the double. Most winners had proved themselves at two, with 18 of the last 27 having won a Group race including 13 at the highest level. Seven of those (Churchill, Dawn Approach, Frankel, Rock Of Gibraltar, Pennekamp, Zafonic and Rodrigo De Triano) had won the Dewhurst, while Saxon Warrior and Camelot have followed up victories in the Racing Post Trophy after a long blank since High Top in 1973. Favourites had a desperate record until five of the last eight winners hit back for punters. There have been just four British-trained winners in 14 years, with only Frankel and Haafhd following up victory in one of the domestic trials since Mystiko in 1991.

2008 Natagora

1,000 Guineas (1m) Newmarket

Year	Winner	Trainer	Jockey	SP	draw/ran
2009	**Ghanaati**	B Hills	R Hills	20-1	7/14
2010	**Special Duty**	C Head-Maarek	S Pasquier	9-2f	18/17
2011	**Blue Bunting**	M Al Zarooni	F Dettori	16-1	16/18
2012	**Homecoming Queen**	A O'Brien	R Moore	25-1	16/17
2013	**Sky Lantern**	R Hannon Sr	R Hughes	9-1	7/15
2014	**Miss France**	A Fabre	M Guyon	7-1	4/17
2015	**Legatissimo**	D Wachman	R Moore	13-2	13/13
2016	**Minding**	A O'Brien	R Moore	11-10f	8/16
2017	**Winter**	A O'Brien	W Lordan	9-1	7/14
2018	**Billesdon Brook**	R Hannon	S Levey	66-1	8/15

COURSE FORM is the key factor in this race and is likely to become even more vital with the Fillies' Mile run at Newmarket for the first time in 2011. The 2016 winner Minding followed up victory in that race, while five of the last 17 winners came via the Rockfel; four of the last 16 had been first or second in the Cheveley Park; 2006 winner Speciosa won the Nell Gwyn, in which Sky Lantern was second and Billesdon Brook fourth; Miss France landed the Oh So Sharp Stakes; and Blue Bunting won a Listed race over course and distance the previous October. Punters have hit back a little in recent years, but still ten of the last 20 winners have been priced in double figures and Billesdon Brook was a real skinner last year when the biggest-priced winner in the race's history. French fillies have a good record, with seven winners since 1993 and Miss France the only one of those not to have Group 1 form as a juvenile.

Lockinge Stakes (1m) Newbury

2009	**Virtual**	4	J Gosden	J Fortune	6-1	10/11
2010	**Paco Boy**	5	R Hannon Sr	R Hughes	8-11f	3/9
2011	**Canford Cliffs**	4	R Hannon Sr	R Hughes	4-5f	4/7
2012	**Frankel**	4	Sir H Cecil	T Queally	2-7f	6/6
2013	**Farhh**	5	S bin Suroor	S de Sousa	10-3	5/12
2014	**Olympic Glory**	4	R Hannon	F Dettori	11-8f	3/8
2015	**Night Of Thunder**	4	R Hannon	J Doyle	11-4jf	3/16
2016	**Belardo**	4	R Varian	A Atzeni	8-1	6/12
2017	**Ribchester**	4	R Fahey	W Buick	7-4f	5/8
2018	**Rhododendron**	4	A O'Brien	R Moore	10-3f	2/14

IT'S ESSENTIAL to look for horses who have already shown themselves to be Group 1 milers as 20 of the last 24 winners had won at the top level, all but one over the trip, three of the exceptions had been second. Consequently it has been straightforward to identify the winner as 12 of the last 16 favourites have obliged and two of the exceptions were second in the market. Four-year-olds have by far the strongest record, accounting for 23 of the last 32 winners, and fillies can also do well with four winners in the last 13 years. The Sandown Mile is a popular prep race yet Belardo was only the second horse to do the double with 21 other Sandown winners failing.

Coronation Cup (1m4f) Epsom

2009	**Ask**	6	Sir M Stoute	R Moore	5-1	8/8

RHODODENDRON (near): the fourth filly in 13 years to win the Lockinge Stakes

2010	Fame And Glory	4	A O'Brien	J Murtagh	5-6f	8/9
2011	St Nicholas Abbey	4	A O'Brien	R Moore	Evsf	1/5
2012	St Nicholas Abbey	5	A O'Brien	J O'Brien	8-11f	4/6
2013	St Nicholas Abbey	6	A O'Brien	J O'Brien	3-10f	3/5
2014	Cirrus Des Aigles	8	C Barande-Barbe	C Soumillon	10-11f	7/7
2015	Pether's Moon	5	R Hannon	P Dobbs	11-1	5/4
2016	Postponed	5	R Varian	A Atzeni	8-11f	3/8
2017	Highland Reel	5	A O'Brien	R Moore	9-4f	3/10
2018	Cracksman	4	J Gosden	F Dettori	2-7f	6/6

AIDAN O'BRIEN has trained eight of the last 14 winners, led by St Nicholas Abbey's hat-trick. That horse was favourite on every occasion, as were Cracksman, Highland Reel, Postponed, Cirrus Des Aigles and Fame And Glory in the last nine years, although history shows that the traditionally small field can produce plenty of upsets, which was the case again in 2015 with Pether's Moon. The key is to oppose four-year-olds as youngsters are often well fancied yet only 2-7 shot Cracksman has won since 2011, making it just five in 16 years overall.

The Oaks (1m4f) Epsom

2008 Look Here

2009	Sariska	M Bell	J Spencer	9-4f	5/10
2010	Snow Fairy	E Dunlop	R Moore	9-1	15/15
2011	Dancing Rain	W Haggas	J Murtagh	20-1	7/13
2012	Was	A O'Brien	S Heffernan	20-1	10/12
2013	Talent	R Beckett	R Hughes	20-1	3/11
2014	Taghrooda	J Gosden	P Hanagan	5-1	9/17
2015	Qualify	A O'Brien	C O'Donoghue	50-1	2/11
2016	Minding	A O'Brien	R Moore	10-11f	4/9
2017	Enable	J Gosden	F Dettori	6-1	9/10
2018	Forever Together	A O'Brien	D O'Brien	7-1	3/9

GUARANTEED STAMINA has been more important than proven top-class form in this race, which can make things tricky for punters with five of the last 11 winners priced at least 20-1. Two of Aidan O'Brien's seven winners came via the Guineas, but they are the only winners not to have been tried beyond a mile since Casual Look in 2003. It therefore follows that the 1,000 Guineas has become a weaker guide than was once the case, with Minding the only winner to follow up since Kazzia in 2002 and four failures in that time. Ten of the last 12 winners had never been tried in a Group 1 and seven of them had triumphed over at least 1m2f, although none of the trials stands above any other and too much is often made of the Musidora winner, with three beaten favourites since 2008 and Sariska the only one to double up since Reams Of Verse in 1997.

The Derby (1m4f) Epsom

2008 New Approach

2009	Sea The Stars	J Oxx	M Kinane	11-4	4/12
2010	Workforce	Sir M Stoute	R Moore	6-1	8/12
2011	Pour Moi	A Fabre	M Barzalona	4-1	7/13
2012	Camelot	A O'Brien	J O'Brien	8-13f	5/9
2013	Ruler Of The World	A O'Brien	R Moore	7-1	10/12
2014	Australia	A O'Brien	J O'Brien	11-8f	12/16
2015	Golden Horn	J Gosden	F Dettori	13-8f	8/12
2016	Harzand	D Weld	P Smullen	13-2	9/16

2017	**Wings Of Eagles**		A O'Brien	P Beggy	40-1	14/18
2018	**Masar**		C Appleby	W Buick	16-1	10/12

JUST AS punters thought they had the Derby sussed, along came the biggest-priced winner in more than 40 years in Wings Of Eagles followed by a 16-1 surprise in Masar. Still, the market has proved a strong guide overall in recent times as the previous 13 winners had come from the first three in the market, including six favourites. The resurgence of the 2,000 Guineas as a good trial has played a big part in that, with Masar the fifth top-three finisher from Newmarket to win at Epsom in 11 years following Australia, Camelot, Sea The Stars and New Approach. Of the recognised trials, the Dante (five winners this century) and the Derrinstown (four) are better pointers than those at Chester and, in particular, Lingfield.

Queen Anne Stakes (1m) Royal Ascot

2009	**Paco Boy**	4	R Hannon Sr	R Hughes	10-3	7/9
2010	**Goldikova**	5	F Head	O Peslier	11-8f	10/10
2011	**Canford Cliffs**	4	R Hannon Sr	R Hughes	11-8	6/7
2012	**Frankel**	4	Sir H Cecil	T Queally	1-10f	8/11
2013	**Declaration Of War**	4	A O'Brien	J O'Brien	15-2	6/13
2014	**Toronado**	4	R Hannon	R Hughes	4-5f	8/10
2015	**Solow**	5	F Head	M Guyon	11-8f	4/8
2016	**Tepin**	5	M Casse	J Leparoux	11-2	12/13
2017	**Ribchester**	4	R Fahey	W Buick	11-10f	1/16
2018	**Accidental Agent**	4	E Johnson Houghton	C Bishop	33-1	4/15

FOUR-YEAR-OLDS once considered Classic contenders fit the bill and this age group has taken 23 of the last 30 runnings. No horse older than five has triumphed since 1976 with Goldikova among some top-class ones to fail when defending her crown in 2011. Eight of the last 12 winners ran in the Lockinge at Newbury, which is obviously the key trial – Ribchester, Frankel and Canford Cliffs all did the double – and 13 of the last 15 winners had previously won a Group 1 at some stage. Toronado is the only horse to ever win the race first time out.

St James's Palace Stakes (1m) Royal Ascot

2009	**Mastercraftsman**	A O'Brien	J Murtagh	5-6f	3/10
2010	**Canford Cliffs**	R Hannon Sr	R Hughes	11-4j	4/9
2011	**Frankel**	Sir H Cecil	T Queally	3-10f	5/9
2012	**Most Improved**	B Meehan	K Fallon	9-1	15/16
2013	**Dawn Approach**	J Bolger	K Manning	5-4f	5/9
2014	**Kingman**	J Gosden	J Doyle	8-11f	7/7
2015	**Gleneagles**	A O'Brien	R Moore	8-15f	5/5
2016	**Galileo Gold**	H Palmer	F Dettori	6-1	7/7
2017	**Barney Roy**	R Hannon	J Doyle	5-2	4/8
2018	**Without Parole**	J Gosden	F Dettori	9-4f	2/10

GUINEAS FORM holds the key to this prize and ten of the last 14 winners had come out on top in one of the Classics. The Curragh is just about the best guide as six Irish 2,000 Guineas winners have followed up in that time compared to five from Newmarket and one from Longchamp. Gleneagles and Henrythenavigator had won at Newmarket and the Curragh and Frankel is the only Newmarket winner to follow up without a run in between since Bolkonski in 1975, although Barney Roy came straight from his Guineas second when winning last year. Without Parole was the first winner not to have run in a Group 1 at all since 1990, with Most Improved the only other winner to have skipped the Classics in 20 years.

Prince of Wales's Stakes (1m2f) Royal Ascot

2009	Vision D'Etat	4	E Libaud	O Peslier	4-1	2/8
2010	Byword	4	A Fabre	M Guyon	5-2f	5/12
2011	Rewilding	4	M Al Zarooni	F Dettori	17-2	6/7
2012	So You Think	6	A O'Brien	J O'Brien	4-5f	7/11
2013	Al Kazeem	5	R Charlton	J Doyle	11-4	9/11
2014	The Fugue	5	J Gosden	W Buick	11-2	7/8
2015	Free Eagle	4	D Weld	P Smullen	5-2f	4/9
2016	My Dream Boat	4	C Cox	A Kirby	16-1	3/6
2017	Highland Reel	5	A O'Brien	R Moore	9-4	6/8
2018	Poet's Word	5	Sir M Stoute	J Doyle	11-2	1/7

A RACE that has altered hugely since gaining Group 1 status in 2000 when Dubai Millennium provided one of the outstanding moments in Royal Ascot history. The race now attracts an international field and 12 of the last 19 winners had won a Group 1 outside Britain and Ireland. That also shows the quality required as three of the seven exceptions had won a Group 1 at home and Poet's Word had been second three times at the top level. The Tattersalls Gold Cup is the best pointer with four of the last seven horses to try it managing to complete the double (Decorated Knight in 2017 was the first to try since Al Kazeem in 2013 and came second).

Gold Cup (2m4f) Royal Ascot

2009	Yeats	8	A O'Brien	J Murtagh	6-4f	4/9
2010	Rite Of Passage	6	D Weld	P Smullen	20-1	1/12
2011	Fame And Glory	5	A O'Brien	J Spencer	11-8f	3/15
2012	Colour Vision	4	S Bin Suroor	F Dettori	6-1	5/9
2013	Estimate	4	Sir M Stoute	R Moore	7-2f	5/14
2014	Leading Light	4	A O'Brien	J O'Brien	10-11f	14/13
2015	Trip To Paris	4	E Dunlop	G Lee	12-1	13/12
2016	Order Of St George	4	A O'Brien	R Moore	10-11f	10/17
2017	Big Orange	6	M Bell	J Doyle	5-1	7/14
2018	Stradivarius	4	J Gosden	F Dettori	7-4jf	6/9

A HALF-MILE longer than any other British or Irish Group 1, this race understandably attracts plenty of real specialists, with Royal Rebel, Kayf Tara, Drum Taps and Sadeem all dual winners since 1988 before Yeats became the first ever four-time winner in 2009. His trainer Aidan O'Brien remains the trainer to follow as he has since won with Order Of St George, Leading Light and Fame And Glory, as well as finishing second with Order Of St George, Age Of Aquarius and Kingfisher, and five of his last six winners started their year in the Vintage Crop Stakes at Navan. The other strong trials are the Sagaro Stakes, which has come back into vogue with Estimate and Colour Vision winning both races to match Celeric, Double Trigger, Sadeem, Longboat and Gildoran since the mid-1980s, and the Henry II Stakes, the route taken by eight of the 13 winners prior to Yeats's reign plus Big Orange and Trip To Paris in the last four years. Wherever it's been, 16 of the last 19 winners had been successful over 2m. Four-year-olds have won six of the last seven renewals and any older horse has to have proved themselves at the top level already as

GOLDEN HORN: Eclipse win has sparked a run of success for three-year-olds

eight of the last 11 older winners had previously landed a Group 1 (plus the 2017 winner Big Orange had won the last two runnings of the Goodwood Cup before it was upgraded to a Group 1).

Coronation Stakes (1m) Royal Ascot

2009	**Ghanaati**	B Hills	R Hills	2-1f	5/10
2010	**Lillie Langtry**	A O'Brien	J Murtagh	7-2f	3/13
2011	**Immortal Verse**	R Collet	G Mosse	8-1	11/12
2012	**Fallen For You**	J Gosden	W Buick	12-1	11/10
2013	**Sky Lantern**	R Hannon Sr	R Hughes	9-2jf	16/17
2014	**Rizeena**	C Brittain	R Moore	11-2	7/12
2015	**Ervedya**	J-C Rouget	C Soumillon	3-1	7/9
2016	**Qemah**	J-C Rouget	G Benoist	6-1	11/13
2017	**Winter**	A O'Brien	R Moore	4-9f	7/7
2018	**Alpha Centauri**	J Harrington	C O'Donoghue	11-4f	9/12

A CHAMPIONSHIP race race for three-year-old fillies. The 1,000 Guineas at Newmarket is much the best guide as ten of the last 16 winners had run on the Rowley Mile, with five doing the double (Winter, Sky Lantern, Ghanaati, Attraction and Russian Rhythm). It's generally best to have been off the track since then, though, as just three of the last 24 winners ran in the Newmarket Classic and the Irish 1,000 Guineas at the Curragh, which often counts against many in the field. Any horse who has been stepped up in trip can be opposed as Lush Lashes is the only winner in the last 24 years to have raced over further.

Diamond Jubilee Stakes (6f) Royal Ascot

2009	**Art Connoisseur**	3	M Bell	T Queally	20-1	11/14
2010	**Starspangledbanner**	4	A O'Brien	J Murtagh	13-2j	21/24

2011	**Society Rock**	4	J Fanshawe	P Cosgrave	25-1	3/16
2012	**Black Caviar**	5	P Moody	L Nolen	1-6f	15/14
2013	**Lethal Force**	4	C Cox	A Kirby	11-1	15/18
2014	**Slade Power**	5	E Lynam	W Lordan	7-2f	4/14
2015	**Undrafted**	5	W Ward	F Dettori	14-1	6/15
2016	**Twilight Son**	4	H Candy	R Moore	7-2	3/9
2017	**The Tin Man**	5	J Fanshawe	T Queally	9-2	3/19
2018	**Merchant Navy**	4	A O'Brien	R Moore	4-1	11/12

A RACE whose profile has risen steadily this century and attracts the best sprinters from around the world, most notably the legendary Black Caviar in 2012. Yet despite Black Caviar and the American winner Undrafted in 2015, the percentage call is to side with domestic talent as they are the only winners trained outside Britain and Ireland since Cape Of Good Hope in 2005, during which time several fancied foreign raiders – Take-over Target (twice), J J The Jet Plane, Sacred Kingdom, Star Witness, Brazen Beau and Redkirk Warrior – have been beaten at 4-1 or shorter. In contrast, course form remains critical because, of the last 19 winners at Ascot, nine had already been successful at the course and the same number had managed a top-four finish at Royal Ascot. The race throws up more than its share of shocks, with four winners priced 20-1 or bigger in the last 11 years, but two of those were among a host of unfancied three-year-olds to run well and that age group is now barred from running because of the Commonwealth Cup.

Coral-Eclipse (1m2f) Sandown

2009	**Sea The Stars**	3	J Oxx	M Kinane	4-7f	6/10
2010	**Twice Over**	5	H Cecil	T Queally	13-8f	1/5
2011	**So You Think**	5	A O'Brien	S Heffernan	4-6f	3/5
2012	**Nathaniel**	4	J Gosden	W Buick	7-2	4/9
2013	**Al Kazeem**	5	R Charlton	J Doyle	15-8f	2/7
2014	**Mukhadram**	5	W Haggas	P Hanagan	14-1	10/9
2015	**Golden Horn**	3	J Gosden	F Dettori	4-9f	1/5
2016	**Hawkbill**	3	C Appleby	W Buick	6-1	3/7
2017	**Ulysses**	4	Sir M Stoute	J Crowley	8-1	6/9
2018	**Roaring Lion**	3	J Gosden	O Murphy	7-4f	7/7

TRADITIONALLY THE first clash of the generations. It has suffered a little in recent times from a lack of three-year-old representation, but the tide may be turning again, helped by Golden Horn and Sea The Stars following up Derby victories after the previous four to take their chance – Authorized, Motivator, Benny The Dip and Erhaab – were all beaten. Indeed, following Golden Horn's win, three-year-olds have filled five of the six top-two positions in the last three years. For older horses, the Prince of Wales's Stakes is the key trial, although Al Kazeem is the only horse to do the double since Mtoto in 1987 with many horses beaten at Ascot – most recently Ulysses, Mukhadram, So You Think, Twice Over and David Junior – improving on that form. Fillies are to be avoided as Pebbles in 1985 is the only one to succeed since the 19th century, since when Bosra Sham and Ouija Board were beaten favourites.

July Cup (6f) Newmarket

2009	**Fleeting Spirit**	4	J Noseda	T Queally	12-1	5/13
2010	**Starspangledbanner**	4	A O'Brien	J Murtagh	2-1f	4/14
2011	**Dream Ahead**	3	D Simcock	H Turner	7-1	2/16

2012	**Mayson**	4	R Fahey	P Hanagan	20-1	11/12
2013	**Lethal Force**	4	C Cox	A Kirby	9-2	4/11
2014	**Slade Power**	5	E Lynam	W Lordan	7-4f	13/13
2015	**Muhaarar**	3	C Hills	P Hanagan	2-1jf	7/14
2016	**Limato**	4	H Candy	H Bentley	9-2f	16/18
2017	**Harry Angel**	3	C Cox	A Kirby	9-2	6/10
2018	**US Navy Flag**	3	A O'Brien	R Moore	8-1	12/13

FIVE OF the last 13 winners were following up victories over the same trip at Royal Ascot – four in the Diamond Jubilee Stakes before Muhaarar from the inaugural Commonwealth Cup, in which the 2017 winner Harry Angel had also been second – but surprisingly it pays to ignore Group 1 form in other races as ten of the other 13 winners since 2001 were scoring for the first time at the top level. Indeed, this is a race in which stars are often born with 42 of the 51 winners being aged three or four. Often that's because horses are dropping into sprints having been tried over further as stamina is an important asset on this stiff uphill finish. Greats like Ajdal and Soviet Song are memorable for that many years ago and more recently the likes of US Navy Flag, Limato, Muhaarar and Dream Ahead had run over a mile earlier in the season.

King George VI and Queen Elizabeth Stakes (1m4f) Ascot

2009	**Conduit**	4	Sir M Stoute	R Moore	13-8f	8/9
2010	**Harbinger**	4	Sir M Stoute	O Peslier	4-1	1/6
2011	**Nathaniel**	3	J Gosden	W Buick	11-2	3/5
2012	**Danedream**	4	P Schiergen	A Starke	9-1	4/10
2013	**Novellist**	4	A Wohler	J Murtagh	13-2	3/8
2014	**Taghrooda**	3	J Gosden	P Hanagan	7-2	7/8
2015	**Postponed**	4	L Cumani	A Atzeni	6-1	9/7
2016	**Highland Reel**	4	A O'Brien	R Moore	13-8f	3/7
2017	**Enable**	3	J Gosden	F Dettori	5-4f	7/10
2018	**Poet's Word**	5	Sir M Stoute	J Doyle	7-4	8/7

THIS RACE has suffered from a lack of three-year-old representation in recent years, with Enable, Taghrooda, Nathaniel, Alamshar and Galileo the only horses of that age to come out on top since Lammtarra in 1995. Taghrooda was an even bigger trends-buster as she became the first British-trained three-year-old filly to win any Group 1 over this trip against older males in the worldwide history of the sport – it therefore makes it all the more astonishing that Enable matched her just three years later. Still, it generally pays to look for a four-year-old (the age of 11 of the last 15 winners, with Poet's Word the first to be older since 1999) and one proven at the top level and the trip because since Belmez in 1990 just four winners hadn't previously landed a Group 1 and just five hadn't been first or second in a Group 1 over 1m4f. The Coronation Cup is a poor guide, though, with only Opera House and Daylami doing the double in more than 40 years.

Sussex Stakes (1m) Goodwood

2009	**Rip Van Winkle**	3	A O'Brien	J Murtagh	6-4f	7/8
2010	**Canford Cliffs**	3	R Hannon Sr	R Hughes	4-6f	7/7
2011	**Frankel**	3	Sir H Cecil	T Queally	8-13f	3/4
2012	**Frankel**	4	Sir H Cecil	T Queally	1-20f	3/4
2013	**Toronado**	3	R Hannon Sr	R Hughes	11-4	7/7
2014	**Kingman**	3	J Gosden	J Doyle	2-5f	4/4

2015	**Solow**	5	F Head	M Guyon	2-5f	5/8
2016	**The Gurkha**	3	A O'Brien	R Moore	11-8f	1/10
2017	**Here Comes When**	7	A Balding	J Crowley	20-1	7/7
2018	**Lightning Spear**	7	D Simcock	O Murphy	9-1	4/8

NOT MANY Group 1 races are won by seven-year-olds, let alone twice in a row, but that's what happened when Lightning Spear emulated Here Comes When last year. It was even more unlikely in the Sussex Stakes, which is generally a great race for glamorous three-year-olds as that age group has provided 29 of the 44 winners since it was opened to all ages in 1975. Nine of the last 12 triumphant three-year-olds were favourites and 11 of the last 13 had been first or second in the St James's Palace Stakes, which is the key trial. Eight of the last 11 successful older horses had contested the Queen Anne Stakes, with Solow, Frankel and Ramonti doing the double since 2007. With Royal Ascot form holding up so well, it's perhaps little wonder that eight of the last 11 favourites have obliged, six of them at odds-on.

Nassau Stakes (1m1f192yds) Goodwood

2009	**Midday**	3	H Cecil	T Queally	11-2	10/10
2010	**Midday**	4	H Cecil	T Queally	15-8f	6/7
2011	**Midday**	5	Sir H Cecil	T Queally	6-4f	6/6
2012	**The Fugue**	3	J Gosden	R Hughes	11-4	7/8
2013	**Winsili**	3	J Gosden	W Buick	20-1	15/14
2014	**Sultanina**	4	J Gosden	W Buick	11-2	2/6
2015	**Legatissimo**	3	D Wachman	W Lordan	2-1f	8/9
2016	**Minding**	3	A O'Brien	R Moore	1-5f	1/5
2017	**Winter**	3	A O'Brien	R Moore	10-11f	6/6
2018	**Wild Illusion**	3	C Appleby	W Buick	4-1	6/6

THIS IS another fantastic race for punters as 23 of the last 25 winners emerged from

POET'S WORD: the first five-year-old to win the King George since 1999

the top three in the market including 14 favourites. The key is to side with a top-class three-year-old as the Classic generation have provided 34 of the 44 winners since the race was opened to older fillies in 1975, despite Midday's best efforts in racking up a hat-trick. Preferably they should be dropping down in trip rather than stepping up as Winter and Halfway To Heaven are the only winners to have had their previous runs over a mile since 2004, during which time Minding has followed up victory in the Oaks while Wild Illusion, Legatissimo, The Fugue, Midday and Peeping Fawn all improved on placed efforts at Epsom.

Juddmonte International Stakes (1m2f85yds) York

2009	Sea The Stars	3	J Oxx	M Kinane	1-4f	3/4
2010	Rip Van Winkle	4	A O'Brien	J Murtagh	7-4f	7/9
2011	Twice Over	6	Sir H Cecil	I Mongan	11-2	4/5
2012	Frankel	4	Sir H Cecil	T Queally	1-10f	7/9
2013	Declaration Of War	4	A O'Brien	J O'Brien	7-1	2/6
2014	Australia	3	A O'Brien	J O'Brien	8-13f	6/6
2015	Arabian Queen	3	D Elsworth	S De Sousa	50-1	5/7
2016	Postponed	5	R Varian	A Atzeni	15-8f	6/12
2017	Ulysses	4	Sir M Stoute	J Crowley	4-1	3/7
2018	Roaring Lion	3	J Gosden	O Murphy	3-1	4/8

FAMOUS FOR its many upsets since Brigadier Gerard suffered his only defeat to Roberto in 1972, this race rediscovered its teeth in 2015 when 50-1 shot Arabian Queen stunned the mighty Golden Horn. Otherwise, though, it has turned in punters' favour in recent times with no other winner returned bigger than 8-1 since Ezzoud in 1993 and seven of the last 12 favourites winning. Older horses have dominated the three-year-olds with just seven younger horses triumphing since 1984, all of whom were recent Group 1 winners apart from Arabian Queen with the previous three being Derby winners. The best trial is the Coral-Eclipse, which has provided ten of the last 24 winners, with Roaring Lion the eighth to complete the double in that time and the second in a row.

Yorkshire Oaks (1m3f195yds) York

2009	Dar Re Mi	4	J Gosden	J Fortune	11-2	4/6
2010	Midday	4	H Cecil	T Queally	11-4	6/8
2011	Blue Bunting	3	M Al Zarooni	F Dettori	11-4f	6/8
2012	Shareta	4	A de Royer-Dupre	C Lemaire	2-1	7/6
2013	The Fugue	4	J Gosden	W Buick	2-1f	6/7
2014	Tapestry	3	A O'Brien	R Moore	8-1	6/7
2015	Pleascach	3	J Bolger	K Manning	8-1	8/11
2016	Seventh Heaven	3	A O'Brien	C O'Donoghue	10-3	10/12
2017	Enable	3	J Gosden	F Dettori	1-4f	1/6
2018	Sea Of Class	3	W Haggas	J Doyle	7-4f	5/8

ALWAYS A top-class race, this has been won by the Classic generation 13 times in the last 19 years, including each of the last five. However, Enable is the only Oaks winner to follow up since Alexandrova in 2005, with four beaten in that time – Taghrooda, Was, Snow Fairy and Sariska – three of them when favourite. Significantly, Enable and Alexandrova had won the Irish Oaks in between because that has been a better guide – the last eight Curragh winners to take their chance have finished 11221211, while 2014 heroine Tapestry had finished second in Ireland.

ALPHA DELPHINI: the third Nunthorpe winner in nine years at 40-1 or bigger

Nunthorpe Stakes (5f) York

2009	Borderlescott	7	R Bastiman	N Callan	9-1	2/16
2010	Sole Power	3	E Lynam	W Lordan	100-1	11/12
2011	Margot Did	3	M Bell	H Turner	20-1	11/15
2012	Ortensia	7	P Messara	W Buick	7-2jf	8/19
2013	Jwala	4	R Cowell	S Drowne	40-1	8/17
2014	Sole Power	7	E Lynam	R Hughes	11-4f	10/13
2015	Mecca's Angel	4	M Dods	P Mulrennan	15-2	10/19
2016	Mecca's Angel	5	M Dods	P Mulrennan	9-2	7/19
2017	Marsha	4	Sir M Prescott	L Morris	8-1	8/11
2018	Alpha Delphini	7	B Smart	G Lee	40-1	7/15

THIS HAS become a real race for upsets, none bigger than Sole Power at 100-1 in 2010, and Alpha Delphini was the second 40-1 winner since then. This is because the race isn't often won by a proven top-level sprinter, with nine of the last 17 winners never having previously landed a Group race, let alone a Group 1, even though many had had long careers as six winners in this time were six or older. Furthermore, the King's Stand is less influential than many might think as only Sole Power has done the double since 2000.

Sprint Cup (6f) Haydock

2009	Regal Parade	5	D Nicholls	A Nicholls	14-1	13/14
2010	Markab	7	H Candy	P Cosgrave	12-1	14/13
2011	Dream Ahead	3	D Simcock	W Buick	4-1f	9/16
2012	Society Rock	5	J Fanshawe	K Fallon	10-1	3/13
2013	Gordon Lord Byron	5	T Hogan	J Murtagh	7-2	2/13
2014	G Force	3	D O'Meara	D Tudhope	11-1	10/17
2015	Twilight Son	3	H Candy	F Sweeney	10-1	5/15
2016	Quiet Reflection	3	K Burke	D Costello	7-2f	4/14
2017	Harry Angel	3	C Cox	A Kirby	2-1f	8/11
2018	The Tin Man	6	J Fanshawe	O Murphy	7-1	5/12

THREE-YEAR-OLDS have taken a firm grip on this race in recent times, winning four in a row from 2014 to 2017 and six of the last 11 runnings in all from less than a third of the runners. That has turned the tide back in punters' favour – four of those winning three-year-olds were favourites – but the race is still known for plenty of upsets, with midsummer form often misleading on much softer ground. Ten of the last 17 winners were returned in double figures, including 33-1 Red Clubs in 2007, and the same number were making their breakthrough at the highest level, with Dream Ahead and Harry Angel the only July Cup winners since Ajdal in 1987 and six others beaten in the meantime.

St Leger (1m6f132yds) Doncaster

2009	**Mastery**	S bin Suroor	T Durcan	14-1	7/8
2010	**Arctic Cosmos**	J Gosden	W Buick	12-1	8/10
2011	**Masked Marvel**	J Gosden	W Buick	15-2	3/9
2012	**Encke**	M Al Zarooni	M Barzalona	25-1	1/9
2013	**Leading Light**	A O'Brien	J O'Brien	7-2f	7/11
2014	**Kingston Hill**	R Varian	A Atzeni	9-4f	4/12
2015	**Simple Verse**	R Beckett	A Atzeni	8-1	1/7
2016	**Harbour Law**	L Mongan	G Baker	22-1	9/9
2017	**Capri**	A O'Brien	R Moore	3-1f	9/11
2018	**Kew Gardens**	A O'Brien	R Moore	3-1	8/12

TOP-CLASS horses tend to be kept to shorter trips these days and Capri was an unusual winner in 2017 given he already had an Irish Derby in the bag, making him the first Curragh winner to follow up since Nijinsky, while only one Derby winner has even tried since Reference Point in 1987, with Camelot only second in 2012. Six of the nine winners to come via the Derby since 1997 finished outside the places at Epsom and even four of the nine to have warmed up in the Great Voltigeur in that time were beaten there. Still, 18 of the last 21 winners had won a Group race, with the Gordon Stakes the other key trial. Kingston Hill is the only winner in more than 25 years to have had his prep run over just 1m2f, though during that time only Leading Light warmed up beyond the Leger distance. Simple Verse is the only filly to prevail since User Friendly in 1992.

Prix de l'Arc de Triomphe (1m4f) Longchamp

2009	**Sea The Stars**	3	J Oxx	M Kinane	4-6f	6/19
2010	**Workforce**	3	Sir M Stoute	R Moore	6-1	8/19
2011	**Danedream**	3	P Schiergen	A Starke	20-1	2/16
2012	**Solemia**	4	C Laffon-Parias	O Peslier	33-1	6/18
2013	**Treve**	3	C Head-Maarek	T Jarnet	9-2	15/17
2014	**Treve**	4	C Head-Maarek	T Jarnet	11-1	3/20
2015	**Golden Horn**	3	J Gosden	F Dettori	9-2	14/17
2016	**Found**	4	A O'Brien	R Moore	6-1	12/16*
2017	**Enable**	3	J Gosden	F Dettori	10-11f	2/18*
2018	**Enable**	4	J Gosden	F Dettori	Evsf	6/19

Run at Chantilly in 2016 and 2017

THE PREMIER middle-distance championship of Europe is generally one for the French, with 17 of the last 29 winners trained at home, although the tide is turning. There hasn't been a successful French-trained colt since Rail Link in 2006 and eight of the subsequent 12 winners came from abroad. It follows that the big domestic trials have a poor record, with the Prix Niel, having thrown up ten winners in 13 years up to 2006, drawing a blank since then and the Prix Foy enduring an even worse run, with no winner since

Subotica in 1992. Fillies are enjoying a remarkable period, with eight of the last 11 renewals going to the girls including brilliant dual winners Treve and Enable. Only four horses older than four have won since the Second World War and the losers include two recent favourites in Orfevre and Treve.

Queen Elizabeth II Stakes (1m) Ascot

2009	Rip Van Winkle	3	A O'Brien	J Murtagh	8-13f	4/4
2010	Poet's Voice	3	S Bin Suroor	F Dettori	9-2	7/8
2011	Frankel	3	Sir H Cecil	T Queally	4-11f	2/8
2012	Excelebration	4	A O'Brien	J O'Brien	10-11f	6/8
2013	Olympic Glory	3	R Hannon Sr	R Hughes	11-2	7/12
2014	Charm Spirit	3	F Head	O Peslier	5-1	7/11
2015	Solow	5	F Head	M Guyon	11-10f	2/9
2016	Minding	3	A O'Brien	R Moore	7-4f	8/13
2017	Persuasive	4	J Gosden	F Dettori	8-1	6/15
2018	Roaring Lion	3	J Gosden	O Murphy	2-1f	15/13

THE MILE championship of Europe in which the Classic generation has held sway, with eight victories in the last 11 years extending a long period of superiority. That said, the time of year makes this a tough date for 2,000 Guineas winners, with Frankel and George Washington the only ones to do the double from nine to try in the last 16 years. Similarly, only Frankel and Bahri have followed up St James's Palace Stakes wins since 1995, although seven of the last 16 successful three-year-olds ran in that race before progressing subsequently. Winners tend to be proven at the highest level, with 13 of the last 16 having already won a Group 1, and as a result the 2017 winner Persuasive is the only one not to come from the first three in the market since 2001. Fillies have won two of the last three runnings having previously drawn a blank since 1987.

Champion Stakes (1m2f) Ascot

2009	Twice Over	4	H Cecil	T Queally	14-1	6/14
2010	Twice Over	5	H Cecil	T Queally	7-2	4/10
2011	Cirrus Des Aigles	5	C Barande-Barbe	C Soumillon	12-1	1/12
2012	Frankel	4	Sir H Cecil	T Queally	2-11f	6/8
2013	Farhh	5	S Bin Suroor	S de Sousa	11-4	5/10
2014	Noble Mission	5	Lady Cecil	J Doyle	7-1	5/9
2015	Fascinating Rock	4	D Weld	P Smullen	10-1	7/13
2016	Almanzor	3	J-C Rouget	C Soumillon	11-8f	1/10
2017	Cracksman	3	J Gosden	F Dettori	13-8f	4/10
2018	Cracksman	4	J Gosden	F Dettori	5-6f	8/8

Run at Newmarket un/til 2011

THE SUBJECT of a big-money makeover when switched to Ascot in 2011. Older horses have increasingly come to the fore, accounting for eight of the last ten winners including four five-year-olds. That's a trend likely to grow stronger because, among the 18 successful three-year-olds since 1980, mile form has proved a lot more influential than form over further – 12 of those 18 had won a Classic with New Approach the only one since Time Charter in 1982 to have done it over 1m4f – yet top milers now have the option of the QEII on the same day. This has been the best British Group 1 for French horses, with four winners in the last 13 years extending a long tradition of success.

RACING & FOOTBALL Outlook

Big handicap records

Lincoln (1m) Doncaster

Year	Winner	Age	Weight	Trainer	Jockey	SP	Draw/ran
2009	**Expresso Star**	4	8-12	J Gosden	J Fortune	10-3f	9/20
2010	**Penitent**	4	9-2	W Haggas	J Murtagh	3-1f	1/21
2011	**Sweet Lightning**	6	9-4	M Dods	J Murtagh	16-1	16/21*
2012	**Brae Hill**	6	9-1	R Fahey	T Hamilton	25-1	12/22
2013	**Levitate**	5	8-7	J Quinn	D Egan (3)	20-1	3/22
2014	**Ocean Tempest**	5	9-3	J Ryan	A Kirby	20-1	3/17
2015	**Gabrial**	6	9-0	R Fahey	T Hamilton	12-1	15/22
2016	**Secret Brief**	4	9-4	C Appleby	W Buick	12-1	22/22
2017	**Bravery**	4	9-1	D O'Meara	D Tudhope	20-1	1/22
2018	**Addeybb**	4	9-2	W Haggas	J Doyle	5-1	10/20

*Run at Newcastle in 2011

AS WITH all big handicaps, the rating required to get a run gets higher and higher, so long-standing trends about siding with a progressive horse on a low weight have been rendered obsolete. Even so, a big weight is still a huge disadvantage as the last winner to carry more than 9st 4lb was Babodana in 2004. It's common for runners to come via the all-weather or Dubai, but 13 of the last 17 winners were having their first run of the year and it's wise to side with trainers who have a proven track record of getting one ready as five of the last ten winning trainers – William Haggas (twice), Richard Fahey, John Quinn and Mark Tompkins – had also won the race within the previous seven years. A high draw is a concern as 11 of the last 12 winners at Doncaster came from a stall no higher than 16.

Royal Hunt Cup (1m) Royal Ascot

2009	**Forgotten Voice**	4	9-1	J Noseda	J Murtagh	4-1f	25/25
2010	**Invisible Man**	4	8-9	S Bin Suroor	F Dettori	28-1	7/29
2011	**Julienas**	4	8-8	W Swinburn	E Ahern	12-1	24/28
2012	**Prince Of Johanne**	6	9-3	T Tate	J Fahy	16-1	33/30
2013	**Belgian Bill**	5	8-11	G Baker	J Doyle	33-1	6/28
2014	**Field Of Dream**	7	9-1	J Osborne	A Kirby	20-1	33/28
2015	**GM Hopkins**	4	9-3	J Gosden	R Moore	8-1	11/30
2016	**Portage**	4	9-5	M Halford	J Doyle	10-1	4/28
2017	**Zhui Feng**	4	9-0	A Perrett	M Dwyer	25-1	26/29
2018	**Settle For Bay**	4	9-1	D Marnane	W Lee	16-1	22/30

A REAL puzzle for punters with Forgotten Voice in 2009 the only winning favourite in the last 21 years. A common mistake is to side with a lightly raced improver because experience is in fact a vital commodity – 19 of the last 21 winners had run at least eight times, which is more than many of the beaten favourites. The handicap tends to be condensed, especially after the demise of the Buckingham Palace Stakes, and few runners get in below the 9st barrier, so it's telling that only Portage (with just 9st 5lb) has carried more than 9st 3lb since 2008, making it just three in 30 years to have defied a greater burden. A high draw is generally essential, with only three of the last 16 winners at Ascot overcoming a single-figure berth.

Wokingham (6f) Royal Ascot

Year	Horse		Wt	Trainer	Jockey	SP	Draw
2009	**High Standing**	4	8-12	W Haggas	R Moore	6-1	4/26
2010	**Laddies Poker Two**	5	8-11	J Noseda	J Murtagh	9-2f	26/27
2011	**Deacon Blues**	4	8-13	J Fanshawe	J Murtagh	15-2	11/25
2012	**Dandy Boy**	6	9-8	D Marnane	P Dobbs	33-1	15/28
2013	**York Glory**	5	9-2	K Ryan	J Spencer	14-1	22/26
2014	**Baccarat**	5	9-5	R Fahey	G Chaloner (3)	9-1	27/28
2015	**Interception**	5	9-3	D Lanigan	G Baker	10-1	21/25
2016	**Outback Traveller**	5	9-1	R Cowell	M Harley	10-1	28/28
2017	**Out Do**	8	8-13	D O'Meara	D Tudhope	25-1	1/27
2018	**Bacchus**	4	9-6	B Meehan	J Crowley	33-1	16/28

THIS RACE is run at such a furious gallop that stamina comes to the fore and, while 14 of the last 15 winners had already triumphed over the big-race trip, the exception had done his winning over further and in all ten of those 15 had a 7f victory to their name, with 2015 winner Interception placed four times at 7f, including in a Listed race. Therefore the Victoria Cup, run over 7f at the same track in May, is one of the key trials, along with the 6f handicaps at Newmarket's Guineas meeting and York's Dante meeting. Fresh horses are preferred, with 12 of the last 17 winners having run no more than twice that year,

BACCHUS (right): won the Wokingham first time out, underlining the need for a fresh horse – 12 of the last 17 winners had run no more than twice that year

GOLDEN STEPS: the only Bunbury Cup winner since 2002 not to have already landed a handicap over the specialist trip of seven furlongs

which is remarkable for a sprint handicap in June. There's nothing to fear about a big weight, but only two winners have been older than five since 1999.

Northumberland Plate (2m) Newcastle

Year	Winner	Age	Wt	Trainer	Jockey	SP	Draw
2009	**Som Tala**	6	8-8	M Channon	T Culhane	16-1	4/17
2010	**Overturn**	6	8-7	D McCain	E Ahern	14-1	21/19
2011	**Tominator**	4	8-8	R Hollinshead	P Pickard (3)	25-1	14/19
2012	**Ile De Re**	6	9-3	D McCain	J Crowley	5-2f	9/16
2013	**Tominator**	6	9-10	J O'Neill	G Lee	8-1	4/18
2014	**Angel Gabrial**	5	9-1	R Fahey	G Chaloner (3)	4-1f	1/19
2015	**Quest For More**	5	9-4	R Charlton	G Baker	15-2	3/19
2016	**Antiquarium**	4	9-5	C Appleby	J McDonald	16-1	3/20
2017	**Higher Power**	5	9-9	J Fanshawe	T Queally	11-2	13/20
2018	**Withhold**	5	9-1	R Charlton	R Winston	5-1f	11/20

WITH SO much of the season revolving around Royal Ascot and Newcastle's biggest day of the summer generally coming just a week later, this provides a good opportunity for horses laid out for the race rather than coming here as an afterthought. Just two of the last 16 winners had run at Royal Ascot despite several fancied runners in that time, including four beaten favourites, coming from the royal meeting. Indeed, 11 of those 16 winners were opening their account for the season. The first bend comes shortly after the start, so those drawn high can be disadvantaged, with 12 of the last 20 winners drawn seven or lower, and Overturn used controversial tactics to overcome that in 2010. The Chester Cup is traditionally a strong guide and that has been reinforced recently with Ile De Re doing the double before Tominator and Angel Gabrial stepped up on placed efforts at Chester.

Bunbury Cup (7f) Newmarket

Year	Winner	Age	Wt	Trainer	Jockey	SP	Draw
2009	**Plum Pudding**	6	9-10	R Hannon Sr	R Moore	12-1	15/19
2010	**St Moritz**	4	9-1	M Johnston	F Dettori	4-1f	4/19
2011	**Brae Hill**	5	9-1	R Fahey	B McHugh	11-1	2/20
2012	**Bonnie Brae**	5	9-9	D Elsworth	R Moore	13-2	12/15
2013	**Field Of Dream**	6	9-7	J Osborne	A Kirby	14-1	20/19

2014	**Heaven's Guest**	4	9-3	R Fahey	T Hamilton	12-1	9/13
2015	**Rene Mathis**	5	9-1	R Fahey	P Hanagan	16-1	10/17
2016	**Golden Steps**	5	9-0	M Botti	F Dettori	7-1jf	14/16
2017	**Above The Rest**	6	9-1	D Barron	C Lee (5)	12-1	19/18
2018	**Burnt Sugar**	6	9-1	R Fell	P Hanagan	7-1	16/18

SEVEN FURLONGS tends to be a specialist trip and Golden Steps is the only winner since 2002 not to have already won a 7f handicap. Most major 7f handicaps over the season are run at Ascot, though, and not all horses act at the Berkshire track, so look for class horses who have struggled earlier in the campaign. The last nine winners hadn't won all year – just one of the last 25 had won more than once – and eight of them had been beaten at Ascot, most well down the field, but the last seven were still good enough to be rated at least 98, which tends to put them towards the top of the handicap given a mark of 91 got a run last year. Indeed, big weights shouldn't be feared at all given Mine, a three-time winner between 2002 and 2006, twice defied a burden of at least 9st 9lb and has been emulated by Bonnie Brae and Plum Pudding since then.

John Smith's Cup (1m2f85yds) York

2009	**Sirvino**	4	8-8	T Brown	N Brown (3)	16-1	16/18
2010	**Wigmore Hall**	3	8-5	M Bell	M Lane (3)	5-1	13/19
2011	**Green Destiny**	4	8-13	W Haggas	A Beschizza (3)	6-1	17-19
2012	**King's Warrior**	5	8-9	P Chapple-Hyam	R Havlin	33-1	19/18
2013	**Danchai**	4	8-11	W Haggas	A Atzeni	10-1	16/19
2014	**Farraaj**	5	9-11	R Varian	A Atzeni	6-1	22/16
2015	**Master Carpenter**	4	9-4	R Millman	P Makin	14-1	1/17
2016	**Educate**	7	9-8	I Mohammed	T Brown	18-1	14/19
2017	**Ballet Concerto**	4	9-3	Sir M Stoute	J Doyle	8-1	11/20
2018	**Euchen Glen**	5	9-3	J Goldie	A Rawlinson	20-1	3/19

LIKE THE Northumberland Plate, this is another handicap in which missing Royal Ascot helps, in keeping with 11 of the last 16 winners whereas 14 of the last 17 beaten favourites registered a top-four finish there. Combine that with a young improver and you might well be on to a winner, with Educate the only winner older than five – and just four of that age successful – since Vintage Premium in 2002 despite three-year-olds struggling desperately to get a run. Indeed, subsequent Grade 1 winner Wigmore Hall was the only three-year-old when successful in 2010 and none have made the field since. This is run on one of the best Saturdays of the summer and, with many top jockeys engaged elsewhere, it provides an opportunity for some younger riders as six of the last 13 winners were partnered by an apprentice.

Stewards' Cup (6f) Goodwood

2009	**Genki**	5	9-1	R Charlton	S Drowne	14-1	17/26
2010	**Evens And Odds**	6	9-1	D Nicholls	B Cray (5)	20-1	11/28
2011	**Hoof It**	4	10-0	M Easterby	K Fallon	13-2jf	18/27
2012	**Hawkeyethenoo**	6	9-9	J Goldie	G Lee	9-1	4/27
2013	**Rex Imperator**	4	9-4	W Haggas	N Callan	12-1	26/27
2014	**Intrinsic**	4	8-11	R Cowell	R Hughes	6-1	22/24
2015	**Magical Memory**	3	8-12	C Hills	F Dettori	6-1f	1/27
2016	**Dancing Star**	3	8-12	A Balding	D Probert	9-2f	4/27
2017	**Lancelot Du Lac**	7	9-5	D Ivory	F Dettori	25-1	15/26
2018	**Gifted Master**	5	9-11	H Palmer	J Watson (5)	20-1	25/26

THIS IS a major betting heat with a strong ante-post market and the betting has become a good guide as seven of the last nine winners were 12-1 or shorter, although the last two provided some relief for bookmakers. This is a race for established sprint handicappers and even the two three-year-old winners in the last four years had landed the big 6f handicap for that age group at Newmarket's July meeting. Fifteen of the last 21 older winners came via the Wokingham, though none of them had won at Royal Ascot and all but two had another run in between. That run tends to have been a good one as nine of the last 16 winners finished first or second in their prep race, which is amazing given the competitiveness of sprint handicaps. Only two winners since 1984 carried more than 9st 7lb, with Jason Watson's 5lb claim taking Gifted Master below that threshold last year.

Ebor (1m6f) York

2009	Sesenta	5	8-8	W Mullins	G Carroll (5)	25-1	16/19
2010	Dirar	5	9-1	G Elliott	J Spencer	14-1	22/20
2011	Moyenne Corniche	6	8-13	B Ellison	D Swift (3)	25-1	10/20
2012	Willing Foe	5	9-2	S Bin Suroor	F Dettori	12-1	16/19
2013	Tiger Cliff	4	9-0	Lady Cecil	T Queally	5-1	18/14
2014	Mutual Regard	5	9-9	J Murtagh	L Steward (5)	20-1	16/19
2015	Litigant	7	9-1	J Tuite	O Murphy	33-1	6/19
2016	Heartbreak City	6	9-6	T Martin	A McNamara (5)	15-2	15/20
2017	Nakeeta	6	9-5	I Jardine	C Rodriguez (5)	12-1	18/19
2018	Muntahaa	5	9-9	J Gosden	J Crowley	11-1	21/20

ONE OF the oldest and most famous handicaps, first run in 1847, this race received a massive cash injection last year, making it a £1 million race. Muntahaa was the first winner of the newly enriched Ebor and was a Group horse running in a handicap for the first time in more than two years under a big weight, so it remains to be seen whether the new prize-money will change the strongest trend in the race because prior to that a light weight had been a big help. Just four winners have carried more than 9st 2lb since 1998 and Muntahaa was the first in that time with more than 9st 4lb (after taking into account claims) despite the handicap becoming more and more condensed. A shrewd trainer will use a claimer to bring the weight down, with five of the last ten winners partnered by such a rider. Progressive horses are always preferred as just five winners have been older than five since Sea Pigeon in 1979 and ten of the last 15 had raced no more than nine times on the Flat in Britain or Ireland.

Ayr Gold Cup (6f) Ayr

2009	Jimmy Styles	5	9-2	C Cox	F Dettori	14-1	15/26
2010	Redford	5	9-2	D Nicholls	F Dettori	14-1	17/26
2011	Our Jonathan	4	9-6	K Ryan	F Norton	11-1	12/26
2012	Captain Ramius	6	9-0	K Ryan	P Smullen	16-1	8/26
2013	Highland Colori	5	9-4	A Balding	O Murphy (5)	20-1	19/26
2014	Louis The Pious	6	9-4	D O'Meara	J Doyle	10-1	19/27
2015	Don't Touch	3	9-1	R Fahey	T Hamilton	6-1f	8/25
2016	Brando	4	9-10	K Ryan	T Eaves	11-1	8/23
2017	Donjuan Triumphant	4	9-10	A Balding	PJ McDonald	13-2	4/17*
2018	Baron Bolt	5	9-3	P Cole	C Noble (5)	28-1	21/25
2018	Son Of Rest	4	9-3	J Stack	C Hayes	5-1f	17/25

Run at Haydock as the 32Red Gold Cup in 2017

A HISTORIC race first run in 1804, this produced a dead-heat last year as Son Of Rest

MUNTAHAA (right): the first winner of the newly enriched £1 million Ebor

just about landed a massive gamble, continuing a fightback for punters after Don't Touch in 2015 had been the only other successful favourite in the last 20 years and Donjuan Triumphant in 2017 the only other winner priced in single figures in that time. Son Of Rest was 10lb well in and, while bigger weights have been defied more in recent years, the percentage call is to avoid horses who have been hit by the handicapper for winning form – nine of the last 17 winners hadn't even won in any of their four most recent outings. Nine of the last 13 runnings have gone to major northern yards, with Kevin Ryan leading the way with four victories.

Cambridgeshire (1m1f) Newmarket

2009	**Supaseus**	6	9-1	H Morrison	T Block	16-1	7/32
2010	**Credit Swap**	5	8-7	M Wigham	J Crowley	14-1	3/35
2011	**Prince Of Johanne**	5	8-12	T Tate	J Fahy (3)	40-1	31/32
2012	**Bronze Angel**	3	8-8	M Tregoning	W Buick	9-1	21/33
2013	**Educate**	4	9-9	I Mohammed	J Murtagh	8-1f	4/33
2014	**Bronze Angel**	5	8-13	M Tregoning	L Steward (5)	14-1	11/31
2015	**Third Time Lucky**	3	8-4	R Fahey	A Beschizza	14-1	7/34
2016	**Spark Plug**	5	9-4	B Meehan	J Fortune	12-1	28/31
2017	**Dolphin Vista**	4	8-10	M Meade	G Wood (3)	50-1	29/34
2018	**Wissahickon**	3	9-5	J Gosden	F Dettori	11-1	21/33

THE FIRST leg of the Autumn Double. Because of its unusual distance and its straight course, this has thrown up a number of specialists down the years, with dual winner Bronze Angel being the most obvious recent example, so consider horses who have run well in the race before. Many of the runners are milers racing over an extra furlong, but stronger stayers often come to the fore and 12 of the last 17 winners had triumphed over 1m2f while Spark Plug had been second in a Listed race at the trip. Experience of a big field is vital and 13 of the last 15 winners had won a race of at least 13 runners, 11 of them in a handicap. Big weights spell trouble as Educate is the only horse to carry more than 9st 5lb to victory since Beauchamp Pilot in 2002.

Cesarewitch (2m2f) Newmarket

2009	Darley Sun	3	8-6	D Simcock	A Atzeni (3)	9-2f	8/32
2010	Aaim To Prosper	7	8-2	B Meehan	L-P Beuzelin (3)	16-1	3/32
2011	Never Can Tell	4	8-11	J Osborne	F Dettori	25-1	36/33
2012	Aaim To Prosper	8	9-10	B Meehan	K Fallon	66-1	1/34
2013	Scatter Dice	4	8-8	M Johnston	S de Sousa	66-1	18/33
2014	Big Easy	7	8-7	P Hobbs	T Queally	10-1	2/33
2015	Grumeti	7	8-2	A King	A Beschizza	50-1	15/34
2016	Sweet Selection	4	8-8	H Morrison	S de Sousa	7-1	23/33
2017	Withhold	4	8-8	R Charlton	S de Sousa	5-1f	24/34
2018	Low Sun	5	9-2	W Mullins	S Heffernan	11-1	13/33

THE SECOND leg of the Autumn Double. Generally punters are too swayed by a young improver as 2009 winner Darley Sun is one of only two successful three-year-olds in 25 years, with Southern France last year and St Michel in 2016 the latest beaten favourites from the Classic generation. Indeed, Darley Sun and Withhold in 2017 were rare winning favourites, with winners returned twice at 66-1 and twice at 50-1 since 2008. One of the big-priced winners, Aaim To Prosper, reinforced the significance of previous form in the race as he followed up his victory two years earlier. Scatter Dice is the only winner since 1995 not to have already been successful over at least 2m and the success of jumps yards reinforces the importance of proven stamina as just four of the last 23 runnings didn't have a recognised hurdler in the first two. The Northumberland Plate is the best trial having thrown up nine of the last 23 winners. Don't read too much into the draw as jockeys have increasingly worked out how to overcome a high berth, although seven of the last 11 winners were still drawn no higher than 18.

November Handicap (1m4f) Doncaster

2009	Charm School	4	8-12	J Gosden	J Fortune	17-2	14/23
2010	Times Up	4	8-13	J Dunlop	D O'Neill	14-1	9/22
2011	Zuider Zee	4	8-13	J Gosden	R Havlin	8-1	20/23
2012	Art Scholar	5	8-7	M Appleby	F Norton	20-1	9/23
2013	Conduct	6	9-2	W Haggas	S Sanders	8-1	21/23
2014	Open Eagle	5	8-12	D O'Meara	D Tudhope	15-2f	18/23
2015	Litigant	7	9-10	J Tuite	G Baker	10-1	12/22
2016	Prize Money	3	9-1	S bin Suroor	G Wood (5)	4-1	12/15
2017	Saunter	4	8-13	I Williams	J Crowley	6-1	14/23
2018	Royal Line	4	9-8	J Gosden	R Havlin	9-1	23/23

THE LAST big betting heat of the season and one that has changed in recent years due to the lack of three-year-olds able to get a run. When Malt Or Mash won in 2007 that age group had won 14 of the last 24 renewals and three-year-olds still have to be feared if getting in, as Prize Money proved in 2016 – bear in mind he had run just once as a two-year-old and four of the previous eight had been unraced so all were therefore late developers. However, four of the last seven winners were at least five, a massive change given just five of the previous 32 had been older than four. A big weight remains a drawback as nine of the last 12 winners carried less than 9st once taking into account jockeys' claims. Favourites have a desperate record, with Open Eagle the only one to oblige since 1995.

Big-Race Dates, Fixtures and Track Facts

Fixtures

Key - Flat, **Jumps**

March

| 30 | Sat | Kempton, Southwell, Doncaster, **Stratford**, **Uttoxeter** |
| 31 | Sun | Doncaster, **Ascot** |

April

1	Mon	Newcastle, Ayr, **Ludlow**
2	Tue	Lingfield, Wolverhampton, Musselburgh
3	Wed	Southwell, Kempton, **Market Rasen**, **Wincanton**
4	Thu	**Aintree**, Southwell, Chelmsford, **Taunton**
5	Fri	**Aintree**, Wolverhampton, Leicester, **Sedgefield**
6	Sat	**Aintree**, Lingfield, Wolverhampton, **Chepstow**, **Newcastle**
7	Sun	**Ffos Las**, **Plumpton**
8	Mon	Redcar, Windsor, **Kelso**
9	Tue	Pontefract, **Exeter**, **Southwell**
10	Wed	Lingfield, Kempton, Nottingham, **Warwick**
11	Thu	Chelmsford, Newcastle, **Towcester**, **Wetherby**
12	Fri	Kempton, Newbury, **Ayr**, **Fontwell**
13	Sat	Wolverhampton, Newbury, Thirsk, **Ayr**, **Bangor** ✖
14	Sun	**Stratford**, **Wincanton**
15	Mon	Pontefract, Windsor, **Hexham**
16	Tue	Wolverhampton, Newmarket, **Exeter**
17	Wed	Southwell, Beverley, Newmarket, **Cheltenham**
18	Thu	Chelmsford, Newmarket, Ripon, **Cheltenham**
19	Fri	Lingfield, Newcastle, Bath
20	Sat	Kempton, Musselburgh, Brighton, Nottingham, **Carlisle**, **Haydock**, **Newton Abbot**
21	Sun	Southwell, **Ffos Las**, **Market Rasen**, **Plumpton**
22	Mon	Wolverhampton, Redcar, **Chepstow**, **Fakenham**, **Huntingdon**, **Plumpton**
23	Tue	Lingfield, Wolverhampton, Yarmouth, **Ludlow**, **Sedgefield**
24	Wed	Epsom, **Fontwell**, **Perth**, **Southwell**, **Taunton**
25	Thu	Chelmsford, Beverley, **Perth**, **Warwick**, **Kempton**
26	Fri	Doncaster, Sandown, **Perth**, **Chepstow**, **Towcester**
27	Sat	Wolverhampton, Haydock, Leicester, Ripon, Doncaster, **Sandown**
28	Sun	Salisbury, Wetherby
29	Mon	Southwell, Wolverhampton, Ayr, Thirsk, Windsor ✖
30	Tue	Chelmsford, Brighton, Nottingham, Yarmouth, Ayr

May

| 1 | Wed | Southwell, Ascot, Pontefract, Bath, Brighton |
| 2 | Thu | Southwell, Chelmsford, Musselburgh, Redcar, Salisbury |

 3 Fri ....Newcastle, Chepstow, Lingfield, Musselburgh, **Cheltenham**
 4 Sat ....Goodwood, Newmarket, Thirsk, Doncaster, **Uttoxeter**, **Hexham** ✗
 5 Sun ....Hamilton, Newmarket
 6 Mon ....Bath, Beverley, Windsor, **Kempton**, **Warwick**
 7 Tue ....Wolverhampton, Wetherby, **Ayr**, **Fakenham**, **Exeter**
 8 Wed........................ Southwell, Chester, **Kelso**, **Newton Abbot**, **Fontwell**
 9 Thu.................Chelmsford, Chester, **Huntingdon**, **Worcester**, **Wincanton**
10 Fri ....Wolverhampton, Ascot, Chester, Nottingham, Ripon,
 ....**Market Rasen**
11 Sat.....................Ascot, Lingfield, Nottingham, Thirsk, **Hexham**, **Warwick**,✗
 .... **Haydock**
12 Sun.. **Ludlow**, **Plumpton**
13 Mon .... Wolverhampton, Musselburgh, Windsor, **Kempton**, **Towcester**
14 Tue ....Beverley, Chepstow, **Sedgefield**, **Southwell**, **Wincanton**
15 Wed.................................Yarmouth, York, Bath, **Newton Abbot**, **Perth**
16 Thu.. Salisbury, York, Newmarket, **Perth**, **Fontwell**
17 Fri ....Newbury, Newmarket, York, Hamilton, **Aintree**
18 Sat................ Newbury, Newmarket, Thirsk, Doncaster, **Bangor**, **Uttoxeter** ✗
19 Sun...Ripon, **Market Rasen**, **Stratford**
20 Mon.................................... Carlisle, Redcar, Leicester, Windsor, **Towcester**
21 Tue ....Wolverhampton, Brighton, Nottingham, **Hexham**, **Huntingdon**
22 Wed...........................Kempton, Ayr, Yarmouth, **Warwick**, **Southwell**
23 Thu.....................Chelmsford, Chepstow, Goodwood, Lingfield, Sandown
24 Fri .... Bath, Goodwood, Haydock, Pontefract, **Worcester**
25 Sat...... Chester, Goodwood, Haydock, York, Salisbury, **Cartmel**, **Ffos Las**
26 Sun...**Fontwell**, **Kelso**, **Uttoxeter**
27 Mon..........Chelmsford, Leicester, Redcar, Windsor, **Cartmel**, **Huntingdon**
28 Tue ....Southwell, Brighton, Leicester, Redcar, Ayr
29 Wed......................Beverley, Hamilton, **Newton Abbot**, **Cartmel**, **Warwick**
30 Thu...............................Lingfield, Wetherby, Yarmouth, Carlisle, Sandown
31 Fri ....Wolverhampton, Chelmsford, Carlisle, Epsom, Doncaster,
 .... **Stratford**

June

 1 Sat...........................Doncaster, Epsom, Musselburgh, Lingfield, **Hexham**,
 ....**Worcester**, **Stratford**
 2 Sun...Nottingham, **Fakenham**
 3 Mon......................... Wolverhampton, Brighton, Thirsk, Windsor, Lingfield, ✗
 .... Newcastle, **Bangor**, **Southwell**
 5 Wed................... Kempton, Nottingham, Ripon, **Fontwell**, **Newton Abbot**
 6 Thu................................. Chelmsford, Hamilton, Haydock, Ripon, **Ffos Las**
 7 Fri ....Brighton, Bath, Goodwood, Haydock, **Market Rasen**, **Uttoxeter**
 8 Sat........Beverley, Chelmsford, Haydock, Newmarket, Chepstow, Lingfield
 9 Sun... Goodwood, **Perth**
10 Mon...................................... Leicester, Pontefract, Windsor, **Stratford**
11 Tue ....Lingfield, Salisbury, Carlisle, Thirsk ✗
12 Wed.............................Kempton, Haydock, Yarmouth, Hamilton, **Fontwell**
13 Thu.........................Newbury, Nottingham, Yarmouth, Haydock, **Uttoxeter**
14 Fri ....Chepstow, Sandown, York, Goodwood, **Aintree**, **Newton Abbot**

ROYAL ASCOT: get set for another host of thrillers from June 18-22

15	Sat	Bath, Chester, Sandown, York, Leicester, **Hexham**, **Worcester**
16	Sun	Doncaster, Salisbury
17	Mon	Carlisle, Catterick, Nottingham, Windsor
18	Tue	Royal Ascot, Thirsk, Beverley, Brighton, **Stratford**
19	Wed	Royal Ascot, Chelmsford, Hamilton, Ripon, **Uttoxeter**
20	Thu	Royal Ascot, Chelmsford, Lingfield, Ripon, **Ffos Las**
21	Fri	Royal Ascot, Redcar, Ayr, Goodwood, Newmarket, **Market Rasen**
22	Sat	Royal Ascot, Ayr, Newmarket, Redcar, Haydock, Lingfield, **Perth**
23	Sun	Pontefract, **Hexham**, **Worcester**
24	Mon	Wolverhampton, Chepstow, Windsor, **Southwell**
25	Tue	Beverley, Brighton, Newbury, **Newton Abbot**
26	Wed	Kempton, Carlisle, Salisbury, Bath, **Worcester**
27	Thu	Newcastle, Newmarket, Nottingham, Hamilton, Leicester
28	Fri	Newcastle, Doncaster, Yarmouth, Chester, Newmarket, **Cartmel**
29	Sat	Chester, Newcastle, Newmarket, Windsor, York, Doncaster, Lingfield
30	Sun	Windsor, **Cartmel**, **Uttoxeter**

July

1	Mon	Wolverhampton, Pontefract, Catterick, Windsor
2	Tue	Brighton, Hamilton, Chepstow, **Stratford**
3	Wed	Kempton, Musselburgh, Thirsk, Bath, **Worcester**
4	Thu	Haydock, Yarmouth, Epsom, Newbury, **Perth**
5	Fri	Chelmsford, Doncaster, Sandown, Beverley, Haydock, **Newton Abbot**
6	Sat	Chelmsford, Beverley, Haydock, Leicester, Sandown, Carlisle, Nottingham

183

 7 Sun...Ayr, **Market Rasen**
 8 Mon... Ayr, Ripon, Windsor, **Worcester**
 9 Tue ....Wolverhampton, Pontefract, Brighton, **Uttoxeter**
10 Wed......................................Kempton, Catterick, Lingfield, Yarmouth, Bath
11 Thu................................Carlisle, Doncaster, Newmarket, Epsom, Newbury
12 Fri.......................... Ascot, Newmarket, York, Chepstow, Chester, **Ffos Las**
13 Sat..........................Ascot, Chester, Newmarket, York, Hamilton, Salisbury,
 .... **Newton Abbot**
14 Sun.. **Perth**, **Stratford**
15 Mon..Wolverhampton, Ayr, Ripon, Windsor
16 Tue .... Bath, Beverley, Nottingham, **Southwell**
17 Wed................. Wolverhampton, Catterick, Lingfield, Yarmouth, **Uttoxeter**
18 Thu............................. Chepstow, Hamilton, Leicester, Epsom, **Worcester**
19 Fri .... Haydock, Newbury, Nottingham, Hamilton, Newmarket, Pontefract
20 Sat................Newbury, Newmarket, Ripon, Doncaster, Haydock, **Cartmel**,
 ....**Market Rasen**
21 Sun...Redcar, **Newton Abbot**, **Stratford**
22 Mon.................................... Ayr, Beverley, Windsor, **Cartmel**
23 Tue ....Wolverhampton, Chelmsford, Musselburgh, **Southwell**
24 Wed...................................... Bath, Catterick, Lingfield, Leicester, Sandown
25 Thu........................ Sandown, Yarmouth, Doncaster, Newbury, **Worcester**
26 Fri.....................Ascot, Thirsk, Chepstow, Newmarket, York, **Uttoxeter**✗
27 Sat.........Newcastle, Ascot, Chester, Newmarket, York, Lingfield, Salisbury
28 Sun... Pontefract, **Uttoxeter**
29 Mon.................................... Ayr, Ffos Las, Windsor, **Newton Abbot**
30 Tue .... Beverley, Goodwood, Yarmouth, **Perth**, **Worcester**
31 Wed................................Goodwood, Redcar, Leicester, Sandown, **Perth**

August

 1 Thu...........................Goodwood, Nottingham, Epsom, Ffos Las, **Stratford**
 2 Fri.............. Wolverhampton, Goodwood, Bath, Musselburgh, Newmarket,
 ....**Bangor**
 3 Sat......................Chelmsford, Doncaster, Goodwood, Newmarket, Thirsk,✗
 .... Hamilton, Lingfield
 4 Sun.. Chester, **Market Rasen**
 5 Mon..Kempton, Ripon, Carlisle, Windsor
 6 Tue .... Catterick, Newbury, Nottingham, Ripon
 7 Wed.................................. Kempton, Bath, Brighton, Pontefract, Yarmouth
 8 Thu........................... Newcastle, Brighton, Haydock, Yarmouth, Sandown
 9 Fri........Chelmsford, Brighton, Musselburgh, Thirsk, Haydock, Newmarket✗
10 Sat.......... Chelmsford, Ascot, Haydock, Newmarket, Redcar, Ayr, Lingfield
11 Sun...Leicester, Windsor
12 Mon.................................... Wolverhampton, Ayr, Catterick, Windsor
13 Tue .... Lingfield, Ffos Las, Nottingham, Carlisle
14 Wed................. Kempton, Beverley, Salisbury, **Newton Abbot**, **Worcester**
15 Thu.............................Lingfield, Beverley, Salisbury, Chepstow, Yarmouth
16 Fri.............................Wolverhampton, Chelmsford, Newbury, Nottingham,
 .... Newmarket, Thirsk ✗

17 Sat............................Doncaster, Newbury, Newmarket, Ripon, Bath, **Perth**,
....**Market Rasen**
18 Sun..Pontefract, **Southwell**
19 Mon..Lingfield, Catterick, Windsor, **Bangor**
20 Tue ....Kempton, Brighton, Hamilton, Yarmouth, **Newton Abbot**
21 Wed...Kempton, Bath, Carlisle, York, **Worcester**
22 Thu.............................Chepstow, York, Leicester, **Stratford**, **Fontwell**
23 Fri.............Chelmsford, Ffos Las, Newmarket, York, Goodwood, Salisbury
24 Sat.............Chelmsford, Goodwood, Newmarket, York, Redcar, Windsor,
....**Cartmel**
25 Sun..Beverley, Goodwood, Yarmouth
26 Mon...................................Southwell, Chepstow, Epsom, Ripon, **Cartmel**
27 Tue ....Epsom, Ripon, Bath, Musselburgh
28 Wed.....................Kempton, Catterick, Lingfield, Musselburgh, **Worcester**
29 Thu...........................Chelmsford, Carlisle, Ffos Las, **Fontwell**, **Sedgefield**
30 Fri.........Newcastle, Wolverhampton, Sandown, Thirsk, Hamilton, **Bangor**✗
31 Sat...................Wolverhampton, Chelmsford, Lingfield, Beverley, Chester,
....Sandown, **Newton Abbot**

September

1 Sun...Brighton, **Worcester**
2 Mon..Brighton, Chepstow, Windsor, **Hexham**
3 Tue ....Catterick, Goodwood, Kempton, Salisbury
4 Wed.....................Chelmsford, Bath, Hamilton, **Southwell**, **Uttoxeter**
5 Thu.......................Chelmsford, Haydock, Salisbury, Lingfield, **Sedgefield**
6 Fri..............................Newcastle, Kempton, Ascot, Haydock, Musselburgh
7 Sat..............Kempton, Wolverhampton, Ascot, Haydock, Thirsk, **Stratford**✗
8 Sun...York, **Fontwell**
9 Mon...............................Wolverhampton, Brighton, **Newton Abbot**, **Perth**
10 Tue ....Catterick, Leicester, **Worcester**, **Kelso**
11 Wed...............................Kempton, Carlisle, Doncaster, **Uttoxeter**
12 Thu...............................Chelmsford, Chepstow, Doncaster, Epsom
13 Fri.................................Chester, Doncaster, Sandown, Salisbury
14 Sat..............Chelmsford, Bath, Chester, Doncaster, Lingfield, Musselburgh
15 Sun..Bath, Ffos Las
16 Mon.................................Kempton, Brighton, Thirsk, **Worcester** ✗
17 Tue ....Newcastle, Chepstow, Redcar, Yarmouth
18 Wed...................................Beverley, Sandown, Yarmouth, **Kelso**
19 Thu................................Chelmsford, Southwell, Ayr, Pontefract, Yarmouth
20 Fri.......................................Newcastle, Ayr, Newbury, **Newton Abbot**
21 Sat.......Chelmsford, Wolverhampton, Ayr, Catterick, Newbury, Newmarket
22 Sun...Hamilton, **Plumpton**
23 Mon.................................Kempton, Hamilton, Leicester, **Warwick**
24 Tue ....Lingfield, Chelmsford, Beverley, **Warwick**
25 Wed.............................Kempton, Newcastle, Goodwood, Redcar, **Perth**
26 Thu.......................Chelmsford, Southwell, Newmarket, Pontefract, **Perth**
27 Fri..Newcastle, Haydock, Newmarket, **Worcester**
28 Sat......Chelmsford, Chester, Haydock, Newmarket, Ripon, **Market Rasen**

29 Sun..Epsom, Musselburgh
30 Mon................................. Wolverhampton, Bath, Hamilton, **Newton Abbot**

October

1 Tue .... Kempton, Ayr, **Sedgefield, Southwell**
2 Wed................... Kempton, Newcastle, Nottingham, **Bangor, Huntingdon**
3 Thu.................Lingfield, Chelmsford, Wolverhampton, Salisbury, **Warwick**
4 Fri..Southwell, Ascot, **Fontwell, Hexham**
5 Sat......................... Wolverhampton, Ascot, Newmarket, Redcar, **Fontwell**
6 Sun...**Kelso**, Uttoxeter
7 Mon..Newcastle, Pontefract, Windsor, **Stratford**
8 Tue ....Chelmsford, Brighton, Catterick, Leicester
9 Wed...................... Kempton, Newcastle, Nottingham, **Ludlow, Towcester**
10 Thu........................... Kempton, Southwell, Ayr, **Exeter, Worcester**
11 Fri..Newcastle, Newmarket, York, **Chepstow**
12 Sat.....................Wolverhampton, Newmarket, York, **Chepstow, Hexham**
13 Sun...Goodwood, **Newton Abbot**
14 Mon............................Wolverhampton, Musselburgh, Windsor, Yarmouth
15 Tue ....Kempton, Leicester, **Hereford, Huntingdon**
16 Wed.............................Kempton, Southwell, Bath, Nottingham, **Wetherby**
17 Thu............. Chelmsford, Wolverhampton, Brighton, **Carlisle, Wincanton**
18 Fri........................... Newcastle, Haydock, Redcar, **Fakenham, Uttoxeter**
19 Sat................Wolverhampton, Ascot, Catterick, **Ffos Las, Market Rasen**,
.... **Stratford**
20 Sun..**Kempton**, Sedgefield
21 Mon............................. Southwell, Pontefract, Windsor, **Plumpton**
22 Tue ....Newcastle, Kempton, Yarmouth, **Exeter**
23 Wed............ Kempton, Wolverhampton, Newmarket, **Fontwell, Worcester**
24 Thu................. Chelmsford, Wolverhampton, **Carlisle, Ludlow, Southwell**
25 Fri... Newcastle, Doncaster, Newbury, **Cheltenham**
26 Sat......................... Chelmsford, Doncaster, Newbury, **Cheltenham, Kelso**
27 Sun..**Aintree, Wincanton**
28 Mon... Kempton, Leicester, Redcar, **Ayr**
29 Tue .... Southwell, Catterick, **Bangor, Chepstow**
30 Wed............Kempton, Wolverhampton, Nottingham, **Fakenham, Taunton**
31 Thu................. Lingfield, Chelmsford, Kempton, **Newton Abbot, Stratford**

November

1 Fri..Newcastle, Newmarket, **Uttoxeter, Wetherby**
2 Sat...................................Chelmsford, Newmarket, **Ascot, Ayr, Wetherby**
3 Sun...**Carlisle, Huntingdon**
4 Mon........................... Kempton, Newcastle, **Hereford, Plumpton**
5 Tue ....Southwell, Kempton, Redcar, **Exeter**
6 Wed.... Kempton, Wolverhampton, Nottingham, **Chepstow, Musselburgh**
7 Thu............ Chelmsford, Southwell, **Market Rasen, Newbury**, Sedgefield
8 Fri...Newcastle, **Fontwell, Hexham, Warwick**
9 Sat...............................Southwell, Doncaster, **Aintree, Kelso, Wincanton**
10 Sun...**Ffos Las, Sandown**
11 Mon...**Carlisle, Kempton, Stratford**

12	Tue	Hereford, Huntingdon, **Lingfield**
13	Wed	**Ayr, Bangor, Exeter**
14	Thu	**Ludlow, Sedgefield, Taunton**
15	Fri	**Cheltenham, Newcastle, Southwell**
16	Sat	Lingfield, Wolverhampton, **Cheltenham, Uttoxeter, Wetherby**
17	Sun	**Cheltenham, Fontwell**
18	Mon	Wolverhampton, Southwell, **Leicester, Plumpton**
19	Tue	Kempton, Chelmsford, **Fakenham, Lingfield**
20	Wed	Kempton, **Chepstow, Hexham, Warwick**
21	Thu	Newcastle, Chelmsford, **Market Rasen, Wincanton**
22	Fri	Newcastle, **Ascot, Catterick, Ffos Las**
23	Sat	Lingfield, Wolverhampton, **Ascot, Haydock, Huntingdon**
24	Sun	**Exeter, Uttoxeter**
25	Mon	**Kempton, Ludlow, Musselburgh**
26	Tue	Wolverhampton, **Sedgefield, Southwell**
27	Wed	Southwell, Kempton, **Hereford, Wetherby**
28	Thu	Lingfield, Chelmsford, **Taunton, Towcester**
29	Fri	Southwell, Kempton, **Doncaster, Newbury**
30	Sat	Wolverhampton, **Bangor, Doncaster, Newbury, Newcastle**

December

1	Sun	**Carlisle**, Leicester
2	Mon	Wolverhampton, **Musselburgh, Plumpton**
3	Tue	Wolverhampton, **Lingfield, Southwell**
4	Wed	Lingfield, Kempton, **Haydock, Ludlow**
5	Thu	Southwell, **Leicester, Market Rasen, Wincanton**
6	Fri	Newcastle, **Exeter, Sandown, Sedgefield**
7	Sat	Wolverhampton, **Aintree, Chepstow, Sandown, Wetherby**
8	Sun	**Huntingdon, Kelso**
9	Mon	Lingfield, Newcastle, **Musselburgh**
10	Tue	Wolverhampton, **Fontwell, Uttoxeter**
11	Wed	Lingfield, Kempton, **Hexham, Leicester**
12	Thu	Chelmsford, **Newcastle, Taunton, Warwick**
13	Fri	Chelmsford, **Bangor, Cheltenham, Doncaster**
14	Sat	Newcastle, Wolverhampton, **Cheltenham, Doncaster, Hereford**
15	Sun	**Carlisle**, Southwell
16	Mon	Wolverhampton, **Ffos Las, Plumpton**
17	Tue	**Catterick, Fakenham, Lingfield**
18	Wed	Lingfield, Newcastle, **Ludlow, Newbury**
19	Thu	Southwell, Wolverhampton, **Exeter, Towcester**
20	Fri	Southwell, Wolverhampton, **Ascot, Uttoxeter**
21	Sat	Lingfield, **Ascot, Haydock, Newcastle**
26	Thu	Wolverhampton, **Fontwell, Huntingdon, Kempton, Market Rasen, Sedgefield, Wetherby, Wincanton**
27	Fri	Wolverhampton, **Chepstow, Kempton, Wetherby**
28	Sat	Lingfield, **Catterick, Leicester, Newbury**
29	Sun	Southwell, **Doncaster, Kelso**
30	Mon	Lingfield, **Haydock, Taunton**
31	Tue	Lingfield, **Uttoxeter, Warwick**

Big-race dates

March
30 Mar	Doncaster	Lincoln (Heritage Handicap)

April
13 Apr	Newbury	Fred Darling Stakes (Group 3)
13 Apr	Newbury	Greenham Stakes (Group 3)
13 Apr	Newbury	John Porter Stakes (Group 3)
16 Apr	Newmarket	Nell Gwyn Stakes (Group 3)
17 Apr	Newmarket	Earl of Sefton Stakes (Group 3)
18 Apr	Newmarket	Craven Stakes (Group 3)
19 Apr	Lingfield	All-Weather Championship Finals
26 Apr	Sandown	Gordon Richards Stakes (Group 3)
26 Apr	Sandown	bet365 Mile (Group 2)

May
1 May	Ascot	Sagaro Stakes (Group 3)
4 May	Newmarket	2,000 Guineas (Group 1)
4 May	Newmarket	Dahlia Stakes (Group 3)
5 May	Newmarket	1,000 Guineas (Group 1)
5 May	Newmarket	Jockey Club Stakes (Group 2)
8 May	Chester	Chester Vase (Group 3)
9 May	Chester	Ormonde Stakes (Group 3)
10 May	Chester	Chester Cup (Heritage Handicap)
10 May	Chester	Huxley Stakes (Group 3)
11 May	Ascot	Victoria Cup (Heritage Handicap)
11 May	Lingfield	Derby Trial (Group 3)
15 May	York	Duke of York Stakes (Group 2)
15 May	York	Musidora Stakes (Group 3)
16 May	York	Dante Stakes (Group 2)
16 May	York	Middleton Stakes (Group 3)
17 May	York	Yorkshire Cup (Group 2)
18 May	Newbury	Lockinge Stakes (Group 1)
25 May	Haydock	Temple Stakes (Group 2)
25 May	Haydock	Sandy Lane Stakes (Group 2)
30 May	Sandown	Henry II Stakes (Group 2)
30 May	Sandown	Brigadier Gerard Stakes (Group 3)
31 May	Epsom	The Oaks (Group 1)
31 May	Epsom	Coronation Cup (Group 1)

June
1 Jun	Epsom	The Derby (Group 1)
1 Jun	Epsom	Princess Elizabeth Stakes (Group 3)
8 Jun	Haydock	John of Gaunt Stakes (Group 3)
8 Jun	Haydock	Pinnacle Stakes (Group 3)
18 Jun	Royal Ascot	King's Stand Stakes (Group 1)
18 Jun	Royal Ascot	Queen Anne Stakes (Group 1)
18 Jun	Royal Ascot	St James's Palace Stakes (Group 1)
18 Jun	Royal Ascot	Coventry Stakes (Group 2)
19 Jun	Royal Ascot	Prince of Wales's Stakes (Group 1)
19 Jun	Royal Ascot	Queen Mary Stakes (Group 2)
19 Jun	Royal Ascot	Duke of Cambridge Stakes (Group 2)
19 Jun	Royal Ascot	Jersey Stakes (Group 3)

19 Jun	Royal Ascot	Royal Hunt Cup (Heritage Handicap)
20 Jun	Royal Ascot	Gold Cup (Group 1)
20 Jun	Royal Ascot	Ribblesdale Stakes (Group 2)
20 Jun	Royal Ascot	Norfolk Stakes (Group 2)
21 Jun	Royal Ascot	Coronation Stakes (Group 1)
21 Jun	Royal Ascot	Commonwealth Cup (Group 1)
21 Jun	Royal Ascot	King Edward VII Stakes (Group 2)
21 Jun	Royal Ascot	Albany Stakes (Group 3)
22 Jun	Royal Ascot	Diamond Jubilee Stakes (Group 1)
22 Jun	Royal Ascot	Hardwicke Stakes (Group 2)
22 Jun	Royal Ascot	Wokingham (Heritage Handicap)
29 Jun	Newcastle	Northumberland Plate (Heritage Handicap)
29 Jun	Newcastle	Chipchase Stakes (Group 3)
29 Jun	Newmarket	Criterion Stakes (Group 3)

July

6 Jul	Sandown	Coral-Eclipse Stakes (Group 1)
6 Jul	Haydock	Lancashire Oaks (Group 2)
11 Jul	Newmarket	Princess of Wales's Stakes (Group 2)
11 Jul	Newmarket	July Stakes (Group 2)
12 Jul	Newmarket	Falmouth Stakes (Group 1)
12 Jul	Newmarket	Duchess of Cambridge Stakes (Group 2)
12 Jul	York	Summer Stakes (Group 3)
13 Jul	Newmarket	July Cup (Group 1)
13 Jul	Newmarket	Superlative Stakes (Group 2)
13 Jul	Newmarket	Bunbury Cup (Heritage Handicap)
13 Jul	York	John Smith's Cup (Heritage Handicap)
20 Jul	Newbury	Hackwood Stakes (Group 3)
27 Jul	Ascot	King George VI and Queen Elizabeth Stakes (Group 1)
27 Jul	Ascot	Summer Mile (Group 2)
27 Jul	York	York Stakes (Group 2)
30 Jul	Goodwood	Goodwood Cup (Group 2)
30 Jul	Goodwood	Lennox Stakes (Group 2)
30 Jul	Goodwood	Vintage Stakes (Group 2)
31 Jul	Goodwood	Sussex Stakes (Group 1)
31 Jul	Goodwood	Molecomb Stakes (Group 3)

August

1 Aug	Goodwood	Nassau Stakes (Group 1)
1 Aug	Goodwood	Richmond Stakes (Group 2)
2 Aug	Goodwood	Betfred Mile (Heritage Handicap)
2 Aug	Goodwood	King George Stakes (Group 2)
2 Aug	Goodwood	Oak Tree Stakes (Group 3)
3 Aug	Goodwood	Stewards' Cup (Heritage Handicap)
3 Aug	Goodwood	Gordon Stakes (Group 3)
10 Aug	Ascot	Shergar Cup Day
10 Aug	Haydock	Rose of Lancaster Stakes (Group 3)
10 Aug	Newmarket	Sweet Solera Stakes (Group 3)
15 Aug	Salisbury	Sovereign Stakes (Group 3)
17 Aug	Newbury	Hungerford Stakes (Group 2)
17 Aug	Newbury	Geoffrey Freer Stakes (Group 3)
21 Aug	York	Juddmonte International (Group 1)
21 Aug	York	Great Voltigeur Stakes (Group 2)
21 Aug	York	Acomb Stakes (Group 3)
22 Aug	York	Yorkshire Oaks (Group 1)
22 Aug	York	Lowther Stakes (Group 2)
23 Aug	York	Nunthorpe Stakes (Group 1)

23 Aug	York	Lonsdale Cup (Group 2)
23 Aug	York	Gimcrack Stakes (Group 2)
24 Aug	York	Ebor (Heritage Handicap)
24 Aug	York	City of York Stakes (Group 2)
24 Aug	Goodwood	Celebration Mile (Group 2)
24 Aug	Goodwood	Prestige Stakes (Group 3)
24 Aug	Windsor	Winter Hill Stakes (Group 3)
31 Aug	Sandown	Solario Stakes (Group 3)

September

7 Sep	Haydock	Sprint Cup (Group 1)
7 Sep	Kempton	Sirenia Stakes (Group 3)
7 Sep	Kempton	September Stakes (Group 3)
12 Sep	Doncaster	May Hill Stakes (Group 2)
12 Sep	Doncaster	Park Hill Stakes (Group 2)
13 Sep	Doncaster	Doncaster Cup (Group 2)
13 Sep	Doncaster	Flying Childers Stakes (Group 2)
14 Sep	Doncaster	St Leger (Group 1)
14 Sep	Doncaster	Park Stakes (Group 2)
14 Sep	Doncaster	Champagne Stakes (Group 2)
14 Sep	Doncaster	Portland (Heritage Handicap)
21 Sep	Ayr	Ayr Gold Cup (Heritage Handicap)
21 Sep	Ayr	Firth Of Clyde Stakes (Group 3)
21 Sep	Newbury	Mill Reef Stakes (Group 2)
21 Sep	Newbury	World Trophy (Group 3)
21 Sep	Newbury	Arc Trial (Group 3)
26 Sep	Newmarket	Tattersalls Stakes (Group 3)
27 Sep	Newmarket	Rockfel Stakes (Group 2)
27 Sep	Newmarket	Joel Stakes (Group 2)
28 Sep	Newmarket	Cambridgeshire (Heritage Handicap)
28 Sep	Newmarket	Middle Park Stakes (Group 1)
28 Sep	Newmarket	Cheveley Park Stakes (Group 1)
28 Sep	Newmarket	Royal Lodge Stakes (Group 2)

October

5 Oct	Newmarket	Sun Chariot Stakes (Group 1)
5 Oct	Ascot	Cumberland Lodge Stakes (Group 3)
5 Oct	Ascot	Bengough Stakes (Group 3)
11 Oct	Newmarket	Fillies' Mile (Group 1)
11 Oct	Newmarket	Challenge Stakes (Group 2)
11 Oct	Newmarket	Cornwallis Stakes (Group 3)
11 Oct	Newmarket	Oh So Sharp Stakes (Group 3)
12 Oct	Newmarket	Cesarewitch (Heritage Handicap)
12 Oct	Newmarket	Dewhurst Stakes (Group 1)
12 Oct	Newmarket	Autumn Stakes (Group 3)
12 Oct	Newmarket	Darley Stakes (Group 3)
19 Oct	Ascot	Queen Elizabeth II Stakes (Group 1)
19 Oct	Ascot	Champion Stakes (Group 1)
19 Oct	Ascot	Champions Sprint (Group 1)
19 Oct	Ascot	Champions Filly & Mare Stakes (Group 1)
19 Oct	Ascot	Champions Long Distance Cup (Group 2)
26 Oct	Doncaster	Vertem Futurity Trophy (Group 1)
26 Oct	Newbury	Horris Hill Stakes (Group 3)
26 Oct	Newbury	St Simon Stakes (Group 3)

November

| 9 Nov | Doncaster | November (Heritage Handicap) |

Track Facts

WANT TO size up the layout and undulations of the course where your fancy's about to line up? Over the next 30-odd pages, we bring you three-dimensional maps of all Britain's Flat tracks, allowing you to see at a glance the task facing your selection. The maps come to you courtesy of the Racing Post's website (www.racingpost.com).

We've listed the top dozen trainers and jockeys at each course, ranked by strike-rate, with a breakdown of their relevant statistics over the last four years. We've also included addresses, phone numbers, directions and fixture lists for each track, together with Racing Post standard times for all you clock-watchers.

ASCOT

Ascot, Berkshire SL5 7JX
Tel 0870 7227 227

How to get there Road: M4 junction 6 or M3 junction 3 on to A332. Rail: Frequent service from Reading or Waterloo

Features RH, stiff climb for final mile on round course

2019 Fixtures May 1, 10-11, June 18-22, July 12-13, 26-27, August 10, September 6-7, October 4-5, 19

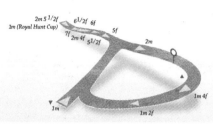

○ Winning Post
◄ Startpoint
▲ Highest Point
▼ Lowest Point
➤ Open ditch
⟁ Water jump
⚑ Fence

Racing Post standard times

5f	59.5	1m2f	2min5
6f	1min12.4	1m4f	2min28.9
7f	1min25.6	2m	3min22
1m (str)	1min38.8	2m4f	4min20
1m (rnd)	1min39.8	2m5f159yds	4min45

Trainers	Wins-Runs	%	2yo	3yo+	£1 level stks
John Gosden	33-212	16	5-19	28-193	-28.88
A P O'Brien	27-175	15	7-32	20-143	-4.59
Richard Hannon	20-254	8	12-89	8-165	-108.00
Charlie Appleby	20-127	16	7-23	13-104	-12.85
William Haggas	19-142	13	3-21	16-121	-26.06
Mark Johnston	18-190	9	9-56	9-134	-74.88
Sir Michael Stoute	18-128	14	2-6	16-122	+12.57
Roger Varian	12-102	12	1-14	11-88	-50.27
Saeed bin Suroor	11-89	12	2-13	9-76	-23.70
Jamie Osborne	11-43	26	0-10	11-33	+54.25
Andrew Balding	10-135	7	0-13	10-122	-83.50
Roger Charlton	9-58	16	2-7	7-51	-17.50
Clive Cox	8-94	9	3-24	5-70	-20.00

Jockeys	Wins-Rides	%	£1 level stks	Best Trainer	W-R
Ryan Moore	42-214	20	-27.07	A P O'Brien	24-96
William Buick	35-196	18	-0.73	Charlie Appleby	13-80
Frankie Dettori	26-139	19	-12.38	John Gosden	16-62
Jamie Spencer	21-178	12	+9.57	Jamie Osborne	3-7
James Doyle	20-155	13	-27.97	Saeed bin Suroor	3-33
Andrea Atzeni	15-144	10	-41.59	Roger Varian	5-51
Adam Kirby	14-149	9	-21.80	Clive Cox	7-52
Silvestre De Sousa	13-167	8	-67.55	Mark Johnston	3-23
Martin Harley	12-108	11	+23.00	William Haggas	3-4
Jim Crowley	11-165	7	-64.00	Owen Burrows	2-13
Oisin Murphy	8-121	7	-29.63	Hugo Palmer	1-1
Fran Berry	6-80	8	-23.00	Mick Quinn	2-3
Luke Morris	6-73	8	-22.55	Sir Mark Prescott Bt	2-15

Favourites

2yo	35.4%	-5.98	3yo	30.8%	-17.74	TOTAL	31.5%	-12.42

Whitletts Road Ayr KA8 0JE.
Tel 01292 264 179

How to get there

Road: south from
Glasgow on A77
or A75, A70, A76.
Rail: Ayr, bus
service from
station on big
race days

Features LH

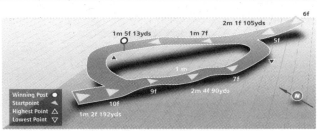

2019 Fixtures

April 1, 29-30, May 22, 28, June 21-22,
July 7-8, 15, 22, 29, August 10, 12,
September 19-21, October 1, 10

Racing Post standard times

5f	57.7	1m2f192yds	2min17.5
6f	1min10	1m5f13yds	2min47
7f50yds	1min28	1m7f	3min15
1m	1min38	2m1f105yds	3min49
1m1f20yds	1min51	2m4f90yds	4min31
1m2f	2min6		

Trainers	Wins-Runs	%	2yo	3yo+	£1 level stks
Keith Dalgleish	52-409	13	13-75	39-334	+36.89
Jim Goldie	45-475	9	0-7	45-468	-65.67
Richard Fahey	30-299	10	9-72	21-227	-94.37
Michael Dods	28-249	11	7-44	21-205	-8.88
David O'Meara	26-172	15	0-14	26-158	-25.75
K R Burke	20-110	18	7-32	13-78	-15.27
Iain Jardine	19-178	11	1-20	18-158	-40.25
Ruth Carr	19-147	13	0-0	19-147	+1.45
R Mike Smith	18-147	12	0-5	18-142	+58.50
Linda Perratt	16-268	6	0-12	16-256	-119.50
Adrian Paul Keatley	13-69	19	0-3	13-66	+5.88
Kevin Ryan	11-132	8	7-40	4-92	-52.63
Tim Easterby	11-114	10	0-12	11-102	-19.09

Jockeys	Wins-Rides	%	£1 level stks	Best Trainer	W-R
Daniel Tudhope	33-178	19	+42.25	David O'Meara	14-77
Paul Mulrennan	32-216	15	-19.96	Michael Dods	12-97
Phillip Makin	31-168	18	+46.85	Keith Dalgleish	19-94
P J McDonald	26-209	12	-19.35	R Mike Smith	8-39
James Sullivan	25-217	12	+4.53	Ruth Carr	17-111
Graham Lee	23-198	12	+25.45	Keith Dalgleish	5-33
Joe Fanning	21-180	12	-64.04	Keith Dalgleish	5-46
Connor Beasley	14-158	9	-83.94	Keith Dalgleish	6-47
Callum Rodriguez	13-88	15	+35.58	Michael Dods	6-39
Ben Curtis	13-81	16	-17.18	K R Burke	5-12
Tony Hamilton	12-141	9	-57.75	Richard Fahey	7-88
Jason Hart	12-96	13	+24.75	Keith Dalgleish	3-18
David Allan	12-94	13	+9.66	Tim Easterby	6-54

Favourites

2yo	31%	-16.21		3yo	27%	-34.59	TOTAL 28.5%	-98.94

BATH

Lansdown, Bath, Glos BA1 9BU
Tel 01291 622 260

How to get there
Road: M4, Jctn
18, then A46
south.
Rail: Bath Spa,
special bus
service to course
on race days

Features LH
uphill 4f straight

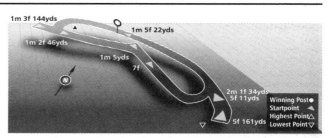

1m 3f 144yds
1m 5f 22yds
1m 2f 46yds
1m 5yds
7f
2m 1f 34yds
5f 11yds
5f 161yds

Winning Post ●
Startpoint ◄
Highest Point △
Lowest Point ▽

2019 Fixtures April 19, May 1, 6, 15, 24, June 7, 15, 26, July 3, 10, 16, 24, August 2, 7, 17, 21, 27, September 4, 14-15, 30, October 16

Racing Post standard times

5f11yds	1min0.8	1m3f144yds	2min28
5f161yds	1min9.6	1m5f22yds	2min48.5
1m5yds	1min39	2m1f34yds	3min40
1m2f46yds	2min8		

Trainers	Wins-Runs	%	2yo	3yo+	£1 level stks
Malcolm Saunders	28-126	22	0-2	28-124	+25.91
Mick Channon	24-117	21	7-28	17-89	+8.50
Richard Hannon	23-136	17	11-63	12-73	-26.24
Clive Cox	18-91	20	7-21	11-70	-12.08
Ronald Harris	16-134	12	2-19	14-115	-2.00
Charles Hills	16-72	22	4-20	12-52	+5.30
Tony Carroll	14-117	12	0-7	14-110	-1.17
Rod Millman	14-91	15	1-14	13-77	+43.63
Mark Johnston	13-63	21	4-17	9-46	-19.79
Roger Charlton	13-41	32	3-7	10-34	+19.83
Sir Mark Prescott Bt	12-31	39	0-4	12-27	-5.08
Brian Meehan	11-49	22	4-22	7-27	+19.73
Andrew Balding	10-71	14	2-12	8-59	-8.59

Jockeys	Wins-Rides	%	£1 level stks	Best Trainer	W-R
Silvestre De Sousa	28-124	23	-18.34	Mark Johnston	6-14
Luke Morris	25-173	14	-60.66	Sir Mark Prescott Bt	12-28
Steve Drowne	19-107	18	+58.88	George Baker	5-19
Adam Kirby	19-65	29	+31.91	Clive Cox	10-30
David Probert	13-107	12	-41.78	Ed de Giles	3-3
Oisin Murphy	13-97	13	+7.68	Rod Millman	3-7
Tom Marquand	13-84	15	+11.37	Richard Hannon	4-21
Josephine Gordon	13-80	16	+27.67	Malcolm Saunders	3-12
Franny Norton	13-71	18	-17.38	Malcolm Saunders	2-3
George Baker	13-37	35	+8.58	Roger Charlton	3-7
Charles Bishop	12-82	15	+6.75	Mick Channon	7-22
Fran Berry	12-75	16	+5.03	Jonjo O'Neill	3-8
Dane O'Neill	12-60	20	+8.80	Richard Hannon	2-3

Favourites

2yo	41.4% +0.74	3yo	39%	-23.91	TOTAL 35.4%	-57.56

York Road, Beverley, E Yorkshire
HU17 8QZ. Tel 01482 867 488

BEVERLEY

How to get there
Road: Course is
signposted from
the M62. Rail:
Beverley, bus
service to course
on race days

Features RH,
uphill finish

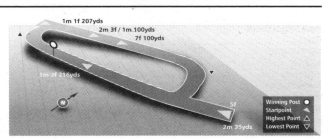

1m 1f 207yds
2m 3f / 1m 100yds
7f 100yds
1m 3f 216yds
5f
2m 35yds

Winning Post ●
Startpoint ◄
Highest Point △
Lowest Point ▽

2019 Fixtures
April 17, 25, May 6, 14, 29, June 8, 18,
25, July 5-6, 16, 22, 30, August 14-15,
25, 31, September 18, 24

Racing Post standard times

5f	1min1	1m4f16yds	2min34.2
7f100yds	1min30	2m35yds	3min30
1m100yds	1min43	2m3f100yds	4min17
1m1f207yds	2min1.3		

Trainers	Wins-Runs	%	2yo	3yo+	£1 level stks
Richard Fahey	42-295	14	17-113	25-182	-107.36
Mark Johnston	40-218	18	19-74	21-144	-39.64
David O'Meara	35-215	16	2-39	33-176	-4.54
Tim Easterby	31-263	12	3-70	28-193	-97.08
Kevin Ryan	20-150	13	9-51	11-99	+19.33
Les Eyre	13-96	14	1-11	12-85	-1.20
Richard Guest	12-54	22	2-4	10-50	+50.50
Karen Tutty	11-70	16	0-1	11-69	+31.25
Michael Dods	11-59	19	6-21	5-38	-4.75
David Loughnane	11-42	26	0-4	11-38	+76.75
Ollie Pears	10-104	10	1-25	9-79	+9.75
Ann Duffield	10-102	10	5-53	5-49	-54.38
Brian Ellison	10-100	10	5-27	5-73	-27.31

Jockeys	Wins-Rides	%	£1 level stks	Best Trainer	W-R
Joe Fanning	38-218	17	-37.91	Mark Johnston	27-140
Daniel Tudhope	36-138	26	+58.93	David O'Meara	17-81
David Allan	29-235	12	-90.20	Tim Easterby	16-126
Ben Curtis	23-116	20	+20.53	Brian Ellison	5-22
Paul Mulrennan	22-143	15	-29.69	Michael Dods	9-33
Paul Hanagan	22-123	18	-33.67	Richard Fahey	17-81
Tony Hamilton	21-144	15	-28.03	Richard Fahey	13-92
Graham Lee	19-173	11	-76.52	Bryan Smart	5-24
P J McDonald	15-170	9	-95.13	Ann Duffield	7-50
Tom Eaves	13-194	7	-86.84	Kevin Ryan	6-44
Andrew Mullen	11-141	8	-28.65	Ollie Pears	3-32
Phillip Makin	10-86	12	-34.65	Keith Dalgleish	3-19
Jason Hart	10-84	12	-28.53	John Quinn	5-35

Favourites

2yo	36%	-22.92		3yo	40.7%	+10.66	TOTAL	35.2%	-37.43

BRIGHTON

Freshfield Road, Brighton, E Sussex
BN2 2XZ. Tel 01273 603 580

How to get there
Road:
Signposted from
A23 London
Road and A27.
Rail: Brighton,
bus to course on
race days

Features LH,
undulating, sharp

5f 59yds	
5f 213yds	6f 209yds
	7f 214yds
	1 m 1f 209yds
	1m 3f 196yds

Winning Post ●
Startpoint ◄
Highest Point △
Lowest Point ▽

2019 Fixtures April 20, 30, May 1, 21,
28, June 3, 7, 18, 25, July 2, 9, August
7-9, 20, September 1-2, 9, 16, October
8, 17

Racing Post standard times

5f59yds	1min0.4	7f214yds	1min33
5f213yds	1min8.4	1m1f209yds	1min59.4
6f209yds	1min20.5	1m3f196yds	2min28.8

Trainers	Wins-Runs	%	2yo	3yo+	£1 level stks
Richard Hannon	28-118	24	12-50	16-68	+45.81
Tony Carroll	27-182	15	0-3	27-179	-8.29
Gary Moore	27-176	15	4-20	23-156	-1.40
Richard Hughes	20-78	26	4-18	16-60	+10.57
John Gallagher	17-89	19	1-7	16-82	+39.00
Eve Johnson Houghton	17-75	23	1-15	16-60	+0.79
Mick Channon	14-110	13	3-27	11-83	-13.25
Philip Hide	14-73	19	1-4	13-69	-9.81
John Bridger	12-104	12	0-5	12-99	-16.17
Mark Johnston	12-74	16	5-32	7-42	-31.11
John Berry	11-32	34	0-0	11-32	+40.20
Paul Cole	10-35	29	3-7	7-28	+19.88
Luca Cumani	10-24	42	2-7	8-17	+5.36

Jockeys	Wins-Rides	%	£1 level stks	Best Trainer	W-R
Jim Crowley	33-136	24	-0.15	Paul Cole	3-4
Silvestre De Sousa	24-127	19	-22.06	Mark Johnston	3-17
Luke Morris	23-144	16	-11.26	Sir Mark Prescott Bt	6-16
David Probert	23-110	21	+21.41	Andrew Balding	4-14
Adam Kirby	23-78	29	+30.89	Clive Cox	8-16
Shane Kelly	22-121	18	-27.94	Richard Hughes	16-50
Hector Crouch	19-148	13	+6.75	Gary Moore	13-91
Tom Marquand	19-118	16	+11.05	Richard Hannon	11-39
Pat Cosgrave	19-91	21	+29.97	Luca Cumani	3-7
Jason Watson	17-73	23	+1.16	Philip Hide	3-12
William Carson	15-141	11	-40.58	John Bridger	8-52
J F Egan	15-89	17	-18.55	John Berry	6-14
George Downing	11-80	14	+6.00	Tony Carroll	9-66

Favourites

2yo	41.4% -16.13		3yo	31.6% -47.50	TOTAL	32.9% -102.26

Durdar Road, Carlisle, Cumbria,
CA2 4TS. Tel 01228 554 700

CARLISLE

How to get there
Road: M6 Jctn
42, follow signs
on Dalston Road.
Rail: Carlisle, 66
bus to course on
race days

Features RH,
undulating, uphill
finish

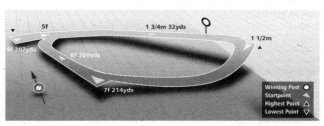

2019 Fixtures May 20, 30-31, June
11, 17, 26, July 6, 11, August 5, 13,
21, 29, September 11

Racing Post standard times

5f	1min	1m1f61yds	1min55.2
5f193yds	1min12.2	1m3f107yds	2min23.5
6f192yds	1min25.7	1m6f32yds	3min2.5
7f200yds	1min38.5	2m1f52yds	3min46

Trainers	Wins-Runs	%	2yo	3yo+	£1 level stks
Richard Fahey	27-203	13	10-75	17-128	-68.01
Keith Dalgleish	24-193	12	2-35	22-158	-40.04
Tim Easterby	21-188	11	2-47	19-141	-58.03
K R Burke	21-96	22	14-46	7-50	+44.82
Mark Johnston	20-101	20	6-37	14-64	-9.51
Michael Dods	13-108	12	7-34	6-74	-39.63
Kevin Ryan	12-86	14	5-30	7-56	-19.45
Ann Duffield	10-61	16	6-30	4-31	+9.98
Brian Ellison	8-54	15	1-12	7-42	-13.19
Iain Jardine	7-59	12	0-9	7-50	-18.50
Alan Swinbank	7-48	15	0-5	7-43	+20.50
Roger Fell	7-39	18	0-1	7-38	+2.00
Nigel Tinkler	7-29	24	1-6	6-23	+27.00

Jockeys	Wins-Rides	%	£1 level stks	Best Trainer	W-R
Ben Curtis	33-109	30	+153.12	K R Burke	6-22
Paul Mulrennan	21-126	17	-27.13	Michael Dods	10-43
Tony Hamilton	18-111	16	-14.51	Richard Fahey	11-72
Joe Fanning	14-104	13	-19.01	Mark Johnston	10-47
Graham Lee	13-110	12	-35.50	Keith Dalgleish	2-11
Phillip Makin	12-93	13	-13.18	Keith Dalgleish	9-61
P J McDonald	12-88	14	-27.02	Ann Duffield	4-29
Rachel Richardson	11-80	14	+4.00	Tim Easterby	7-52
David Allan	10-72	14	-20.90	Tim Easterby	8-53
Connor Beasley	8-80	10	-31.00	Keith Dalgleish	3-13
Franny Norton	8-58	14	-30.13	Mark Johnston	5-33
Daniel Tudhope	8-54	15	-14.08	David O'Meara	2-24
Andrew Mullen	7-65	11	-6.50	Keith Dalgleish	2-7

Favourites

2yo	48.6%	+12.75	3yo	40.9%	+17.59	TOTAL 36.4%	-3.87

CATTERICK

Catterick Bridge, Richmond, N Yorks
DL10 7PE. Tel 01748 811 478

How to get there
Road: A1, exit 5m south of Scotch Corner. Rail: Darlington or Northallerton and bus

Features LH, undulating, tight

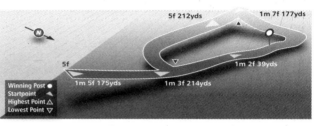

2019 Fixtures
June 17, July 1, 10, 17, 24, August 6, 12, 19, 28, September 3, 10, 21, October 8, 19, 29

Racing Post standard times

5f	58.3	1m3f214yds	2min33
5f212yds	1min11.3	1m5f175yds	2min57
7f	1min23.3	1m7f177yds	3min23

Trainers	Wins-Runs	%	2yo	3yo+	£1 level stks
Richard Fahey	31-179	17	13-71	18-108	-15.78
John Quinn	26-140	19	7-40	19-100	+19.80
Tim Easterby	22-193	11	3-40	19-153	-44.15
Ruth Carr	18-123	15	1-4	17-119	-21.50
Keith Dalgleish	18-83	22	5-28	13-55	+52.83
Mark Johnston	17-120	14	13-62	4-58	-57.76
David O'Meara	16-149	11	6-34	10-115	-61.07
Brian Ellison	12-81	15	3-12	9-69	-12.85
Michael Easterby	11-108	10	0-14	11-94	-31.88
Michael Bell	11-28	39	1-7	10-21	+18.14
Ann Duffield	10-91	11	2-37	8-54	+16.08
Scott Dixon	9-103	9	1-9	8-94	-43.09
Michael Appleby	9-89	10	1-9	8-80	-30.79

Jockeys	Wins-Rides	%	£1 level stks	Best Trainer	W-R
P J McDonald	26-153	17	+19.77	Mark Johnston	5-19
James Sullivan	23-167	14	-34.72	Ruth Carr	14-91
Jason Hart	21-130	16	+11.75	John Quinn	13-66
Paul Mulrennan	19-99	19	-10.83	Paul Midgley	3-8
David Allan	18-157	11	+0.30	Tim Easterby	7-73
Ben Curtis	15-116	13	-32.34	Brian Ellison	5-24
Joe Fanning	12-107	11	-28.63	Mark Johnston	3-47
Daniel Tudhope	12-85	14	-31.54	David O'Meara	6-51
Graham Lee	11-134	8	-82.90	Chris Wall	1-1
Tom Eaves	11-110	10	-19.51	Declan Carroll	2-9
Phillip Makin	11-82	13	-34.46	Keith Dalgleish	5-26
Jack Garritty	11-65	17	+10.50	Richard Fahey	2-11
Connor Beasley	11-59	19	+101.50	Keith Dalgleish	6-14

Favourites

2yo	45.5% +2.16	3yo	32.7% -24.17	TOTAL	35.1% -21.19

CHELMSFORD

Great Leighs, CM3 1QP.
Tel 01245 362 412

How to get there
Road: M11 Jctn 8, A120 towards Chelmsford, signposted from A131. Rail: Chelmsford, bus to course on racedays

Features LH, Polytrack, 1m circuit with wide sweeping bends

2019 Fixtures April 4, 11, 18, 25, 30, May 2, 9, 23, 27, 31, June 6, 8, 19-20, July 5-6, 23, August 3, 9-10, 16, 23-24, 29, 31, September 4-5, 12, 14, 19, 21, 24, 26, 28, October 3, 8, 17, 24, 26, 31, November 2, 7, 19, 21, 28, December 12-13

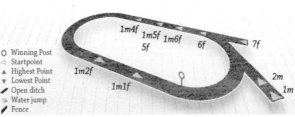

	Winning Post
O	Startpoint
▲	Highest Point
▼	Lowest Point
✔	Open ditch
	Water jump
✔	Fence

Racing Post standard times

5f	59.6
6f	1min12.3
1m	1min39
1m2f	2min6.5
1m6f	3min0.6
2m	3min28

Trainers	Wins-Runs	%	2yo	3yo+	£1 level stks
Mark Johnston	58-355	16	24-117	34-238	-69.40
David Simcock	44-219	20	6-25	38-194	+19.59
Saeed bin Suroor	43-137	31	10-31	33-106	-9.05
Stuart Williams	41-262	16	5-26	36-236	+5.88
William Haggas	40-150	27	11-45	29-105	-4.08
Michael Appleby	39-389	10	0-19	39-370	-145.88
John Gosden	39-168	23	9-59	30-109	-37.43
Marco Botti	38-271	14	12-79	26-192	-30.21
Derek Shaw	37-275	13	1-28	36-247	+4.79
Jamie Osborne	33-236	14	6-66	27-170	-2.98
Chris Dwyer	33-202	16	3-25	30-177	+23.04
Richard Hannon	31-263	12	15-118	16-145	-91.86
Dean Ivory	28-203	14	0-23	28-180	-38.93

Jockeys	Wins-Rides	%	£1 level stks	Best Trainer	W-R
Luke Morris	80-732	11	-291.43	Sir Mark Prescott Bt	22-109
Jim Crowley	59-257	23	+42.62	Hugo Palmer	7-14
Silvestre De Sousa	57-285	20	-9.73	Chris Dwyer	15-63
Adam Kirby	55-330	17	-93.83	Ian Williams	4-7
Oisin Murphy	51-276	18	-39.41	Andrew Balding	11-43
Martin Harley	48-320	15	-31.98	David Simcock	8-21
Ryan Moore	36-87	41	+35.57	Sir Michael Stoute	10-28
James Doyle	34-128	27	-24.47	William Haggas	7-16
Martin Lane	32-187	17	+38.03	Derek Shaw	11-53
Franny Norton	31-225	14	-36.01	Mark Johnston	15-93
Robert Havlin	30-194	15	-47.54	John Gosden	17-67
Joe Fanning	27-191	14	-47.37	Mark Johnston	18-103
Josephine Gordon	26-297	9	-118.72	Phil McEntee	8-70

Favourites
2yo	43.5% +12.51	3yo	36.1% -95.74	TOTAL	36.3% -147.78

CHEPSTOW

Chepstow, Monmouthshire,
NP16 6BE. Tel 01291 622 260

How to get there
Road: M4 Jct 22 on
west side of Severn
Bridge, A48 north,
A446. Rail: Chep-
stow, bus to course
on race days

Features LH,
undulating

2019 Fixtures May
3, 14, 23, June 8, 14, 24, July 2, 12,
18, 26, August 15, 22, 26, September
2, 12, 17

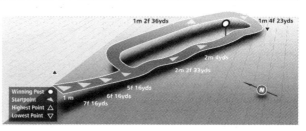

Racing Post standard times

5f16yds	58.3	1m2f36yds	2min6.5
6f16yds	1min9.8	1m4f23yds	2min34
7f16yds	1min21.5	2m49yds	3min28
1m14yds	1min33.5	2m2f	3min52

Trainers	Wins-Runs	%	2yo	3yo+	£1 level stks
Richard Hannon	20-123	16	12-47	8-76	-36.94
David Evans	19-174	11	4-51	15-123	-39.70
John O'Shea	17-117	15	0-0	17-117	+14.33
Andrew Balding	17-92	18	2-16	15-76	-7.70
Eve Johnson Houghton	16-58	28	5-18	11-40	+13.68
Ed de Giles	15-59	25	0-4	15-55	+52.25
Ralph Beckett	14-51	27	2-13	12-38	-10.58
Ronald Harris	11-117	9	0-20	11-97	-12.15
Richard Price	11-74	15	0-2	11-72	-26.18
Clive Cox	11-47	23	3-12	8-35	+3.89
Bernard Llewellyn	10-85	12	0-0	10-85	-1.08
Mick Channon	10-79	13	2-24	8-55	-12.90
John Flint	9-60	15	0-0	9-60	+2.75

Jockeys	Wins-Rides	%	£1 level stks	Best Trainer	W-R
Tom Marquand	22-127	17	+3.63	Richard Price	7-21
Luke Morris	20-143	14	-18.76	John O'Shea	4-16
David Probert	20-133	15	-31.16	Patrick Chamings	3-10
Franny Norton	17-86	20	+25.55	Paul Henderson	4-7
Oisin Murphy	13-66	20	+6.66	Andrew Balding	3-16
Dane O'Neill	12-62	19	-3.56	Richard Hannon	2-3
Callum Shepherd	12-54	22	+38.50	Ed de Giles	8-24
Richard Kingscote	12-43	28	+17.29	K R Burke	2-3
John Fahy	11-54	20	+48.38	Eve Johnson Houghton	5-13
Liam Keniry	10-86	12	-25.90	Neil Mulholland	2-2
Edward Greatrex	9-107	8	-51.05	Andrew Balding	4-15
Charles Bishop	9-69	13	-9.25	Eve Johnson Houghton	6-18
Rossa Ryan	9-40	23	+10.15	John O'Shea	4-12

Favourites

2yo	38%	-13.44		3yo	35.5%	-27.97	TOTAL	34.6% -47.28

Steam Mill Street, Chester, CH1 2LY
Tel 01244 304 600

CHESTER

How to get there
Road: Inner Ring
Road and A458
Queensferry
Road.
Rail: Chester
General, bus to
city centre

Features LH, flat,
very sharp

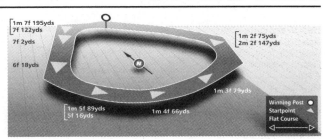

2019 Fixtures May 8-10, 25, June 15, 28-29, July 12-13, 27, August 4, 31, September 13-14, 28

Racing Post standard times

5f16yds	59.6	1m3f79yds	2min22.7
5f110yds	1min5.6	1m4f66yds	2min34.6
6f18yds	1min13.1	1m5f89yds	2min48
7f2yds	1min24.3	1m7f195yds	3min24
7f122yds	1min31.4	2m2f147yds	4min1
1m2f75yds	2min7.9		

Trainers	Wins-Runs	%	2yo	3yo+	£1 level stks
Richard Fahey	52-419	12	10-73	42-346	-61.55
Mark Johnston	33-196	17	12-61	21-135	-37.51
Andrew Balding	33-150	22	6-24	27-126	+53.10
Tom Dascombe	30-240	13	15-93	15-147	-87.54
Tim Easterby	15-103	15	1-14	14-89	+2.25
Sir Michael Stoute	10-39	26	1-3	9-36	-11.04
A P O'Brien	10-29	34	0-0	10-29	-4.08
Richard Hannon	9-71	13	6-31	3-40	-18.50
Kevin Ryan	9-61	15	3-9	6-52	-11.34
Ian Williams	8-62	13	1-2	7-60	-21.75
Brian Ellison	8-58	14	0-4	8-54	-0.50
William Haggas	8-29	28	3-5	5-24	-4.68
Ralph Beckett	6-43	14	1-2	5-41	-18.13

Jockeys	Wins-Rides	%	£1 level stks	Best Trainer	W-R
Franny Norton	37-237	16	-77.65	Mark Johnston	21-121
Richard Kingscote	32-168	19	-0.51	Tom Dascombe	20-112
David Probert	15-87	17	-11.96	Andrew Balding	12-59
Ryan Moore	13-40	33	-5.83	A P O'Brien	10-18
Paul Hanagan	9-77	12	-28.65	Richard Fahey	6-59
Paddy Mathers	9-70	13	-8.25	Richard Fahey	9-55
J F Egan	8-91	9	-34.50	Saeed bin Suroor	2-5
Jack Garritty	8-61	13	-16.09	Richard Fahey	6-37
Graham Lee	8-41	20	+20.85	Ed Dunlop	1-1
Adam McNamara	8-34	24	+9.17	Richard Fahey	8-31
Connor Murtagh	7-58	12	-8.75	Richard Fahey	7-40
Shane Gray	6-56	11	-17.75	Kevin Ryan	6-25
David Nolan	6-53	11	+3.38	Richard Fahey	4-38

Favourites

2yo	36.6% -12.66	3yo	30.8% -23.64	TOTAL	31.1% -53.48

DONCASTER

Leger Way, Doncaster
DN2 6BB. Tel 01302 320066/7

How to get there
Road: M18 Jct 3,
A638, A18 to Hull.
Rail: Doncaster
Central

Features LH, flat

2019 Fixtures
March 30-31,
April 26-27, May
4, 18, 31, June 1,
16, 28-29, July 5, 11, 20, 25, August 3,
17, September 11-14, October 25-26,
November 9

1m 6f 132yds — 2m 110yds — 2 1/4m — 5f — 5f 140yds — 6f 110yds — 6f — 7f — 1 m — 1 1/2m — 1m 2f 60yds — 1m — Winning Post — Startpoint — Highest Point — Lowest Point

Racing Post standard times

5f	57.9	1m (Rnd)	1min36.2
5f140yds	1min6.2	1m2f60yds	2m6
6f	1min10.5	1m4f	2min29
6f110yds	1min17	1m6f132yds	3min3
7f	1min23.3	2m110yds	3min33
1m (Str)	1min36	2m2f	3min52

Trainers	Wins-Runs	%	2yo	3yo+	£1 level stks
Roger Varian	33-128	26	3-26	30-102	+41.48
Richard Fahey	32-360	9	9-94	23-266	-96.12
Richard Hannon	29-243	12	13-117	16-126	-19.77
Mark Johnston	23-149	15	12-71	11-78	-28.35
Sir Michael Stoute	23-61	38	4-14	19-47	+52.95
John Gosden	22-117	19	9-37	13-80	-30.70
David O'Meara	20-211	9	4-11	16-200	-66.09
Charlie Appleby	20-90	22	7-35	13-55	-0.48
William Haggas	17-91	19	9-26	8-65	-29.54
David Simcock	17-78	22	2-12	15-66	+8.20
Saeed bin Suroor	17-52	33	4-13	13-39	+10.54
Ralph Beckett	14-82	17	4-25	10-57	-9.87
Ian Williams	14-61	23	0-3	14-58	+15.53

Jockeys	Wins-Rides	%	£1 level stks	Best Trainer	W-R
Andrea Atzeni	40-162	25	+60.28	Roger Varian	17-58
Jamie Spencer	28-144	19	+38.32	David Simcock	10-30
Ryan Moore	24-107	22	-8.13	Sir Michael Stoute	7-18
P J McDonald	22-152	14	+48.13	Mark Johnston	6-25
William Buick	22-110	20	+8.22	Charlie Appleby	9-47
Daniel Tudhope	21-133	16	+8.00	David O'Meara	5-60
James Doyle	20-124	16	-57.06	Charlie Appleby	4-16
Silvestre De Sousa	17-116	15	-25.03	Mark Johnston	3-16
Oisin Murphy	15-112	13	-54.44	Ralph Beckett	5-13
Paul Hanagan	14-135	10	-46.53	Richard Fahey	4-58
Graham Lee	13-150	9	-60.88	Jedd O'Keeffe	2-19
Tony Hamilton	13-117	11	-5.97	Richard Fahey	8-84
Jim Crowley	13-99	13	-50.34	Ian Williams	3-4

Favourites

2yo	45.5%	+18.32	3yo	39.3%	+12.05	TOTAL	35.5%	-19.59

Epsom Downs, Surrey, KT18 5LQ
Tel 01372 726 311

EPSOM

How to get there
Road: M25 Jct 8
(A217) or 9 (A24),
2m south of
Epsom on B290.
Rail: Epsom
and bus, Epsom
Downs or
Tattenham
Corner

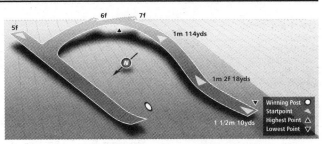

Features LH,
undulating

2019 Fixtures April 24, May 31, June
1, July 4, 11, 18, August 1, 26-27,
September 12, 29

Racing Post standard times

5f	54.9	1m114yds	1min41.8
6f	1min7	1m2f18yds	2min5.3
7f	1min20	1m4f10yds	2min33.6

Trainers	Wins-Runs	%	2yo	3yo+	£1 level stks
Mark Johnston	20-102	20	12-26	8-76	-15.58
Mick Channon	12-51	24	1-15	11-36	+21.53
Andrew Balding	11-77	14	1-9	10-68	+19.21
John Gosden	11-40	28	0-5	11-35	-3.96
Richard Fahey	10-92	11	1-15	9-77	-12.63
Eve Johnson Houghton	8-39	21	0-5	8-34	+1.48
Roger Varian	8-25	32	0-3	8-22	+7.38
Richard Hannon	7-71	10	5-28	2-43	-30.75
Jim Boyle	7-54	13	0-9	7-45	-6.00
Ralph Beckett	6-42	14	1-4	5-38	-6.75
Hughie Morrison	6-24	25	3-4	3-20	+20.50
Saeed bin Suroor	6-19	32	2-4	4-15	+0.24
Gary Moore	5-65	8	0-7	5-58	-16.90

Jockeys	Wins-Rides	%	£1 level stks	Best Trainer	W-R
Silvestre De Sousa	34-118	29	+53.62	Mark Johnston	6-27
Charles Bishop	13-29	45	+35.64	Mick Channon	5-14
Franny Norton	12-44	27	+21.93	Mark Johnston	9-26
Jim Crowley	10-65	15	-26.60	Charlie Appleby	1-1
Frankie Dettori	9-33	27	-3.51	John Gosden	8-16
Andrea Atzeni	8-58	14	-28.12	Roger Varian	5-14
David Probert	8-51	16	-5.75	Patrick Chamings	2-4
Hector Crouch	6-44	14	+5.67	Gary Moore	5-29
Harry Bentley	6-40	15	-11.92	David O'Meara	3-8
James Doyle	6-36	17	-10.50	John Gosden	2-4
Edward Greatrex	6-31	19	+28.46	Andrew Balding	4-9
Oisin Murphy	5-71	7	-36.63	Andrew Balding	2-17
William Buick	5-36	14	-6.25	Charlie Appleby	2-17

Favourites

| 2yo | 37.2% -8.15 | | 3yo | 33.9% -7.73 | | TOTAL | 33.5% | -27.90 |

FFOS LAS

Trimsaran, Carmarthenshire, SA17 4DE
Tel: 01554 811092

How to get there
Road: M4 Jctn
48 and follow the
A4138 to Llanelli.
Rail: Llanelli,
Kidwelly or
Carmarthen

Features LH, flat,
galloping

2019 Fixtures
July 29, August 1, 13, 23, 29,
September 15

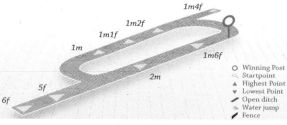

O Winning Post
⌐ Startpoint
▲ Highest Point
▼ Lowest Point
✦ Open ditch
↘ Water jump
✦ Fence

Racing Post standard times

5f	57	1m4f	2min34
6f	1min8.5	1m6f	3min
1m	1min38	2m	3min28.5
1m2f	2min6		

Trainers	Wins-Runs	%	2yo	3yo+	£1 level stks
David Evans	15-107	14	7-41	8-66	+14.25
Andrew Balding	15-51	29	3-13	12-38	+32.52
Rod Millman	8-41	20	1-17	7-24	-8.75
Richard Hughes	5-25	20	1-9	4-16	+10.18
Richard Hannon	4-34	12	3-24	1-10	-20.50
William Muir	4-31	13	3-12	1-19	-7.25
Hughie Morrison	4-19	21	0-2	4-17	+3.00
Roger Charlton	4-14	29	1-3	3-11	-2.63
Tony Carroll	3-27	11	0-1	3-26	-7.00
Bernard Llewellyn	3-26	12	0-0	3-26	+7.00
Ronald Harris	3-25	12	1-4	2-21	+0.50
Ralph Beckett	3-22	14	1-8	2-14	-9.59
Charles Hills	3-20	15	2-8	1-12	+10.50

Jockeys	Wins-Rides	%	£1 level stks	Best Trainer	W-R
Liam Keniry	11-59	19	+33.50	Andrew Balding	3-13
David Probert	10-38	26	+5.73	Andrew Balding	7-19
Shane Kelly	8-37	22	-8.07	Richard Hughes	4-17
Oisin Murphy	7-33	21	-1.63	Dominic Ffrench Davis	1-1
Kieran Shoemark	7-33	21	+0.13	David Evans	2-4
Fran Berry	6-32	19	-3.09	David Evans	3-6
Jim Crowley	6-23	26	-9.13	David Evans	2-3
Luke Morris	6-18	33	+15.75	Sir Mark Prescott Bt	2-4
Steve Drowne	5-41	12	+37.00	Charles Hills	1-1
Martin Dwyer	5-38	13	-5.08	William Muir	2-12
Tom Marquand	5-24	21	+9.23	Ali Stronge	1-1
George Baker	4-18	22	-3.75	Alexandra Dunn	1-1
Rossa Ryan	4-17	24	+15.00	David Flood	1-1

Favourites

2yo	34.1%	-11.44		3yo	30%	-27.50		TOTAL	35.3%	-24.74

Chichester, W Sussex,
PO18 0PS. Tel 01243 755 022

GOODWOOD

How to get there
Road: signposted
from A27 south
and A285 north.
Rail: Chichester,
bus to course on
race days

Features RH,
undulating

2019 Fixtures
May 4, 23-25, June 7, 9, 14, 21, July
30-31, August 1-3, 23-25, September
3, 25, October 13

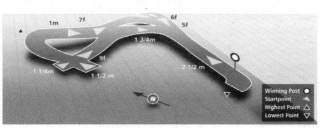

Racing Post standard times

5f	57	1m3f	2min21
6f	1min9.7	1m4f	2min34
7f	1min24	1m6f	2min58.5
1m	1min36.7	2m	3min21
1m1f	1min51.4	2m4f	4min14
1m1f192yds	2min4		

Trainers	Wins-Runs	%	2yo	3yo+	£1 level stks
Mark Johnston	39-251	16	14-77	25-174	+44.08
Richard Hannon	33-298	11	18-131	15-167	-94.97
Mick Channon	24-173	14	13-58	11-115	+9.83
William Haggas	21-98	21	3-17	18-81	-5.68
Sir Michael Stoute	20-93	22	1-3	19-90	-18.80
Charlie Appleby	17-87	20	9-28	8-59	-19.92
John Gosden	16-91	18	4-16	12-75	-37.64
Andrew Balding	15-139	11	1-32	14-107	-54.76
David Simcock	15-103	15	1-7	14-96	+22.50
Roger Varian	11-69	16	3-13	8-56	-17.00
Charles Hills	10-106	9	3-39	7-67	-60.42
Ian Williams	10-52	19	0-0	10-52	+21.15
Henry Candy	10-52	19	0-9	10-43	-0.57

Jockeys	Wins-Rides	%	£1 level stks	Best Trainer	W-R
Jim Crowley	34-215	16	-52.40	Charles Hills	6-19
Ryan Moore	22-105	21	-24.96	Sir Michael Stoute	7-25
Andrea Atzeni	20-130	15	+41.26	Roger Varian	6-38
Silvestre De Sousa	20-126	16	-3.52	Mick Channon	8-29
William Buick	20-96	21	+30.63	Charlie Appleby	12-42
James Doyle	17-130	13	-20.40	Mark Johnston	3-14
Joe Fanning	17-109	16	+2.65	Mark Johnston	13-76
Frankie Dettori	16-92	17	+19.70	John Gosden	4-27
Oisin Murphy	13-135	10	-64.63	David Simcock	4-16
Harry Bentley	13-103	13	+14.13	Henry Candy	4-9
Pat Cosgrave	13-76	17	+127.50	William Haggas	6-20
Adam Kirby	12-85	14	-7.25	Clive Cox	3-25
Jamie Spencer	12-83	14	-6.38	David Simcock	4-21

Favourites

2yo	41.8% +1.80	3yo	39.6% +28.63	TOTAL	38.6% +49.36

HAMILTON

Bothwell Road, Hamilton, Lanarkshire
ML3 0DW. Tel 01698 283 806

How to get there
Road: M74 Jct 5,
off the A74. Rail:
Hamilton West

Features RH,
undulating, dip
can become
testing in wet
weather

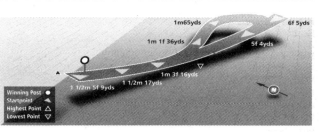

2019 Fixtures
May 5, 17, 29, June 6, 12, 19, 27,
July 2, 13, 18-19, August 3, 20, 30,
September 4, 22-23, 30

Racing Post standard times

5f4yds	58.2	1m3f16yds	2min20
6f5yds	1min10	1m4f17yds	2min33.7
1m65yds	1min45	1m5f9yds	2min47.5
1m1f36yds	1min55.5		

Trainers	*Wins-Runs*	%	*2yo*	*3yo+*	*£1 level stks*
Keith Dalgleish	51-390	13	8-74	43-316	-45.99
Richard Fahey	31-229	14	8-72	23-157	-70.63
Kevin Ryan	28-115	24	10-29	18-86	+33.96
Mark Johnston	27-165	16	13-58	14-107	-42.84
David O'Meara	24-119	20	1-13	23-106	-18.65
John Patrick Shanahan	19-96	20	0-3	19-93	+4.14
Tim Easterby	18-77	23	3-9	15-68	+27.15
Iain Jardine	17-138	12	3-18	14-120	+36.30
Michael Dods	12-62	19	3-9	9-53	-6.59
Jim Goldie	11-133	8	0-3	11-130	-47.50
Rebecca Bastiman	9-57	16	0-0	9-57	-3.63
Paul Midgley	8-65	12	0-2	8-63	-16.75
Ruth Carr	7-72	10	0-2	7-70	+19.00

Jockeys	*Wins-Rides*	%	*£1 level stks*	*Best Trainer*	*W-R*
Joe Fanning	38-237	16	-50.78	Mark Johnston	22-121
Graham Lee	24-150	16	-34.02	Paul Midgley	3-14
Connor Beasley	21-147	14	+8.00	Keith Dalgleish	11-52
Daniel Tudhope	21-103	20	+5.93	David O'Meara	10-45
Paul Mulrennan	17-129	13	-34.48	Michael Dods	5-22
P J McDonald	17-115	15	-9.98	Mark Johnston	4-9
Tony Hamilton	15-96	16	-10.07	Richard Fahey	10-55
James Sullivan	14-155	9	+3.00	Ruth Carr	5-57
Phillip Makin	14-110	13	-30.05	Keith Dalgleish	8-69
Shane Gray	14-77	18	+24.53	Kevin Ryan	7-24
Rowan Scott	13-121	11	-35.58	Keith Dalgleish	7-55
Andrew Mullen	12-86	14	-21.00	Michael Dods	2-5
Jamie Gormley	12-74	16	-18.71	Iain Jardine	4-39

Favourites

2yo	37.5% -14.64	3yo	41.6% +0.96	TOTAL 33.3%	-73.25

Newton-Le-Willows, Merseyside
WA12 0HQ. Tel 01942 725 963

HAYDOCK

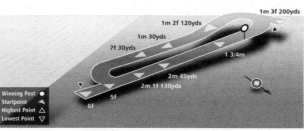

How to get there
Road: M6 Jct 23,
A49 to Wigan.
Rail: Wigan & 320
bus or Newton-le-
Willows

Features LH, flat,
easy turns, suits
the galloping type

2019 Fixtures
April 27, May 24-25, June 6-8, 12-13,
22, July 4-6, 19-20, August 8-10,
September 5-7, 27-28, October 18

Racing Post standard times

5f	58.5	1m2f95yds	2min9
5f (Inner)	58	1m3f200yds	2min26.5
6f	1min11	1m6f	2min54
6f (Inner)	1min10.3	2m45yds	3min24
7f	1min26	2m1f130yds	3min51
1m	1min38		

Trainers	Wins-Runs	%	2yo	3yo+	£1 level stks
Tom Dascombe	53-300	18	15-102	38-198	+101.95
Mark Johnston	32-184	17	15-65	17-119	-2.22
William Haggas	30-105	29	4-20	26-85	+0.86
Richard Fahey	26-292	9	9-75	17-217	-131.89
David O'Meara	21-187	11	0-5	21-182	-17.53
John Gosden	21-76	28	10-26	11-50	+4.19
Richard Hannon	20-177	11	8-73	12-104	-37.44
Hugo Palmer	18-56	32	7-15	11-41	+84.20
Tim Easterby	17-178	10	3-38	14-140	-13.50
K R Burke	16-157	10	3-50	13-107	-30.17
Clive Cox	12-46	26	4-14	8-32	+31.82
Andrew Balding	11-81	14	4-9	7-72	-31.55
Roger Varian	11-79	14	1-18	10-61	-35.58

Jockeys	Wins-Rides	%	£1 level stks	Best Trainer	W-R
Richard Kingscote	61-307	20	+74.18	Tom Dascombe	43-218
Daniel Tudhope	25-147	17	-2.87	David O'Meara	13-75
Paul Hanagan	19-145	13	-54.53	Richard Fahey	8-51
Franny Norton	19-128	15	-22.13	Mark Johnston	14-66
William Buick	16-74	22	-11.26	Charlie Appleby	7-32
Graham Lee	14-130	11	-57.71	Kevin Ryan	3-12
Adam Kirby	14-83	17	+2.37	Clive Cox	9-17
Pat Cosgrave	14-53	26	+11.49	William Haggas	10-26
Frankie Dettori	14-38	37	+6.03	John Gosden	6-13
Silvestre De Sousa	13-67	19	-4.13	Mark Johnston	4-15
Joe Fanning	12-63	19	+8.63	Mark Johnston	5-29
Jim Crowley	12-58	21	-7.64	Hugo Palmer	2-2
Ben Curtis	11-108	10	-11.38	Brian Ellison	3-18

Favourites

2yo	36.1%	-23.50		3yo	33.2%	-41.09		TOTAL	33.6%	-67.26

KEMPTON

Staines Rd East, Sunbury-On-Thames
TW16 5AQ. Tel 01932 782 292

How to get there
Road: M3 Jct 1,
A308 to Kingston-
on-Thames. Rail:
Kempton Park
from Waterloo

Features RH,
Polytrack, sharp

2019 Fixtures
March 30, April
3, 10, 12, 20, May 22, June 5, 12, 26,
July 3, 10, August 5, 7, 14, 20-21,
28, September 3, 6-7, 11, 16, 23, 25,
October 1-2, 9-10, 15-16, 22-23, 28,
30-31, November 4-6, 19-20, 27, 29,
December 4, 11

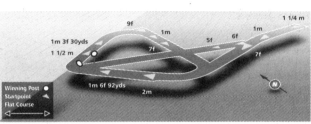

Racing Post standard times

5f	58.8	1m2f	2min4
6f	1min10.6	1m3f	2min17
7f	1min23.7	1m4f	2min30
1m	1min36.6	2m	3min22.5

Trainers	Wins-Runs	%	2yo	3yo+	£1 level stks
Richard Hannon	57-483	12	28-227	29-256	-138.08
John Gosden	56-215	26	24-109	32-106	+28.63
Charlie Appleby	42-125	34	25-75	17-50	-26.26
James Fanshawe	40-236	17	5-36	35-200	-49.72
Roger Varian	37-170	22	16-77	21-93	-13.45
Ralph Beckett	31-219	14	15-94	16-125	-17.01
Roger Charlton	31-180	17	9-68	22-112	-16.04
Andrew Balding	28-255	11	6-55	22-200	-75.62
Marco Botti	28-254	11	8-90	20-164	-60.49
William Haggas	27-135	20	9-52	18-83	-33.41
Tony Carroll	26-355	7	0-22	26-333	-144.38
Hugo Palmer	26-161	16	11-75	15-86	-18.56
Saeed bin Suroor	26-113	23	8-41	18-72	-37.51

Jockeys	Wins-Rides	%	£1 level stks	Best Trainer	W-R
Luke Morris	70-756	9	-178.56	Sir Mark Prescott Bt	13-94
Jim Crowley	68-463	15	-116.30	Amanda Perrett	8-40
Adam Kirby	64-502	13	-147.17	Clive Cox	13-88
Oisin Murphy	64-449	14	-71.82	Andrew Balding	9-68
James Doyle	55-210	26	+5.85	Saeed bin Suroor	8-29
Robert Havlin	46-314	15	-56.25	John Gosden	27-100
Tom Marquand	42-420	10	-37.13	Richard Hannon	8-110
Martin Harley	42-269	16	+34.94	James Tate	6-23
Liam Keniry	41-504	8	-116.46	Ed Walker	7-60
George Baker	41-262	16	-64.63	Gary Moore	7-37
Andrea Atzeni	39-159	25	+16.35	Roger Varian	14-53
William Buick	36-133	27	-38.22	Charlie Appleby	23-62
David Probert	34-353	10	-49.50	Andrew Balding	6-69

Favourites

2yo	42.7%	-7.55	3yo	37.2%	-24.46	TOTAL 35.9% -70.49

LEICESTER

London Road, Oadby, Leicester,
LE2 4QH. Tel 0116 271 6515

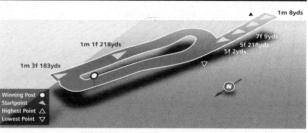

How to get there
Road: M1 Jct 21,
A6, 2m south of
city. Rail:
Leicester, bus

Features RH,
straight mile is
downhill for first
4f, then uphill to
finish

2019 Fixtures April 5, 27, May 20,
27-28, June 10, 15, 27, July 6, 18, 24,
31, August 11, 22, September 10, 23,
October 8, 15, 28

Racing Post standard times

5f2yds	59	1m60yds	1min42.5
5f218yds	1min10.5	1m1f218yds	2min4.5
7f9yds	1min23	1m3f183yds	2min29.3
1m8yds	1min41		

Trainers	Wins-Runs	%	2yo	3yo+	£1 level stks
Richard Fahey	28-143	20	11-54	17-89	+17.80
Mark Johnston	26-116	22	8-52	18-64	-1.61
Richard Hannon	25-174	14	16-86	9-88	-48.35
Mick Channon	15-71	21	8-33	7-38	+32.17
Charles Hills	13-63	21	3-27	10-36	+11.13
Sir Michael Stoute	13-62	21	2-23	11-39	-14.07
Roger Varian	12-68	18	2-19	10-49	-28.58
David Evans	11-102	11	4-37	7-65	-26.25
David O'Meara	10-73	14	0-7	10-66	-28.00
Saeed bin Suroor	10-38	26	2-10	8-28	+2.25
Hughie Morrison	9-43	21	0-6	9-37	+26.00
Michael Appleby	8-114	7	1-19	7-95	-49.25
Clive Cox	8-74	11	3-28	5-46	-26.02

Jockeys	Wins-Rides	%	£1 level stks	Best Trainer	W-R
Silvestre De Sousa	33-131	25	+40.99	Mark Johnston	8-25
Jim Crowley	21-104	20	+17.73	Charles Hills	6-12
Paul Hanagan	19-85	22	+23.93	Richard Fahey	9-30
Andrea Atzeni	15-81	19	-31.04	Roger Varian	8-35
Jamie Spencer	13-68	19	-13.01	Michael Bell	4-11
Ryan Moore	12-70	17	-35.29	Sir Michael Stoute	4-20
Fran Berry	12-67	18	+13.75	David Evans	3-10
James Doyle	12-57	21	-0.98	Saeed bin Suroor	4-10
Oisin Murphy	11-95	12	-48.25	Ralph Beckett	2-7
Adam Kirby	10-98	10	-43.02	Clive Cox	5-38
Liam Keniry	9-58	16	-2.88	Andrew Balding	2-9
William Buick	9-46	20	-13.87	Charlie Appleby	3-16
Sean Levey	9-43	21	+18.38	Richard Hannon	7-32

Favourites

2yo	30.6% -37.60		3yo	36.7% -6.20	TOTAL	32.8% -66.34

LINGFIELD Turf

Racecourse Road, Lingfield
RH7 6PQ. Tel 01342 834 800

How to get there
Road: M25 Jctn 6, south on A22, then B2029. Rail: Lingfield from London Bridge or Victoria

Features LH, undulating

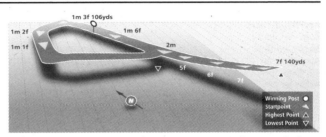

2019 Fixtures
May 3, 11, 23, 30, June 8, 11, 22, 29, July 10, 17, 24, 27, August 3, 10, 28, September 5, 14

Racing Post standard times

5f	56.9	1m2f	2min6.7
6f	1min9.4	1m3f106yds	2min27
7f	1min21	1m6f	3min
7f140yds	1min28	2m	3min27.5
1m1f	1min53		

Trainers	Wins-Runs	%	2yo	3yo+	£1 level stks
William Haggas	21-47	45	10-16	11-31	+34.71
Richard Hannon	20-126	16	6-46	14-80	-17.76
John Bridger	15-103	15	3-16	12-87	+47.13
Jim Boyle	14-57	25	2-11	12-46	+50.50
Andrew Balding	11-45	24	1-6	10-39	+5.50
Gary Moore	10-74	14	1-8	9-66	-21.25
David Evans	10-67	15	6-30	4-37	+5.78
Roger Varian	9-36	25	2-10	7-26	-5.97
Mick Channon	8-91	9	5-30	3-61	-52.04
Richard Hughes	8-52	15	3-15	5-37	-16.26
John Best	7-47	15	1-13	6-34	-6.52
Jonathan Portman	7-39	18	1-8	6-31	+16.85
John Ryan	7-38	18	1-8	6-30	+23.00

Jockeys	Wins-Rides	%	£1 level stks	Best Trainer	W-R
Silvestre De Sousa	24-95	25	-25.75	Ed Dunlop	3-5
Pat Cosgrave	22-91	24	+2.56	William Haggas	10-20
Oisin Murphy	20-97	21	-23.56	Andrew Balding	4-12
Jim Crowley	19-75	25	-4.11	David Evans	2-2
Luke Morris	13-93	14	-49.35	Sir Mark Prescott Bt	6-16
Adam Kirby	12-51	24	+0.81	David Evans	2-4
Harry Bentley	12-49	24	+17.25	Ed Vaughan	5-11
Martin Dwyer	10-71	14	-28.89	Sylvester Kirk	2-2
Hector Crouch	10-68	15	+2.73	Gary Moore	5-26
Edward Greatrex	10-51	20	+38.99	Archie Watson	2-8
James Doyle	10-36	28	-8.55	Charlie Appleby	2-3
David Probert	9-74	12	+15.30	Andrew Balding	3-12
Kieran O'Neill	8-79	10	+26.25	John Bridger	4-16

Favourites

2yo	45.8%	-2.55		3yo	33.9%	-42.70		TOTAL	37.9%	-48.10

LINGFIELD AW

Features LH, Polytrack, tight

2019 Fixtures
April 2, 6, 10, 19, 23, June 4, 20, August 13, 15, 19, 31, September 24, October 3, 31, November 23, 28, December 4, 9, 11, 18, 21, 28, 30-31

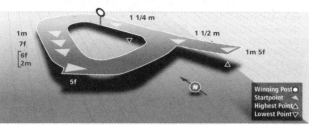

Racing Post standard times

5f	57.5	1m2f	2min1.8
6f	1min9.6	1m4f	2min28
7f	1min22.2	1m5f	2min40.5
1m	1min35.3	2m	3min16

Trainers	Wins-Runs	%	2yo	3yo+	£1 level stks
Richard Hannon	52-320	16	17-93	35-227	+17.81
Mark Johnston	45-247	18	9-41	36-206	-23.19
Charlie Appleby	42-129	33	3-19	39-110	+10.76
John Gosden	35-174	20	9-48	26-126	-31.17
David Evans	33-234	14	6-28	27-206	-56.01
William Haggas	31-120	26	10-36	21-84	+1.53
Andrew Balding	30-203	15	2-19	28-184	-56.56
Ralph Beckett	29-131	22	4-21	25-110	-21.25
Gary Moore	28-245	11	0-15	28-230	-83.30
Simon Dow	27-190	14	4-20	23-170	+2.02
Archie Watson	27-114	24	5-21	22-93	+23.63
Jamie Osborne	26-218	12	2-36	24-182	-35.36
Stuart Williams	24-161	15	2-10	22-151	+0.33

Jockeys	Wins-Rides	%	£1 level stks	Best Trainer	W-R
Adam Kirby	109-551	20	-81.48	Charlie Appleby	14-33
Luke Morris	99-757	13	-174.00	Sir Mark Prescott Bt	19-91
Jim Crowley	61-298	20	+2.12	Amanda Perrett	10-26
George Baker	58-304	19	-11.53	Gary Moore	9-52
Oisin Murphy	53-305	17	-2.82	Andrew Balding	11-58
Joe Fanning	43-219	20	+4.15	Mark Johnston	25-108
Tom Marquand	39-286	14	+7.44	Richard Hannon	9-62
Robert Havlin	38-297	13	-62.48	John Gosden	23-83
Liam Keniry	35-363	10	-68.02	John Butler	7-24
Martin Harley	34-255	13	-50.49	Tom Dascombe	4-5
James Doyle	33-109	30	-3.94	Saeed bin Suroor	8-15
Shane Kelly	32-379	8	-196.02	Richard Hughes	11-103
David Probert	30-277	11	-90.29	Andrew Balding	10-60

Favourites

2yo	33.3%	-36.04	3yo	37.4%	-85.82	TOTAL	35.5%	-182.57

MUSSELBURGH

Linkfield Road EH21 7RG
Tel 0131 665 2859

How to get there
Road: M8 Jct 2,
A8 east, follow
Ring Road, A1
east. Rail:
Musselburgh
from Edinburgh
Waverley

Features RH, flat,
tight

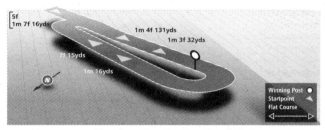

2019 Fixtures April 2, 20, May 2-3, 13, June 1, July 3, 23, August 2, 9, 27-28, September 6, 14, 29, October 14

Racing Post standard times

5f	58	1m3f32yds	2min22
7f30yds	1min26.8	1m4f100yds	2min40
1m	1min38.8	1m6f	1min59.2
1m1f	1min51.1	2m	3min25

Trainers	Wins-Runs	%	2yo	3yo+	£1 level stks
Keith Dalgleish	42-339	12	12-70	30-269	-98.28
Mark Johnston	37-189	20	13-66	24-123	-35.69
Richard Fahey	34-189	18	10-48	24-141	+30.83
Kevin Ryan	19-87	22	5-21	14-66	+24.88
Jim Goldie	17-224	8	0-6	17-218	-66.88
Iain Jardine	15-155	10	1-18	14-137	-78.73
Tim Easterby	15-120	13	4-19	11-101	-34.30
Rebecca Bastiman	14-79	18	0-2	14-77	+12.75
Linda Perratt	12-173	7	1-7	11-166	-16.50
David O'Meara	12-109	11	4-26	8-83	-50.60
Ruth Carr	10-83	12	0-0	10-83	-9.50
John Quinn	10-67	15	3-18	7-49	-11.22
Michael Easterby	10-54	19	0-3	10-51	+11.50

Jockeys	Wins-Rides	%	£1 level stks	Best Trainer	W-R
Joe Fanning	47-263	18	-83.61	Mark Johnston	29-121
Paul Mulrennan	23-158	15	-30.29	Alistair Whillans	4-13
Phillip Makin	21-129	16	+5.59	Keith Dalgleish	12-63
Connor Beasley	20-124	16	+42.46	Richard Guest	4-15
David Allan	16-93	17	+22.88	Tim Easterby	7-49
Daniel Tudhope	16-60	27	+25.03	David O'Meara	6-29
James Sullivan	15-122	12	+9.50	Ruth Carr	7-53
P J McDonald	14-136	10	-60.38	Linda Perratt	3-22
Jason Hart	13-104	13	-25.00	John Quinn	5-29
Paul Hanagan	12-75	16	-2.55	Richard Fahey	10-51
Ben Curtis	12-58	21	+3.96	William Haggas	3-5
Andrew Mullen	11-94	12	-12.68	Michael Appleby	5-15
Graham Lee	10-121	8	-64.18	Bryan Smart	2-9

Favourites

2yo	38%	-7.96		3yo	36.4%	-9.89		TOTAL	32.9%	-42.41

Newbury, Berkshire, RG14 7NZ
Tel: 01635 400 15 or 01635 550 354

NEWBURY

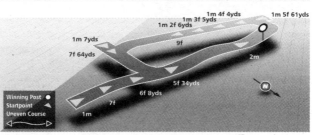

How to get there
Road: M4 Jct 13
and A34 south.
Rail: Newbury
Racecourse

Features LH,
wide, flat

2019 Fixtures
April 12-13, May
17-18, June 13,
25, July 4, 11, 19-20, 25, August 6,
16-17, September 20-21, October
25-26

Racing Post standard times

5f34yds	59.6	1m1f	1min50
6f8yds	1min10.5	1m2f6yds	2min3
7f	1min22.8	1m3f5yds	2min17
7f64yds	1min28	1m4f4yds	2min30.3
1m	1min35.8	1m5f61yds	2min47.5
1m7yds	1min36.5	2m	3min23.5

Trainers	Wins-Runs	%	2yo	3yo+	£1 level stks
Richard Hannon	43-414	10	24-231	19-183	-96.80
John Gosden	37-159	23	15-56	22-103	+17.42
William Haggas	36-149	24	10-63	26-86	+16.25
Andrew Balding	16-151	11	3-50	13-101	+3.93
Brian Meehan	15-160	9	7-87	8-73	+25.38
Charles Hills	15-152	10	8-67	7-85	-18.13
Sir Michael Stoute	15-105	14	5-21	10-84	-36.71
Charlie Appleby	14-48	29	4-17	10-31	+5.24
Ralph Beckett	13-112	12	6-42	7-70	-22.96
Roger Varian	12-90	13	3-29	9-61	-21.00
Mark Johnston	12-75	16	6-32	6-43	-0.53
Roger Charlton	11-86	13	3-29	8-57	-3.64
Eve Johnson Houghton	10-85	12	2-31	8-54	+22.38

Jockeys	Wins-Rides	%	£1 level stks	Best Trainer	W-R
Frankie Dettori	33-120	28	+38.33	John Gosden	17-53
James Doyle	28-163	17	-37.16	William Haggas	7-22
Jim Crowley	27-200	14	+15.24	William Haggas	5-16
Ryan Moore	24-152	16	-53.65	Sir Michael Stoute	10-48
William Buick	19-82	23	+23.74	Charlie Appleby	9-17
Silvestre De Sousa	16-116	14	+24.50	Mick Channon	3-18
Oisin Murphy	15-177	8	-79.71	John Gosden	2-2
Paul Hanagan	15-76	20	+15.50	William Haggas	3-8
Pat Dobbs	14-142	10	-23.25	Richard Hannon	7-70
Adam Kirby	13-152	9	-57.75	Luca Cumani	3-8
Jamie Spencer	13-96	14	-11.63	Luca Cumani	4-13
Andrea Atzeni	12-121	10	-21.75	Roger Varian	6-38
Pat Cosgrave	12-93	13	-26.00	William Haggas	6-39

Favourites

2yo	32.9%	-25.13	3yo	27.3%	-37.92	TOTAL 29.2% -85.53

NEWCASTLE

High Gosforth Park NE3 5HP
Tel: 0191 236 2020 or 236 5508

How to get there
Road:
Signposted from
A1. Rail:
Newcastle
Central, metro to
Regent Centre or
Four Lane End
and bus

O Winning Post
◁ Startpoint
▲ Highest Point
▼ Lowest Point

Features LH,
Tapeta, easy bends with uphill straight

2019 Fixtures April 1, 11, 19, May 3,
June 3, 27-29, July 27, August 8, 30,
September 6, 17, 20, 25, 27, October
2, 7, 9, 11, 18, 22, 25, November 1, 4,
8, 21-22, December 6, 9, 14, 18

Racing Post standard times

5f	58	1m4f98yds	2min36.5
6f	1min10.2	2m56yds	3min27
7f	1min24		
1m	1min36.5		
1m2f	2min6		

Trainers	*Wins-Runs*	%	*2yo*	*3yo+*	*£1 level stks*
Richard Fahey	46-370	12	15-115	31-255	-39.88
Jim Goldie	28-238	12	1-4	27-234	+22.33
John Gosden	26-75	35	12-28	14-47	-3.77
Michael Easterby	25-183	14	5-31	20-152	+81.08
Mark Johnston	24-227	11	9-94	15-133	-74.52
David O'Meara	20-247	8	3-32	17-215	-75.65
Kevin Ryan	20-173	12	5-36	15-137	-35.19
Richard Guest	19-167	11	0-15	19-152	-43.30
Michael Dods	19-160	12	5-40	14-120	-24.49
Hugo Palmer	19-81	23	8-30	11-51	+0.28
William Haggas	19-49	39	6-18	13-31	+9.23
James Bethell	18-112	16	1-19	17-93	+31.20
Iain Jardine	17-201	8	0-12	17-189	-32.25

Jockeys	*Wins-Rides*	%	*£1 level stks*	*Best Trainer*	*W-R*
Joe Fanning	41-280	15	-34.00	Mark Johnston	11-92
P J McDonald	39-367	11	-97.51	James Bethell	7-39
Luke Morris	34-250	14	-49.00	Sir Mark Prescott Bt	15-51
Ben Curtis	32-270	12	-29.14	K R Burke	7-26
Callum Rodriguez	27-127	21	+88.82	Michael Dods	10-37
Kevin Stott	26-153	17	-0.83	Kevin Ryan	8-57
Josephine Gordon	26-152	17	-24.94	Hugo Palmer	10-38
Andrew Mullen	25-306	8	-53.92	Tom Tate	7-20
Paul Mulrennan	24-285	8	-87.20	Michael Dods	6-66
Paul Hanagan	24-169	14	-45.13	Richard Fahey	12-80
Tony Hamilton	22-244	9	-59.88	Richard Fahey	14-128
Daniel Tudhope	22-171	13	-85.34	Jim Goldie	4-12
Graham Lee	19-319	6	-145.29	Bryan Smart	3-33

Favourites

2yo	41.5%	-0.23	3yo	39.4%	+4.56	TOTAL 34.9%	-49.27

Westfield House, The Links,
Newmarket, Suffolk. CB8 0TG

NEWMARKET

Rowley Mile

How to get there
Road: from
south M11 Jct
9, then A11,
otherwise A14
and A11. Rail:
Newmarket

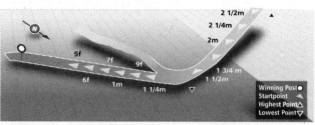

Features RH, wide, galloping,
uphill finish

2019 Fixtures April 16-18, May 4-5,
16-18, June 8, September 21, 26-28,
October 5, 11-12, 23, November 1-2

Racing Post standard times

5f	57.5	1m2f	2min0.5
6f	1min10.1	1m4f	2min28
7f	1min22.5	1m6f	2min53.5
1m	1min35.1	2m	3min19
1m1f	1min47.8	2m2f	3min45

Trainers	Wins-Runs	%	2yo	3yo+	£1 level stks
John Gosden	52-261	20	20-93	32-168	+21.59
Charlie Appleby	44-161	27	13-59	31-102	+30.66
A P O'Brien	29-131	22	17-73	12-58	+24.01
Richard Hannon	26-267	10	8-123	18-144	-3.13
Mark Johnston	25-211	12	13-89	12-122	-17.75
Roger Varian	19-162	12	6-51	13-111	-22.50
Saeed bin Suroor	17-111	15	7-32	10-79	-7.88
William Haggas	15-145	10	4-60	11-85	-40.71
Sir Michael Stoute	14-138	10	1-40	13-98	-61.63
Ralph Beckett	13-98	13	5-31	8-67	-12.09
Mick Channon	12-90	13	1-34	11-56	-3.38
Charles Hills	11-130	8	2-47	9-83	-73.93
Hugo Palmer	11-100	11	6-43	5-57	-18.93

Jockeys	Wins-Rides	%	£1 level stks	Best Trainer	W-R
William Buick	52-240	22	+53.46	Charlie Appleby	33-113
Ryan Moore	46-255	18	-64.72	A P O'Brien	20-68
Frankie Dettori	43-203	21	+54.53	John Gosden	31-102
James Doyle	26-196	13	-70.78	Saeed bin Suroor	9-40
Jim Crowley	22-185	12	-73.88	Owen Burrows	3-15
Andrea Atzeni	19-203	9	-71.00	Roger Varian	9-78
Silvestre De Sousa	19-171	11	-43.33	Roger Varian	3-14
Pat Cosgrave	15-101	15	-18.67	William Haggas	6-39
Oisin Murphy	14-144	10	-43.78	Andrew Balding	6-43
Harry Bentley	13-91	14	-18.59	Ralph Beckett	6-22
Adam Kirby	12-131	9	-45.90	Charlie Appleby	4-10
Joe Fanning	11-104	11	+29.00	Mark Johnston	7-73
Jamie Spencer	10-156	6	-73.25	Kevin Ryan	3-11

Favourites

2yo	35.5%	-23.17	3yo	32.6%	-14.94	TOTAL	32.6%	-45.58

NEWMARKET

Westfield House, The Links,
Newmarket, Suffolk. CB8 0TG

July Course

How to get there
See previous
page

Features RH,
wide, galloping,
uphill finish

2019 Fixtures
June 21-22, 27-
29, July 11-13,
19-20, 26-27,
August 2-3, 9-10,
16-17, 23-24

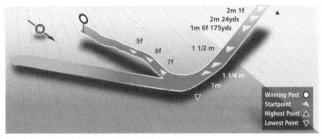

Racing Post standard times

5f	57.2	1m110yds	1min43	1m6f175yds	3min3
6f	1min10.1	1m2f	2min1.5	2m24yds	3min20
7f	1min23	1m4f	2min26.5		
1m	1min36	1m5f	2min40		

Trainers	*Wins-Runs*	%	*2yo*	*3yo+*	*£1 level stks*
Richard Hannon	40-308	13	23-159	17-149	-60.65
Charlie Appleby	37-156	24	23-85	14-71	-10.80
Mark Johnston	36-179	20	11-60	25-119	+1.51
John Gosden	32-173	18	11-69	21-104	-31.43
Charles Hills	16-125	13	6-40	10-85	-22.13
William Haggas	16-108	15	3-30	13-78	-26.61
Saeed bin Suroor	16-75	21	4-19	12-56	-6.88
Richard Fahey	15-126	12	5-33	10-93	+10.75
Andrew Balding	15-91	16	3-23	12-68	+12.79
Ralph Beckett	13-68	19	3-27	10-41	+1.62
Sir Michael Stoute	12-102	12	5-35	7-67	-63.08
Michael Bell	12-101	12	3-41	9-60	-4.50
Roger Varian	9-80	11	1-23	8-57	-37.34

Jockeys	*Wins-Rides*	%	*£1 level stks*	*Best Trainer*	*W-R*
James Doyle	50-205	24	+28.35	Charlie Appleby	11-31
William Buick	26-140	19	-37.17	Charlie Appleby	13-60
Harry Bentley	25-134	19	+11.28	Ralph Beckett	4-16
Ryan Moore	22-123	18	-30.63	A P O'Brien	7-22
Dane O'Neill	20-122	16	+3.00	Charles Hills	4-15
Silvestre De Sousa	19-140	14	-47.81	Mark Johnston	3-12
Frankie Dettori	18-111	16	-26.58	John Gosden	7-37
Andrea Atzeni	17-119	14	-35.15	Roger Varian	5-28
Jim Crowley	17-104	16	-20.52	Mark Johnston	4-11
Adam Kirby	14-121	12	-55.42	Charlie Appleby	4-10
Paul Hanagan	14-95	15	-8.01	Richard Fahey	3-21
Robert Havlin	14-67	21	-4.48	John Gosden	13-38
Oisin Murphy	13-78	17	-16.27	Andrew Balding	5-9

Favourites

2yo	47.4%	+20.83		3yo	33.4%	-26.13		TOTAL	38%	+17.98

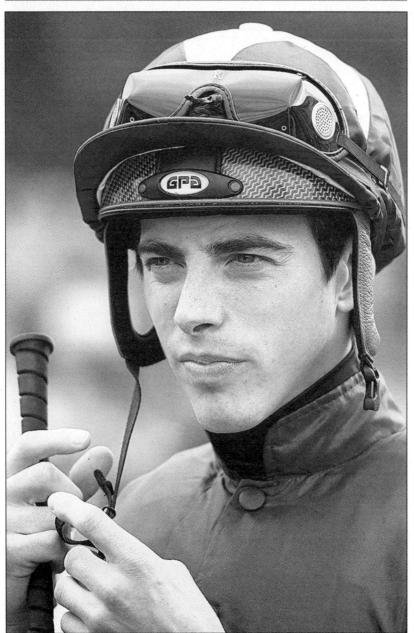

JAMES DOYLE: no jockey rides the July Course better than him

NOTTINGHAM

Colwick Park, Nottingham,
NG2 4BE. Tel 0115 958 0620

How to get there
Road: M1 Jct 25,
A52 east to B686,
signs for Trent
Bridge, then
Colwick Park.
Rail:
Nottingham

Features LH, flat,
easy turns

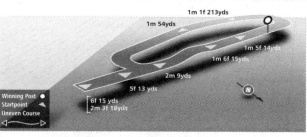

2019 Fixtures April 10,
20, 30, May 10-11, 21,
June 2, 5, 13, 17, 27, July
6, 16, 19, August 1, 6, 13,
16, October 2, 9, 16, 30,
November 6

Racing Post standard times

5f13yds	58.4	1m2f50yds (Inner)	2min8.6
5f13yds (Inner)	59.8	1m6f15yds	2min57
6f15yds	1min12.2	2m9yds	3min24
1m75yds	1min42	2m9yds (Inner)	3min32
1m75yds (Inner)	1min43.5	2m2f18yds	3min55
1m2f50yds	2min6		

Trainers	Wins-Runs	%	2yo	3yo+	£1 level stks
Richard Fahey	32-177	18	11-65	21-112	+53.51
Michael Appleby	28-210	13	1-19	27-191	-11.93
Richard Hannon	20-139	14	9-70	11-69	-35.49
Roger Varian	17-92	18	4-35	13-57	-18.87
Mark Johnston	16-117	14	11-62	5-55	-46.43
Mick Channon	16-108	15	8-40	8-68	+58.73
John Gosden	16-104	15	8-45	8-59	-11.23
Sir Michael Stoute	16-69	23	2-13	14-56	+14.21
Ralph Beckett	12-67	18	3-29	9-38	+6.63
William Haggas	12-66	18	3-24	9-42	-17.21
Hughie Morrison	12-56	21	0-11	12-45	+29.50
K R Burke	11-81	14	3-17	8-64	+5.25
Clive Cox	11-74	15	3-20	8-54	-16.75

Jockeys	Wins-Rides	%	£1 level stks	Best Trainer	W-R
Silvestre De Sousa	29-163	18	-21.00	Mick Channon	4-15
Jim Crowley	27-83	33	+68.08	Ian Williams	4-6
Paul Hanagan	22-99	22	+20.37	Richard Fahey	10-37
Oisin Murphy	18-93	19	+43.79	Hughie Morrison	4-9
Andrew Mullen	17-116	15	+37.57	Michael Appleby	10-62
Andrea Atzeni	16-84	19	-13.06	Roger Varian	8-38
James Doyle	15-50	30	+5.54	John Gosden	3-8
Luke Morris	14-130	11	-6.79	Scott Dixon	2-2
Franny Norton	14-100	14	+15.57	Mark Johnston	7-39
Sean Levey	14-56	25	+28.82	Richard Hannon	12-42
Harry Bentley	12-57	21	-21.98	Charles Hills	2-2
William Buick	12-45	27	+11.58	Charlie Appleby	5-15
Tony Hamilton	11-90	12	+33.00	Richard Fahey	9-54

Favourites

2yo	35.8%	-16.96	3yo	37.3%	+9.14	TOTAL	34.4%	-25.25

33 Ropergate, Pontefract,
WF8 1LE. Tel 01977 703 224

PONTEFRACT

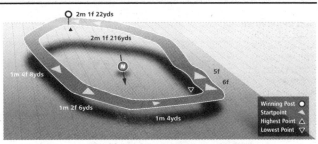

How to get there
Road: M62 Jct
32, then A539.
Rail: Pontefract
Monkhill or
Pontefract Baghill
from Leeds

Features LH,
undulating, sharp
home turn, last
half-mile all uphill

2019 Fixtures April 9, 15, May 1, 24,
June 10, 23, July 1, 9, 19, 28, August
7, 18, September 19, 26, October 7,
21

Racing Post standard times

5f	1min1.8	1m4f8yds	2min35.5
6f	1min14.6	2m1f22yds	3min41
1m4yds	1min42.6	2m1f216yds	3min51
1m2f6yds	2min9.4	2m5f122yds	4min41

Trainers	Wins-Runs	%	2yo	3yo+	£1 level stks
Richard Fahey	42-262	16	16-83	26-179	-1.58
Mark Johnston	30-160	19	13-55	17-105	-50.68
Tim Easterby	20-162	12	1-38	19-124	-30.67
David O'Meara	16-146	11	0-15	16-131	-51.00
Kevin Ryan	13-89	15	4-25	9-64	+0.71
Micky Hammond	12-128	9	1-10	11-118	-37.75
Mick Channon	12-47	26	5-15	7-32	+52.50
Sir Michael Stoute	12-45	27	0-5	12-40	-8.31
Richard Whitaker	11-47	23	2-5	9-42	+20.58
Michael Easterby	10-79	13	0-8	10-71	-13.42
Charlie Appleby	9-24	38	3-9	6-15	+1.07
Michael Dods	8-109	7	0-16	8-93	-63.33
Ruth Carr	8-74	11	0-0	8-74	-8.25

Jockeys	Wins-Rides	%	£1 level stks	Best Trainer	W-R
Silvestre De Sousa	27-113	24	-6.57	Mark Johnston	9-32
Daniel Tudhope	25-135	19	-7.33	David O'Meara	12-73
Graham Lee	19-185	10	-36.25	Mick Channon	4-14
Paul Hanagan	19-102	19	+34.55	Richard Fahey	12-68
Franny Norton	18-97	19	-9.81	Mark Johnston	13-60
P J McDonald	16-134	12	-30.89	Mark Johnston	3-16
Tony Hamilton	16-131	12	-40.84	Richard Fahey	16-85
David Allan	16-110	15	+15.50	Tim Easterby	12-75
Paul Mulrennan	13-126	10	-55.83	Michael Dods	6-47
Ben Curtis	13-78	17	+24.08	David Barron	3-7
Graham Gibbons	11-72	15	-17.55	Michael Easterby	3-12
Joe Fanning	11-72	15	+12.53	Les Eyre	2-9
Richard Kingscote	10-55	18	+1.44	Tom Dascombe	3-26

Favourites

2yo	42%	+1.73		3yo	34.7%	-24.38		TOTAL	35.2%	-17.12

REDCAR

Redcar, Teesside,
TS10 2BY. Tel 01642 484 068

How to get there
Road: A1, A168,
A19, then A174.
Rail: Redcar
Central from
Darlington

Features LH, flat,
galloping

2019 Fixtures
April 8, 22, May
2, 20, 27-28, June 21-22, July 21, 31,
August 10, 24, September 17, 25,
October 5, 18, 28, November 5

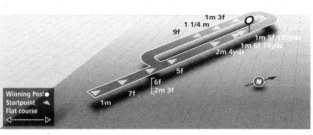

Racing Post standard times

5f	57	1m3f	2min16
6f	1min9.5	1m5f135yds	2min51
7f	1min22	1m6f19yds	2min57.5
1m	1min35	2m4yds	3min22
1m1f	1min48	2m3f	4min8
1m2f	2min3		

Trainers	Wins-Runs	%	2yo	3yo+	£1 level stks
Richard Fahey	38-259	15	17-120	21-139	-40.85
David O'Meara	32-212	15	6-37	26-175	-15.36
Tim Easterby	26-324	8	2-92	24-232	-121.19
Kevin Ryan	22-136	16	8-53	14-83	-30.65
Michael Dods	21-174	12	7-59	14-115	-12.34
Mark Johnston	17-103	17	5-41	12-62	-7.00
William Haggas	12-31	39	5-16	7-15	+2.67
Ruth Carr	11-134	8	0-2	11-132	-54.75
Keith Dalgleish	11-81	14	5-33	6-48	+17.75
Michael Easterby	10-115	9	1-29	9-86	-49.63
David Barron	10-87	11	2-18	8-69	+0.75
Declan Carroll	10-67	15	4-16	6-51	+18.25
Nigel Tinkler	8-122	7	1-32	7-90	-32.50

Jockeys	Wins-Rides	%	£1 level stks	Best Trainer	W-R
David Allan	27-223	12	-43.94	Tim Easterby	14-118
Daniel Tudhope	26-129	20	+38.58	David O'Meara	13-71
Paul Mulrennan	21-173	12	-72.25	Michael Dods	9-53
Jason Hart	21-137	15	-7.14	John Quinn	5-35
Graham Lee	19-197	10	-66.94	Keith Dalgleish	3-8
Kevin Stott	19-96	20	+15.88	Kevin Ryan	12-38
Tony Hamilton	17-127	13	-35.49	Richard Fahey	15-70
Andrew Mullen	15-158	9	-7.00	Michael Dods	3-22
Phillip Makin	15-113	13	-32.89	David O'Meara	4-18
Paul Hanagan	15-88	17	-23.33	Richard Fahey	7-43
Joe Fanning	14-88	16	+2.68	Mark Johnston	6-34
Ben Curtis	13-128	10	-69.10	William Haggas	3-4
P J McDonald	12-148	8	-50.75	Ann Duffield	3-32

Favourites

2yo	39.6%	+0.98	3yo	38.2%	+2.38	TOTAL	35.7% +9.19

77 North Street, Ripon, N Yorkshire
HG4 1DS. Tel 01765 602 156 or 01765 603 696

RIPON

How to get there
Road: A1, then
B6265. Rail:
Harrogate, bus to
Ripon centre, 1m
walk

Features RH,
sharp

2019 Fixtures
April 18, 27, May
10, 19, June 5-6, 19-20, July 8, 15, 20,
August 5-6, 17, 26-27, September 28

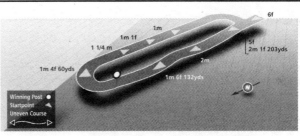

Racing Post standard times

5f	58	1m2f	2min4.5
6f	1min10.3	1m4f10yds	2min33.4
1m	1min38.1	2m	3min26.5
1m1f	1min52	2m1f203yds	3min53
1m1f170yds	2min1.3		

Trainers	Wins-Runs	%	2yo	3yo+	£1 level stks
Tim Easterby	39-341	11	7-82	32-259	-62.16
Richard Fahey	37-278	13	10-86	27-192	-72.59
David O'Meara	35-235	15	5-27	30-208	+16.38
Mark Johnston	30-169	18	13-50	17-119	+26.62
William Haggas	15-35	43	2-9	13-26	+10.82
Ruth Carr	12-88	14	0-1	12-87	+53.50
Keith Dalgleish	9-70	13	0-22	9-48	-15.13
Nigel Tinkler	9-58	16	1-21	8-37	-0.67
Roger Varian	9-36	25	1-5	8-31	-12.26
David Barron	8-83	10	2-14	6-69	-34.00
Richard Whitaker	8-63	13	1-6	7-57	+28.00
John Quinn	8-61	13	2-23	6-38	+4.10
Kevin Ryan	7-95	7	1-22	6-73	-44.25

Jockeys	Wins-Rides	%	£1 level stks	Best Trainer	W-R
Silvestre De Sousa	32-84	38	+34.84	Mark Johnston	6-16
David Allan	28-203	14	-33.68	Tim Easterby	21-167
Paul Mulrennan	21-111	19	+2.91	Bryan Smart	3-12
Daniel Tudhope	21-110	19	-9.01	David O'Meara	11-74
Tony Hamilton	18-135	13	-27.03	Richard Fahey	13-86
Franny Norton	17-98	17	+10.67	Mark Johnston	13-61
P J McDonald	15-143	10	-46.92	Ann Duffield	4-32
Paul Hanagan	12-82	15	-23.77	Richard Fahey	8-54
Graham Lee	11-95	12	-14.46	Mick Channon	2-3
Jason Hart	11-86	13	-7.42	John Quinn	5-30
David Nolan	11-68	16	+4.04	David O'Meara	6-35
Phillip Makin	10-114	9	-42.50	Keith Dalgleish	6-26
Ben Curtis	10-86	12	-20.00	David Barron	2-13

Favourites

2yo	42.7% -1.48	3yo	35.6% -19.30	TOTAL	34.3% -35.36

SALISBURY

Netherhampton, Salisbury, Wilts
SP2 8PN. Tel 01722 326 461

How to get there
Road: 2m west
of Salisbury on
A3094. Rail:
Salisbury, bus

Features RH,
uphill finish

2019 Fixtures
April 28, May 2,
16, 25, June 11,
16, 26, July 13, 27, August 14-15, 23,
September 3, 5, 13, October 3

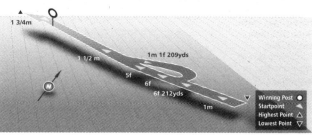

Racing Post standard times

5f	59.8	1m1f198yds	2min5.8
6f	1min12.3	1m4f	2min33
6f212yds	1min26.5	1m6f21yds	3min
1m	1min39.5		

Trainers	Wins-Runs	%	2yo	3yo+	£1 level stks
Richard Hannon	45-307	15	26-148	19-159	-28.24
Andrew Balding	25-144	17	9-44	16-100	-8.72
Ralph Beckett	16-112	14	5-38	11-74	-28.29
Clive Cox	15-94	16	6-33	9-61	-25.52
Rod Millman	12-124	10	6-48	6-76	-42.38
Mick Channon	12-120	10	3-45	9-75	-25.90
Charles Hills	11-77	14	0-27	11-50	-9.90
Sir Michael Stoute	11-66	17	1-14	10-52	-17.19
John Gosden	11-38	29	2-9	9-29	+36.36
Roger Charlton	10-55	18	2-16	8-39	-19.46
Roger Varian	9-51	18	2-11	7-40	+0.73
William Haggas	9-35	26	2-16	7-19	-5.83
David Evans	8-96	8	5-48	3-48	+4.91

Jockeys	Wins-Rides	%	£1 level stks	Best Trainer	W-R
Oisin Murphy	20-122	16	+26.63	Andrew Balding	6-30
Jim Crowley	19-132	14	-21.44	Charles Hills	3-14
Pat Dobbs	17-135	13	-63.58	Richard Hannon	9-55
Tom Marquand	17-124	14	+14.61	Richard Hannon	9-54
David Probert	12-98	12	-31.32	Andrew Balding	8-51
Sean Levey	12-86	14	-24.70	Richard Hannon	12-76
Silvestre De Sousa	12-59	20	-6.64	Mick Channon	3-24
Andrea Atzeni	11-47	23	+14.64	Roger Varian	3-11
Ryan Moore	10-45	22	-16.86	Sir Michael Stoute	4-17
Robert Havlin	10-35	29	+43.61	John Gosden	8-20
Charles Bishop	9-72	13	-22.62	Mick Channon	3-23
Kieran Shoemark	9-62	15	-13.52	Roger Charlton	4-18
Dane O'Neill	8-66	12	-24.05	Henry Candy	2-15

Favourites

2yo	33.6%	-25.55	3yo	33.6%	-26.00	TOTAL 34.2% -46.61

Esher, Surrey, KT10 9AJ.
Tel 01372 463 072 or 01372 464 348

SANDOWN

How to get there
Road: M25 Jct 10
then A3. Rail:
Esher from
Waterloo

Features RH, last
7f uphill

2019 Fixtures
April 26, May 23,
30, June 14-15,
July 5-6, 24-25, 31, August 8, 30-31,
September 13, 18

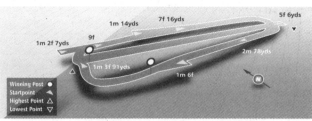

Racing Post standard times

5f6yds	59.8	1m2f7yds	2min5.8
7f16yds	1min27	1m3f91yds	2min23
1m14yds	1min39.9	1m6f	2min58.3
1m1f	1min52.9	2m78yds	3min34

Trainers	Wins-Runs	%	2yo	3yo+	£1 level stks
Richard Hannon	30-220	14	14-89	16-131	-11.22
John Gosden	25-111	23	7-29	18-82	-9.42
Sir Michael Stoute	24-92	26	0-12	24-80	+20.98
Roger Varian	16-66	24	1-12	15-54	-5.63
Andrew Balding	14-132	11	3-33	11-99	-8.73
Clive Cox	14-90	16	4-21	10-69	+11.56
William Haggas	14-56	25	5-13	9-43	-2.74
Mark Johnston	13-92	14	8-31	5-61	-38.54
Roger Charlton	11-55	20	1-9	10-46	-14.11
Charlie Appleby	10-57	18	5-21	5-36	-3.60
Ralph Beckett	8-72	11	1-16	7-56	-24.55
Brian Meehan	7-65	11	1-21	6-44	-27.17
Henry Candy	7-47	15	1-8	6-39	+1.79

Jockeys	Wins-Rides	%	£1 level stks	Best Trainer	W-R
Ryan Moore	33-136	24	+17.70	Sir Michael Stoute	14-41
James Doyle	22-113	19	-24.96	Charlie Appleby	4-15
Silvestre De Sousa	22-87	25	+16.43	Mark Johnston	6-17
Jim Crowley	21-161	13	-20.73	Owen Burrows	3-15
Andrea Atzeni	21-102	21	-23.95	Roger Varian	7-27
Oisin Murphy	16-132	12	-23.00	Joseph Tuite	2-3
Frankie Dettori	16-79	20	-12.38	John Gosden	7-37
William Buick	15-105	14	-26.85	Charlie Appleby	6-33
Adam Kirby	11-108	10	-62.22	Clive Cox	7-38
Fran Berry	10-68	15	+10.08	Henry Candy	3-12
Charles Bishop	10-58	17	+5.25	Eve Johnson Houghton	5-28
George Baker	10-38	26	+1.16	Roger Charlton	3-4
Pat Dobbs	7-89	8	-27.75	Richard Hannon	4-42

Favourites

2yo	41.7%	-1.08		3yo	40.8%	+21.69	
					TOTAL	40.9%	+42.54

SOUTHWELL

Rolleston, Newark, Notts
NG25 0TS. Tel 01636 814 481

**How to get
there** Road: A1
to Newark, then
A617 or M1 to
Nottingham, then
A612. Rail:
Rolleston

Features LH,
Fibresand, sharp

Please note there
are no turf fixtures scheduled this
year. Stats relate to all-weather only.

2019 Fixtures March 30, April 3-4,
17, 21, 29, May 1-2, 8, 28, July 26,
September 19, 26, October 4, 10, 16,
21, 29, November 5, 7, 9, 18, 27, 29,
December 5, 19-20, 29

Inside Lane: Turf Course
Outside Lane: All Weather
Winning Post ●
Startpoint ▲
Flat Course

Racing Post standard times

5f	58	1m4f	2min35
6f	1min14	1m5f	2min50.5
7f	1min27	1m6f	3min2
1m	1min39.8	2m	3min34
1m3f	2min22.3	2m2f	4min4

Trainers	Wins-Runs	%	2yo	3yo+	£1 level stks
Michael Appleby	86-607	14	4-34	82-573	-168.74
Scott Dixon	40-482	8	3-40	37-442	-50.35
Richard Fahey	29-154	19	6-36	23-118	-5.54
David Evans	27-184	15	3-20	24-164	+8.04
Derek Shaw	23-191	12	0-2	23-189	+40.83
K R Burke	21-114	18	2-19	19-95	+105.36
David Barron	21-92	23	2-6	19-86	+7.23
Declan Carroll	20-101	20	0-0	20-101	+22.88
Conor Dore	19-133	14	0-1	19-132	+3.63
Andrew Balding	18-78	23	0-5	18-73	-16.92
Julia Feilden	16-98	16	1-3	15-95	+30.19
Roy Bowring	14-109	13	0-1	14-108	-25.45
Brian Ellison	14-102	14	1-9	13-93	-40.56

Jockeys	Wins-Rides	%	£1 level stks	Best Trainer	W-R
Luke Morris	49-389	13	-146.00	Scott Dixon	10-74
Andrew Mullen	40-353	11	-152.54	Michael Appleby	17-156
Ben Curtis	34-211	16	+45.25	Brian Ellison	5-19
Alistair Rawlinson	30-190	16	-9.82	Michael Appleby	25-150
Kieran O'Neill	25-240	10	+73.95	Scott Dixon	20-177
Joe Fanning	24-182	13	-43.56	Mark Johnston	6-33
Tom Eaves	21-229	9	-5.33	James Given	4-37
Tony Hamilton	21-171	12	+17.25	Derek Shaw	8-47
Paul Mulrennan	19-133	14	+34.39	Conor Dore	7-34
J F Egan	19-105	18	+3.63	David Evans	8-41
Silvestre De Sousa	19-85	22	+11.85	Chris Dwyer	5-17
P J McDonald	18-151	12	-45.22	Philip Kirby	3-6
Oisin Murphy	18-85	21	-12.37	Andrew Balding	9-30

Favourites

2yo	27.9% -22.79	3yo	36.1% -34.94	TOTAL	32.7% -146.57

Station Road, Thirsk, N Yorkshire,
YO7 1QL. Tel 01845 522 276

THIRSK

How to get there
Road: A61 from
A1 in the west
or A19 in the
east. Rail: Thirsk,
10min walk

Features LH,
sharp, tight turns

2019 Fixtures
April 13, 29, May
4, 11, 18, June 3, 11, 18, July 3, 26,
August 3, 9, 16, 30, September 7, 16

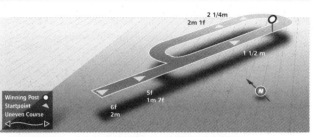

Racing Post standard times

5f	58	1m	1min36.5
6f	1min10.6	1m4f	2min32
7f	1min24	2m	3min23

Trainers	Wins-Runs	%	2yo	3yo+	£1 level stks
Richard Fahey	38-229	17	13-86	25-143	+8.42
David O'Meara	25-197	13	4-28	21-169	-31.05
Tim Easterby	24-285	8	5-83	19-202	-29.38
Michael Dods	21-188	11	4-45	17-143	-30.03
Kevin Ryan	18-158	11	6-42	12-116	-39.21
Paul Midgley	12-70	17	0-7	12-63	+25.75
Keith Dalgleish	12-54	22	3-17	9-37	+50.96
Ruth Carr	11-163	7	0-3	11-160	-52.14
Brian Ellison	11-84	13	1-13	10-71	+9.88
Michael Appleby	11-63	17	1-4	10-59	+109.25
Bryan Smart	10-57	18	4-15	6-42	+27.00
William Haggas	10-35	29	4-13	6-22	-10.63
John Quinn	9-88	10	2-23	7-65	-30.05

Jockeys	Wins-Rides	%	£1 level stks	Best Trainer	W-R
Paul Mulrennan	28-185	15	+16.63	Michael Dods	11-80
Daniel Tudhope	25-131	19	-7.62	David O'Meara	17-84
David Allan	22-186	12	-0.75	Tim Easterby	10-119
Graham Lee	18-173	10	-44.68	Bryan Smart	4-22
P J McDonald	14-182	8	-52.30	Ann Duffield	4-22
Tom Eaves	14-163	9	+12.07	James Given	2-16
Ben Curtis	14-139	10	-42.08	Brian Ellison	4-24
Phillip Makin	14-97	14	-16.13	John Davies	3-14
Tony Hamilton	13-155	8	-64.33	Richard Fahey	10-80
Paul Hanagan	12-77	16	-2.80	Richard Fahey	11-44
Kevin Stott	12-66	18	+10.98	Kevin Ryan	5-26
Joe Fanning	12-55	22	+9.42	Keith Dalgleish	2-3
James Sullivan	11-191	6	-72.64	Ruth Carr	7-124

Favourites

2yo	41.1% -1.28	3yo	38.2% -4.00		TOTAL 37%	+18.87

WETHERBY

York Road, Wetherby, West Yorks
L22 5EJ. Tel: 01937 582 035

How to get there Road: A1, A58 from Leeds, B1224 from York. Rail: Leeds, Harrogate, York.

Features LH, 1m4f circuit

2019 Fixtures April 28, May 7, 30

○ Winning Post
◁ Startpoint
▲ Highest Point
▼ Lowest Point
✐ Open ditch
≈ Water jump
✐ Fence

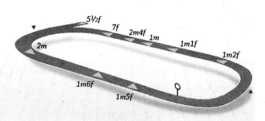

Racing Post standard times

5f110yds	1min4.8	1m2f	2min4.5
7f	1min25.2	1m6f	2min56
1m	1min38.3		

Trainers	Wins-Runs	%	2yo	3yo+	£1 level stks
Richard Fahey	6-29	21	2-8	4-21	+16.25
Tim Easterby	5-32	16	0-5	5-27	+11.80
David O'Meara	5-28	18	0-3	5-25	+45.75
Ruth Carr	3-21	14	0-0	3-21	-2.00
Kevin Ryan	3-19	16	1-2	2-17	+24.50
Mark Johnston	3-15	20	1-5	2-10	+10.10
Declan Carroll	3-11	27	0-0	3-11	+11.00
John Gosden	3-4	75	0-0	3-4	+8.00
Michael Dods	2-18	11	0-2	2-16	-1.00
Roger Fell	2-16	13	0-1	2-15	-5.00
Antony Brittain	2-10	20	0-0	2-10	+5.50
Tony Coyle	2-10	20	0-1	2-9	+3.50
John Davies	2-10	20	0-0	2-10	+1.50

Jockeys	Wins-Rides	%	£1 level stks	Best Trainer	W-R
P J McDonald	7-39	18	+40.50	David Loughnane	2-3
Tony Hamilton	5-39	13	-13.50	Roger Fell	2-13
James Sullivan	5-32	16	+17.00	Ruth Carr	3-16
Paul Mulrennan	5-25	20	+6.10	John Mackie	1-1
Daniel Tudhope	5-18	28	+58.75	David O'Meara	3-10
Ben Curtis	4-30	13	-5.50	William Haggas	1-1
Tom Eaves	4-29	14	+38.50	David Brown	2-2
Joe Fanning	4-26	15	+27.00	Mark Johnston	2-7
Phillip Makin	4-25	16	+3.00	David O'Meara	2-4
David Allan	4-25	16	+1.55	Alan Swinbank	1-1
Paul Hanagan	4-20	20	+7.17	Richard Fahey	2-7
Cam Hardie	3-19	16	-0.63	John Quinn	1-1
Jack Garritty	3-14	21	+6.00	Jedd O'Keeffe	2-6

Favourites

2yo	40%	+0.73	3yo	28.2%	-10.41	TOTAL 27.6%	-17.43

Maidenhead Road, Windsor, Berks
SL4 5JJ. Tel 01753 498 400

WINDSOR

How to get there
Road: M4 Jctn 6,
A355, A308. Rail:
Paddington to
Windsor Central/
Waterloo to Wind-
sor Riverside

Features Figure
of eight, flat, long
straight

2019 Fixtures April 8, 15, 29, May 6,
13, 20, 27, June 3, 10, 17, 24, 29-30,
July 1, 8, 15, 22, 29, August 5, 11-12,
19, 24, September 2, October 7, 14,
21

Racing Post standard times

5f10yds	59.2	1m2f7yds	2min5
6f	1min10.5	1m3f135yds	2min25
1m67yds	1min41.1		

Trainers	Wins-Runs	%	2yo	3yo+	£1 level stks
Richard Hannon	49-304	16	26-134	23-170	-43.78
Clive Cox	33-156	21	9-28	24-128	+2.09
Roger Varian	22-76	29	1-8	21-68	-5.45
David Evans	19-211	9	9-84	10-127	-100.33
Ed Walker	19-89	21	4-23	15-66	-6.50
John Gosden	19-63	30	4-11	15-52	-10.22
Ralph Beckett	18-96	19	4-22	14-74	-21.66
Charles Hills	17-116	15	4-43	13-73	+0.25
Henry Candy	16-90	18	2-15	14-75	-9.00
Roger Charlton	16-80	20	2-19	14-61	-16.21
Saeed bin Suroor	15-40	38	4-8	11-32	+4.92
William Haggas	14-56	25	3-19	11-37	-18.21
Andrew Balding	13-122	11	5-23	8-99	-55.90

Jockeys	Wins-Rides	%	£1 level stks	Best Trainer	W-R
Adam Kirby	47-233	20	-7.72	Clive Cox	24-88
James Doyle	29-128	23	-36.48	Saeed bin Suroor	7-15
Jamie Spencer	25-144	17	+1.34	Ed Walker	5-11
Tom Marquand	23-199	12	-88.65	Richard Hannon	12-84
Oisin Murphy	22-190	12	-84.23	Ralph Beckett	4-10
Andrea Atzeni	22-98	22	-11.88	Roger Varian	10-38
David Probert	21-181	12	-1.36	Andrew Balding	8-58
Jim Crowley	21-125	17	-25.41	Ralph Beckett	4-4
George Baker	20-102	20	-16.21	Ed Walker	4-10
Harry Bentley	20-91	22	+16.25	Henry Candy	3-7
Sean Levey	18-109	17	+29.72	Richard Hannon	13-80
Pat Dobbs	17-110	15	-27.70	Ralph Beckett	4-19
Pat Cosgrave	16-136	12	-46.56	William Haggas	8-31

Favourites

2yo	48.3% +8.23	3yo 40.9% +9.55	TOTAL 39.4% +6.07	

WOLVES

Dunstall Park, Gorsebrook Road, Wolverhampton, West Midlands. WV6 0PE. Tel 08702 202 442

How to get there
Road: A449, close to M6, M42 and M54. Rail: Wolverhampton

Features LH, sharp, relaid with Tapeta in 2014

2019 Fixtures
April 2, 5-6, 13, 16, 22-23, 27, 29, May 7, 10, 13, 21, 31, June 3, 24, July 1, 9, 15, 17, 23, August 2, 12, 16, 30-31, September 7, 9, 21, 30, October 3, 5, 12, 14, 17, 19, 23-24, 30, November 6, 16, 18, 23, 26, 30, December 2-3, 7, 10, 14, 16, 19-20, 26-27

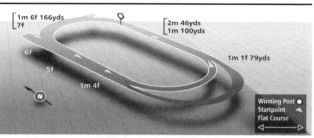

Racing Post standard times

5f20yds	1min0.5	1m1f103yds	1min57.3
5f216yds	1min13.2	1m4f50yds	2min35.3
7f32yds	1min27	1m5f194yds	2min58.5
1m141yds	1min46.7	2m119yds	3min36

Trainers	Wins-Runs	%	2yo	3yo+	£1 level stks
David Evans	61-551	11	7-111	54-440	-119.97
Richard Fahey	57-462	12	11-138	46-324	-123.41
Michael Appleby	52-489	11	1-13	51-476	-137.90
Tom Dascombe	52-343	15	13-103	39-240	+81.27
Mark Johnston	50-365	14	14-112	36-253	-101.95
Daniel Mark Loughnane	49-546	9	0-43	49-503	-133.52
John Gosden	44-139	32	18-60	26-79	-4.62
Tony Carroll	40-412	10	1-21	39-391	-101.92
Charlie Appleby	40-124	32	9-39	31-85	-19.00
David O'Meara	39-358	11	2-47	37-311	-105.77
Richard Hannon	38-241	16	17-114	21-127	-53.86
Jamie Osborne	37-299	12	11-79	26-220	-123.01
William Haggas	33-105	31	13-38	20-67	-3.46

Jockeys	Wins-Rides	%	£1 level stks	Best Trainer	W-R
Luke Morris	133-1045	13	-269.43	Sir Mark Prescott Bt	24-116
Adam Kirby	115-531	22	-16.20	Jamie Osborne	10-32
Richard Kingscote	73-452	16	-71.13	Tom Dascombe	34-197
Joe Fanning	63-464	14	-116.79	Mark Johnston	20-149
Martin Harley	55-325	17	+3.03	Marco Botti	6-14
Oisin Murphy	51-275	19	-38.25	Andrew Balding	7-28
Stevie Donohoe	49-375	13	-49.53	Ian Williams	14-83
Silvestre De Sousa	45-221	20	-25.88	Chris Dwyer	7-22
Josephine Gordon	43-382	11	-82.97	Hugo Palmer	10-31
Pat Cosgrave	43-199	22	+35.03	George Baker	6-15
Tony Hamilton	41-300	14	-70.26	Richard Fahey	28-182
Robert Winston	41-242	17	-32.69	Dean Ivory	16-64
Franny Norton	38-342	11	-138.67	Mark Johnston	16-83

Favourites

2yo	41.2% -4.70	3yo	37.4% -80.50	TOTAL	35.9% -138.71

North Denes, Great Yarmouth, Norfolk
NR30 4AU. Tel 01493 842 527

YARMOUTH

How to get there
Road: A47 to end, A1064. Rail: Great Yarmouth, bus

Features LH, flat

2019 Fixtures
April 23, 30, May 15, 22, 30, June 12-13, 28, July 4, 10, 17, 25, 30, August 7-8, 15, 20, 25, September 17-19, October 14, 22

Racing Post standard times

5f43yds	1min0.5	1m2f21yds	2min5
6f3yds	1min11	1m3f101yds	2min23.5
7f3yds	1min23.6	1m6f17yds	2min59
1m3yds	1min36.5	2m	3min24.5
1m1f	1min50	2m2f51yds	3min56

Trainers	Wins-Runs	%	2yo	3yo+	£1 level stks
William Haggas	27-112	24	12-53	15-59	-10.38
David Simcock	23-85	27	5-18	18-67	+40.63
John Gosden	20-60	33	9-35	11-25	+26.52
Roger Varian	18-80	23	6-32	12-48	-11.22
Chris Dwyer	16-92	17	2-14	14-78	+40.63
Stuart Williams	13-80	16	0-12	13-68	-15.00
Michael Bell	12-67	18	4-31	8-36	+7.18
John Ryan	11-105	10	2-25	9-80	-27.70
Hugo Palmer	11-45	24	4-17	7-28	+18.19
Michael Appleby	10-102	10	0-7	10-95	-30.79
Chris Wall	10-69	14	1-10	9-59	-32.82
Sir Michael Stoute	10-54	19	3-26	7-28	-22.74
Mark Johnston	10-53	19	5-15	5-38	+44.45

Jockeys	Wins-Rides	%	£1 level stks	Best Trainer	W-R
Silvestre De Sousa	40-177	23	+2.19	Chris Dwyer	7-40
Jamie Spencer	39-159	25	+52.84	David Simcock	12-34
Andrea Atzeni	25-88	28	+6.69	Roger Varian	12-38
Frankie Dettori	15-32	47	+22.60	John Gosden	8-15
James Doyle	14-54	26	+12.85	Hugo Palmer	3-8
Ryan Moore	14-51	27	-11.38	William Haggas	4-13
Pat Cosgrave	13-79	16	+10.70	William Haggas	6-28
Luke Morris	12-123	10	-68.69	Sir Mark Prescott Bt	3-23
Josephine Gordon	12-93	13	-22.06	Hugo Palmer	4-14
Stevie Donohoe	12-84	14	+5.25	Charlie Fellowes	7-24
Martin Harley	11-103	11	-47.25	David Simcock	3-5
Jim Crowley	11-64	17	-25.53	Owen Burrows	4-9
Oisin Murphy	10-39	26	+1.38	Brian Meehan	1-1

Favourites

2yo	44.2%	+0.63	3yo	41.9%	+19.68	
					TOTAL 38.8%	-4.27

YORK

Knavesmire Road, York, YO23 1EX
Tel 01904 620 911

How to get there
Road: Course
is south of city.
From north, A1,
A59 to York,
northern bypass
from A19 to A64.
Otherwise, A64.
Rail: York, bus

Features LH, flat

2019 Fixtures May 15-17, 25, June
14-15, 29, July 12-13, 26-27, August
21-24, September 8

Racing Post standard times

5f	57.5	1m208yds	1min49
5f89yds	1min2.7	1m2f88yds	2min7
6f	1min10	1m4f	2min28.1
7f	1min22.3	1m6f	2min57
1m	1min37	2m88yds	3min29

Trainers	*Wins-Runs*	%	*2yo*	*3yo+*	*£1 level stks*
Richard Fahey	36-500	7	16-161	20-339	-145.25
William Haggas	28-150	19	10-39	18-111	-20.95
Tim Easterby	24-286	8	3-51	21-235	-36.50
Mark Johnston	24-216	11	12-89	12-127	+16.76
David O'Meara	21-330	6	0-25	21-305	-119.00
John Gosden	21-73	29	0-5	21-68	+12.65
Kevin Ryan	19-226	8	11-77	8-149	-79.00
Sir Michael Stoute	16-81	20	1-2	15-79	+4.71
Michael Dods	14-85	16	0-7	14-78	+15.92
Charlie Appleby	13-61	21	5-12	8-49	+0.30
Ralph Beckett	11-65	17	2-12	9-53	+32.08
Andrew Balding	10-93	11	1-19	9-74	+23.00
Richard Hannon	9-117	8	7-59	2-58	-44.00

Jockeys	*Wins-Rides*	%	*£1 level stks*	*Best Trainer*	*W-R*
James Doyle	21-114	18	+0.10	Saeed bin Suroor	5-17
Frankie Dettori	21-95	22	+3.73	John Gosden	12-36
Paul Hanagan	17-192	9	-50.25	Richard Fahey	10-112
Daniel Tudhope	17-188	9	-35.75	David O'Meara	9-120
P J McDonald	15-126	12	+70.85	Mark Johnston	5-29
Phillip Makin	14-127	11	+12.13	David O'Meara	5-39
William Buick	14-100	14	-6.58	Charlie Appleby	8-34
Jim Crowley	13-99	13	+45.75	Sir Michael Stoute	3-11
Oisin Murphy	12-72	17	+38.08	Andrew Balding	4-17
Silvestre De Sousa	11-131	8	-2.63	Mark Johnston	5-37
Andrea Atzeni	11-111	10	-51.88	Roger Varian	5-35
David Allan	10-162	6	-59.50	Tim Easterby	7-124
James Sullivan	10-85	12	+32.50	Tom Tate	3-14

Favourites

2yo	29.6%	-19.57	3yo	35.4% +15.93	TOTAL 28.8%	-21.26

ROARING LION: helped to take John Gosden's recent York strike-rate to 29 per cent with his wins in last season's Dante Stakes and Juddmonte Internarional

Win - free form!

THIS YEAR'S QUIZ could hardly be more simple, and the prize should prove invaluable to our lucky winner. We're offering a free subscription to The Flat Form Book, the BHA's official form book – every week from May to November, you could be getting the previous week's results in full, together with notebook comments highlighting future winners, adjusted Official Ratings and Racing Post Ratings. The winner will also get a copy of last year's complete form book.

All you have to do is this: identify the three horses pictured on the following pages. The theme honours the legendary Mark Johnston with three of his leading performers from last season – the Derby runner-up, the Coronation Stakes runner-up and the Vintage Stakes winner. If you think you know the answer, write their names in the box below in the order in which they appear.

Send your answers along with your details on the entry form below, to:

2019 Flat Annual Competition, Racing & Football Outlook, Floor 7, Vivo Building, South Bank Central, 30 Stamford Street, London, SE1 9LS.
Entries must reach us no later than first post on May 9. The winner's name and the right answers will be printed in the RFO's May 14 edition.

Six runners-up will each receive a copy of last year's form book.

Name ....

Address ....

....

Town ....

Postcode ....

In the event of more than one correct entry, the winner will be drawn at random from the correct entries. The Editor's decision is final and no correspondence will be entered into.

BETTING CHART

ON	ODDS	AGAINST
50	Evens	50
52.4	11-10	47.6
54.5	6-5	45.5
55.6	5-4	44.4
58	11-8	42
60	6-4	40
62	13-8	38
63.6	7-4	36.4
65.3	15-8	34.7
66.7	2-1	33.3
68	85-40	32
69.2	9-4	30.8
71.4	5-2	28.6
73.4	11-4	26.6
75	3-1	25
76.9	100-30	23.1
77.8	7-2	22.2
80	4-1	20
82	9-2	18
83.3	5-1	16.7
84.6	11-2	15.4
85.7	6-1	14.3
86.7	13-2	13.3
87.5	7-1	12.5
88.2	15-2	11.8
89	8-1	11
89.35	100-12	10.65
89.4	17-2	10.6
90	9-1	10
91	10-1	9
91.8	11-1	8.2
92.6	12-1	7.4
93.5	14-1	6.5
94.4	16-1	5.6
94.7	18-1	5.3
95.2	20-1	4.8
95.7	22-1	4.3
96.2	25-1	3.8
97.2	33-1	2.8
97.6	40-1	2.4
98.1	50-1	1.9
98.5	66-1	1.3
99.0	100-1	0.99

The table above (often known as the 'Field Money Table') shows both bookmakers' margins and how much a backer needs to invest to win £100. To calculate a bookmaker's margin, simply add up the percentages of all the odds on offer. The sum by which the total exceeds 100% gives the 'over-round' on the book. To determine what stake is required to win £100 (includes returned stake) at a particular price, just look at the relevant row, either odds-against or odds-on.

RULE 4 DEDUCTIONS

When a horse is withdrawn before coming under starter's orders, but after a market has been formed, bookmakers are entitled to make the following deductions from win and place returns (excluding stakes) in accordance with Tattersalls' Rule 4(c).

Odds of withdrawn horse	*Deduction from winnings*
(1) 3-10 or shorter	75p in the £
(2) 2-5 to 1-3	70p in the £
(3) 8-15 to 4-9	65p in the £
(4) 8-13 to 4-7	60p in the £
(5) 4-5 to 4-6	55p in the £
(6) 20-21 to 5-6	50p in the £
(7) Evens to 6-5	45p in the £
(8) 5-4 to 6-4	40p in the £
(9) 13-8 to 7-4	35p in the £
(10) 15-8 to 9-4	30p in the £
(11) 5-2 to 3-1	25p in the £
(12) 100-30 to 4-1	20p in the £
(13) 9-2 to 11-2	15p in the £
(14) 6-1 to 9-1	10p in the £
(15) 10-1 to 14-1	5p in the £
(16) longer than 14-1	no deductions

(17) When more than one horse is withdrawn without coming under starter's orders, total deductions shall not exceed 75p in the £.

Starting-price bets are affected only when there was insufficient time to form a new market.

Feedback!

If you have any comments or criticism about this book, or suggestions for future editions, please tell us.

Write   Nick Watts/Dylan Hill
2019 Flat Annual
Racing & Football Outlook
Floor 7, Vivo Building, South Bank Central
30 Stamford Street
London SE1 9LS

email   rfo@rfoutlook.co.uk

Horse index

All horses discussed, with page numbers, except for references in the Group 1 and two-year-old form sections (pages 80-111), which have their own indexes